THE TEMPLE:
ITS MINISTRY AND SERVICES

THE TEMPLE

ITS MINISTRY AND SERVICES

Updated Edition

ALFRED EDERSHEIM

HENDRICKSON PUBLISHERS

The Temple: Its Ministry and Services, Updated Edition
Alfred Edersheim

Copyright © 1994 by Hendrickson Publishers, Inc.
P.O. Box 3473
Peabody, Massachusetts 01961-3473
All rights reserved.

Printed in the United States of America

Hardcover edition: ISBN 1-56563-136-6
Paperback edition: ISBN 1-56563-006-8

Fourth printing — June 1998

CONTENTS

PREFACE

✣

It has been my wish in this book, to take the reader back nineteen centuries; to show him Jerusalem as it was, when our Lord passed through its streets, and the Sanctuary, when He taught in its porches and courts; to portray, not only the appearance and structure of the Temple, but to describe its ordinances and worshippers, the ministry of its priesthood, and the ritual of its services. In so doing, I have hoped, not only to illustrate a subject, in itself most interesting to the Bible-student, but also, and chiefly, to sketch, in one important aspect, the religious life of the period in which our blessed Lord lived upon earth, the circumstances under which He taught, and the religious rites by which He was surrounded; and whose meaning, in their truest sense, He came to fulfil.

The Temple and its services form, so to speak, part of the life and work of Jesus Christ; part also of His teaching, and of that of His apostles. What connects itself so closely with Him must be of deepest interest. We want to be able, as it were, to enter Jerusalem in His train, along with those who on that Palm-Sunday cried, 'Hosanna to the Son of David;' to see its streets and buildings; to know exactly how the Temple looked, and to find our way through its gates, among its porches, courts, and chambers; to be present in spirit at its services; to witness the Morning and the Evening Sacrifice; to mingle with the crowd of worshippers at the great Festivals, and to stand by the side of those who offered sacrifice or free-will offering, or who awaited the solemn purification which would

One day as he was teaching the people in the temple courts and preaching the gospel, the chief priests and the teachers of the law, together with the elders, came up to him (Luke 20:1).

The crowds that went ahead of him and those that followed shouted,
  "Hosanna to the Son of David!"
"Blessed is he who comes in the name of the Lord!"
"Hosanna in the highest!" (Matt. 21:9).

I did not see a temple in the city, because the Lord God Almighty and the Lamb are its temple (Rev. 21:22).

restore them to the fellowship of the Sanctuary. We want to *see* these rites, as it were, before us—to hear the Temple-music, to know the very Psalms that were chanted, the prayers that were offered, the duties of the priesthood, the sacrificial worship in which they engaged, and the very attitude of the worshippers— in short, all those details which in their combination enable us vividly to realise the scenes, as if we ourselves were present in them. For, amidst them all, we ever see that one great outstanding Personality, Whose presence filled that house with glory.

The New Testament transports us into almost every one of the scenes described in this book. It also makes frequent reference to them for illustration. We see the father of John ministering in his course in the burning of incense; the Virgin-Mother at her purification, presenting her First-born; the child Jesus among the Rabbis; the Master teaching in the porches of the Temple, sitting in the Treasury, attending the various festivals, giving His sanction to the purifications by directing the healed leper to the priest, and, above all, as at the Feast of Tabernacles, applying to Himself the significant rites of the Sanctuary. And, as we follow on, we witness the birth of the Church on the day of Pentecost; we mark the frequent illustrations of spiritual realities by Temple-scenes, in the writings of the apostles, but more especially in the Book of Revelation, whose imagery is so often taken from them; and we still look for the accomplishment of the one yet unfulfilled type—the Feast of Tabernacles, as the grand harvest-festival of the Church.

I have thus placed the permanent *Christian* interest in the foreground, because it occupied that place in my own mind. At the same time, from the nature of the subject, I hope the volume may fulfil yet another and kindred purpose. Although it does not profess to be a Handbook of Biblical Antiquities, nor a treatise on the types of the Old Testament, both these subjects had to be constantly referred to. But to realise the gorgeous Temple ritual, in all its details, possesses more than a merely historical interest. We are indeed fascinated by it; we live over again, if not

the period of Israel's temporal glory, yet that of deepest interest to us; and we can vividly represent to ourselves what the Temple had been before its services
had for ever passed away. But beyond this, stretching
far back through the period of prophets and kings,
and reaching up to the original revelation of Jehovah
amid the awful grandeur of Sinai, our holiest recol-
lections, and the very springs of our religious life rise
among these ordinances and types, which we here see
fully developed and carried out, and that under the
very light of His Presence, to Whom they all had
pointed. I say not, whether or how far later Jewish
practice may have misapprehended the original import
or the meaning of the Divine ordinances. That was
beyond my present task. But an accurate acquaintance with the sacrificial services at the time of Christ
must not only tend to correct mistakes, but throw a
fresh and vivid light upon all, and influence our views
of what the Levitical ordinances were intended to be
and to teach.

To have thus stated my object in this book, is
also to have indicated its difficulties. Yet abundant
materials for such a work, though scattered far and
wide, are within our reach. Not to speak of contemporary writings, as those of Josephus and Philo, and
references in the New Testament itself, we have in the
Mishnah a body of authoritative traditions, reaching
up, not only to Temple-times, but even to the days
of Jesus Christ.[1] On this source of information, of

---

[1]Quite a different estimate must be formed of the *Gemara* (which in a general way may
be described as a twofold commentary—the Jerusalem and Babylonian *Gemara*—upon the
Mishnah), not only from its much later date, but also from the strange and heterogeneous *con-
geries* which are found in the many folios of the Talmud. Judaism was, at the time of its compi-
lation, already thoroughly ossified; and the trustworthiness of tradition greatly impaired not
merely by the long interval of time that had elapsed, but by dogmatic predilections and prejudices, and by the not unnatural wish to foist comparatively recent views, practices, and prayers
upon Temple-times. Indeed, the work wants in its greatest part even the local colouring of the
Mishnah—an element of such importance in Eastern traditions, where, so to speak, the colours
are so fast, that, for example, to this day the modern Arab designations of places and localities
have preserved the original Palestinian names, and not those more recent Greek or Roman with
which successive conquerors had overlaid them.

course in conjunction with the Old Testament itself, I have been chiefly dependent.

While thus deriving my materials at first hand, I have also thankfully made use of any and every help within my reach. Foremost I place here the writings of Maimonides, not only because he is of greatest authority among the Jews, but because his vast and accurate knowledge of these subjects, and the clearness and subtlety of his intellect, entitle him to that position. Next to him come the numerous writers on Biblical Antiquities, in Latin and German; works on Typology—scientific and popular; treatises on the Life and Times of our Lord; histories of the Jewish Nation, or of Judaism; commentaries on such passages in the Old and New Testament as bore on these subjects; and numerous treatises on cognate points. In my study of ancient Jerusalem, I had the benefit of the labours of recent explorers, from Robinson and Barclay to the volumes published under the auspices of the Palestine Exploration Fund.

To the Cyclopaedias of Winer, Herzog, Ersch and Gruber, Dr. Smith, and Kitto (the third edition), I have been greatly indebted. The last-named of these works has the special merit of a series of articles on Jewish subjects (as I may designate them), written in quite an original manner, and with most competent knowledge. Although, as will appear from the text, I have been obliged frequently to differ from their writer, yet these articles must, from the fulness and ability of their treatment, be of very great use to the student. Lightfoot's *Horae Hebraicae et Talmudicae* are known to every scholar. Not so, perhaps, his small learned treatise *De ministerio templi*. The title and many of the subjects are similar to those treated in the present volume. But the learned reader will at once perceive that the plan and execution are quite different, though the work has been of great service to me. Perhaps I ought not here to omit such names as Relandus, Buxtorf, Otho, Schöttgen, Meuschen, Goodwin, Hottinger, Wagenseil, and Lundius; and, among modern writers, Bähr, Keil, Kurtz, de Wette, Saalschütz, Zunz, Jost, Geiger, Herzfeld, and Grätz, of whose works I have, I may say, *constantly* availed myself. Many others have been consulted, some of which are quoted in the foot-notes, while others are not expressly referred to, as not adding anything material to our knowledge.

In general, I should explain, that I have acted on the principle of giving the *minimum* of references possible. It would have been easy to have multiplied them almost indefinitely. But I wished to avoid cumbering my pages with an array of authorities, which too often give a mere appearance of learning; and, while they are not needed by scholars, may tend to interfere with the more general and popular use of such a work. For a similar reason, I have throughout avoided the use of Hebrew and even Greek letterpress. To print an expression in Hebrew letters could not be necessary for students, while the general reader, whom it too often bewilders by a show of knowledge, must in such case necessarily pass it over, unnoticed and unknown.

While this book embodies the studies of many years, I have during its actual composition deemed no labour nor pains irksome in comparing the results of my own investigations with those of all, within reach, who were entitled to such consideration. Thus much for the matter of the book. As to its form, some subjects may be touched in it which do not equally interest all readers;[2] others may appear to have been treated with too little or else with too much detail; objections may be raised to interpretations of types, or even to the general view of the Old Testament which has been taken throughout. My aim has been to make the book as complete and generally useful as I could, and clearly to express my convictions as to the meaning of the Old Testament. But on one point especially I would wish to be quite explicit. At the close of these studies, I would say, with humble and

---

[2]Thus Chapters 1 and 2, which give a description of ancient Jerusalem and of the structure and arrangements of the Temple, may not interest some readers, yet it could neither be left out, nor put in a different part of the book. Those for whom this subject has no attractions may, therefore, begin with Chapter 3.

heartfelt thankfulness, that step by step my Christian faith has only been strengthened by them, that, as I proceeded, the conviction has always been deepened that Christ is indeed 'the end of the Law for righteousness,' to Whom all the ordinances of the Old Testament had pointed, and in Whom alone, alike the people and the history of Israel find their meaning. Viewed in this light, the Temple-services are not so many strange or isolated rites, for the origin of which we must look among neighbouring nations, or in the tendencies natural to men during the infancy of their history. Rather, all now becomes one connected whole—the design and execution bearing even stronger evidence to its Divine authorship than other of God's works,—where every part fits into the other, and each and all point with unswerving steadfastness to Him in Whom the love of God was fully manifested, and its purposes towards the world entirely carried out. From first to last, the two dispensations are substantially one; Jehovah, the God of Israel, is also the God and Father of our Lord and Saviour Jesus Christ—*Novum Testamentum in Vetere latet; Vetus in Novo patet.*   A.E.

1

A First View of Jerusalem, and of the Temple

❇

As he approached Jerusalem and saw the city, he wept over it. —Luke 19:41.

The Charm of Jerusalem

In every age, the memory of Jerusalem has stirred the deepest feelings. Jews, Christians, and Mohammedans turn to it with reverent affection. It almost seems as if in some sense each could call it his 'happy home,' the 'name ever dear' to him. For our holiest thoughts of the past, and our happiest hopes for the future, connect themselves with 'the city of our God.' We know from many passages of the Old Testament, but especially from the Book of Psalms, with what ardent longing the exiles from Palestine looked towards it; and during the long centuries of

Model of the Temple in Jerusalem

They were looking intently up into the sky as he was going, when suddenly two men dressed in white stood beside them. "Men of Galilee," they said, "why do you stand here looking into the sky? This same Jesus, who has been taken from you into heaven, will come back in the same way you have seen him go into heaven" (Acts 1:10–11).

*Then Melchizedek king of Salem brought out bread and wine. He was priest of God Most High, and he blessed Abram, saying,
"Blessed be Abram by
   God Most High,
   Creator of heaven and
   earth.
And blessed be God
   Most High,
   who delivered your
   enemies into your
   hand."
Then Abram gave him a tenth of everything (Gen. 14:18–20).*

dispersion and cruel persecution, up to this day, the same aspirations have breathed in almost every service of the synagogue, and in none more earnestly than in that of the paschal night, which to us is for ever associated with the death of our Saviour. It is this one grand presence there of 'the Desire of all nations,' which has for ever cast a hallowed light round Jerusalem and the Temple, and given fulfilment to the prophecy—'Many people shall go and say, Come ye, and let us go up to the mountain of Jehovah, to the house of the God of Jacob; and He will teach us of His ways, and we will walk in His paths: for out of Zion shall go forth the law, and the word of Jehovah from Jerusalem' (Isaiah 2:3). His feet have trodden the busy streets of Jerusalem, and the shady recesses of the Mount of Olives; His figure has 'filled with glory' the Temple and its services; His person has given meaning to the land and the people; and the decease which He accomplished at Jerusalem has been for the life of all nations. These facts can never be past—they are eternally present; not only to our faith, but also to our hope; for He 'shall so come in like manner' as the 'men of Galilee' had on Mount Olivet 'seen Him go into heaven.'

ANCIENT MEMORIES

But our memories of Jerusalem stretch far back beyond these scenes. In the distance of a remote antiquity we read of Melchisedek, the typical priest-king of Salem, who went out to meet Abraham, the ancestor of the Hebrew race, and blessed him. A little later, and this same Abraham was coming up from Hebron on his mournful journey, to offer up his only son. A few miles south of the city, the road by which he travelled climbs the top of a high promontory, that juts into the deep Kedron valley. From this spot, through the cleft of the mountains which the Kedron has made for its course, one object rose up straight before him. It was *Moriah*, the mount on which the sacrifice of Isaac was to be offered. Here Solomon afterwards built the Temple. For over Mount Moriah David had seen the hand of the destroying angel stayed, probably just above where afterwards from the large altar of burnt-offering the smoke of count-less sacrifices rose day by day. On the opposite hill of Zion, separated only by a ravine from Moriah, stood the city and the palace of David, and close by the site of the Temple the tower of David. After that period an ever-shifting historical panorama passes before our view, unchanged only in this, that, amidst all the varying events, Jerusalem remains the one centre of interest and attraction, till we come to that Presence which has made it, even in its desolateness, 'Hephzibah,' 'sought out,' 'a city not forsaken' (Isaiah 62:4).

Cairn Altar

ORIGIN OF THE NAME

The Rabbis have a curious conceit about the origin of the name Jerusalem, which is commonly taken to mean, 'the foundation,' 'the abode,' or 'the inheritance of peace.' They make it a compound of *Jireh* and *Shalem,* and say that Abraham called it 'Jehovah-Jireh,' while Shem had named it *Shalem,* but that God combined the two into Jireh-Shalem, Jerushalaim, or Jerusalem (*Ber. R.*). There was certainly something peculiar in the choice of Palestine to be the country of the chosen people, as well as of Jerusalem to be its capital. The political importance of the land must be judged from its situation rather than its size. Lying midway between the east and the west, and placed between the great military monarchies, first of Egypt and Assyria, and then of Rome and the East, it naturally became the battle-field of the nations and the highway of the world. As for Jerusalem, its situation was entirely unique. Pitched on a height of about 2,610 feet above the level of the sea, its climate was more healthy, equable, and temperate than that of any other part of the country. From the top of Mount Olivet an unrivalled view of the most interesting localities in the land might be obtained. To the east the eye would wander over the intervening plains to Jericho, mark the tortuous windings of Jordan, and the sullen grey of the Dead Sea, finally resting on Pisgah and the mountains of Moab and Ammon. To

Jerusalem

the south, you might see beyond 'the king's gardens,' as far as the grey tops of 'the hill-country of Judaea.' Westwards, the view would be arrested by the mountains of *Bether* (Song of Solomon 2:17), whilst the haze in the distant horizon marked the line of the Great Sea. To the north, such well-known localities met the eye as Mizpeh, Gibeon, Ajalon, Michmash, Ramah, and Anathoth. But, above all, just at your feet, the Holy City would lie in all her magnificence, like 'a bride adorned for her husband.'

THIS SITUATION OF JERUSALEM

'Beautiful for situation, the joy of the whole earth, is Mount Zion, on the sides of the north, the city of the Great King....Walk about Zion, and go round about her: tell the towers thereof. Mark ye well her bulwarks, consider her palaces.' If this could be said of Jerusalem even in the humbler days of her native monarchy (Psalm 48:2, 12, 13),[1] it was emphatically true at the times when Jesus 'beheld the city,' after Herod the Great had adorned it with his wonted splendour. As the pilgrim bands 'came up' from all parts of the country to the great feasts, they must have stood enthralled when its beauty first burst

---

[1] The psalm was probably written during the reign of Jehoshaphat.

upon their gaze.[2] Not merely remembrances of the past, or the sacred associations connected with the present, but the grandeur of the scene before them must have kindled their admiration into enthusiasm. For Jerusalem was a city of palaces, and right royally enthroned as none other. Placed on an eminence higher than the immediate neighbourhood, it was cut off and isolated by deep valleys on all sides but one, giving it the appearance of an immense natural fortress. All round it, on three sides, like a natural fosse, ran the deep ravines of the Valley of Hinnom and of the Black Valley, or Kedron, which merged to the south of the city, descending in such steep declivity that where the two meet is 670 feet below the point whence each had started.[3] Only on the north-west was the city, as it were, bound to the mainland. And as if to give it yet more the character of a series of fortress-islands, a deep natural cleft—the Tyropoeon —ran south and north right through the middle of the city, then turned sharply westwards, separating Mount Zion from Mount Acra. Similarly, Acra was divided from Mount Moriah, and the latter again by an artificial valley from Bezetha, or the New Town. Sheer up from these encircling ravines rose the city of marble and cedar-covered palaces. Up that middle cleft, down in the valley, and along the slopes of the hills, crept the busy town, with its streets, markets, and bazaars. But alone, and isolated in its grandeur, stood the Temple Mount. Terrace upon terrace its courts rose, till, high above the city, within the enclosure of marble cloisters, cedar-roofed and richly ornamented, the Temple itself stood out a mass of snowy marble and of gold, glittering in the sunlight against the half-encircling green background of Olivet. In all his wanderings the Jew had not seen a city like his own Jerusalem. Not Antioch in Asia, not even imperial Rome herself, excelled it in architectural

*That is where the tribes
go up,
the tribes of the LORD,
to praise the name of the
LORD
according to the statute
given to Israel
(Ps. 122:4).*

---

[2] See the 'Songs of Degrees,' or rather 'Psalms of Ascent' (to the feasts), specially Psalm 122.

[3] In fact, the valley of Hinnom and the glen of Kedron were really one. For this and other topographical details the reader is referred to *The Recovery of Jerusalem*, by Capts. Wilson and Warren, R.E.

splendour. Nor has there been, either in ancient or modern times, a sacred building equal to the Temple, whether for situation or magnificence; nor yet have there been festive throngs like those joyous hundreds of thousands who, with their hymns of praise, crowded towards the city on the eve of a Passover. No wonder that the song burst from the lips of those pilgrims:

> 'Still stand our feet
> Within thy gates, Jerusalem!
> Jerusalem, ah! thou art built
> As a city joined companion-like together'
> (Psalm 122:2, 3).[4]

Mount of Olives from the Golden Gate

*After Jesus had said this, he went on ahead, going up to Jerusalem. As he approached Bethphage and Bethany at the hill called the Mount of Olives, he sent two of his disciples...
(Luke 19:28–29).*

From whatever side the pilgrim might approach the city, the first impression must have been solemn and deep. But a social surprise awaited those who came, whether from Jericho or from Galilee, by the well-known road that led over the Mount of Olives. From the south, beyond royal Bethlehem—from the west, descending over the heights of Beth-horon—or from the north, journeying along the mountains of Ephraim, they would have seen the city first vaguely looming in the grey distance, till, gradually approaching, they had become familiar with its outlines. It was far otherwise from the east. A turn in the road, and the city, hitherto entirely hid from view, would burst upon them suddenly, closely, and to most marked advantage. It was by this road Jesus made His triumphal entry from Bethany on the week of His Passion.[5] Up from 'the house of dates' the broad, rough road wound round the shoulder of Olivet. Thither the wondering crowd from Bethany followed Him, and there the praising multitude from the city met Him. They had come up that same Olivet, so familiar to them all. For did it not seem almost to form part of the city itself, shutting it off like a screen from the desert land that descended beyond to Jordan and the Dead Sea?

---

[4] The allusion is to the various hills which, 'like companions,' are joined together to form 'the city.'

[5] See the glowing description in Stanley's *Sinai and Palestine*.

MOUNT OF OLIVES

From the Temple Mount to the western base of Olivet, it was not more than 100 or 200 yards straight across, though, of course, the distance to the summit was much greater, say about half a mile. By the nearest pathway it was only 918 yards from the city gate to the principal summit.[6] Olivet was always fresh and green, even in earliest spring or during parched summer—the coolest, the pleasantest, the most sheltered walk about Jerusalem. For across this road the Temple and its mountain flung their broad shadows, and luxuriant foliage spread a leafy canopy overhead. They were not gardens, in the ordinary Western sense, through which one passed, far less orchards; but something peculiar to those climes, where Nature everywhere strews with lavish hand her flowers, and makes her gardens—where the garden bursts into the orchard, and the orchard stretches into the field, till, high up, olive and fig mingle with the darker cypress and pine. The stony road up Olivet wound along terraces covered with olives, whose silver and dark green leaves rustled in the breeze. Here gigantic gnarled fig-trees twisted themselves out of rocky soil; there clusters of palms raised their knotty stems high up into waving plumed tufts, or spread, bush-like, from the ground, the rich-coloured fruit bursting in clusters from the pod. Then there were groves of myrtle, pines, tall, stately cypresses, and on the summit itself two gigantic cedars. To these shady retreats the inhabitants would often come from Jerusalem to take pleasure or to meditate, and there one of their most celebrated Rabbis was at one time wont in preference to teach.[7] Thither, also, Christ with His disciples often resorted.

Coming from Bethany the city would be for some time completely hidden from view by the inter-

Cultivated palm

---

[6]'By the longer footpath it is 1,310 yards, and by the main camel road perhaps a little farther.' Josephus calculates the distance from the city evidently to the top of Mount Olivet at 1,010 yards, or 5 furlongs. See *City of the Great King*, p. 59.

[7]R. Jochanan ben Saccai, who was at the head of the Sanhedrim immediately before and after the destruction of Jerusalem.

vening ridge of Olivet. But at a sudden turn of the road, where 'the descent of the Mount of Olives' begins, all at once a first glimpse of Jerusalem is caught, and that quite close at hand. True, the configuration of Olivet on the right would still hide the Temple and most part of the city; but across Ophel, the busy suburb of the priests, the eye might range to Mount Zion, and rapidly climb its height to where Herod's palace covered the site once occupied by that of David. A few intervening steps of descent, where the view of the city has again been lost, and the pilgrim would hurry on to that ledge of rock. What a panorama over which to roam with hungry eagerness! At one glance he would see before him the whole city—its valleys and hills, its walls and towers, its palaces and streets, and its magnificent Temple—almost like a vision from another world. There could be no difficulty in making out the general features of the scene. Altogether the city was only thirty-three stadia, or about four English miles, in circumference. Within this compass dwelt a population of 600,000 (according to Tacitus), but, according to the Jewish historian, amounting at the time of the Passover to between two and three millions, or about equal to that of London.[8]

Each day Jesus was teaching at the temple, and each evening he went out to spend the night on the hill called the Mount of Olives (Luke 21:37).

THE WALLS

The first feature to attract attention would be the city walls, at the time of Christ only two in number.[9] The first, or old wall, began at the north-western angle of Zion, at the tower of *Hippicus,* and ran along

---

[8]Mr. Fergusson, in Smith's *Dictionary of the Bible,* i, p. 1025, controverts these numbers, on the ground of the population of modern cities within a given area. But two millions represent not the ordinary population, only the festive throngs at the Passover. Taking into consideration Eastern habits—the sleeping on the roof, and possibly the camping out—the computation is not extravagant. Besides, however untruthful Josephus was, he may, as a general rule, be trusted where official numbers, capable of verification, are concerned. In fact, taking into account this extraordinary influx, the Rabbis distinctly state, that during the feasts—except on the first night—the people might camp *outside* Jerusalem, but within the limits of a sabbath-day's journey. This, as Otho well remarks (*Lex. Rabb.* p. 195), also explains how, on such occasions, our Lord so often retired to the Mount of Olives.

[9]The third, largest, and strongest wall, which enclosed *Bezetha,* or the New Town, was built by Herod Agrippa, twelve years after the date of the crucifixion.

the northern brow of Zion, where it crossed the cleft, and joined the western colonnade of the Temple at the 'Council-house.' It also enclosed Zion along the west and the south, and was continued eastward around Ophel, till it merged in the south-eastern angle of the Temple. Thus the first wall would defend Zion, Ophel, and, along with the Temple walls, Moriah also. The second wall, which commenced at a gate in the first wall, called 'Gennath,' ran first north, and then east, so as to enclose Acra, and terminated at the Tower of Antonia. Thus the whole of the old city and the Temple were sufficiently protected.

Tower of Antonia

TOWER OF ANTONIA

The Tower of Antonia was placed at the north-western angle of the Temple, midway between the castle of the same name and the Temple. With the former it communicated by a double set of cloisters, with the latter by a subterranean passage into the Temple itself, and also by cloisters and stairs descending into the northern and the western porches of the Court of the Gentiles. Some of the most glorious traditions in Jewish history were connected with this castle, for there had been the ancient 'armoury of David,' the palace of Hezekiah and of Nehemiah, and the fortress of the Maccabees. But in the days of Christ Antonia was occupied by a hated Roman garrison, which kept watch over Israel, even in its sanctuary. In fact, the Tower of Antonia overlooked and commanded the Temple, so that a detachment of soldiers could at any time rush down to quell a riot, as on the occasion when the Jews had almost killed Paul (Acts 21:31). The city walls were further defended by towers—sixty in the first, and forty in the second wall. Most prominent among them were Hippicus, Phasaelus, and Mariamne, close by each other, to the north-west of Zion—all compactly built of immense marble blocks, square, strongly fortified, and surmounted by buildings defended by battlements and turrets.[10] They were built by Herod, and named after

The whole city was aroused, and the people came running from all directions. Seizing Paul, they dragged him from the temple, and immediately the gates were shut. While they were trying to kill him, news reached the commander of the Roman troops that the whole city of Jerusalem was in an uproar. He at once took some officers and soldiers and ran down to the crowd. When the rioters saw the commander and his soldiers, they stopped beating Paul (Acts 21:30–32).

---

[10]For particulars of these forts, see Josephus's *Wars*, 5.156–171.

the friend and the brother he had lost in battle, and the wife whom his jealousy had killed.

THE FOUR HILLS

If the pilgrim scanned the city more closely, he would observe that it was built on four hills. Of these, the western, or ancient Zion, was the highest, rising about 200 feet above Moriah, though still 100 feet lower than the Mount of Olives. To the north and the east, opposite Zion, and divided from it by the deep Tyropoeon Valley, were the crescent-shaped Acra and Moriah, the latter with Ophel as its southern outrunner. Up and down the slopes of Acra the Lower City crept. Finally, the fourth hill, Bezetha (from *bezaion*, marshy ground), the New Town, rose north of the Temple Mount and of Acra, and was separated from them by an artificial valley. The streets, which, as in all Eastern cities, were narrow, were paved with white marble. A somewhat elevated footway ran along for the use of those who had newly been purified in the Temple, while the rest walked in the roadway below. The streets derived their names mostly from the gates to which they led, or from the various *bazaars*. Thus there were 'Water-street,' 'Fish-street,' 'East-street,' etc. The 'Timber Bazaar' and that of the 'Tailors' were in the New City; the Grand Upper Market on Mount Zion. Then there were the 'Wool' and the 'Braziers' Bazaar;' 'Baker-street,' 'Butcher-street,' 'Strangers-street,' and many others similarly named. Nor would it have been difficult to identify the most prominent buildings in the city. At the north-western angle of Mount Zion, the ancient Salem and Jebus, on the site of the castle of David, was the grand palace of Herod, generally occupied by the Roman procurators during their temporary sojourn in Jerusalem. It stood high up, just within shelter of the great towers which Herod had reared—a marvel of splendour, of whose extent, strength, height, rooms, towers, roofs, porticoes, courts, and adjacent gardens Josephus speaks in such terms of admiration.

Street of a Jewish city

Excavations on southeastern hill of Jerusalem

HIGH-PRIEST'S PALACE

At the opposite, or north-eastern corner of Mount Zion, was the palace of the High-priest. Being built on the slope of the hill, there was under the principal apartments a lower story, with a porch in front, so that we can understand how on that eventful night Peter was '*beneath* in the palace' (Mark 14:66). Beyond it, probably on the slope of the Acra, was the Repository of the Archives, and on the other side of the cleft, abutting on the Temple, with which it was probably connected by a colonnade, the Council Chamber of the Sanhedrim. Following the eastern brow of Mount Zion, south of the High-priest's palace, and opposite the Temple, was the immense Xystus, which probably extended into the Tyropoeon. Whatever may have been its original purpose,[11] it was afterwards used as a place of public meetings, where, on great occasions, the populace was harangued. Here Peter probably addressed the three thousand converts on the day of Pentecost when the multitude had hurried thither from the

When the day of Pentecost came, they were all together in one place. Suddenly a sound like the blowing of a violent wind came from heaven and filled the whole house where they were sitting (Acts 2:1–2).

---

[11]Barclay suggests that the Xystus had originally been the heathen gymnasium built by the infamous high-priest Jason. (*City of the Great King*, p. 101.)

Temple on hearing 'the mighty rushing sound.' The Xystus was surrounded by a covered colonnade. Behind it was the palace of Agrippa, the ancient palace of David and of the Maccabees, and again, in the rear of it, that of Bernice. On Acra stood afterwards the palaces of certain foreign princes, such as those of Queen Helena, King Monobasus, and other proselytes. In this quarter, or even beyond it to the north-west, one would naturally look for the Theatre and the Amphitheatre, which, being so essentially un-Jewish, must have been located as far as possible from the Temple. The space around the Temple was no doubt kept clear of buildings. On the south-eastern corner behind it was the great Sheep Market, and to the south of it the Hippodrome. Originally, 'the king's house by the horse-gate,' built by Solomon, and the royal stables, had occupied the southern area of the Temple Mount, where Herod afterwards built the 'Royal Porch.' For the Temple of Solomon was 300 feet shorter, from north to south, than that of Herod. Transversely, between Xystus and the Fish Gate, lay the quarter of *Maktesh* (Zeph. 1:10, 11), occupied by various bazaars, chiefly connected with the Temple. Lastly, south of the Temple, but on the same hill, was *Ophel*, the crowded suburb of the priests.

In this hasty survey of the city no notice has been taken of the magnificent monuments and pillars erected in various parts of Jerusalem, nor of its synagogues, of which tradition fixes the number at from 460 to 480; nor of many public buildings; nor yet of such sacred spots as the Pool of Siloam, or that of Bethesda, on which the memory loves to dwell. In sharp contrast to all this beauty and magnificence must have been the great walls and towers, and the detached forts, which guarded either the Temple or access to the various hills on which the city rose, such as Millo, Ophel, and others. Of these the highest and strongest was the L-shaped Tower of Antonia, which rose to a height of 105 feet, being itself reared on a rock 75 feet high. Indeed, the towers and the castle of Antonia, with its squares, outbuildings, and colonnades, must have looked almost like a small town, on its rocky height. Beyond the city, numerous large gates opened everywhere into the country, upon the slopes and crests of hills covered by delicious gardens and dotted with beautiful villas.

THE SHUSHAN GATE

Such must have been a first view of Jerusalem, as 'beheld' from the Mount of Olives, on which we are supposed to have taken our stand. If Jewish tradition on the subject may be trusted, a gate opened upon this Mount of Olives through the eastern wall of the Temple.[12] It is called 'the Shushan Gate,' from the sculptured representation over it of the city to which so many Jewish memories attached. From this gate an arched roadway, by which the priests brought out the 'red heifer,' and on the Day of Atonement the scape-goat, is said to have conducted to the Mount of Olives. Near the spot where the red heifer was burned were extensive lavatories, and booths for the sale of articles needed for various purifications. Up a crest, on one of the most commanding elevations, was the Lunar Station, whence, by fire signals, the advent of each new moon was telegraphed from hill to hill into far countries. If Jewish tradition may further be trusted, there was also an unused gate in the Temple towards the north—*Tedi* or *Tere*—and two gates towards the south. We know for certain of only a subterranean passage which led from the fortress Antonia on the 'north-western angle' of the Temple into the Temple Court, and of the cloisters with stairs descending into the porches, by one of which the chief captain Lysias rushed to the rescue of Paul, when nearly killed by the infuriated multitude. Dismissing all doubtful questions, we are sure that at any rate five gates opened into the outer Temple enclosure or Court of the Gentiles—one from the south, and four—and these the principal—from the west. That southern gate was double, and must have chiefly served the convenience of the priests. Coming from Ophel, they would pass

...but for the tower itself, when Herod the king of the Jews had fortified it more firmly than before, in order to secure and guard the temple, he gratified Antonius, who was his friend, and the Roman ruler, and then gave it the name of the Tower of Antonia (Jos. Antiquities 15.409).

---

[12]In the chamber above this gate two standard measures were kept, avowedly for the use of the workmen employed in the Temple. (*Chel.* xvii. 9.)

through its gigantic archway and vestibule (40 feet each way), and then by a double tunnel nearly 200 feet long, whence they emerged at a flight of steps leading straight up from the Court of the Gentiles into that of the priests, close to the spot where they would officiate.[13]

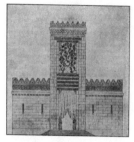

Front elevation of Temple

But to join the great crowd of worshippers we have to enter the city itself. Turning our back on Mount Zion, we now face eastwards to Mount Moriah. Though we look towards the four principle entrances to the Temple, yet what we see within those walls on the highest of the terraces is not the front but the back of the sanctuary. It is curious how tradition is here in the most palpable error in turning to the east in worship. The Holy Place itself faced eastwards, and was approached from the east; but most assuredly the ministering priests and the worshippers looked not towards the east, but towards the west.

THE TEMPLE PLATEAU

The Temple plateau had been artificially levelled at immense labour and cost, and enlarged by gigantic substructures. The latter served also partly for the purpose of purification, as otherwise there might have been some dead body beneath, which, however great the distance from the surface, would, unless air had intervened, have, according to tradition, defiled the whole place above. As enlarged by Herod the Great, the Temple area occupied an elongated square of from 925 to 950 feet and upwards.[14] Roughly calculating it at about 1,000 feet, this would give an extent more than one-half greater than the length of St. Peter's at Rome, which measures 613 feet, and

[13]Jewish tradition mentions the following five as the outer gates of the Temple: that of *Shushan* to the east, of *Tedi* to the north, of *Copponus* to the west, and the two *Huldah* gates to the south. The Shushan gate was said to have been lower than the others, so that the priests at the end of the 'heifer-bridge' might look over it into the Temple. In a chamber above the Shushan gate, the standard measures of the 'cubit' were kept.

[14]Many modern writers have computed the Temple area at only 606 feet, while Jewish authorities make it much larger than we have stated it. The computation in the text is based on the latest and most trustworthy investigations, and fully borne out by the excavations made on the spot by Capts. Wilson and Warren.

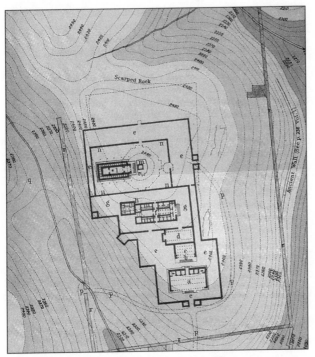

Temple Plateau, showing elevation

nearly double our own St. Paul's, whose extreme length is 520$\frac{1}{2}$ feet. And then we must bear in mind that the Temple plateau was not merely about 1,000 feet in length, but a square of nearly 1,000 feet! It was not, however, in the centre of this square, but towards the north-west, that the Temple itself and its special courts were placed. Nor, as already hinted, were they all on a level, but rose terrace upon terrace, till the sacred edifice itself was reached, its porch protruding, 'shoulder-like,' on either side—perhaps rising into two flanking towers—and covering the Holy and Most Holy Places. Thus must the 'golden fane' have been clearly visible from all parts; the smoke of its sacrifices slowly curling up against the blue Eastern sky, and the music of its services wafted across the busy city, while the sunlight glittered on its gilt roofs, or shone from its pavement of tesselated marble, or threw great shadows on Olivet behind.

FABLES OF THE RABBIS

Assuredly, when the Rabbis thought of their city in her glory, they might well say: 'The world is like unto an eye. The ocean surrounding the world is the white of the eye; its black is the world itself; the pupil is Jerusalem; but the image within the pupil is the sanctuary.' In their sorrow and loneliness they have written many fabled things of Jerusalem, of which some may here find a place, to show with what halo of reverence they surrounded the loving memories of the past. Jerusalem, they say, belonged to no tribe in particular—it was all Israel's. And this is in great measure literally true; for even afterwards, when ancient Jebus became the capital of the land, the boundary line between Judah and Benjamin ran right through the middle of the city and of the Temple; so that, according to Jewish tradition, the porch and the sanctuary itself were in Benjamin, and the Temple courts and altar in Judah. In Jerusalem no house might be hired. The houses belonged as it were to all; for they must all be thrown open, in free-hearted hospitality, to the pilgrim-brethren that came up to the feast. Never had any one failed to find in Jerusalem the means of celebrating the paschal festivities, nor yet had any lacked a bed on which to rest. Never did serpent or scorpion hurt within her precincts; never did fire desolate her streets, nor ruin occur. No ban ever rested on the Holy City. It was Levitically more sacred than other cities, since there alone the paschal lamb, the thank-offerings, and the second tithes might be eaten. Hence they carefully guarded against all possibility of pollution. No dead body might remain in the city overnight; no sepulchres were there, except those of the house of David and of the prophetess Huldah. No even domestic fowls might be kept, nor vegetable gardens be planted, lest the smell of decaying vegetation should defile the air; nor yet furnaces be built, for fear of smoke. Never had adverse accident interrupted the services of the sanctuary, nor profaned the offerings. Never had rain extinguished the fire on the altar, nor contrary wind driven back the smoke of the sacrifices; nor yet,

In the days of her affliction and wandering Jerusalem remembers all the treasures that were hers in days of old (Lam. 1:7a).

however great the crowd of worshippers, had any failed for room to bow down and worship the God of Israel!

Thus far the Rabbis. All the more impressive is their own admission and their lament—so significant as viewed in the light of the Gospel: 'For three years and a half abode the Shechinah' (or visible Divine presence) 'on the Mount of Olives,'—waiting whether Israel would repent—'and calling upon them, "Seek ye the Lord while He may be found, call upon Him while He is near." And when all was in vain, then the Shechinah returned to its own place!'

O God, the nations have invaded your inheritance; they have defiled your holy temple, they have reduced Jerusalem to rubble (Ps. 79:1).

JERUSALEM IN RUINS

The Shechinah *has* withdrawn to its own place! Both the city and the Temple have been laid 'even with the ground,' because Jerusalem knew not the time of her visitation (Luke 19:44). 'They have laid Jerusalem on heaps' (Ps. 79:1). 'The stones of the sanctuary are poured out in the top of every street' (Lam. 4:1). All this, and much more, did the Saviour,

Western wall of the Temple, with the Wailing Place of the Jews

As he approached Jerusalem and saw the city, he wept over it and said, "If you, even you, had only known on this day what would bring you peace— but now it is hidden from your eyes" (Luke 19:41–42).

the rightful King of Israel, see in the near future, when 'He beheld the city, and wept over it.' And now we must search very deep down, sinking the shaft from 60 to over 125 feet through the rubbish of accumulated ruins, before reaching at last the ancient foundations.[15] And there, close by where once the royal bridge spanned the deep chasm and led from the City of David into the royal porch of the Temple, is 'the Jews' Wailing Place,' where the mourning heirs to all this desolation reverently embrace the fallen stones, and weep unavailing tears—unavailing because the present is as the past, and because what brought that judgment and sorrow is unrecognised, unrepented, unremoved. Yet—'Watchman, what of the night? Watchman, what of the night? The watchman said, The morning cometh, and also the night. If ye will inquire, inquire! Return, come!'

---

[15] *Recovery of Jerusalem*, p. 185.

2
WITHIN THE HOLY PLACE

✣

"Not one stone here will be left on another; every one will be thrown down."—Matthew 24:2.

'THE ROYAL BRIDGE'

Of the four principal entrances into the Temple —all of them from the west—the most northerly descended, perhaps by flights of steps, into the Lower City; while two others led into the suburb, or *Parbar*, as it is called. But by far the most magnificent avenue was that at the south-western angle of the Temple. Probably this was 'the ascent...into the house of the Lord,' which so astounded the Queen of Sheba (1 Kings 10:5).[1] It would, indeed, be difficult to exaggerate the splendour of this approach. A colossal bridge on arches spanned the intervening Valley of the Tyropoeon, connecting the ancient City of David with what is called the 'Royal Porch of the Temple.' From its ruins we can reconstruct this bridge. Each arch spanned 41½ feet, and the spring-stones measured 24 feet in length by 6 in thickness. It is almost impossible to realise these proportions, except by a comparison with other buildings. A single stone 24 feet long! Yet these were by no means the largest in the masonry of the Temple. Both at the south-eastern and the south-western angles stones have been found

When the queen of Sheba saw all the wisdom of Solomon and the palace he had built, the food on his table, the seating of his officials, the attending servants in their robes, his cupbearers, and the burnt offerings he made at the temple of the LORD, she was overwhelmed (1 Kgs. 10:4–5).

---

[1]According to Mr. Lewin, however (*Siege of Jerusalem*, p. 270), this celebrated 'ascent' to the house of the Lord went up by a double subterranean passage, 250 feet long and 62 feet wide, by a flight of steps from the new palace of Solomon, afterwards occupied by the 'Royal Porch,' right into the inner court of the Temple.

measuring from 20 to 40 feet in length, and weighing above 100 tons.

THE TEMPLE PORCHES

The view from this 'Royal Bridge' must have been splendid. It was over it that they led the Saviour, in sight of all Jerusalem, to and from the palace of the high-priest, that of Herod, the meeting-place of the Sanhedrim, and the judgment-seat of Pilate. Here the city would have lain spread before us like a map. Beyond it the eye would wander over straggling suburbs, orchards, and many gardens—fairest among them the royal gardens to the south, the 'garden of

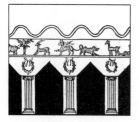

Corinthian columns

roses,' so celebrated by the Rabbis—till the horizon was bounded by the hazy outline of mountains in the distance. Over the parapet of the bridge we might have looked into the Tyropoeon Valley below, a depth of not less than 225 feet. The roadway which spanned this cleft for a distance of 354 feet, from Mount Moriah to Mount Zion opposite, was 50 feet broad, that is, about 5 feet wider than the central avenue of the Royal Temple-Porch into which it led. These 'porches,' as they are called in the New Testament, or cloisters, were among the finest architectural features of the Temple. They ran all round the inside of its wall, and bounded the outer enclosure of the Court of the Gentiles. They consisted of double rows of Corinthian pillars, all monoliths, wholly cut out of one block of marble, each pillar being 37^1/$_2$ feet high. A flat roof, richly ornamented, rested against the wall, in which also the outer row of pillars was inserted. Possibly there may have been towers[2] where one colonnade joined the other. But the 'Royal Porch,' by which we are supposed to have entered the Temple, was the most splendid, consisting not as the others, of a double, but of a *treble* colonnade, formed of 162 pillars, ranged in four rows of 40 pillars each, the two odd pillars serving as a kind of screen, where the 'Porch' opened upon the bridge. Indeed, we may regard the Royal Porch as consisting

---

[2]The suggestion is that of Dr. Barclay, in his *City of the Great King.*

of a central nave 45 feet wide, with gigantic pillars 100 feet high, and of two aisles 30 feet wide, with pillars 50 feet high.[3] By very competent authorities this Royal Porch, as its name indicates, is regarded as occupying the site of the ancient palace of Solomon, to which he 'brought up' the daughter of Pharaoh. Here also had been the 'stables of Solomon.' When Herod the Great rebuilt the Temple, he incorporated with it this site of the ancient royal palace. What the splendour and height[4] of this one porch in the Temple must have been is best expressed in the words of Captain Wilson:[5] 'It is almost impossible to realise the effect which would be produced by a building longer and higher than York Cathedral, standing on a solid mass of masonry almost equal in height to the tallest of our church spires.' And this was only one of the porches which formed the southern enclosure of the first and outermost court of the Temple—that of the Gentiles. The view from the top of this colonnade into Kedron was to the stupendous depth of 450 feet. Here some have placed that pinnacle of the Temple to which the tempter brought our Saviour.

Solomon made an alliance with Pharaoh king of Egypt and married his daughter. He brought her to the City of David until he finished building his palace and the temple of the LORD, and the wall around Jerusalem (1 Kgs. 3:1).

Solomon's Porch

---

[3] Mr. Fergusson, in Smith's *Dictionary of the Bible,* vol. 3, p. 1462.
[4] Professor Porter has calculated it at 440 feet.
[5] *Recovery of Jerusalem,* p. 9.

Then came the Feast of Dedication at Jerusalem. It was winter, and Jesus was in the temple area walking in Solomon's Colonnade (John 10:22–23).

These halls or porches around the Court of the Gentiles must have been most convenient places for friendly or religious intercourse—for meetings or discussions.[6] Here Jesus, when still a child, was found by His parents disputing with the doctors; here He afterwards so often taught the people; and here the first assemblies of the Christians must have taken place when, 'continuing daily with one accord in the Temple,…praising God, and having favour with all the people,…the Lord added to the church daily such as should be saved.' Especially do we revert to Solomon's Porch, that ran along the eastern wall of the Temple, and faced its great entrance. It was the only remnant left of the Temple built by the wise King of Israel. In this porch 'Jesus walked' on that 'Feast of the Dedication' (John 10:23), when He 'told it plainly,' 'I and my Father are one;' and it was thither 'that all the people ran together' when 'the notable miracle' on the lame man had been wrought at the 'Beautiful Gate of the Temple.'

COURT OF THE GENTILES

It was the rule when entering the Temple to pass in by the right, and when leaving it to go out by the left hand. The great Court of the Gentiles,[7] which formed the lowest or outer enclosure of the Sanctuary, was paved with the finest variegated marble. According to Jewish tradition, it formed a square of 750 feet. Its name is derived from the fact that it was open to all—Jews or Gentiles—provided they observed the prescribed rules of decorum and reverence. In this court tradition places eating and sleeping apartments for the Levites, and a synagogue. But, despite pharisaic punctiliousness, the noise, especially on the eve of the Passover, must have been most disturbing. For there the oxen, sheep, and doves selected as fit for sacrifices were sold as in a market; and here were those tables of the money-changers

---

[6]According to *Succ.* iv. 1, benches or seats were placed there.

[7]We have adopted this name as in common use, though Relandus (*Antiq.* p. 78) rightly objects that the only term for it used in Jewish writings is the 'mountain of the house.'

Inscription warning Gentiles against entry into Temple

which the Lord overthrew when He drove from His Father's house them that bought and sold (Matt. 21:12; John 2:14).[8] Within a short distance, in the court, a marble screen 4½ feet high, and beautifully ornamented, bore Greek and Latin inscriptions, warning Gentiles not to proceed, on pain of death. One of those very tablets, bearing almost the same words as those given by Josephus, has been discovered in late excavations. It was because they thought Paul had infringed this order, that the infuriated multitude 'went about to kill him' (Acts 21:31). Beyond this enclosure a flight of fourteen steps, each 9 inches high, led up to a terrace 15 feet broad, called the 'Chel,' which bounded the *inner* wall of the Temple. We are now approaching the Sanctuary itself, which consisted, first, of three courts, each higher than the former, and, beyond them, of the Holy and Most Holy Places, with their outbuildings. Entering by the principal gate on the *east* we pass, first into the Court of the Women, thence into that of Israel, and from

---

[8]Compare also especially *Jer. Chag.* 78*a*.

the latter into that of the Priests. This would have been, so to speak, the natural way of advancing. But there was a nearer road into the Court of the Priests. For both north and south, along the terrace, flights of steps led up to three gates (both north and south), which opened into the Court of the Priests, while a fourth gate (north and south) led into the middle of the Court of the Women. Thus there were nine gates opening from 'the Terrace' into the Sanctuary—the principal one from the east, and four north and south, of which one (north and south) also led into the Court of the Women, and the other three (north and south) into that of the Priests.

Interior of Golden Gate

One day Peter and John were going up to the temple at the time of prayer—at three in the afternoon. Now a man crippled from birth was being carried to the temple gate called Beautiful, where he was put every day to beg from those going into the temple courts…

Then Peter said, "Silver or gold I do not have, but what I have I give you. In the name of Jesus Christ of Nazareth, walk." Taking him by the right hand, he helped him up, and instantly the man's feet and ankles became strong. He jumped to his feet and began to walk. Then he went with them into the temple courts, walking and jumping, and praising God (Acts 3:1–2, 6–8).

THE 'BEAUTIFUL GATE'

These eight side gates, as we may call them, were all two-leaved, wide, high, with superstructures and chambers supported by two pillars, and covered with gold and silver plating. But far more magnificent than any of them was the ninth or *eastern* gate, which formed the principal entrance into the Temple. The ascent to it was from the terrace by twelve easy steps. The gate itself was made of dazzling Corinthian brass, most richly ornamented; and so massive were its double doors that it needed the united strength of twenty men to open and close them. This was the 'Beautiful Gate;' and on its steps had they been wont these many years to lay the lame man, just as privileged beggars now lie at the entrance to Continental cathedrals. No wonder that all Jerusalem knew him; and when on that sunny afternoon Peter and John joined the worshippers in the Court of the Women, not alone, but in company with the well-known cripple, who, after his healing, was 'walking and leaping and praising God,' universal 'wonder and amazement' must have been aroused. Then, when the lame man, still 'holding by' the apostles, again descended these steps, we can readily understand how all the people would crowd around in Solomon's Porch, close by, till the sermon of Peter—so fruitful in its spiritual results—was interrupted by the Temple police, and the sudden imprisonment of the apostles.

COURT OF THE WOMEN

The Court of the Women obtained its name, not from its appropriation to the exclusive use of women, but because they were not allowed to proceed farther, except for sacrificial purposes. Indeed, this was probably the common place for worship, the females occupying, according to Jewish tradition, only a raised gallery along three sides of the court. This court covered a space upwards of 200 feet square. All around ran a simple colonnade, and within it, against the wall, the thirteen chests, or 'trumpets,' for charitable contributions were placed.[9] These thirteen chests were narrow at the mouth and wide at the bottom, shaped like trumpets, whence their name. Their specific objects were carefully marked on them. Nine were for the receipt of what was legally due by worshippers; the other four for strictly voluntary gifts. Trumpets 1 and 2 were appropriated to the half-shekel Temple-tribute of the current and of the past year. Into Trumpet 3 those women who had to bring turtledoves for a burnt- and a sin-offering dropped their equivalent in money, which was daily taken out and a corresponding number of turtledoves offered. This not only saved the labour of so many separate sacrifices, but spared the modesty of those who might not wish to have the occasion or the circumstances of their offering to be publicly known. Into this trumpet Mary the mother of Jesus must have dropped the value of her offering (Luke 2:22, 24) when the aged Simeon took the infant Saviour 'in his arms, and blessed God.' Trumpet 4 similarly received the value of the offerings of young pigeons. In Trumpet 5 contributions for the wood used in the Temple; in Trumpet 6 for the incense, and in Trumpet 7 for the golden vessels for the ministry were deposited. If a man had put aside a certain sum for a sin-offering, and any money was left over after its purchase, it was cast into Trumpet 8. Similarly, Trumpets 9, 10, 11, 12, and 13 were destined for what was left over from trespass-offerings, offerings of birds, the offering of

As he looked up, Jesus saw the rich putting their gifts into the temple treasury. He also saw a poor widow put in two very small copper coins. "I tell you the truth," he said, "this poor widow has put in more than all the others (Luke 21:1–3).

Ancient horns and curved trumpets

---

[9]It was probably into one of these that the poor widow dropped her 'two mites' (Luke 21:2).

the Nazarite, of the cleansed leper, and voluntary offerings. In all probability this space where the thirteen Trumpets were placed was the 'treasury,' where Jesus taught on that memorable Feast of Tabernacles (John 7; 8; see specially 8:20). We can also understand how, from the peculiar and known destination of each of these thirteen 'trumpets,' the Lord could distinguish the contributions of the rich who cast in 'of their abundance' from that of the poor widow who of her 'penury' had given 'all the living' that she had (Mark 12:41; Luke 21:1). But there was also a special treasury-chamber, into which at certain times they carried the contents of the thirteen chests; and, besides, what was called 'a chamber of the silent,' where devout persons secretly deposited money, afterwards secretly employed for educating children of the pious poor.

He spoke these words while teaching in the temple area near the place where the offerings were put. Yet no one seized him, because his time had not yet come (John 8:20).

So when you give to the needy, do not announce it with trumpets, as the hypocrites do in the synagogues and on the streets, to be honored by men. I tell you the truth, they have received their reward in full (Matt. 6:2).

It is probably in ironical allusion to the form and name of these treasure-chests that the Lord, making use of the word 'trumpet,' describes the conduct of those who, in their almsgiving, sought glory from men as 'sounding a trumpet' before them (Matt. 6:2)—that is, carrying before them, as it were, in full display one of these trumpet-shaped alms-boxes (literally called in the Talmud, 'trumpets'), and, as it were, sounding it.[10]

THE CHAMBERS

In each of the four corners of the Court of the Women were chambers, or rather unroofed courts, each said to have been 60 feet long. In that at the right hand (on the north-east), the priests who were unfit for other than menial services on account of bodily blemishes, picked the worm-eaten wood from that destined for the altar. In the court at the farther angle (north-west) the purified lepers washed before

---

[10]The allusion is all the more pointed, when we bear in mind that each of these trumpets had a mark to tell its special object. It seems strange that this interpretation should not have occurred to any of the commentators, who have always found the allusion such a *crux interpretum*. An article in the *Bible Educator* has since substantially adopted this view, adding that trumpets were blown when the alms were collected. But for the latter statement there is no historical authority whatever, and it would contravene the religious spirit of the times.

presenting themselves to the priests at the Gate of Nicanor. At the left (south-east) the Nazarites polled their hair, and cooked their peace-offerings; while in a fourth court (at the south-west) the oil and wine were kept for the drink-offerings. The musical instruments used by the Levites were deposited in two rooms under the Court of the Israelites, to which the access was from the Court of the Women.

Of course the western colonnade of this court was open. Thence fifteen easy steps led through the so-called Gate of Nicanor[11] into the Court of Israel. On these steps the Levites were wont on the Feast of Tabernacles to sing the fifteen 'Psalms of Degrees,' or ascent (Pss. 120 to 134), whence some have derived their name. Here, or, rather, in the Gate of Nicanor, all that was ordered to be done 'before the Lord' took place. There the cleansed leper and the women coming for purification presented themselves to the priests, and there also the 'water of jealousy' was given to the suspected wife.

Ancient musical instruments

I rejoiced with those who said to me,
"Let us go to the house of the Lord."
Our feet are standing in your gates,
O Jerusalem
(Ps. 122:1–2).

COURT OF ISRAEL

Perhaps it will be most convenient for practical purposes to regard the two Courts of Israel and of the Priests as in reality forming only *one*, divided into two parts by a low balustrade $1\frac{1}{2}$ feet high. Thus viewed, this large double court, inclusive of the Sanctuary itself, would measure $280\frac{1}{2}$ feet in length by $202\frac{1}{2}$ feet in breadth. Of this a narrow strip, $16\frac{1}{2}$ feet long, formed the Court of Israel. Two steps led up from it to the Court of the Priests. Here you mounted again by three low semicircular steps to a kind of pulpit or platform, where, as well as on the 'fifteen steps,' the Levites sang and played during the ordinary service. The *priests*, on the other hand, occupied, while pronouncing the blessing, the steps at the other end of the court which led up to the Temple porch. A similar arrangement existed in the great court as in that of the Women. Right and left of the Nicanor

---

[11]Jost (*Gesch. d. Jud.*, vol. i, p. 142) calls the Nicanor the gate of Corinthian brass. On the origin of the name see Herzfeld, *Gesch. d. V. Isr.*, vol. i, p. 344.

Gate were receptacles for the priestly vestments (one for each of the four kinds, and for the twenty-four courses of priests: 4 x 24 = 96).

Next came the chamber of the high-priest's meat-offering (Lev. 6:20), where each morning before going to their duties the officiating priesthood gathered from the so-called 'Beth-ha-Moked,' or 'house of stoves.' The latter was built on arches, and contained a large dining-hall that communicated with four other chambers. One of these was a large apartment where fires were continually burning for the use of the priests who ministered barefoot. There also the heads of the ministering courses slept, and here, in a special receptacle under the pavement, the keys of the Temple were hung up at night. Of the other three chambers of the Beth-Moked, one was appropriated to the various counterfoils given as a warrant when a person had paid his due for a drink-offering. In another the shewbread was prepared, while yet a third served for the lambs (at least six in number) that were always kept ready for the regular sacrifice. Here also a passage led to the well-lit sub-terranean bath for the use of the priests. Besides the Beth-Moked there were, north and south of the court, rooms for storing the salt for the altar, for salting the skins of sacrifices, for washing 'their inwards,' for storing the 'clean' wood, for the machinery by which the laver was supplied with water, and finally the chamber 'Gazith,' or Hall of Hewn Stones, where the Sanhedrim was wont to meet. Above some of these chambers were other apartments, such as those in which the high-priest spent the week before the Day of Atonement in study and meditation.

The fire on the altar must be kept burning; it must not go out. Every morning the priest is to add firewood and arrange the burnt offering on the fire and burn the fat of the fellowship offerings on it. The fire must be kept burning on the altar continuously; it must not go out (Lev. 6:12–13).

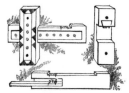

Egyptian key

THE CHAMBERS

The account which Jewish tradition gives of these gates and chambers around the Court of the Priests is somewhat conflicting, perhaps because the same chambers and gates may have borne different names. It may, however, be thus summarised. Entering the Great Court by the Nicanor Gate, there was at the right hand the Chamber of Phinehas with

its 96 receptacles for priests' vestments, and at the left
the place where the high-priest's daily meat-offering
was prepared, and where every morning before day-
break all the ministering priests met, after their
inspection of the Temple and before being told off
to duty. Along the southern side of the court were
the Water-gate, through which at the Feast of
Tabernacles the pitcher with water was brought from
the Pool of Siloam, with a chamber above it, called
Abtinas,[12] where the priests kept guard at night; then
the Gate of the Firstlings, through which the firstlings
fit to be offered were brought; and the Wood-gate,
through which the altar-wood was carried. Alongside
these gates were *Gazith,* the hall of square polished
stones, where the Sanhedrim sat; the chamber *Golah,*
for the water apparatus which emptied and filled the
laver; and the wood-chamber. Above and beyond it
were the apartments of the high-priest and the council-
chamber of the 'honourable councillors,' or priestly
council for affairs strictly connected with the Temple.
On the northern side of the Priests' Court were the
gate Nitzutz (Spark Gate), with a guard-chamber
above for the priests, the Gate of Sacrifices, and the
Gate of Beth-Moked. Alongside these gates were the
chamber for salting the sacrifices; that for salting the
skins (named *Parvah* from its builder), with bath-
rooms for the high-priest above it; and finally the
Beth-Moked with its apartments. The two largest of
these buildings—the council-chamber of the Sanhedrim
at the south-eastern,[13] and the Beth-Moked at the
north-western angle of the court—were partly built

---

[12]The Talmud (*Yoma* 19*a*) expresses a doubt as to its exact localisation.

[13]It is very strange what mistakes are made about the localisation of the rooms and courts connected with the Temple. Thus the writer of the article 'Sanhedrim' in Kitto's *Encycl.,* vol. iii, p. 766, says that the hall of the Sanhedrim 'was situate in the centre of the south side of the Temple-court, the northern part extending to the Court of the Priests, and the southern part to the Court of the Israelites.' But the Court of Israel and that of the Priests did *not* lie north and south, but east and west, as a glance at the Temple plan will show! The hall of the Sanhedrim extended indeed *south,* though certainly not to the Court of Israel, but to the *Chel* or terrace. The authorities quoted in the article 'Sanhedrim' do not bear out the writer's conclusions. It ought to be remarked that about the time of Christ the Sanhedrim removed its sittings from the Hall of Square Stones to another on the east of the Temple-court.

Altar of Burnt Offerings and Altar of Incense

into the court and partly out on 'the terrace.' This, because none other than a prince of the house of David might sit down within the sacred enclosure of the Priests' Court. Probably there was a similar arrangement for the high-priest's apartments and the priests' council-chamber, as well as for the guard-chambers of the priests, so that at each of the four corners of the court the apartments would abut upon 'the terrace.'[14] All along the colonnades, both around the Court of the Gentiles and that of the Women, there were seats and benches for the accommodation of the worshippers.

THE ALTAR

The most prominent object in the Court of the Priests was the immense altar of unhewn stones,[15] a

---

[14]We know that the two priestly guard-chambers above the Water-gate and Nitzutz opened also upon the terrace. This may explain how the Talmud sometimes speaks of six and sometimes of eight gates opening from the Priests' Court upon the terrace, or else gates 7 and 8 may have been those which opened from the terrace north and south into the Court of the Women.

[15]They were 'whitened' twice a year. Once in seven years the high-priest was to inspect the Most Holy Place, through an opening made from the room above. If repairs were required, the workmen were let down through the ceiling in a sort of cage, so as not to see anything but what they were to work at.

square of not less than 48 feet, and, inclusive of 'the horns,' 15 feet high. All around it a 'circuit' ran for the use of the ministering priests, who, as a rule, always passed round by the right, and retired by the left.[16] As this 'circuit' was raised 9 feet from the ground, and 1¹/₂ feet high, while the 'horns' measured 1¹/₂ feet in height, the priests would have only to reach 3 feet to the top of the altar, and 4¹/₂ feet to that of each 'horn.' An inclined plane, 48 feet long by 24 wide, into which about the middle two smaller 'descents' merged, led up to the 'circuit' from the south. Close by was the great heap of salt, from which every sacrifice must be salted with salt.[17] On the altar, which at the top was only 36 feet wide, three fires burned, one (east) for the offerings, the second (south) for the incense, the third (north) to supply the means for kindling the other two. The four 'horns' of the altar were straight, square, hollow prominences, that at the south-west with two openings, into whose silver funnels the drink-offerings, and, at the Feast of Tabernacles, the water from the Pool of Siloam, were poured. A red line all round the middle of the altar marked that *above* it the blood of sacrifices intended to be eaten, *below* it that of sacrifices wholly consumed, was to be sprinkled. The system of drainage into chambers below and canals, all of which could be flushed at will, was perfect; the blood and refuse being swept down into Kedron and towards the royal gardens. Finally, north of the altar were all requisites for the sacrifices—six rows, with four rings each, of ingenious mechanism, for fastening the sacrifices; eight marble tables for the flesh, fat, and cleaned 'inwards;' eight low columns, each with three hooks, for hanging up the pieces; a marble table for laying them out, and one of silver for the gold and silver vessels of the service.

Build an altar of acacia wood, three cubits high; it is to be square, five cubits long and five cubits wide. Make a horn at each of the four corners, so that the horns and the altar are of one piece, and overlay the altar with bronze (Exod. 27:1–2).

---

[16]The three exceptions to this are specially mentioned in the Talmud. The high-priest both ascended and descended by the right.

[17]Also a receptacle for such sin-offerings of birds as had become spoiled. This inclined plane was kept covered with salt, to prevent the priests, who were barefooted, from slipping.

THE LAVER

Molten Sea or Great Laver

Then the LORD said to Moses, "Make a bronze basin, with its bronze stand, for washing. Place it between the Tent of Meeting and the altar, and put water in it" (*Exod. 30:17–18*).

Between the altar and porch of the Temple, but placed towards the south, was the immense laver of brass, supported by twelve colossal lions, which was drained every evening, and filled every morning by machinery, and where twelve priests could wash at the same time. Indeed, the water supply to the Sanctuary is among the most wonderful of its arrangements. That of the Temple is designated by Captain Wilson as the 'low-level supply,' in contradistinction to the 'high-level aqueduct,' which collected the water in a rock-hewn tunnel four miles long, on the road to Hebron, and then wound along so as to deliver water to the upper portion of the city. The 'low-level' aqueduct, which supplied the Temple, derived its waters from three sources—from the hills about Hebron, from Etham, and from the three pools of Solomon. Its total length was over forty miles. The amount of water it conveyed may be gathered from the fact that the surplusage of the waters of Etham is calculated, when drained into the lower pool of Gihon, to have presented when full, 'an area of nearly four acres of water.'[18] And, as if this had not been sufficient, 'the ground is perfectly honeycombed with a series of remarkable rock-hewn cisterns, in which the water brought by an aqueduct from Solomon's Pools, near Bethlehem, was stored. The cisterns appear to have been connected by a system of channels cut out of the rock; so that when one was full the surplus water ran into the next, and so on, till the final overflow was carried off by a channel into the Kedron. One of the cisterns—that known as the Great Sea—would contain two million gallons; and the total number of gallons which could be stored probably exceeded ten millions.' There seems little doubt that the drainage of Jerusalem was 'as well managed as the water supply; the mouth of the main drain being in the valley of the Kedron, where the sewerage was probably used as manure for the gardens.'

---

[18]See Barclay, *City of the Great King*, pp. 292–336.

THE GREAT STONES

The mind becomes bewildered at numbers, the accuracy of which we should hesitate to receive if they were not confirmed by modern investigations. We feel almost the same in speaking of the proportions of the Holy House itself. It was built on immense foundations of solid blocks of white marble covered with gold, each block measuring, according to Josephus, 67^1/$_2$ by 9 feet. Mounting by a flight of twelve steps to the 'Porch,' we notice that it projected 30 feet on each side beyond the Temple itself. Including these projections, the buildings of the Temple were 150 feet long, and as many broad. Without them the breadth was only 90, and the length 120 feet. Of these 60 feet in length, from east to west, and 30 feet in breadth, belonged to the Holy Place; while the Most Holy was 30 feet long, and as many broad. There were, therefore, on either side of the Sanctuary, as well as behind it, 30 feet to spare, which were occupied by side buildings three stories high, each containing five rooms, while that at the back had eight. These side-buildings, however, were lower than the Sanctuary itself, over which also superstructures had been reared. A gabled cedar roof, with golden spikes on it, and surrounded by an elegant balustrade, surmounted the whole.

Now the temple was built of stones that were white and strong, and each of their length was twenty-five cubits, their height was eight, and their breadth about twelve... (Jos. Antiquities 15.392).

THE VEIL

The entrance to the 'Porch,' which was curiously roofed, was covered by a splendid veil. Right and left were depositories for the sacrificial knives. Within the 'Porch' a number of 'dedicated' gifts were kept, such as the golden candelabra of the proselyte queen of Adiabene, two golden crowns presented by the Maccabees, etc. Here were also two tables—one of marble, on which they deposited the new shewbread; the other of gold, on which they laid the old as it was removed from the Holy Place. Two-leaved doors,[19] with gold plating, and covered by a rich Babylonian

---

[19]There was also a small wicket gate by which he entered who opened the large doors from within.

*You brought a vine out
   of Egypt;
you drove out the nations
   and planted it.
You cleared the ground
   for it,
and it took root and filled
   the land.
The mountains were
   covered with its shade,
the mighty cedars with its
   branches.
It sent out its boughs to
   the Sea,
its shoots as far as the
   River (Ps. 80:8–11).*

*At that moment the curtain
of the temple was torn in
two from top to bottom.
The earth shook and the
rocks split (Matt 27:51).*

curtain of the four colours of the Temple ('fine linen, blue, scarlet, and purple'), formed the entrance into the Holy Place. Above it hung that symbol of Israel (Ps. 80:8; Jer. 2:21; Ezek. 19:10; Joel 1:7), a gigantic vine of pure gold, and made of votive offerings—each cluster the height of a man. In the Holy Place were, to the south, the golden candlestick; to the north, the table of shewbread; and beyond them the altar of incense, near the entrance to the Most Holy. The latter was now quite empty, a large stone, on which the high-priest sprinkled the blood on the Day of Atonement, occupying the place where the ark with the mercy-seat had stood. A wooden partition separated the Most Holy from the Holy Place; and over the door hung the veil which was 'rent in twain from the top to the bottom' when the way into the holiest of all was opened on Golgotha (Matt. 27:51).[20]

Such was the Temple as restored by Herod—a work which occupied forty-six years to its completion. Yet, though the Rabbis never weary praising its splendour, not with one word do any of those who were contemporary indicate that its restoration was carried out by Herod the Great.[21] So memorable an event in their history is passed over with the most absolute silence. What a complete answer does this afford to the objection sometimes raised from the silence of Josephus about the person and mission of Jesus!

OUR LORD'S PREDICTION

With what reverence the Rabbis guarded their Temple will be described in the sequel. The readers of the New Testament know how readily any supposed infringement of its sanctity led to summary popular vengeance. To the disciples of Jesus it seemed difficult to realise that such utter ruin as their Master foretold could so soon come over that beautiful and glorious

---

[20]The Rabbis speak of two veils, and say that the high-priest went in by the southern edge of the first veil, then walked along till he reached the northern corner of the second veil, by which he entered the Most Holy Place.

[21]The first mention occurs in the Babylon Talmud, and then neither gratefully nor graciously. (*Taan.* 23*a*; *Baba B.* 3*b*; 4*a*; *Succ.* 51*b*.)

house. It was the evening of the day in which He had predicted the utter desolation of Jerusalem. All that day He had taught in the Temple, and what He had said, not only there, but when, on beholding the city, He wept over it, seems to have filled their minds alike with awe and with doubt. And now He, with His disciples, had 'departed from the Temple.' Once more they lingered in sweet retirement 'on the Mount of Olives' (Matt. 24:1, 3). 'The purple light on the mountains of Moab was fast fading out. Across the city the sinking sun cast a rich glow over the pillared cloisters of the Temple, and over the silent courts as they rose terrace upon terrace. From where they stood they could see over the closed Beautiful Gate, and right to the entrance to the Holy Place, which now glittered with gold; while the eastern walls and the deep valley below were thrown into a solemn shadow, creeping, as the orb sunk lower, further and further towards the summit of Olivet, irradiated with one parting gleam of roseate light, after all below was sunk in obscurity.'[22]

Then it was and there that the disciples, looking down upon the Temple, pointed out to the Master: 'What manner of stones and what buildings are here.' The view from that site must have rendered belief in the Master's prediction even more difficult and more sad. A few years more, and it was all literally fulfilled! It may be, as Jewish tradition has it, that ever since the Babylonian captivity the 'Ark of the Covenant' lies buried and concealed underneath the wood-court at the north-eastern angle of the Court of the Women. And it may be that some at least of the spoils which Titus carried with him from Jerusalem—the seven-branched candlestick, the table of shewbread, the priests' trumpets, and the identical golden mitre which Aaron had worn on his forehead—are hidden somewhere in the vaults beneath the site of the Temple, after having successfully gone to Rome, to Carthage, to Byzantium, to Ravenna, and thence to

Jesus left the temple and was walking away when his disciples came up to him to call his attention to its buildings. "Do you see all these things?" he asked. "I tell you the truth, not one stone here will be left on another; every one will be thrown down."

As Jesus was sitting on the Mount of Olives, the disciples came to him privately. "Tell us," they said, "when will this happen, and what will be the sign of your coming and of the end of the age?" (Matt. 24:1–3).

---

[22]Bartlett, *Jerusalem Revisited,* p. 115.

Jerusalem. But of 'those great buildings' that once stood there, there is 'not left one stone upon another' that has not been 'thrown down.'

3

TEMPLE ORDER, REVENUES, AND MUSIC

✴

The high priest carries the blood of animals into the Most Holy Place as a sin offering, but the bodies are burned outside the camp. And so Jesus also suffered outside the city gate to make the people holy through his own blood.—Hebrews 13:11-12.

SECOND TEMPLE INFERIOR IN GLORY

To the devout and earnest Jew the second Temple must, 'in comparison of' 'the house in her first glory,' have indeed appeared 'as nothing' (Hag. 2:3). True, in architectural splendour the second, as restored by Herod, far surpassed the first Temple.[1] But, unless faith had recognised in Jesus of Nazareth 'the Desire of all nations,' who should 'fill this house with glory' (Hag. 2:7), it would have been difficult to draw other than sad comparisons. Confessedly, the real elements of Temple-glory no longer existed. The Holy of Holies was quite empty, the ark of the covenant, with the cherubim, the tables of the law, the book of the covenant, Aaron's rod that budded, and the pot of manna, were no longer in the sanctuary. The fire that had descended from heaven upon the altar was extinct. What was far more solemn, the visible presence of God in the Shechinah was wanting.[2] Nor could the will of God be now ascertained through the Urim and Thummim, nor even the high-

Who of you is left who saw this house in its former glory? How does it look to you now? Does it not seem to you like nothing? (Hag. 2:3).

---

[1] The Talmud expressly calls attention to this, and mentions as another point of pre-eminence, that whereas the first Temple stood 410, the second lasted 420 years.

[2] The following five are mentioned by the Rabbis as wanting in the last Temple: the ark, the holy fire, the Shechinah, the spirit of prophecy, and the Urim and Thummim.

priest be anointed with the holy oil, its very composition being unknown. Yet all the more jealously did the Rabbis draw lines of fictitious sanctity, and guard them against all infringement.

LINES OF SANCTITY

In general, as the camp in the wilderness had really consisted of three parts—the camp of Israel, that of the Levites, and that of God—so they reckoned three corresponding divisions of the Holy City. From the gates to the Temple Mount was regarded as the camp of Israel; thence to the gate of Nicanor represented the camp of Levi; while the rest of the sanctuary was 'the camp of God.' It is in allusion to this that the writer of the Epistle to the Hebrews compares Christ's suffering 'without the gate' of Jerusalem to the burning of the sin-offerings 'without the camp.' According to another Rabbinical arrangement different degrees of sanctity attached to different localities. The first, or lowest degree, belonged to the land of Israel, whence alone the first sheaf at the Passover, the firstfruits, and the two wave-loaves at Pentecost might be brought; the next degree to walled cities in Palestine, where no leper nor dead body (Luke 7:12) might remain; the third to Jerusalem itself, since, besides many prohibitions to guard its purity, it was only there lawful to partake of peace-offerings, of the firstfruits, and of 'the second tithes.' Next came, successively, the Temple Mount, from which all who were in a state of Levitical uncleanness were excluded; 'the Terrace,' or 'Chel,' from which, besides Gentiles, those who had become defiled by contact with a dead body were shut out; the Court of the Women, into which those who had been polluted might not come, even if they 'had washed,' till after they were also Levitically fit to eat of 'things sacred,' that is, after sunset of the day on which they had washed; the Court of Israel, into which those might not enter who, though delivered from their uncleanness, had not yet brought the offering for their purifi-

Breastplate of the High Priest. The main purpose of the breastplate was to provide a receptacle for the sacred lot, the mysterious Urim and Thummim.

Also put the Urim and the Thummim in the breastpiece, so they may be over Aaron's heart whenever he enters the presence of the LORD. Thus Aaron will always bear the means of making decisions for the Israelites over his heart before the LORD (Exod. 28:30).

cation;[3] the Court of the Priests, ordinarily accessible only to the latter; the space between the altar and the Temple itself, from which even priests were excluded if their bearing showed that they did not realise the solemnity of the place; the Temple, into which the priests might only enter after washing their hands and feet; and, lastly, the Most Holy Place, into which the high-priest alone was allowed to go, and that only once a year.

Rules of the Rabbis

From these views of the sanctity of the place, it will readily be understood how sufficient outward reverence should have been expected of all who entered upon the Temple Mount. The Rabbis here also lay down certain rules, of which some are such as a sense of propriety would naturally suggest, while others strangely remind us of the words of our Saviour. Thus no one was to come to it except for strictly religious purposes, and neither to make the Temple Mount a place of thoroughfare, nor use it to shorten the road. Ordinarily the worshippers were to enter by the right and to withdraw by the left, avoiding both the direction and the gate by which they had come. But mourners and those under ecclesiastical discipline were to do the reverse, so as to meet the stream of worshippers, who might address to them either words of sympathy ('He who dwelleth in this house grant thee comfort!'), or else of admonition ('He who dwelleth in this house put it into thy mind to give heed to those who would restore thee again!'). As already stated, it was expressly prohibited to sit down in the Court of Priests, an exception being only made in favour of princes of the house of David, probably to vindicate their consistency, as such instances were recorded in the past history of Israel. Alike the ministering priests and the worshippers were to walk backwards when leaving the immediate

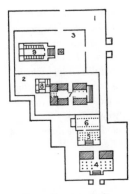

Great Court including royal buildings

---

[3]This class would include the following four cases: the cleansed leper, a person who had had an issue, a woman that had been in her separation, and one who had just borne a child. Further explanations of each case are given in subsequent chapters.

The LORD said to him:
"I have heard the prayer
and plea you have made
before me; I have conse-
crated this temple, which
you have built, by putting
my Name there forever.
My eyes and my heart
will always be there"
(1 Kgs. 9:3).

neighbourhood where the holy service was performed, and at the Gate of Nicanor each one was to stand with his head bent. It need scarcely be said that reverence in gesture and deportment was enjoined while on the Temple Mount. But even when at a distance from Jerusalem and the Temple, its direction was to be noted, so as to avoid in every-day life anything that might seem incongruous with the reverence due to the place of which God had said, 'Mine eyes and mine heart shall be there perpetually' (1 Kgs. 9:3). Probably from a similar feeling of reverence, it was ordered, that when once a week the sanctuary was thoroughly cleaned, any repairs found needful should be executed if possible by priests or else by Levites, or at least by Israelites, and only in case of extreme necessity by workmen not Levitically 'clean.'

Other Rabbinical ordinances, however, are not so easily explained, unless on the ground of the avoidance of every occupation and undertaking other than worship. Thus 'no man might go on the Temple Mount with his staff,' as if on business or pleasure; nor yet 'with shoes on his feet'—sandals only being allowed; nor 'with the dust upon his feet;' nor 'with his scrip,' nor 'with money tied to him in his purse.' Whatever he might wish to contribute either to the Temple, or for offerings, or for the poor must be carried by each 'in his hand,' possibly to indicate that the money about him was exclusively for an immediate sacred purpose. It was probably for similar reasons that Jesus transferred these very ordinances to the disciples when engaged in the service of the *real* Temple. The direction, 'Provide neither gold, nor silver, nor brass in your purses, nor scrip for your journey, neither two coats, neither shoes, nor yet staves,' must mean, Go out in the same spirit and manner as you would to the Temple services, and fear not—'for the workman is worthy of his meat' (Matt. 10:9, 10). In other words: Let this new Temple service be your only thought, undertaking, and care.[4]

---

[4]On the reverence due in prayer, see a subsequent chapter.

WILFUL PROFANITY

But, guard it as they might, it was impossible wholly to preserve the sanctuary from profanation. For wilful, conscious, high-handed profanity, whether in reference to the Temple or to God, the law does not appear to have provided any atonement or offering. To this the Epistle to the Hebrews alludes in the well-known passage, so often misunderstood, 'For if we sin wilfully after that we have received the knowledge of the truth, there remaineth no more sacrifice for sins, but a certain fearful looking for of judgment and fiery indignation, which shall devour the adversaries' (Heb. 10:26, 27). In point of fact, these terms of threatening correspond to two kinds of Divine punishment frequently mentioned in the Old Testament. The one, often referred to in the warning 'that he die not,' is called by the Rabbis, 'death by the hand of Heaven or of God;' the other is that of being 'cut off.' It is difficult to distinguish exactly between these two. Tradition enumerates thirty-six offences to which the punishment of 'cutting off' attaches. From their graver nature, as compared with the eleven offences on which 'death by the hand of God' was to follow, we gather that 'cutting off' must have been the severer of the two punishments, and it may correspond to the term 'fiery indignation.' Some Rabbis hold that 'death by the hand of God' was a punishment which ended with this life, while 'cutting off' extended beyond it. But the best authorities maintain, that whereas death by the hand of Heaven fell upon the guilty individual alone, 'the cutting off' extended to the children also, so that the family would become extinct in Israel. Such Divine punishment is alluded to in 1 Cor. 16:22, under the well-known Jewish expression, 'Anathema Maranatha'—literally, Anathema when the Lord cometh!

If anyone does not love the Lord—a curse be on him. Come, O Lord! (1 Cor. 16:22).

ITS PENALTIES

To these two Divine punishments corresponded other two by the hand of man—the 'forty stripes save one,' and the so-called 'rebels' beating.' The distinction between them is easily explained. The former

If the guilty man deserves to be beaten, the judge shall make him lie down and have him flogged in his presence with the number of lashes his crime deserves, but he must not give him more than forty lashes. If he is flogged more than that, your brother will be degraded in your eyes (Deut. 25:2–3).

They got up, drove him out of the town, and took him to the brow of the hill on which the town was built, in order to throw him down the cliff. But he walked right through the crowd and went on his way (Luke 4:29–30).

At this, they picked up stones to stone him, but Jesus hid himself, slipping away from the temple grounds (John 8:59).

When Phinehas son of Eleazar, the son of Aaron, the priest, saw this, he left the assembly, took a spear in his hand and followed the Israelite into the tent. He drove the spear through both of them—through the Israelite and into the woman's body (Num. 25:7–8a).

were only inflicted after a regular judicial investigation and sentence, and for the breach of some negative precept or prohibition; while the latter was, so to speak, in the hands of the people, who might administer it on the spot, and without trial, if any one were caught in supposed open defiance of some positive precept, whether of the Law of Moses or of the traditions of the elders. The reader of the New Testament will remember such popular outbursts, when the men of Nazareth would have cast Jesus over the brow of the hill on which their city was built (Luke 4:29), and when on at least two occasions the people took up stones in the Temple to stone Him (John 8:59; 10:31). It is a remarkable fact, that when the Lord Jesus and when His martyr Stephen were before the Sanhedrim (Matt. 26:59, 68; Acts 7:57, 58), the procedure was in each case in direct contravention of all the rules of the Rabbinical criminal law. In each case the sitting terminated in 'the rebels' beating,' both when they 'buffeted the Master' and 'smote Him with the palms of their hands,' and when 'they ran upon' Stephen 'with one accord, and cast him out of the city, and stoned him.' For the rebels' beating was really unto death. The same punishment was also to have been inflicted upon Paul, when, on the charge of having brought a Gentile beyond the enclosure in the court open to such, 'the people ran together, and they took Paul, and drew him out of the Temple,' and 'went about to kill him.' This summary mode of punishing supposed 'rebellion' was probably vindicated by the example of Phinehas, the son of Eleazar (Num. 25:7, 8). On the other hand, the mildness of the Rabbinical law, where religious feelings were not involved, led to modifications of the punishment prescribed in Deut. 25:2, 3. Thus because the words were, 'by a certain number, forty stripes he may give him,' instead of a simple direction to give the forty stripes, the law was construed as meaning a number near to forty, or thirty-nine, which accordingly was the severest corporeal punishment awarded at one time. If the number of stripes were less than thirty-nine, it must still be some multiple of three, since, as the scourge was composed of three separate thongs (the middle one of calf's leather, the other two of asses', with a reference to Isaiah 1:3), each stroke of the scourge in reality inflicted three stripes. Hence the greatest number of strokes administered at one time amounted to only thirteen. The law also most particularly defined and modified every detail, even to the posture of the criminal. Still this punishment, which St. Paul underwent not less than five times at the hands of the Jews (2 Cor. 11:24), must have been very severe. In general, we can only hope that it was not so often administered as Rabbinical writings seem to imply. During the scourging, Deut. 28:58, 59, and at its close Ps. 78:38, were read to the culprit. After the punishment he was not to be reproached, but received as a brother.[5]

Scourge

NECESSITY FOR DISCIPLINE

That strict discipline both in regard to priests and worshippers would, however, be necessary, may be inferred even from the immense number of worshippers which thronged Jerusalem and the Temple. According to a late computation, the Temple could have held 'within its colossal girdle' 'two amphitheatres of the size of the Coliseum.' As the latter is reckoned to have been capable, inclusive of its arena and passages, of accommodating 109,000 persons, the calculation that the Temple might contain at one time about 210,000 persons seems by no means exaggerated.[6] It will readily be believed what immense wealth this multitude must have brought to the great national sanctuary.

The ox knows his master, the donkey his owner's manger, but Israel does not know, my people do not understand (Isa. 1:3).

Five times I received from the Jews the forty lashes minus one (2 Cor. 11:24).

---

[5]Further details belong to the criminal jurisprudence of the Sanhedrim.

[6]See *Edinburgh Review* for January, 1873, p. 18. We may here insert another architectural comparison from the same interesting article, which, however, is unfortunately defaced by many and serious mistakes on other points. 'The length of the eastern wall of the sanctuary,' writes the reviewer, 'was more than double that of the side of the Great Pyramid; its height nearly one-third of the Egyptian structure from the foundation. If to this great height of 152 feet of solid wall you add the descent of 114 feet to the bed of the Kedron, and the further elevation of 160 feet attained by the pinnacle, we have a total of 426 feet, which is only 59 feet less than the Great Pyramid.'

THE TEMPLE TREASURY

Indeed, the Temple treasury had always been an object of cupidity to foreigners. It was successively plundered by Syrians and Romans,[7] though at the last siege the flames deprived Titus and his soldiers of this booty. Even so liberal and enlightened a statesman as Cicero inveighed, perhaps on the ground of exaggerated reports, against the enormous influx of gold from all lands to Jerusalem. From Biblical history we know how liberal were the voluntary contributions at the time of Moses, of David, and again of Joash (2 Chron. 24) and of Josiah (2 Kgs. 22). Such offerings to the Temple treasury continued to the last a very large source of revenue. They might be brought either in the form of vows or of free gifts. Any object, or even a person, might be dedicated by vow to the altar. If the thing vowed were suitable, it would be used; if otherwise, sold, and its value given to the treasury. Readers of the New Testament know how fatally such spurious liberality interfered with the most sacred duties of life (Matt. 15:5). From Jewish tradition we gather that there must have been quite a race for distinction in this respect. The wood, the incense, the wine, the oil, and all the other things requisite for the sacred services, as well as golden and silver vessels, were contributed with lavish hand. Certain families obtained by their zeal special privileges, such as that the wood they brought should always be first used for the altar fire; and the case of people leaving the whole of their fortune to the Temple is so often discussed (Shek. iv.), that it must have been a by no means uncommon occurrence. To this practice Christ may have referred in denouncing the Scribes and Pharisees who 'devour widows' houses, and for a pretence make long prayers'[8] (Matt. 23:14). For a good deal of this money went in the end from the Temple

A proclamation was then issued in Judah and Jerusalem that they should bring to the LORD the tax that Moses the servant of God had required of Israel in the desert. All the officials and all the people brought their contributions gladly, dropping them into the chest until it was full (2 Chron. 24:9–10).

But you say that if a man says to his father or mother, 'Whatever help you might otherwise have received from me is a gift devoted to God,' he is not to 'honor his father' with it. Thus you nullify the word of God for the sake of your tradition (Matt. 15:5–6).

Woe to you, teachers of the law and Pharisees, you hypocrites! You devour widows' houses and for a show make lengthy prayers. Therefore you will be punished more severely (Matt. 23:14 [NIV^mg]).

---

[7]The history of the Temple treasury would form an interesting subject, on which for the present we cannot enter.

[8]On the other hand, there are not a few passages in the *Mishnah* inveighing against vows, and showing how absolution from them may be obtained. A full treatment of the subject belongs to Jewish antiquities and Rabbinical jurisprudence.

treasury to them, although there is no evidence of their intriguing for personal gifts.

THE TRIBUTE MONEY

Besides these votive offerings, and the sale of the surplusage of incense, flour, etc., the people were wont on the Sabbaths and feast-days to bring voluntary contributions 'in their hand' to the Temple.[9] Another and very large source of revenue was from the profit made by the meat-offerings, which were prepared by the Levites, and sold every day to the offerers. But by far the largest sum was derived from the half-shekel of Temple tribute, which was incumbent on every male Israelite of age, including proselytes and even manumitted slaves. As the shekel of the sanctuary was double the ordinary, the half-shekel due to the Temple treasury amounted to about 1s.4d. (two *denarii* or a *didrachma*). Hence, when Christ was challenged at Capernaum (Matt. 17:24) for this payment, He directed Peter to give the *stater*, or two didrachmas, for them both. This circumstance also enables us to fix the exact date of this event. For annually, on the 1st of Adar (the month before the Passover), proclamation was made throughout the country by messengers sent from Jerusalem of the approaching Temple tribute. On the 15th of Adar the money-changers opened stalls throughout the country to change the various coins, which Jewish residents at home or settlers abroad might bring, into the ancient money of Israel. For custom had it that nothing but the regular half-shekel of the sanctuary could be received at the treasury. On the 25th of Adar business was only transacted within the precincts of Jerusalem and of the Temple, and after that date those who had refused to pay the impost could be proceeded against at law, and their goods distrained (Shek. i. 3), the only exception being in favour of priests, and that 'for the sake of peace,' that is, lest their office should come in disrepute. From heathens or Samaritans no tribute money was to be received, the general rule in refer-

After Jesus and his disciples arrived in Capernaum, the collectors of the two—drachma tax came to Peter and asked, "Doesn't your teacher pay the temple tax?"
"Yes, he does," he replied (Matt. 17:24–25a).

On the 15th thereof the tables [of the money—changers] were set up in the provinces; and on the 25th thereof they were set up in the Temple. After they were set up in the Temple they began to exact pledges. From whom did they exact pledges? From levites, Israelites, proselytes, and freed slaves, but not from women, slaves, or minors...They did not exact pledges from the priests, in the interests of peace (Mishnah, Šeqalim i.3).

---

[9] The subject of 'Vows' will be again and more fully treated in a subsequent chapter.

But Zerubbabel, Jeshua and the rest of the heads of the families of Israel answered, "You have no part with us in building a temple to our God. We alone will build it for the Lord, the God of Israel, as King Cyrus, the king of Persia, commanded us" (Ezra 4:3).

When it was almost time for the Jewish Passover, Jesus went up to Jerusalem. In the temple courts he found men selling cattle, sheep and doves, and others sitting at tables exchanging money. So he made a whip out of cords, and drove all from the temple area, both sheep and cattle; he scattered the coins of the money changers and overturned their tables (John 2:13–15).

ence to all their offerings being this: 'A votive and a free-will offering they receive at their hands; but whatever is not either a votive or a free-will offering (does not come under either category) is not received at their hands.' In support, Ezra 4:3 was quoted (Shek. i. 5). The law also fixed the rate of discount which the money-changers were allowed to charge those who procured from them the Temple coin, perhaps to obviate suspicion of, or temptation to usury—a sin regarded as one of the most heinous civil offences.

ANNUAL SUM OF TRIBUTE

The total sum derived annually from the Temple tribute has been computed at about £76,000.[10] As the bankers were allowed to charge a silver *meah,* or about one-fourth of a denar[11] (2*d.*) on every half-shekel, their profits must have amounted to nearly £9,500, or, deducting a small sum for exceptional cases, in which the *meah* was not to be charged,[12] say about £9,000—a very large sum, considering the value of money in a country where a labourer received a *denar* (8*d.*) for a day's work (Matt. 20:2), and the 'good Samaritan' left only two *denars* (1*s.* 4*d.*) in the inn for the keep of the sick man (Luke 10:35). It must therefore have been a very powerful interest which Jesus attacked, when in the Court of the Temple He 'poured out the changers' money, and overthrew the tables' (John 2:15), while at the same time He placed Himself in direct antagonism to the sanctioned arrangements of the Sanhedrim, whom He virtually charged with profanity.

TRIBUTE ENFORCED BY LAW

It had only been about a century before, during the reign of Salome-Alexandra (about 78 B.C.), that the Pharisaical party, being then in power, had carried

---

[10]See Winer, *Real-Wörterb.* ii. 589.

[11]Ersch's *Encycl.* (Art. Juden, p. 31) computes it at one-fifth; Zunz (*Zur Gesch. u. Litt.,* p. 539) at one-third of a *denar.* We have adopted the view of Winer.

[12]These are mentioned in Shek. i. 7. Our deduction is very liberal.

an enactment by which the Temple tribute was to be enforced at law. It need scarcely be said that for this there was not the slightest Scriptural warrant. Indeed, the Old Testament nowhere provided legal means for enforcing any payment for religious purposes. The law stated what was due, but left its observance to the piety of the people, so that alike the provision for the Temple and for the priesthood must have varied with the religious state of the nation (Mal. 3:8–10). But, irrespective of this, it is matter of doubt whether the half-shekel had ever been intended as an annual payment.[13] Its first enactment was under exceptional circumstances (Exod. 30:12), and the mode in which, as we are informed, a similar collection was made during the reign of Joash, suggests the question whether the original institution by Moses was not treated rather as affording a precedent than as laying down a binding rule (2 Chron. 24:6–11). At the time of Nehemiah (Neh. 10:32–34) we read only of a self-imposed 'ordinance,' and at the rate of a third, not a half-shekel. But long before the coming of Christ very different views prevailed. 'The dispersed abroad' regarded the Temple as the one bond of their national as well as their religious life. Patriotism and religion swelled their gifts, which far exceeded the legal dues. Gradually they came to regard the Temple tribute as, in the literal sense of the words, 'a ransom for their souls' (Exod. 30:12). So many were the givers and so large their gifts that they were always first brought to certain central places, whence the most honourable of their number carried them as 'sacred ambassadors' to Jerusalem. The richest contributions came from those crowded Jewish settlements in Mesopotamia and Babylon, to which 'the dispersed' had originally been transported. Here special treasuries for their reception had been built in the cities of Nisibis and Nehardea, whence a large armed escort annually accompanied the 'ambassadors' to Palestine. Similarly, Asia Minor, which at one time contributed nearly £8,000 a year, had its central collecting places. In the

"Will a man rob God? Yet you rob me.
"But you ask, 'How do we rob you?'
"In tithes and offerings. You are under a curse— the whole nation of you— because you are robbing me. Bring the whole tithe into the storehouse, that there may be food in my house. Test me in this," says the LORD Almighty, "and see if I will not throw open the floodgates of heaven and pour out so much blessing that you will not have room enough for it" (Mal. 3:8–10).

We assume the responsibility for carrying out the commands to give a third of a shekel each year for the service of the house of our God: for the bread set out on the table; for the regular grain offerings and burnt offerings; for the offerings on the Sabbaths, New Moon festivals and appointed feasts; for the holy offerings; for sin offerings to make atonement for Israel; and for all the duties of the house of our God (Neh. 10:32–33).

---

[13]See Michaelis, *Mos. Recht.* vol. iii, pp. 150, etc., and Saalschütz, *Das Mos. Recht.*, p. 292.

LIQUID MEASURE							
1 log (לֹג, lōgh, Lev 14 10)					approximately	1	pint
4 logs, 1 kab (קַב, ḳabh, 2 K 6 25)					"	2	qts.
12 "	3 kabs, 1 hin (הִין, hin, Ex 30 24)				"	1½	gals.
72 "	18 "	6 hins, 1 bath (בַּת, bath, Ezk 45 10)			"	9	"
720 "	180 "	60 "	10 baths, 1 homer or kor (חֹמֶר, ḥōmer, כֹּר, kōr, Ezk 45 14)		"	90	"

DRY MEASURE								
1 log						approximately	1	pint
4 logs, 1 kab						"	2	qts.
7⅓ "	1 omer (עֹמֶר, 'ōmer, Ex 16 16)					"	3	qts., 1⅓ pts.
24 "	6 kabs,	3⅓ omers, 1 seah (סְאָה, se'āh, 1 K 18 32)				"	1½	pecks
72 "	18 "	10 "	3 seahs, 1 ephah (אֵפָה, 'ēphāh, Ex 16 36)			"	4½	"
360 "	90 "	50 "	15 "	5 ephahs, 1 lethech (לֶתֶךְ, lethekh, Hos 3 2)		"	5	bu., 2⅓ pecks
720 "	180 "	100 "	30 "	10 "	2 lethechs, 1 homer or kor (Ezk 45 14)	"	11	bu., 1 peck

Weights and measures

Temple these moneys were emptied into three large chests, which were opened with certain formalities at each of the three great feasts. According to tradition these three chests held three seahs each (the seah = 1 peck 1 pint), so that on the three occasions of their opening twenty-seven seahs of coin were taken.

HOW THE MONEY WAS SPENT

The Temple revenues were in the first place devoted to the purchase of all *public* sacrifices, that is, those offered in the name of the *whole congregation* of Israel, such as the morning and evening sacrifices, the festive sacrifices, etc. This payment had been one of the points in controversy between the Pharisees and the Sadducees. So great importance was attached to it, that all Israel should appear represented in the purchase of the public sacrifices, that when the three chests were emptied they took expressly from one 'for the land of Israel,' from another 'for the neighbouring lands' (that is, for the Jews there resident), and from the third 'for distant lands.' Besides, the Temple treasury defrayed all else necessary for the services of the sanctuary; all Temple repairs, and the salaries of a large staff of regular officials, such as those who prepared the shewbread and the incense; who saw to the correctness of the copies of the law used in the synagogues; who examined into the Levitical fitness of sacrifices; who instructed the priests in their various duties (*Ketuv* cvi. 1); who made the curtains, etc.,—not omitting, according to their own testimony, the fees of the Rabbis. And after all this lavish expenditure there was not only enough to pay for the repairs of the city-walls, the roads, and public buildings, etc., about Jerusalem, but sufficient to accumulate immense wealth in the treasury!

THE TEMPLE HYMNODY

To the wealth and splendour of the Temple corresponded the character of its services. The most important of these, next to the sacrificial rites, was the hymnody of the sanctuary. We can conceive what it must have been in the days of David and of Solomon. But even in New Testament times it was such that St. John could find no more adequate imagery to portray heavenly realities and final triumph of the Church than that taken from the service of praise in the Temple. Thus, when first 'the twenty-four elders,' representing the chiefs of the twenty-four courses of the priesthood, and afterwards the 144,000, representing redeemed Israel in its fulness (12 x 12,000), sing 'the new song'—the former in heaven, the latter on Mount Zion—they appear, just as in the Temple services, as 'harpers, harping with their harps' (Rev. 5:8; 14:2, 3). Possibly there may also be an analogy between the time when these 'harpers' are introduced and the period in the Temple-service when the music began—just as the joyous drink-offering was poured out. There is yet a third reference in the Book of Revelation to 'the harps of God' (Rev. 15:2), with most pointed allusion, not to the ordinary, but to the Sabbath services in the Temple. In this case 'the harpers' are all they 'that had gotten the victory over the beast.' The Church, which has come out of great tribulation, stands victorious 'on the sea of glass;' and the saints, 'having the harps of God,' sing 'the song of Moses, the servant of God.' It is the Sabbath of the Church; and as on the Sabbath, besides the psalm for the day (Ps. 92) at the ordinary sacrifice, they sung at the additional Sabbatic sacrifice (Num. 28:9, 10), in the morning, the Song of Moses, in Deut. 32, and in the evening that in Exod. 15, so the victorious Church celebrates her true Sabbath of rest by singing this same 'Song of Moses and of the Lamb,' only in

And I heard a sound from heaven like the roar of rushing waters and like a loud peal of thunder. The sound I heard was like that of harpists playing their harps (Rev. 14:2).

And I saw what looked like a sea of glass mixed with fire and, standing beside the sea, those who had been victorious over the beast and his image and over the number of his name. They held harps given them by God (Rev. 15:2).

I will proclaim the name of the LORD.
Oh, praise the greatness of our God!
He is the Rock, his works are perfect,
and all his ways are just.
A faithful God who does no wrong,
upright and just is he (Deut. 32:3–4).

language that expresses the fullest meaning of the Sabbath songs in the Temple.

INSTRUMENTAL MUSIC

Then Moses and the Israelites sang this song to the LORD:
"I will sing to the LORD, for he is highly exalted. The horse and its rider he has hurled into the sea" (Exod. 15:1).

...and that they had the plainest instances in their forefathers, who, by their righteousness, and exerting themselves on behalf of their own laws, and their own children, had frequently conquered many ten thousands,—for innocence is the strongest army (Jos. Antiquities 12.291).

Properly speaking, the real service of praise in the Temple was only with the voice. This is often laid down as a principle by the Rabbis. What instrumental music there was, served only to accompany and sustain the song. Accordingly, none other than Levites might act as choristers, while other distinguished Israelites were allowed to take part in the instrumental music. The blasts of the trumpets, blown by priests only, formed—at least in the second Temple—no part of the instrumental music of the service, but were intended for quite different purposes. Even the posture of the performers showed this, for while the Levites stood at their desks facing towards the sanctuary, or westwards, the priests, with their silver trumpets, stood exactly in the opposite direction, on the west side of the rise of the altar, by the 'table of the fat,' and looking eastwards or down the courts. On ordinary days the priests blew seven times, each time three blasts—a short sound, an alarm, and again a sharp short sound (Thekiah, Theruah, and Thekiah),[14] or, as the Rabbis express it, 'An alarm in the midst and a plain note before and after it.' According to tradition, they were intended symbolically to proclaim the kingdom of God, Divine Providence, and the final judgment. The first three blasts were blown when the great gates of the Temple—especially that of Nicanor—were opened. Then, when the drink-offering was poured out, the Levites sung the psalm of the day in three sections. After each section there was a pause, when the priests blew three blasts, and the people worshipped. This

Levite

---

[14]Inferring from the present usage in the Synagogue, Saalschütz (*Gesch. d. Musik bei d. Hebr.*) has thus marked them—

The Thekiah: and the Theruah:

was the practice at the evening, as at the morning sacrifice. On the eve of the Sabbath a threefold blast of the priests' trumpets summoned the people, far as the sound was carried over the city, to prepare for the holy day, while another threefold blast announced its actual commencement. On Sabbaths, when, besides the ordinary, an additional sacrifice was brought, and the 'Song of Moses' sung—not the whole every Sabbath, but divided into six parts, one for every Sabbath,— the priests sounded their trumpets additional three times in the pauses of the Sabbath psalm.[15]

THE INFLUENCE OF DAVID

The music of the Temple owed its origin to David, who was not only a poet and a musical composer, but who also invented musical instruments (Amos 6:5; 1 Chron. 23:5), especially the ten-stringed *Nevel* or lute (Ps. 33:2; 144:9). From the Book of Chronicles we know how fully this part of the service was cultivated, although the statement of Josephus (*Ant.* 8.94), that Solomon had provided forty thousand harps and lutes, and two hundred thousand silver trumpets, is evidently a gross exaggeration. The Rabbis enumerate thirty-six different instruments, of which only fifteen are mentioned in the Bible, and of these five in the Pentateuch. As in early Jewish poetry there was neither definite and continued metre (in the modern sense), nor regular and premeditated rhyme, so there was neither musical notation, nor yet any artificial harmony. The melody was simple, sweet, and sung in unison to the accompaniment of instrumental music. Only one pair of brass cymbals were allowed to be used.[16] But this 'sounding brass' and 'tinkling cymbal' formed no part of the Temple music itself, and served only as the signal to begin that part of the service. To this the apostle seems to refer when, in 1 Cor. 13:1, he compares the gift of 'tongues' to the sign or signal by which the real music of the Temple was introduced.

Cymbals and drum

You strum away on your harps like David
and improvise on musical instruments
(Amos 6:5).

Praise the LORD with the harp;
make music to him on the ten–stringed lyre
(Ps. 33:2).

If I speak in the tongues of men and of angels, but have not love, I am only a resounding gong or a clanging cymbal (1 Cor. 13:1).

---

[15]All these regulations are stated in *Mishnah, Succah,* v. 5. Further details about Temple hymns and Temple music are given in the description of the daily service, and in that of the Sabbath and the various feast-days.

[16]For particulars on all points connected with Jewish art, poetry, and science, I must refer to my *History of the Jewish Nation.*

THE HARP AND LUTE

That music was chiefly sustained by the harp (Kinnor) and the lute (Nevel). Of the latter (which was probably used for solos) not less than two nor more than six were to be in the Temple orchestra; of the former, or harp, as many as possible, but never less than nine. There were, of course, several varieties both of the Nevel and the Kinnor. The chief difference between these two kinds of stringed instruments lay in this, that in the Nevel (lute or guitar) the strings were drawn over the sounding-board, while in the Kinnor they stood out free, as in our harps.[17] Of wind-instruments we know that, besides their silver trumpets, the priests also blew the Shophar or horn, notably at the new moon, on the Feast of the New Year (Ps. 81:3), and to proclaim the Year of Jubilee (Lev. 25:9), which, indeed, thence derived its name. Originally the Shophar was probably a ram's horn, but afterwards it was also made of metal. The Shophar was chiefly used for its loud and far-sounding tones (Exod. 19:16, 19; 20:18; Isa. 58:1). At the Feast of the New Year, one priest with a Shophar was placed between those who blew the trumpets; while on fast-days a priest with a Shophar stood on each side of them—the tones of the Shophar being prolonged beyond those of the trumpets. In the synagogues out of Jerusalem the Shophar alone was blown at the New Year, and on fast-days only trumpets.

Stringed instruments

Begin the music, strike the tambourine,
play the melodious harp and lyre.
Sound the ram's horn at the New Moon,
and when the moon is full, on the day of our Feast (Ps. 81:2–3).

THE FLUTE

The flute (or reed pipe) was played in the Temple on twelve special festivities.[18] These were: the day of killing the first, and that of killing the second Passover, the first day of unleavened bread, Pentecost, and the eight days of the Feast of Tabernacles. Quite in accordance with the social character of these feasts,

---

[17] The opposite is in the generally received opinion. But see the article 'Music,' by Leyrer, in Herzog's *Encycl.*

[18] The flute was used in Alexandria to accompany the hymns at the love feasts of the early Christians, up to the year 190, when Clement of Alexandria introduced the harp in its place. See Leyrer *u. s.*

the flute was also used by the festive pilgrim-bands on their journey to Jerusalem, to accompany 'the Psalms of Degrees,' or rather of 'Ascent' (Isa. 30:29), sung on such occasions. It was also customary to play it at marriage feasts and at funerals (Matt. 9:23); for according to Rabbinical law every Jew was bound to provide at least two flutes and one mourning woman at the funeral of his wife. In the Temple, not less than two nor more than twelve flutes were allowed, and the melody was on such occasions to close with the notes of one flute alone. Lastly, we have sufficient evidence that there was a kind of organ used in the Temple (the *Magrephah*), but whether merely for giving signals or not, cannot be clearly determined.

Wind instruments and sistrum

THE HUMAN VOICE

As already stated, the service of praise was mainly sustained by the human voice. A good voice was the one qualification needful for a Levite. In the second Temple female singers seem at one time to have been employed (Ezra 2:65; Neh. 7:67). In the Temple of Herod their place was supplied by Levite boys. Nor did the worshippers any more take part in the praise, except by a responsive Amen. It was otherwise in the first Temple, as we gather from 1 Chron. 16:36, from the allusion in Jer. 33:11, and also from such Psalms as 26:12; 68:26. At the laying of the foundation of the second Temple, and at the dedication of the wall of Jerusalem, the singing seems to have been antiphonal, or in responses (Ezra 3:10, 11; Neh. 12:27, 40), the two choirs afterwards apparently combining, and singing in unison in the Temple itself. Something of the same kind was probably also the practice in the first Temple. What the melodies were to which the Psalms had been sung, it is, unfortunately, now impossible to ascertain. Some of the music still used in the synagogue must date from those times, and there is no reason to doubt that in the so-called Gregorian *tones* we have also preserved to us a close approximation to the ancient hymnody of the Temple, though certainly not without considerable alterations.

And you will sing as on the night you celebrate a holy festival; your hearts will rejoice as when people go up with flutes to the mountain of the LORD, to the Rock of Israel (Isa. 30:29).

Praise be to the LORD, the God of Israel, from everlasting to everlasting.
Then all the people said "Amen" and "Praise the LORD" (1 Chron. 16:36).

Then I heard what sounded like a great multitude, like the roar of rushing waters and like loud peals of thunder, shouting: "Hallelujah!
For our Lord God Almighty reigns"
(Rev. 19:6).

But how solemn must have been the scene when, at the dedication of Solomon's Temple during the service of praise, 'the house was filled with a cloud, even the house of Jehovah; so that the priests could not stand to minister by reason of the cloud: for the glory of Jehovah had filled the house of God!' (2 Chron. 5:13, 14). Such music, and such responsive singing, might well serve, in the Book of Revelation, as imagery of heavenly realities (Rev. 4:8, 11; 5:9, 12; 7:10–12), especially in that description of the final act of worship in Rev. 14:1–5, where at the close of their antiphony the two choirs combine, as at the dedication of the second Temple, to join in this grand unison, 'Alleluia: for the Lord God omnipotent reigneth' (Rev. 19:6, 7; comp. also Rev. 5:13).

4

THE OFFICIATING PRIESTHOOD

❋

Day after day every priest stands and performs his religious duties; again and again he offers the same sacrifices, which can never take away sins.
—Hebrews 10:11.

THE PRIESTHOOD

Among the most interesting glimpses of early life in the church is that afforded by a small piece of rapidly-drawn scenery which presents to our view 'a great company of the priests,' 'obedient to the faith' (Acts 6:7). We seem to be carried back in imagination to the time when Levi remained faithful amidst the general spiritual defection (Exod. 32:26), and then through the long vista of devout ministering priests to reach the fulfilment of this saying of Malachi— part admonition, and part prophecy: 'For the priest's lips should keep knowledge, and they should seek the law at his mouth: for he is the messenger of the Lord of hosts' (Mal. 2:7). We can picture to ourselves how they who ministered in holy things would at eventide, when the Temple was deserted of its worshippers, gather to speak of the spiritual meanings of the services, and to consider the wonderful things which had taken place in Jerusalem, as some alleged, in ful- filment of those very types that formed the essence of their office and ministry. 'For this thing was not done in a corner.' The trial of Jesus, His condemnation by the Sanhedrim, and His being delivered up to the Gentiles, must have formed the theme of frequent and anxious discussion in the Temple. Were not their own chief priests implicated in the matter? Did not

So he stood at the entrance to the camp and said, "Whoever is for the LORD, come to me." And all the Levites rallied to him (Exod. 32:26).

When Judas, who had betrayed him, saw that Jesus was condemned, he was seized with remorse and returned the thirty silver coins to the chief priests and the elders. "I have sinned," he said, "for I have betrayed innocent blood."

"What is that to us?" they replied. "That's your responsibility."

So Judas threw the money into the temple and left. Then he went away and hanged himself (Matt. 27:3–5).

Judas on that fatal day rush into the Temple, and wildly cast the 'price of blood' into the 'treasury'? On the other hand, was not one of the principal priests and a member of the priestly council, Joseph of Arimathea, an adherent of Christ? Did not the Sanhedrist Nicodemus adopt the same views, and even Gamaliel advise caution? Besides, in the 'porches' of the Temple, especially in that of Solomon, 'a notable miracle' had been done in 'that Name,' and there also its all-prevailing power was daily proclaimed. It specially behoved the priesthood to inquire well into the matter; and the Temple seemed the most appropriate place for its discussion.

THE NUMBER OF PRIESTS

The number of priests to be found at all times in Jerusalem must have been very great, and Ophel a densely inhabited quarter. According to Jewish tradition, half of each of the twenty-four 'courses,' into which the priesthood were divided, were permanently resident in Jerusalem; the rest scattered over the land. It is added, that about one half of the latter had settled in Jericho, and were in the habit of supplying the needful support to their brethren while officiating in Jerusalem. Of course such statements must not be taken literally, though no doubt they are substantially correct. When a 'course' was on duty, all its members were bound to appear in the Temple. Those who stayed away, with such 'representatives of the people' (or 'stationary men') as, like them, had been prevented from 'going up' to Jerusalem in their turn, had to meet in the synagogues of their district to pray and to fast each day of their week of service, except on the sixth, the seventh, and the first—that is, neither on the Sabbath, nor on the days preceding and succeeding it, as the 'joy' attaching to the Sabbath rendered a fast immediately before or after it inappropriate.

SYMBOLISM OF THE PRIESTHOOD

It need scarcely be said, that everything connected with the priesthood was intended to be symbolical and typical—the office itself, its functions, even its dress and outward support. The fundamental design of Israel itself was to be unto Jehovah 'a kingdom of priests and an holy nation' (Exod. 19:5, 6). This, however, could only be realised in 'the fulness of time.' At the very outset there was the barrier of sin; and in order to gain admittance to the ranks of Israel, when 'the sum of the children of Israel was taken after their number,' every man had to give the half-shekel, which in after times became the regular Temple contribution, as 'a ransom (covering) for his soul unto Jehovah' (Exod. 30:12, 13). But even so Israel was sinful, and could only approach Jehovah in the way which He Himself opened, and in the manner which He appointed. Direct choice and appointment by God were the conditions alike of the priesthood, of sacrifices, feasts, and of every detail of service.

When you take a census of the Israelites to count them, each one must pay the LORD a ransom for his life at the time he is counted. Then no plague will come on them when you number them. Each one who crosses over to those already counted is to give a half shekel, according to the sanctuary shekel, which weighs twenty gerahs. This half shekel is an offering to the LORD (Exod. 30:12–13).

MEDIATION

The fundamental ideas which underlay all and connected it into a harmonious whole, were *reconciliation* and *mediation:* the one expressed by typically atoning sacrifices, the other by a typically intervening priesthood. Even the Hebrew term for priest (*Cohen*) denotes in its root-meaning 'one who stands up for another, and mediates in his cause.'[1] For this purpose God chose the *tribe of Levi,* and out of it again the *family of Aaron,* on whom He bestowed the 'priest's office as a gift' (Num. 18:7). But the whole characteristics and the functions of the priesthood centered in the *person of the high-priest.* In accordance with their Divine 'calling' (Heb. 5:4) was the special and exceptional provision made for the support of the priesthood. Its principle was thus expressed: 'I am thy part and thine inheritance among the children of Israel;' and its joyousness, when realised in its full meaning and application, found vent in such words as Ps. 16:5, 6: 'Jehovah is the portion of mine inheritance

But only you and your sons may serve as priests in connection with everything at the altar and inside the curtain. I am giving you the service of the priesthood as a gift. Anyone else who comes near the sanctuary must be put to death (Num. 18:7).

No one takes this honor upon himself; he must be called by God, just as Aaron was (Heb. 5:4).

---

[1]This root-meaning (through the Arabic) of the Hebrew word for priest, as one intervening, explains its occasional though very rare application to others than priests, as, for example, to the sons of David (2 Sam. 8:18), a mode of expression which is thus correctly paraphrased in 1 Chron. 18:17: 'And the sons of David were at the hand of the king.'

and of my cup: Thou maintainest my lot. The lines are fallen unto me in pleasant places; yea, I have a goodly heritage.'

HOLINESS

But there was yet another idea to be expressed by the priesthood. The object of reconciliation was *holiness.* Israel was to be 'a holy nation'—reconciled through the 'sprinkling of blood;' brought near to, and kept in fellowship with God by that means. The priesthood, as the representative offerers of that blood and mediators of the people, were also to show forth the 'holiness' of Israel. Every one knows how this was symbolised by the gold-plate which the high-priest wore on his forehead, and which bore the words: 'Holiness unto Jehovah.' But though the high-priest in this, as in every other respect, was the fullest embodiment of the functions and the object of the priesthood, the same truth was also otherwise shown forth. The *bodily qualifications* required in the priesthood, the kind of *defilements* which would temporarily or wholly interrupt their functions, their *mode of ordination,* and even every portion, material, and colour of their *distinctive dress* were all intended to express in a symbolical manner this characteristic of holiness. In all these respects there was a difference between Israel and the tribe of Levi; between the tribe of Levi and the family of Aaron; and, finally, between an ordinary priest and the high-priest, who most fully typified our Great High-priest, in whom all these symbols have found their reality.

High Priest in his robes

Make a plate of pure gold and engrave on it as on a seal: HOLY TO THE LORD… It will be on Aaron's forehead, and he will bear the guilt involved in the sacred gifts the Israelites consecrate, whatever their gifts may be. It will be on Aaron's forehead continually so that they will be acceptable to the LORD (Exod. 28:36, 38).

THE TWENTY-FOUR COURSES

This much it seemed necessary to state for the general understanding of the matter. Full details belong to the exposition of the meaning and object of the Levitical priesthood, as instituted by God, while our present task rather is to trace its further development to what it was at the time when Jesus was in the Temple. The first peculiarity of post-Mosaic times which we here meet, is the arrangement of the priesthood into 'twenty-four courses,' which undoubtedly dates from the times of David. But Jewish tradition would make it even much older. For, according to the Talmud, it should be traced up to Moses, who is variously supposed to have arranged the sons of Aaron into eight or else sixteen courses (four, or else eight, of Eleazar; and the other four, or else eight, of Ithamar), to which, on the one supposition, Samuel and David each added another eight 'courses,' or, on the other, Samuel and David, in conjunction, the eight needed to make up the twenty-four mentioned in 1 Chron. 24. It need scarcely be told that, like many similar statements, this also is simply an attempt to trace up every arrangement to the fountain-head of Jewish history, in order to establish its absolute authority.[2]

The priests:
the descendants of
Jedaiah (through the
family of Jeshua)   *973*
  of Immer   *1,052*
  of Pashhur   *1,247*
  of Harim   *1,017*
(Ezra 2:36–39).

THE COURSES AFTER THE CAPTIVITY

The institution of David and of Solomon continued till the Babylonian captivity. Thence, however, only four out of the twenty-four 'courses' returned: those of Jedaiah, Immer, Pashur, and Harim (Ezra 2:36–39), the course of 'Jedaiah' being placed first because it was of the high-priest's family, 'of the house of Jeshua,' 'the son of Jozadak' (Ezra 3:2; Hag. 1:1; 1 Chron. 6:15). To restore the original number, each of these four families was directed to draw five lots for those which had not returned, so as to form once more twenty-four courses, which were to bear the ancient names. Thus, for example, Zacharias, the father of John the Baptist, really belonged not to the family of Abijah (1 Chron. 24:10), which had not returned from Babylon, but to the 'course of Abia,' which had been formed out of some other family, and only bore the ancient name (Luke 1:5). Like the priests, the Levites had at the time of King David been arranged into twenty-four 'courses,' which were to act as 'priests' assistants' (1 Chron. 23:4, 28), as 'singers and musicians' (1 Chron. 25:6), as 'gate-keepers and

David said, "Of these, twenty-four thousand are to supervise the work of the temple of the LORD and six thousand are to be officials and judges. Four thousand are to be gatekeepers and four thousand are to praise the LORD with the musical instruments I have provided for that purpose"
(1 Chron. 23:4–5).

---

[2]Curiously enough, here also the analogy between Rabbinism and Roman Catholicism holds good. Each claims for its teaching and practices the so-called principle of catholicity— 'semper, ubique, ab omnibus' ('always, everywhere, by all'), and each invents the most curious historical fables in support of it!

guards' (1 Chron. 26:6 and following), and as 'officers and judges.' Of these various classes, that of the 'priests' assistants' was by far the most numerous,[3] and to them the charge of the Temple had been committed in subordination to the priests. It had been their duty to look after the sacred vestments and vessels; the store-houses and their contents; and the preparation of the shewbread, of the meat-offerings, of the spices, etc. They were also generally to assist the priests in their work, to see to the cleaning of the sanctuary, and to take charge of the treasuries (1 Chron. 23:28–32).

IN THE TEMPLE OF HEROD

Of course these services, as also those of the singers and musicians, and of the porters and guards, were retained in the Temple of Herod. But for the employment of Levites as 'officers and judges' there was no further room, not only because such judicial functions as still remained to the Jews were in the hands of the Sanhedrim and its subordinate authorities, but also because in general the ranks of the Levites were so thinned. In point of fact, while no less than 4,289 priests had returned from Babylon, the number of Levites was under 400 (Ezra 2:40–42; Neh. 7:43–45), of whom only 74 were 'priests' assistants.' To this the next immigration, under Ezra, added only 38, and that though the Levites had been specially searched for (Ezra 8:15, 18, 19). According to tradition, Ezra punished them by depriving them of their tithes. The gap in their number was filled up by 220 Nethinim (Ezra 8:20), literally, 'given ones,' probably originally strangers and captives[4] as in all likelihood the Gibeonites had been the first 'Nethinim' (Josh. 9:21, 23, 27). Though the Nethinim, like the Levites and priests, were freed from all taxation (Ezra 7:24), and perhaps also from military service (Jos. *Ant.*

---

[3]Apparently it numbered 24,000, out of a total of 38,000 Levites.
[4]This is also confirmed by their foreign names (Ezra 2:43–58). The total number of Nethinim who returned from Babylon was 612—392 with Zerubbabel (Ezra 2:58; Neh. 7:60), and 220 with Ezra (Ezra 8:20).

3.287–288; 4.67), the Rabbinists held them in the lowest repute—beneath a bastard, though above a proselyte—forbade their intermarrying with Israelites, and declared them incapable of proper membership in the congregation.[5]

DUTIES OF PRIESTS AND LEVITES

The duties of priests and Levites in the Temple may be gathered from Scripture, and will be further explained in the course of our inquiries. Generally, it may here be stated that on the Levites devolved the Temple-police, the guard of the gates, and the duty of keeping everything about the sanctuary clean and bright. But as at night the priests kept watch about the innermost places of the Temple, so they also opened and closed all the inner gates, while the Levites discharged this duty in reference to the outer gates, which led upon the Temple Mount (or Court of the Gentiles), and to the 'Beautiful Gate,' which formed the principal entrance into the Court of the Women. The laws of Levitical cleanness, as explained by the Rabbis, were most rigidly enforced upon worshippers and priests. If a leper, or any other who was 'defiled,' had ventured into the sanctuary itself, or any priest officiated in a state of 'uncleanness,' he would, if discovered, be dragged out and killed, without form of process, by 'the rebels' beating.' Minor punishments were awarded to those guilty of smaller offences of the same kind. The Sabbath-rest was strictly enforced, so far as consistent with the necessary duties of the Temple service. But the latter superseded the Sabbath law (Matt. 12:5) and defilement on account of death.[6] If the time for offering a sacrifice was not fixed, so that it might be brought on one day as well as another, then the service did not supersede either the Sabbath or defilement on account of death. But where the time was unalterably fixed, there the higher duty of obedience to a direct command came

…because the tribe of Levi was made free from war and warlike expeditions, and was set apart for the divine worship, lest they should want and seek after the necessaries of life, and so neglect the temple… *(Jos. Antiquities 4.67).*

Or haven't you read in the Law that on the Sabbath the priests in the temple desecrate the day and yet are innocent? (Matt. 12:5).

---

[5]So in many passages of the Talmud.
[6]See Maimonides, *Yad ha Chas. Biath. Mikd.* iv. 9, etc.

in to supersede alike the Sabbath and this one (but only this one) ground of defilement. The same principle applied to worshippers as well as priests.

THE WEEK'S SERVICE

He also made twenty–four parts of the tribe of Levi; and when they cast lots, they came up in the same manner for their courses of eight days: he also honored the posterity of Moses, and made them the keepers of the treasures of God, and of the donations which the king dedicated: he also ordained, that all the tribe of Levi, as well as the priests, should serve God night and day as Moses had enjoined them (Jos. Antiquities 7.367).

Then the LORD said to Aaron, "You and your sons are not to drink wine or other fermented drink whenever you go into the Tent of Meeting, or you will die. This is a lasting ordinance for the generations to come (Lev. 10:8–9).

Each 'course' of priests and of Levites (as has already been stated) came on duty for a week, from one Sabbath to another. The service of the week was subdivided among the various families which constituted a 'course;' so that if it consisted of five 'houses of fathers,' three served each one day, and two each two days; if of six families, five served each one day, and one two days; if of eight families, six served each one day, and the other two in conjunction on one day; or, lastly, if of nine families, five served each one day, and the other four took it two in conjunction for two days.[7] These divisions and arrangements were made by 'the chiefs' or 'heads of the houses of their fathers.' On Sabbaths the whole 'course' was on duty; on feast-days any priest might come up and join in the ministrations of the sanctuary; and at the Feast of Tabernacles all the twenty-four courses were bound to be present and officiate. While actually engaged on service in the Temple, the priests were not allowed to drink wine, either by day or by night. The other 'families' or 'houses' also of the 'course' who were in attendance at Jerusalem, though not on actual duty, were, during their week of ministry, prohibited the use of wine, except at night, because they might have to be called in to assist their brethren of the officiating 'family,' which they could not do if they had partaken of strong drink. The law even made(a somewhat curious) provision to secure that the priests should come up to Jerusalem properly trimmed, washed, and attired, so as to secure the *decorum* of the service.[8]

---

[7]Some have imagined that every 'course' was arranged into six, or else into seven 'families,' but the view in the text expresses most likely the correct tradition.

[8]Comp. Relandus, *Antiq.* p. 169.

THESE FUNCTIONS NOT SACERDOTAL

It would be difficult to conceive arrangements more thoroughly or consistently opposed to what are commonly called 'priestly pretensions,' than those of the Old Testament. The fundamental principle, laid down at the outset, that all Israel were 'a kingdom of priests' (Exod. 19:5, 6), made the priesthood only representatives of the people. Their income, which even under the most favorable circumstances must have been moderate, was, as we have seen, dependent on the varying religious state of the nation, since no law existed by which either the payment of tithes or any other offerings could be enforced. How little power or influence, comparatively speaking, the priesthood wielded, is sufficiently known from Jewish history. Out of actual service neither the priests nor even the high-priest wore a distinctive dress (comp. Acts 23:5; see also chap. 7), and though a number of civil restrictions were laid on priests, there were few corresponding advantages. It is indeed true that alliances with distinguished priestly families were eagerly sought, and that during the troubled period of Syrian domination the high-priest for a time held civil as well as religious rule. But the latter advantage was dearly bought, both as regarded the priests and the nation.

Nor must we forget the powerful controlling influence which Rabbinism exercised. Its tendency, which must never be lost sight of in the study of the state of Palestine at the time of our Lord, was steadily against all privileges other than those gained by traditionary learning and theological ingenuity. The Pharisee, or, rather, the man learned in the traditional law, was everything both before God and before man; 'but this people, who knoweth not the law,' were 'cursed,' plebeians, country people, unworthy of any regard or attention. Rabbinism applied these principles even in reference to the priesthood. It divided all priests into 'learned' and 'unlettered,' and excluded the latter from some of the privileges of their own order. Thus there were certain priestly dues which the people might at will give to any priest they chose. But

Now if you obey me fully and keep my covenant, then out of all nations you will be my treasured possession. Although the whole earth is mine, you will be for me a kingdom of priests and a holy nation.' These are the words you are to speak to the Israelites (Exod. 19:5–6).

Those who were standing near Paul said, "You dare to insult God's high priest?"

Paul replied, "Brothers, I did not realize that he was the high priest; for it is written: 'Do not speak evil about the ruler of your people'" (Acts 23:4–5).

Has any of the rulers or of the Pharisees believed in him? No! But this mob that knows nothing of the law—there is a curse on them (John 7:48–49).

from some of them the 'unlettered' priests were debarred, on the ostensible ground that in their ignorance they might have partaken of them in a state of Levitical uncleanness, and so committed mortal sin.

TRAINING OF PRIESTS

Seven days before the Day of Atonement the High Priest was taken apart from his own house unto the Counsellors' Chamber and another priest was made ready in his stead lest aught should befall him to render him ineligible (Mishnah, Yoma I.1).

In general, the priests had to undergo a course of instruction, and were examined before being allowed to officiate. Similarly, they were subject to the ordinary tribunals, composed of men learned in the law, without regard to their descent from one or another tribe. The ordained 'rulers' of the synagogues, the teachers of the people, the leaders of their devotions, and all other officials were not necessarily 'priests,' but simply chosen for their learning and fitness. Any one whom the 'elders' or 'rulers' deemed qualified for it might, at their request, address to the people on the Sabbath a 'word of exhortation.' Even the high-priest himself was answerable to the Sanhedrim. It is distinctly stated, that 'if he committed an offence which by the law deserved whipping, the Great Sanhedrim whipt him, and then had him restored again to his office.' Every year a kind of ecclesiastical council was appointed to instruct him in his duties for the Day of Atonement, 'in case he were not learned,' or, at any rate, to see to it that he knew and remembered them. Nay, the principle was broadly laid down—that 'a scholar, though he were a bastard, was of far higher value than an unlearned high-priest.' If, besides all this, it is remembered how the political influence of the high-priest had decayed in the days of Herod, and how frequently the occupants of that office changed, through the caprice of the rulers or through bribery, the state of public feeling will be readily understood.

At the same time, it must be admitted, that generally speaking the high-priest would, of necessity, wield very considerable influence, and that, ordinarily, those who held the sacred office were not only 'lettered,' but members of the Sanhedrim. According to Jewish tradition, the high-priest ought, in every respect, to excel all other priests, and if he were poor, the rest were to contribute, so as to secure him an independent fortune. Certain marks of outward respect were also shown him. When he entered the Temple he was accompanied by three persons—one walking at each side, the third behind him. He might, without being appointed to it, officiate in any part of the Temple services; he had certain exceptional rights; and he possessed a house in the Temple, where he lived by day, retiring only at night to his own home, which must be within Jerusalem, and to which he was escorted by the people after the solemnities of the Day of Atonement, which devolved almost exclusively upon him.

In the first place, therefore, history informs us that Aaron, the brother of Moses, officiated to God as a high priest; and that, after his death, his sons succeeded him immediately; and that this dignity hath been continued down from them all to their posterity (Jos. Antiquities 20.225).

OFFICE HEREDITARY

Originally the office of high-priest was regarded as being held for life and hereditary;[9] but the troubles of later times made it a matter of cabal, crime, or bribery. Without here entering into the complicated question of the succession to the high-priesthood, the following may be quoted from the Talmud (Talmud Jer. *Ioma*, i.), without, of course, guaranteeing its absolute accuracy: 'In the first Temple,[10] the high-priests served, the son succeeding the father, and they were eighteen in number. But in the second Temple they got the high-priesthood for money; and there are those who say they destroyed each other by witchcraft, so that some reckon 80 high-priests during that period, others 81, others 82, 83, 84, and even 85.' The Rabbis enumerate 18 high-priests during the first Temple; Lightfoot counts 53 from the return from Babylon to Matthias, when the last war of the Jews began; while Relandius reckons 57. But there is both difficulty and confusion amid the constant changes at the last.

There was not any fixed age for entering on the office of high-priest, any more than on that of an ordinary priest. The Talmudists put it down as twenty years. But the unhappy descendant of the Maccabees, Aristobulus, was only sixteen years of age when his

---

[9]According to the Rabbis, he was appointed by the Sanhedrim.

[10]This, of course, does not include the period before the first Temple was built.

beauty, as he officiated as high-priest in the Temple, roused the jealousy of Herod, and procured his death. The entrance of the Levites is fixed, in the sacred text, at thirty during the wilderness period, and after that, when the work would require less bodily strength, but a larger number of ministers, at twenty-five years of age.[11]

The LORD said to Moses, "This applies to the Levites: Men twenty–five years old or more shall come to take part in the work at the Tent of Meeting, but at the age of fifty, they must retire from their regular service and work no longer (Num. 8:23–25).

DISQUALIFICATIONS FOR THE PRIESTHOOD

No special disqualifications for the Levitical office existed, though the Rabbis insist that a good voice was absolutely necessary. It was otherwise with the priest's office. The first inquiry instituted by the Sanhedrim, who for the purpose sat daily in 'the Hall of Polished Stones,' was into the genealogy of a candidate. Certain genealogies were deemed authoritative. Thus, 'if his father's name were inscribed in the archives of Jeshana at Zipporim, no further inquiry was made.' If he failed to satisfy the court about his perfect legitimacy, the candidate was dressed and veiled in black, and permanently removed. If he passed that ordeal, inquiry was next made as to any physical defects, of which Maimonides enumerates a hundred and forty that permanently, and twenty-two which temporarily disqualified for the exercise of priestly office. Persons so disqualified were, however, admitted to menial offices, such as in the wood-chamber, and entitled to Temple support. Those who had stood the twofold test were dressed in white raiment, and their names properly inscribed. To this pointed allusion is made in Rev. 3:5, 'He that overcometh, the same shall be clothed in white raiment; and I will not blot out his name out of the book of life.'

THE INVESTITURE

Thus received, and afterwards instructed in his duties, the formal admission alike of the priest and of

---

[11]It is thus we reconcile Num. 4:3 with 8:24, 25. In point of fact, these two reasons are expressly mentioned in 1 Chron. 23:24–27, as influencing David still further to lower the age of entrance to twenty.

the high-priest was not, as of old, by anointing, but simply by investiture. For even the composition of the sacred oil was no longer known in the second Temple. They were called 'high-priests by investiture,' and regarded as of inferior rank to those 'by anointing.' As for the common priests, the Rabbis held that they were not anointed even in the first Temple, the rite which was applied to the sons of Aaron being valid also for their descendants. It was otherwise in the case of the high-priest. His investiture was continued during seven days. In olden days, when he was anointed, the sacred oil was not only 'poured over him,' but also applied to his forehead, over the eyes, as tradition has it, after the form of the Greek letter X. The coincidence is certainly curious. This sacred oil was besides only used for anointing such kings as were of the family of David, not other Jewish monarchs, and if their succession had been called in question. Otherwise the royal dignity went, as a matter of course, by inheritance from father to son.

Anointing

So Samuel took the horn of oil and anointed him in the presence of his brothers, and from that day on the Spirit of the LORD came upon David in power. Samuel then went to Ramah (1 Sam. 16:13).

THE DRESS OF THE HIGH-PRIEST

The high-priests 'by investiture' had not any more the real Urim and Thummim (their meaning even being unknown), though a breast-plate, with twelve stones, was made and worn, in order to complete the eight sacred vestments. This was just double the number of those worn by an ordinary priest, viz. the linen breeches, the coat, the girdle, and the bonnet. To these the high-priest added other four distinctive articles of dress, called 'golden vestments,' because, unlike the robes of the ordinary priests, *gold*, the symbol of splendour, appeared in them. They were the *Meïl*, or robe of the ephod, wholly of 'woven work,' of dark blue colour, descending to the knees, and adorned at the hem by alternate blossoms of the pomegranate in blue, purple, and scarlet, and golden bells, the latter, according to tradition, seventy-two in number; the *Ephod* was the breast-plate, the former of the four colours of the sanctuary (white, blue, purple, and scarlet), and inwrought with threads of gold; the *Mitre;* and, lastly, the *Ziz,* or golden frontlet.

High Priest's garment

If either a priest or the high-priest officiated without wearing the full number of his vestments, his service would be invalid, as also if anything, however trifling (such, for instance, as a plaster), had intervened between the body and the dress of the priest. The material of which the four vestments of the ordinary priest were made was 'linen,' or, more accurately, 'byssus,' the white shining cotton-stuff of Egypt. These two qualities of the byssus are specially marked as characteristic,[12] and on them part of the symbolic meaning depended. Hence we read in Rev. 19:8, 'And to her,'—the wife of the Lamb made ready— 'was granted that she should be arrayed in byssus vestments, shining and pure; for the byssus vestment is the righteousness of the saints.'[13]

ALLUSIONS TO THE DRESS IN THE NEW TESTAMENT

We add some further particulars, chiefly in illustration of allusions in the New Testament. The priest's 'coat' was woven of one piece, like the seamless robe of the Saviour (John 19:23). As it was close-fitting, the girdle could not, strictly speaking, have been necessary. Besides, although the account of the Rabbis, that the priest's girdle was three fingers broad and sixteen yards long (!), is exaggerated, no doubt it really reached beyond the feet, and required to be thrown over the shoulder during ministration. Hence its object must chiefly have been symbolical. In point of fact, it may be regarded as the most distinctive priestly vestment, since it was only put on during actual ministration, and put off immediately afterwards. Accordingly, when in Rev. 1:13, the Saviour is seen 'in the midst of the candlesticks,' 'girt about the paps with a golden girdle,' we are to understand by it that our heavenly High-Priest is there engaged in actual ministry for us. Similarly, the girdle is described as 'about the paps,' or (as in Rev. 15:6) about the 'breasts,' as both the girdle of the ordinary

Now the vestment of the high priest being made of linen, signified the earth; the blue denoted the sky, being like lightning in its pomegranates, and in the noise of the bells resembling thunder. And for the ephod, it showed that God had made the universe of four [elements]; and as for the gold interwoven, I suppose it related to the splendor by which all things are enlightened (Jos. Antiquities 3.184).

When the soldiers crucified Jesus, they took his clothes, dividing them into four shares, one for each of them, with the undergarment remaining. This garment was seamless, woven in one piece from top to bottom (John 19:23).

They are to wear linen turbans on their heads and linen undergarments around their waists. They must not wear anything that makes them perspire (Ezek. 44:18).

---

[12]Rev. 15:6, 'clothed in pure and shining linen.'
[13]So literally.

priest and that on the ephod which the high-priest wore were girded there, and not round the loins (compare Ezek. 44:18). Lastly, the expression 'golden girdle' may bear reference to the circumstance that the dress peculiar of the high-priest was called his 'golden vestments,' in contradistinction to the 'linen vestments,' which he wore on the Day of Atonement.

THE BREAST-PLATE

Of the four distinctive articles in the high-priest's dress, the breast-plate, alike from its square form and the twelve jewels on it, bearing the names of the tribes, suggests 'the city four-square,' whose 'foundations' are twelve precious stones (Rev. 21:16, 19, 20).

MITRE

The 'mitre' of the high-priest differed from the head-gear of the ordinary priest, which was shaped like the inverted calyx of a flower, in size and probably also somewhat in shape. According to the Rabbis, it was eight yards high (!!). Fastened to it by two (according to the Rabbis, by three) ribbons of 'blue lace' was the symbol of royalty—the 'golden plate' (or Ziz), on which, 'Holiness unto Jehovah' was graven. This plate was only two fingers wide, and reached from temple to temple.

PHYLACTERIES

Between this plate and the mitre the high-priest is by some supposed to have worn his phylacteries. But this cannot be regarded as by any means a settled point. According to the distinct ceremony of the Talmud,[14] neither priests, Levites, nor the 'stationary men' wore phylacteries during their actual service in the Temple. This is a strong point urged by the modern Karaite Jews against the traditions of the Rabbis. Can it be, that the wearing of phylacteries at the time of Christ was *not* a universally acknowledged obligation, but rather the badge of a party? This would give addi-

The foundations of the city walls were decorated with every kind of precious stone. The first foundation was jasper, the second sapphire, the third chalcedony, the fourth emerald, the fifth sardonyx, the sixth carnelian, the seventh chrysolite, the eighth beryl, the ninth topaz, the tenth chrysoprase, the eleventh jacinth, and the twelfth amethyst (Rev. 21:19–20).

Phylactery

---

[14]Zebach. xix. a. 6. See Jost. *Gesch. d. Judenth.* vol. ii, p. 309.

tional force to the words in which Christ inveighed against those who made broad their phylacteries.

THE ZIZ

According to Josephus, the original Ziz of Aaron still existed in his time, and was carried with other spoils to Rome. There R. Eliezer saw it in the reign of Hadrian. Thence we can trace it, with considerable probability, through many vicissitudes, to the time of Belisarius, and to Byzantium. From there it was taken by order of the emperor to Jerusalem. What became of it afterwards is unknown; possibly it may still be in existence.[15] It only requires to be added that the priests' garments, when soiled, were not washed, but used as wicks for the lamps in the Temple; those of the high-priest were 'hid away.' The high-priest wore 'a fresh suit of linen vestments' each time on the Day of Atonement.

These vestments king Herod kept in that place; and after his death they were under the power of the Romans, until the time of Tiberius Caesar… (Jos. Antiquities 15.404).

THE FOURTEEN OFFICERS

The priesthood ministering in the Temple were arranged into 'ordinary' priests and various officials. Of the latter there were, besides the high-priest,[16] the 'Sagan,' or suffragan priest; two 'Katholikin,' or chief treasurers and overseers; seven 'Ammarcalin,' who were subordinate to the Katholikin, and had chief charge of all the gates; and three 'Gizbarin,' or under-treasurers. These fourteen officers, ranking in the order mentioned, formed the standing 'council of the Temple,' which regulated everything connected with the affairs and services of the sanctuary. Its members were also called 'the elders of the priests,' or 'the counsellors.' This judicatory, which ordinarily did not busy itself with criminal questions, apparently took a leading part in the condemnation of Jesus. But, on the other hand, it is well to remember that they

Common Priest

---

[15]When Josephus speaks of a triple crown worn by the high-priest, this may have been introduced by the Asmoneans when they united the temporal monarchy with the priesthood. Compare Smith's *Dictionary of the Bible*, i, 807a.

[16]The Rabbis speak of a high-priest ordained 'for war,' who accompanied the people to battle, but no historical trace of a distinct office of this kind can be discovered.

were not all of one mind, since Joseph of Arimathea belonged to their number—the title by which he is designated in Mark 15:43 being exactly the same word as that applied in the Talmud to the members of this priestly council.

THEIR DUTIES

It is difficult to specify the exact duties of each of these classes of officials. The 'Sagan' (or 'Segen,' or 'Segan') would officiate for the high-priest, when from any cause he was incapacitated; he would act generally as his assistant, and take the oversight of all the priests, whence he is called in Scripture 'second priest' (2 Kgs. 25:18; Jer. 52:24), and in Talmudical writings 'the Sagan of the priests.'[17] A 'Chananjah' is mentioned in the Talmud as a Sagan, but whether or not he was the 'Annas' of the New Testament must be left undecided. The two Katholikin were to the Sagan what he was to the high-priest, though their chief duty seems to have been about the treasures of the Temple.[18] Similarly, the seven Ammarcalin were assistants of the Katholikin, though they had special charge of the gates, the holy vessels, and the holy vestments; and again the three (or else seven), 'Gizbarin' assistants of the Ammarcalin. The title 'Gizbar' occurs so early as Ezra 1:8; but its exact meaning seems to have been already unknown when the LXX translated that book. They appear to have had charge of all dedicated and consecrated things, of the Temple tribute, of the redemption money, etc., and to have decided all questions connected with such matters.

Joseph of Arimathea, a prominent member of the Council, who was himself waiting for the kingdom of God, went boldly to Pilate and asked for Jesus' body (Mark 15:43).

The commander of the guard took as prisoners Seraiah the chief priest, Zephaniah the priest next in rank and the three doorkeepers (2 Kgs. 25:18).

Cyrus king of Persia had them brought by Mithredath the treasurer [Gizbar], who counted them out to Sheshbazzar the prince of Judah (Ezra 1:8).

LOWER OFFICIALS

Next in rank to these officials were the 'heads of each course' on duty for a week, and then the 'heads of families' of every course. After them followed fifteen overseers, viz. 'the overseer concerning the

---

[17]We may here at once dismiss the theory that the Sagan was the elected successor of the high-priest.

[18]Thus in *Bamidbar Rabba* (sect. 14, fol. 271*a*), Korah is described as Katholicus to the King of Egypt, who 'had the keys of his treasures.' Compare *Buxtorff in vocem*.

times,' who summoned priests and people to their respective duties; the overseer for shutting the doors (under the direction, of course, of the Ammarcalin); the overseer of the guards, or captain of the Temple; the overseer of the singers and of those who blew the trumpets; the overseer of the cymbals; the overseer of the lots, which were drawn every morning; the overseer of the birds, who had to provide the turtledoves and pigeons for those who brought such offerings; the overseer of the seals, who dispensed the four counterfoils for the various meat-offerings suited for different sacrifices; the overseer of the drink-offerings, for a similar purpose to the above; the overseer of the sick, or the Temple physician; the overseer of the water, who had charge of the water-supply and the drainage; the overseer for making the shewbread; for preparing the incense; for making the veils; and for providing the priestly garments. All these officers had, of course, subordinates, whom they chose and employed, either for the day or permanently; and it was their duty to see to all the arrangements connected with their respective departments. Thus, not to speak of instructors, examiners of sacrifices, and a great variety of artificers, there must have been sufficient employment in the Temple for a very large number of persons.

Stone waterpots

SOURCES OF SUPPORT FOR THE PRIESTS

We must not close without enumerating the twenty-four sources whence, according to the Talmud, the priests derived their support.[19] Of these ten were only available while in the Temple itself, four in Jerusalem, and the remaining ten throughout the Holy Land. Those which might only be used in the Temple itself were the priest's part of the sin-offering; that of the trespass-offering for a known, and for a doubtful trespass; public peace-offerings; the leper's log of oil; the two Pentecostal loaves; the

---

[19]The Rabbis also enumerate fifteen functions which were peculiar to the priest's service. But as each of them will find its place in subsequent chapters we do not recount them here. The curious reader is referred to Relandus, *Antiq.* (ed. Buddeus), pp. 176, 177.

shewbread; what was left of meat-offerings, and the omer at the Passover. The four which might be used only in Jerusalem were the firstlings of beasts, the Biccurim,[20] the portion from the thank-offering (Lev. 7:12; 22:29, 30), and from the Nazarite's goat, and the skins of the holy sacrifices. Of the ten which might be used throughout the land, five could be given at will to any priest, viz. the tithe of the tithe, the heave-offering of the dough (Num. 15:20; Rom. 11:16), the first of the fleece and the priest's due of meat (Deut. 18:3). The other five, it was thought, should be given to the priests of the special course on duty for the week, viz. the redemption-money for a first-born son, that for an ass, the 'sanctified field of possession' (Lev. 27:16), what had been 'devoted,' and such possession of 'a stranger' or proselyte as, having been stolen, was restored to the priests after the death of the person robbed, with a fifth part additional. Finally, to an unlettered priest it was only lawful to give the following from among the various dues: things 'devoted,' the first-born of cattle, the redemption of a son, that of an ass, the priest's due (Deut. 18:3), the first of the wool, the 'oil of burning,'[21] the ten things which were to be used in the Temple itself, and the Biccurim. On the other hand, the high-priest had the right to take what portion of the offerings he chose, and one half of the shewbread every Sabbath also belonged to him.

This is the share due the priests from the people who sacrifice a bull or a sheep: the shoulder, the jowls and the inner parts (Deut. 18:3).

If a man dedicates to the LORD part of his family land, its value is to be set according to the amount of seed required for it—fifty shekels of silver to a homer of barley seed (Lev. 27:16).

Thus elaborate in every particular was the system which regulated the admission, the services, and the privileges of the officiating priesthood. Yet it has all vanished, not leaving behind it in the synagogue even a single trace of its complicated and perfect arrangements. These 'old things are passed away,' because they were only 'a shadow of good things to come.' But 'the substance is of Christ,' and 'He abideth an High-Priest for ever.'

---

[20]To prevent mistakes, we may state that the term 'Therumoth' is, in a general way, used to designate the prepared produce, such as oil, flour, wine; and 'Biccurim,' the natural product of the soil, such as corn, fruits, etc.

[21]A term meaning 'defiled *Therumoth.*'

5

SACRIFICES: THEIR ORDER AND THEIR MEANING

> There are...men who offer the gifts prescribed by the law. They serve at a sanctuary that is a copy and shadow of what is in heaven. —Hebrews 8:4-5.

With what shall I come before the LORD and bow down before the exalted God? Shall I come before him with burnt offerings, with calves a year old (Mic. 6:6)?

It is a curious fact, but sadly significant, that modern Judaism should declare neither sacrifices nor a Levitical priesthood to belong to the essence of the Old Testament; that, in fact, they had been foreign elements imported into it—tolerated, indeed, by Moses, but against which the prophets earnestly protested and incessantly laboured.[1] The only arguments by which this strange statement is supported are, that the Book of Deuteronomy contains merely a brief summary, not a detailed repetition, of sacrificial ordinances, and that such passages as Isa. 1:11, etc., Micah 6:6, etc., inveigh against sacrifices offered without real repentance or change of mind. Yet this anti-sacrificial, or, as we may call it, anti-spiritual, tendency is really of much earlier date. For the sacrifices of the Old Testament were not merely outward observances—a sort of work-righteousness which justified the offerer by the mere fact of his obedience—since 'it is not possible that the blood of bulls and of goats should take away sins' (Heb. 10:4).

But those sacrifices are an annual reminder of sins, because it is impossible for the blood of bulls and goats to take away sins (Heb. 10:3–4).

SYMBOLISM OF THE SACRIFICES
The sacrifices of the Old Testament were symbolical and typical. An outward observance without

---

[1]We specially refer to Dr. A. Geiger, one of the ablest Rabbinical writers of Germany, who makes this argument the substance of Lect. v. in his *Judenth. u.s. Gesch.* (*Judaism and its History*).

any real inward meaning is only a ceremony. But a rite which has a present spiritual meaning is a symbol; and if, besides, it also points to a future reality, conveying at the same time, by anticipation, the blessing that is yet to appear, it is a type. Thus the Old Testament sacrifices were not only symbols, nor yet merely predictions by fact (as prophecy is a prediction by word), but they already conveyed to the believing Israelite the blessing that was to flow from the future reality to which they pointed. Hence the service of the letter and the work-righteousness of the Scribes and Pharisees ran directly contrary to this hope of faith and spiritual view of sacrifices, which placed all on the level of sinners to be saved by the substitution of another, to whom they pointed. Afterwards, when the destruction of the Temple rendered its services impossible, another and most cogent reason was added for trying to substitute other things, such as prayers, fasts, etc., in room of the sacrifices. Therefore, although none of the older Rabbis has ventured on such an assertion as that of modern Judaism, the tendency must have been increasingly in that direction. In fact, it had become a necessity—since to declare sacrifices of the essence of Judaism would have been to pronounce modern Judaism an impossibility. But thereby also the synagogue has given sentence against itself, and by disowning sacrifices has placed itself outside the pale of the Old Testament.

Altar–Temple

Sacrifices the Centre of the Old Testament

Every unprejudiced reader of the Bible must feel that sacrifices constitute the centre of the Old Testament. Indeed, were this the place, we might argue from their universality that, along with the acknowledgment of a Divine power, the dim remembrance of a happy past, and the hope of a happier future, sacrifices belonged to the primeval traditions which mankind inherited from Paradise. To sacrifice seems as 'natural' to man as to pray; the one indicates what he feels about himself, the other what he feels about God. The one means a felt need of propitiation; the other a felt sense of dependence.

THE IDEA OF SUBSTITUTION

For the life of a creature is in the blood, and I have given it to you to make atonement for yourselves on the altar; it is the blood that makes atonement for one's life (Lev. 17:11).

Blessed is he
  whose transgressions are forgiven,
whose sins are covered.
Blessed is the man
  whose sin the LORD does not count against him
  and in whose spirit is no deceit (Ps. 32:1–2).

Day after day every priest stands and performs his religious duties; again and again he offers the same sacrifices, which can never take away sins. But when this priest had offered for all time one sacrifice for sins, he sat down at the right hand of God. Since that time he waits for his enemies to be made his footstool, because by one sacrifice he has made perfect forever those who are being made holy (Heb. 10:11–14).

The fundamental idea of sacrifice in the Old Testament is that of substitution, which again seems to imply everything else—atonement and redemption, vicarious punishment and forgiveness. The firstfruits go for the whole products; the firstlings for the flock; the redemption-money for that which cannot be offered; and the life of the sacrifice, which is in its blood (Lev. 17:11), for the life of the sacrificer. Hence also the strict prohibition to partake of blood. Even in the 'Korban,' gift (Mark 7:11) or free-will offering, it is still the gift for the giver. The idea of substitution, as introduced, adopted, and sanctioned by God Himself, is expressed by the sacrificial term rendered in our version 'atonement,' but which really means covering, the substitute in the acceptance of God taking the place of, and so covering, as it were, the person of the offerer. Hence the Scriptural experience: 'Blessed is he whose transgression is forgiven, whose sin is covered…unto whom the Lord imputeth not iniquity' (Ps. 32:1, 2); and perhaps also the Scriptural prayer: 'Behold, O God, our shield, and look upon the face of Thine Anointed' (Ps. 84:9). Such sacrifices, however, necessarily pointed to a mediatorial priesthood, through whom alike they and the purified worshippers should be brought near to God, and kept in fellowship with Him. Yet these priests themselves continually changed; their own persons and services needed purification, and their sacrifices required constant renewal, since, in the nature of it, such substitution could not be perfect. In short, all this was symbolical (of man's need, God's mercy, and His covenant), and typical, till He should come to whom it all pointed, and who had all along given reality to it; He whose Priesthood was perfect, and who on a perfect altar brought a perfect sacrifice, once for all —a perfect Substitute, and a perfect Mediator (Heb. 10:1–24).

THE PASCHAL LAMB

At the very threshold of the Mosaic dispensation stands the sacrifice of the Pascal Lamb connected with the redemption of Israel, and which in many respects must be regarded as typical, or rather anticipatory, of all the others. But there was one sacrifice which, even under the Old Testament, required no renewal. It was when God had entered into covenant relationship with Israel, and Israel became the 'people of God.' Then Moses sprinkled 'the blood of the covenant,' on the altar and on the people (Exod. 24). On the ground of this covenant-sacrifice all others rested (Ps. 50:5). These were, then, either sacrifices of communion with God, or else intended to restore that communion when it had been disturbed or dimmed through sin and trespass: sacrifices *in* communion, or *for* communion with God. To the former class belong the burnt- and the peace-offerings; to the latter, the sin- and the trespass-offerings. But, as without the shedding of blood there is no remission of sin, every service and every worshipper had, so to speak, to be purified by blood, and the mediatorial agency of the priesthood called in to bring near unto God, and to convey the assurance of acceptance.

BLOODY AND UNBLOODY OFFERINGS

The readiest, but perhaps the most superficial, arrangement of sacrifices is into bloody an unbloody. The latter, or 'Minchah,' included, besides the meat- and drink-offering, the first sheaf at the Passover, the two loaves at Pentecost, and the shewbread. The meat-offering was only brought alone in two instances—the priest's offering (Lev. 7:12) and that of jealousy (Num. 5:15), to which Jewish tradition adds the meat-offerings mentioned in Lev. 2. If in Lev. 5:11 a meat-offering is allowed in cases of extreme poverty as a substitute for a sin-offering, this only further proves the substitutionary character of sacrifices. From all this it will be evident that, as a general rule, the meat-offering cannot be regarded as separate from the other or bloody sacrifices. In proof of this, it always varied in quantity, according to the kind of

Gather to me my consecrated ones, who made a covenant with me by sacrifice (Ps. 50:5).

If he offers it as an expression of thankfulness, then along with this thank offering he is to offer cakes of bread made without yeast and mixed with oil, wafers made without yeast and spread with oil, and cakes of fine flour well–kneaded and mixed with oil (Lev. 7:12).

If, however, he cannot afford two doves or two young pigeons, he is to bring as an offering for his sin a tenth of an ephah of fine flour for a sin offering. He must not put oil or incense on it, because it is a sin offering (Lev. 5:11).

sacrifice which is accompanied (Num. 15:1–12; 28:1–12; 29:1, etc.).

THE REQUISITES OF SACRIFICE

The general requisites of all sacrifices were—that they should be brought of such things, in such place and manner, and through such mediatorial agency, as God had appointed. Thus the choice and the appointment of the mode of approaching Him, were to be all of God. Then it was a first principle that every sacrifice must be of such things as had belonged to the offerer. None other could represent him or take his place before God. Hence the Pharisees were right when, in opposition to the Sadducees, they carried it that all public sacrifices (which were offered for the nation as a whole) should be purchased, not from voluntary contributions, but from the regular Temple revenues. Next, all animal sacrifices were to be free of blemishes (of which the Rabbis enumerate seventy-three), and all unbloody offerings to be without admixture of leaven or of honey; the latter probably because, from its tendency to fermentation or corruption, it resembled leaven. For a similar reason salt, as the symbol of incorruption, was to be added to all sacrifices.[2] Hence we read in Mark 9:49: 'For every one shall be salted with fire, and every sacrifice shall be salted with salt;' that is, as the salt is added to the sacrifice symbolically to point to its incorruption, so the reality and permanence of our Christian lives will be brought out by the fire of the great day, when what is wood, hay, and stubble shall be consumed; while that which is real shall prove itself incorruptible, having had the fire applied to it.

THE CREATURES APPOINTED

In Scripture three kinds of four-footed beasts—oxen, sheep and goats; and two of birds—turtle-doves and young pigeons—are appointed for sacrifice.'[3]

Goat. Goats were among the chief possessions of the wealthy in the early ages of the world.

---

[2] The Rabbis speak of the so-called 'salt of Sodom,' probably rock salt from the southern end of the Dead Sea, as used in the sacrifices.

[3] 'The birds' used at the purification of the leper (Lev. 14:4) cannot be regarded as sacrifices.

The latter, except in certain purifications, are only allowed as substitutes for other sacrifices in case of poverty. Hence also no direction is given either as to their age or sex, though the Rabbis hold that the turtle-doves (which were the common birds of passage) should be fully grown, and the domestic pigeons young birds. But, as in the various sacrifices of oxen, sheep, and goats there were differences of age and sex, the Jews enumerated twelve sacrifices, to which as many terms in Scripture correspond. The Paschal lamb and that for the trespass-offerings required to be males, as well as all burnt- and all public sacrifices. The latter 'made void the Sabbath and defilement,' *i.e.* they superseded the law of Sabbath rest (Matt. 12:5), and might be continued, notwithstanding one kind of Levitical defilement—that by death.

If the whole Israelite community sins unintentionally and does what is forbidden in any of the LORD's commands, even though the community is unaware of the matter, they are guilty (Lev. 4:13).

THE ELEVEN SACRIFICES OF THE RABBIS.

The Rabbis, who are very fond of subtle distinctions, also speak of public sacrifices that resembled the private,[4] and of private sacrifices that resembled the public, in that they also 'made void the Sabbath and defilement.'[5] Altogether they enumerate *eleven public* sacrifices, viz. the daily sacrifices; the additional for the Sabbath; for the New Moon; the Passover sacrifices; the lamb when the sheaf was waved; the Pentecostal sacrifices; those brought with the two first loaves; New Year's; Atonement Day sacrifices; those on the first day of, and those on the octave of 'Tabernacles.' *Private* sacrifices they classify as those on account of sins by word or deed; those on account of what concerned the body (such as various defilements); those on account of property (firstlings, tithes); those on account of festive seasons; and those on account of vows or promises. Yet another division of sacrifices was into those *due*, or prescribed, and those *voluntary*. For the latter nothing could be used that had previously been vowed, since it would already belong unto God.

---

[4]When the congregation had sinned through ignorance (Lev. 4:13; Num. 15:24–26).

[5]The Paschal lamb, and the high-priest's bullock for a sin-offering and ram for a burnt-offering on the Day of Atonement.

HOLY AND LESS HOLY

He is to slaughter the lamb in the holy place where the sin offering and the burnt offering are slaughtered. Like the sin offering, the guilt offering belongs to the priest; it is most holy (Lev. 14:13).

Moses said to Aaron and his remaining sons, Eleazar and Ithamar, "Take the grain offering left over from the offerings made to the LORD by fire and eat it prepared without yeast beside the altar, for it is most holy" (Lev. 10:12).

But of far greater importance is the arrangement of sacrifices into the most holy and the less holy, which is founded on Scripture (Lev. 6:17; 7:1; 14:13). Certain meat-offerings (Lev. 2:3, 10; 6:17; 10:12), and all burnt-, sin-, and trespass-sacrifices, as well as all public peace-offerings, were most holy. Such were to be offered or sacrificed in one of the more holy places; they were slain at the north side of the altar[6] (the less holy at the east or south side); and they were either not partaken of at all, or else only by the officiating priests, and within the court of the Temple. The skins of the most holy sacrifices, except such as were wholly burnt, belonged to the priests; those of the less holy to the offerers. In the latter case they also partook of their flesh, the only exception being the firstlings, which were eaten by the priests alone. The Rabbis attach ten comparative degrees of sanctity to sacrifices; and it is interesting to mark that of these the first belonged to the blood of the sin-offering; the second to the burnt-offering; the third to the sin-offering itself; and the fourth to the trespass-offering. Lastly, all sacrifices had to be brought before actual sunset, although the unconsumed flesh might smoulder on the altar till next dawn.

THE ACTS OF SACRIFICE

The Rabbis mention the following five acts as belonging to the offerer of a sacrifice: the laying on of hands, slaying, skinning, cutting up, and washing the inwards. These other five were strictly priestly functions: Catching up the blood, sprinkling it, lighting the altar fire, laying on the wood, bringing up the pieces, and all else done at the altar itself.

The whole service must have been exceedingly solemn. Having first been duly purified, a man brought his sacrifice himself 'before the Lord'— anciently, to 'the door of the Tabernacle' (Lev. 1:3;

---

[6]The reason of this is obscure. Was it that the north was regarded as the symbolical region of cold and darkness? Or was it because during the wilderness-journey the Most Holy Place probably faced north—towards Palestine?

He is to present the bull at the entrance to the Tent of Meeting before the LORD. He is to lay his hand on its head and slaughter it before the LORD (Lev. 4:4).

Bringing the sacrifice

4:4), where the altar of burnt-offering was (Exod. 40:6), and in the Temple into the Great Court. If the sacrifice was most holy, he entered by the northern; if less holy, by the southern gate. Next he placed it so as to face the west, or the Most Holy Place, in order thus literally to bring it before the Lord. To this the apostle refers when, in Rom. 12:1, he beeseecheth us to present our 'bodies a living sacrifice, holy, acceptable to God.'

LAYING ON OF HANDS

But this was only the commencement of the service. Women might bring their sacrifices into the Great Court; but they might not perform the second rite[7]—that of laying on of hands. This meant transmission and delegation, and implied representation; so that it really pointed to the substitution of the sacrifice for the sacrificer. Hence it was always accompanied by confession of sin and prayer. It was thus done. The sacrifice was so turned that the person confessing looked towards the west, while he laid his hands between the horns of the sacrifice,[8] and if the

---

[7]There is, however, one dissentient opinion on this point. See Relandus, *Ant.* p. 277.

[8]If the offerer stood outside the Court of the Priests, on the topmost of the fifteen Levitical steps, or within the Gate of Nicanor, *his hands* at least must be within the Great Court, or the rite was not valid.

The elders of the community are to lay their hands on the bull's head before the LORD, and the bull shall be slaughtered before the LORD (Lev. 4:15).

The goats for the sin offering were brought before the king and the assembly, and they laid their hands on them (2 Chron. 29:23).

Scapegoat
(on which the High Priest laid his hands on the Day of Atonement)

sacrifice was brought by more than one, each had to lay on his hands. It is not quite a settled point whether one or both hands were laid on; but all are agreed that it was to be done 'with one's whole force'—as it were, to lay one's whole weight upon the substitute.[9] If a person under vow had died, his heir-at-law took his place. The only public sacrifices in which hands were laid on were those for sins of public ignorance (Lev. 4:15; 16:21), when the 'elders' acted as representing the people—to which some Rabbinical authorities add public sin-offerings in general,[10]—and the scapegoat on the Day of Atonement, on which the high-priest laid his hands. In all private sacrifices, except firstlings, tithes, and the Paschal lamb, the offerer laid hands on, and, while doing so, repeated the following prayer: 'I entreat, O Jehovah: I have sinned, I have done perversely, I have rebelled, I have committed (naming the sin, trespass, or, in the case of a burnt-offering, the breach of positive or negative command); but I return in repentance, and let this be for my atonement (covering).' According to Maimonides, in peace-offerings a record of God's praise, rather than a confession of sins, was spoken. But, as the principle prevailed that frequent confession even without sacrifice was meritorious, another formula is also recorded, in which the allusion to sacrifices is omitted.

Closely connected with this was 'the lifting and waving' of certain sacrifices. The priest put his hands under those of the offerer, and moved the sacrifice upwards and downwards, right and left; according to Abarbanel also 'forwards and backwards.' The lamb of the leper's trespass-offering was waved before it was slain (Lev. 14:24); private peace-offerings, only after they had been slain; while in public peace-offerings, the practice varied.

---

[9]Children, the blind, the deaf, those out of their mind, and non-Israelites, were not allowed to 'lay on hands.'

[10]On the ground of 2 Chron. 29:23.

SACRIFICES SLAIN BY PRIESTS ONLY

Under ordinary circumstances all public sacrifices, and also always that of the leper, were slain by the priests.[11] The Talmud declares the offering of birds, so as to secure the blood,[12] to have been the most difficult part of a priest's work. For the death of the sacrifice was only a means towards an end, that end being the shedding and sprinkling of the blood, by which the atonement was really made. The Rabbis mention a variety of rules observed by the priest who caught up the blood—all designed to make the best provision for its proper sprinkling.[13] Thus the priest was to catch up the blood in a silver vessel pointed at the bottom, so that it could not be put down, and to keep it constantly stirred, to preserve the fluidity of the blood. In the sacrifice of the red heifer, however, the priest caught the blood directly in his left hand, and sprinkled it with his right towards the Holy Place: while in that of the leper one of the two priests received the blood in the vessel; the other in his hand, from which he anointed the purified leper (Lev. 4:25).

The priest is to take the lamb for the guilt offering, together with the log of oil, and wave them before the LORD as a wave offering (Lev. 14:24).

Then the priest shall take some of the blood of the sin offering with his finger and put it on the horns of the altar of burnt offering and pour out the rest of the blood at the base of the altar (Lev. 4:25).

THE APPLICATION OF THE BLOOD

According to the difference of sacrifices, the blood was differently applied, and in different places. In all burnt-, trespass-, and peace-offerings the blood was thrown directly out of the vessel or vessels in which it had been caught, the priest going first to one corner of the altar and then to the other, and throwing it in the form of the Greek letter Γ, so that each time two sides of the altar were covered. Any blood left after these two 'gifts,' as they were called (which stood for four), was poured out at the base of the altar, whence it flowed into the Kedron. In all sin-offerings the blood was not thrown, but sprinkled, the priest dipping the forefinger of his right hand into

He is to dip his finger into the blood and sprinkle some of it seven times before the LORD, in front of the curtain of the sanctuary (Lev. 4:6).

---

[11]The Hebrew term used for sacrificial slaying is never applied to the ordinary killing of animals.

[12]In the case of birds there was no laying on of hands.

[13]The Rabbis mention five mistakes which might render a sacrifice invalid, none of them the least interesting, except, perhaps, that the gullet might never be wholly severed.

the blood, and then sprinkling it from his finger by a motion of the thumb. According to the importance of the sin-offering, the blood was so applied either to the four horns of the altar of burnt-offering, or else it was brought into the Holy Place itself, and sprinkled first seven times towards the veil of the Most Holy Place (Lev. 4:6, 17), and then on the four horns of the golden altar of incense, beginning at the north-east. Finally, on the Day of Atonement the blood was sprinkled within the Most Holy Place itself. From all sin-offerings the blood of which was sprinkled on the horns of the altar of burnt-offering certain portions were to be eaten, while those whose blood was brought into the Holy Place itself were wholly burnt. But in the sacrifices of firstlings, of tithes of animals, and of the Paschal lamb, the blood was neither thrown nor sprinkled, and only poured out at the base of the altar.

Sprinkling the altar

He is to wash the inner parts and the legs with water, and the priest is to burn all of it on the altar. It is a burnt offering, an offering made by fire, an aroma pleasing to the LORD *(Lev. 1:9).*

You blind men! Which is greater: the gift, or the altar that makes the gift sacred (Matt. 23:19)?

THE FLAYING

On the shedding of blood, which was of the greatest importance—since, according to the Talmud, 'whenever the blood touches the altar the offerer is atoned for'—followed the 'flaying' of the sacrifice and the 'cutting up into his pieces.' All this had to be done in an orderly manner, and according to certain rules, the apostle adopting the sacrificial term when he speaks of 'rightly dividing the word of truth' (2 Tim. 2:15). The 'inwards' and 'legs' having been washed (Lev. 1:9), and dried with sponges, the separate pieces of the sacrifice were brought up by various priests: the calculation of the Rabbis being, that in the case of a sheep or a she-goat six priests carried the sacrifice, one more the meat-, and another the drink-offering (in all eight); while in that of a ram twelve, and in that of a bullock four-and-twenty priests were needed for the service. Next, the sacrificial salt was applied, and then the pieces were first confusedly thrown and then arranged upon the fire.[14] This latter part of the service requires explanation.

The Burning

The common idea that the burning either of part or the whole of the sacrifice pointed to its destruction, and symbolised the wrath of God and the punishment due to sin, does not seem to accord with the statements of Scripture. The term used is not that commonly employed for burning, but means 'causing to smoke,' and the rite symbolises partly the entire surrender of the sacrifice, but chiefly its acceptance on the part of God. Thus the sacrifice consumed by a fire which had originally come down from God Himself—not by strange fire—would ascend 'for a sweet savour unto the Lord' (Lev. 1:9; 4:31). Even the circumstance that the fire for the altar of incense was always taken from that on the altar of burnt-offering, shows that, while that fire might symbolise the presence of a holy Jehovah in His house, it could not refer

He shall remove all the fat, just as the fat is removed from the fellowship offering, and the priest shall burn it on the altar as an aroma pleasing to the LORD. In this way the priest will make atonement for him, and he will be forgiven (Lev. 4:31).

The burnt-offering

---

[14]Whatever was laid upon the altar was regarded as 'sanctified' by it, and could not be again removed, even though it should have become defiled. This explains the words of Christ in Matt. 23:19.

After that, the priest must wash his clothes and bathe himself with water. He may then come into the camp, but he will be ceremonially unclean till evening. The man who burns it must also wash his clothes and bathe with water, and he too will be unclean till evening (Num. 19:7–8).

to the fire of wrath or of punishment.[15] As already stated, those parts of the sin-, trespass-,[16] and public peace-offerings, which were allowed to be eaten, could only be partaken of by the priests (not their families) during their actual ministry, and within the Temple walls. The flesh of these offerings had also to be eaten on the day of the sacrifice, or in the night following; while in other offerings the permission extended to a second day. The Rabbis, however, restrict the eating of the Paschal lamb to midnight. Whatever was left beyond the lawful time had to be burned.

NEW TESTAMENT VIEW OF SACRIFICE AGREES WITH THE SYNAGOGUE

It is deeply interesting to know that the New Testament view of sacrifices is entirely in accordance with that of the ancient Synagogue. At the threshold we here meet the principle: 'There is no atonement except by blood.' In accordance with this we quote the following from Jewish interpreters. Rashi says (on Lev. 17:11): 'The soul of every creature is bound up in its blood; therefore I gave it to atone for the soul of man—that one soul should come and atone for the other.' Similarly Aben Ezra writes: 'One soul is a substitute for the other.' And Moses ben Nachmann: 'I gave the soul for you on the altar, that the soul of the animal should be an atonement for the soul of the man.' These quotations might be almost indefinitely multiplied. Another phase of Scriptural truth appears in such Rabbinical statements as that by the imposition of hands: 'The offerer, as it were, puts away his sins from himself, and transfers them upon the living animal;' and that, 'as often as any one sins with his soul, whether from haste or malice, he puts away his sin from himself, and places it upon the head of his

---

[15]Compare the article in Herzog's *Encyc.* vol. x, p. 633. Some of the sacrifices were burned on the altar of burnt-offering, and some outside the gate; while in certain less holy sacrifices it was allowed to burn what was left anywhere within the city.

[16]Except those for the whole people and for the high-priest, which had to be burned outside the gate.

sacrifice, and it is an atonement for him.' Hence, also, the principle laid down by Abarbanel, that, 'after the prayer of confession (connected with the imposition of hands) the sins of the children of Israel lay on the sacrifice (of the Day of Atonement).' This, according to Maimonides, explains why every one who had anything to do with the sacrifice of the red heifer or the goat on the Day of Atonement, or similar offerings, was rendered unclean; since these animals were regarded as actually sin-bearing. In fact, according to Rabbinical expression, the sin-bearing animal is on that ground expressly designated as something to be rejected and abominable. The Christian reader will here be reminded of the Scriptural statement: 'For He has made Him to be sin for us who knew no sin, that we might be made the righteousness of God in Him.'

Priest with altar, lampstand, and table of shewbread

There is yet one other phase on which the Synagogue lays stress. It is best expressed in the following quotation, to which many similar might be added: 'Properly speaking, the blood of the sinner should have been shed, and his body burned, as those of the sacrifices. But the Holy One—blessed be He!—accepted our sacrifice from us as redemption and atonement. Behold the full grace which Jehovah—blessed be He!—has shown to man! In His compassion and in the fulness of His grace He accepted the soul of the animal instead of his soul, that through it there might be an atonement.' Hence also the principle, so important as an answer to the question, Whether the Israelites of old had understood the meaning of sacrifices? 'He that brought a sacrifice required to come to the knowledge that that sacrifice was his redemption.'[17]

JEWISH LITURGIES

In view of all this, the deep-felt want so often expressed by the Synagogue is most touching. In the liturgy for the Day of Atonement we read: 'While the altar and the sanctuary were still in their places, we

---

[17]David de Pomis. On the whole subject see Wünsche's interesting tractate, *Die Lieden des Messias*, where the quotations are given at length.

The LORD said to Moses, "The tenth day of this seventh month is the Day of Atonement. Hold a sacred assembly and deny yourselves, and present an offering made to the LORD by fire" (Lev. 23:26–27).

were atoned for by the goats, designated by lot. But now for our guilt, if Jehovah be pleased to destroy us, He takes from our hand neither burnt-offering nor sacrifice.' We add only one more out of many similar passages in the Jewish prayer-book: 'We have spoken violence and rebellion; we have walked in a way that is not right....Behold, our transgressions have increased upon us; they press upon us like a burden; they have gone over our heads; we have forsaken Thy commandments, which are excellent. And wherewith shall we appear before Thee, the mighty God, to atone for our transgressions, and to put away our trespasses, and to remove sin, and to magnify Thy grace? Sacrifices and offerings are no more; sin- and trespass-offerings have ceased; the blood of sacrifices is no longer sprinkled; destroyed is Thy holy house, and fallen the gates of Thy sanctuary; Thy holy city lies desolate; Thou hast slain, sent from Thy presence; they have gone, driven forth from before Thy face, the priests who brought Thy sacrifices!' Accordingly, also, the petition frequently recurs: 'Raise up for us a right Intercessor (that it may be true), I have found a ransom (an atonement or covering).' And on the Day of Atonement, as in substance frequently on other occasions, they pray: 'Bring us back in jubilee to Zion, Thy city, and in joy as of old to Jerusalem, the house of Thy holiness! Then shall we bring before Thy face the sacrifices that are due.'

THE EVE OF DAY OF ATONEMENT

Who shall make answer to this deep lament of exiled Judah? Where shall a ransom be found to take the place of their sacrifices? In their despair some appeal to the merits of the fathers or of the pious; others to their own or to Israel's sufferings, or to death, which is regarded as the last expiation. But the most melancholy exhibition, perhaps, is that of an attempted sacrifice by each pious Israelite on the eve of the Day of Atonement. Taking for males a white cock,[18] and for females a hen, the head of the house

---

[18]Because the Hebrew word for 'man' (Gever) is used in the Talmud for 'a cock,' and 'white,' with reference to Isa. 1:18.

prays: 'The children of men who dwell in darkness and in the shadow of death, bound in misery and iron—them will He bring forth from darkness and the shadow of death, and break their bonds asunder. Fools, because of their transgressions and because of their iniquities, are afflicted; their soul abhorreth all manner of meat, and they draw near unto the gates of death. Then they cry unto the Lord in their trouble, that He save them out of their distresses. He sends His word and heals them, and delivers them from their destruction. Then they praise the Lord for His goodness, and for His marvellous works to the children of men. If there be an angel with Him, an intercessor, one among a thousand, to show unto men his righteousness, then He is gracious unto him, and saith, Let him go, that he may not go down into the pit; I have found an atonement (a covering).' Next, the head of the house swings the sacrifice round his head, saying, 'This is my substitute; this is in exchange for me; this is my atonement. This cock goes into death, but may I enter into a long and happy life, and into peace!' Then he repeats this prayer three times, and lays his hands on the sacrifice, which is now slain.

This offering up of an animal not sanctioned by the law, in a place, in a manner, and by hands not authorised by God, is it not a terrible phantom of Israel's dark and dreary night? and does it not seem strangely to remind us of that other terrible night, when the threefold crowing of a cock awakened Peter to the fact of his denial of 'the Lamb of God which taketh away the sin of the world'?

And still the cry of the Synagogue comes to us through these many centuries of past unbelief and ignorance: 'Let one innocent come and make atonement for the guilty!' To which no other response can ever be made than that of the apostle: 'Such an High-Priest became us, who is holy, harmless, undefiled, separate from sinners, and made higher than the heavens!' (Heb. 7:26).

As Simon Peter stood warming himself, he was asked, "You are not one of his disciples, are you?"

He denied it, saying, "I am not."

One of the high priest's servants, a relative of the man whose ear Peter had cut off, challenged him, "Didn't I see you with him in the olive grove?" Again Peter denied it, and at that moment a rooster began to crow (John 18:25–27).

6

THE BURNT-OFFERING,
THE SIN- AND TRESPASS-OFFERING,
AND THE PEACE-OFFERING

Day after day every priest stands and performs his religious duties; again and again he offers the same sacrifices, which can never take away sins. But when this priest had offered for all time one sacrifice for sins, he sat down at the right hand of God.
—Hebrews 10:11-12.

Get rid of the old yeast that you may be a new batch without yeast—as you really are. For Christ, our Passover lamb, has been sacrificed (1 Cor. 5:7).

THE IDEA OF SUBSTITUTION

The question whether or not sacrifices were to cease after the coming of the Messiah is differently answered in the Jewish synagogue, some arguing that only thank- and peace-offerings would then be brought, while the majority expect a revival of the regular sacrificial worship.[1] But on one point the authorities of the old synagogue, previous to their controversy with Christianity, are agreed. As the Old Testament and Jewish tradition taught that the object of a sacrifice was its *substitution* for the offender, so Scripture and the Jewish fathers also teach that the substitute to whom all these types pointed was none other than the Messiah.

It has been well remarked,[2] that the difficulties of modern interpreters of the Messianic prophecies arise chiefly from their not perceiving the unity of the Old Testament in its progressive unfolding of the plan

---

[1]See Wünsche, *u.s.* p. 28. It has been a matter of controversy whether or not, in the first years after the destruction of the Temple, solitary attempts were made by enthusiasts to offer sacrifices. My own conviction is, that no such instance can be historically established. See Derenbourg, *Essai sur l'Hist. de la Pal.* pp. 480–482.

[2]Wünsche, p. 35.

of salvation. Moses must not be read independently of the Psalms, nor yet the Psalms independently of the Prophets. Theirs are not so many unconnected writings of different authorship and age, only held together by the boards of one volume. They form integral parts of one whole, the object of which is to point to the goal of all revelation in the appearing of the Christ. Accordingly, we recognise in the prophetic word, not a change nor a difference, but three well-marked progressive stages, leading up to the sufferings and the glory of Messiah. In the Proto-Evangel, as Gen. 3:15 has been called, and in what follows it, we have as yet only the grand general outlines of the figure. Thus we see a *Person* in the Seed of the woman; *suffering*, in the prediction that His heel would be bruised; and *victory*, in that He would bruise the serpent's head. These merely general outlines are wonderfully filled up in the Book of Psalms. The 'Person' is now 'the son of David;' while alike the sufferings and the victory are sketched in vivid detail in such Psalms as 22, 35, 69, and 102; or else in Psalms 2, 72, 89, 110, and 118—not to speak of other almost innumerable allusions.

CHRIST OUR SUBSTITUTE

One element only was still wanting—that this Son of David, this Sufferer and Conqueror, should be shown to be our *Substitute*, to whom also the sacrificial types had pointed. This is added in the writings of the prophets, especially in those of Isaiah, culminating, as it were, in Isa. 53, around which the details furnished by the other prophets naturally group themselves. The picture is now completed, and so true to the original that, when compared with the reality in the Person and Work of the Lord Jesus Christ, we can have no difficulty in recognising it; and this not so much from one or other outline in prophecy or type, as from their combination and progressive development throughout the Scriptures of the Old Testament, considered as a connected whole.

And I will put enmity between you and the woman, and between your offspring and hers; he will crush your head, and you will strike his heel (Gen. 3:15).

He said to me, "You are my Son; today I have become your Father. Ask of me, and I will make the nations your inheritance, the ends of the earth your possession. You will rule them with an iron scepter; you will dash them to pieces like pottery" (Ps. 2:7b–9).

But he was pierced for our transgressions, he was crushed for our iniquities; the punishment that brought us peace was upon him, and by his wounds we are healed. We all, like sheep, have gone astray, each of us has turned to his own way; and the LORD has laid on him the iniquity of us all (Isa. 53:5–6).

*He was despised and
rejected by men,
a man of sorrows, and
familiar with suffering.
Like one from whom men
hide their faces
he was despised, and we
esteemed him not
(Isa. 53:3).*

As already stated, such early works as the *Targum Jonathan* and the *Jerusalem Targum*[3] frankly adopt the Messianic interpretation of these prophecies. The later Rabbis also admit that this had been the common view of the Jewish fathers; but, on account of 'the sages of the Nazarenes, who apply it to that man whom they hanged in Jerusalem towards the close of the second Temple, and who, according to their opinion, was the Son of the Most Blessed, and had taken human nature in the womb of the Virgin,' they reject that interpretation, and refer the prediction of suffering either to some individual, or mostly to Israel as a nation. But so difficult is it to weaken the language in which the Messiah's vicarious sufferings are described—not less than twelve times in Isa. 52:13 to 53—that some of their commentators have been forced to admit it, sometimes almost unconsciously. The language of Isaiah has even crept into the following Messianic hymnal prayer for the Passover:[4]—

> *'Haste, my Beloved; come, ere ends the
>   vision's day;
> Make haste, and chase Thyself the shadows
>   all away!
> "Despised" is He, but yet "extolled" and "high"
>   shall be;
> "Deal prudently," "sprinkle nations," and
>   "judge" shall He.'*

Thus, if by the universal consent of all who are unprejudiced sacrifices point to substitution, substitution in its turn points to the Person and Work of the Messiah.

It has already been explained that all sacrifices were either such as were offered on the ground of

---

[3]Whatever date may be assigned to these *Targumin*, in their *present* recension, there can be no doubt that they embody the elements of the very earliest Jewish Biblical interpretation. For particulars I must take leave to refer to my *History of the Jewish Nation*, chap. xi: *Theological Science and Religious Belief in Palestine*, p. 407, etc.

[4]According to the English edition of David Levi, this prayer applies to 'the true Messiah.' See Wünsche, p. 28, etc.

communion with God—the burnt- and the peace-offerings; or else such as were intended to restore that communion when it had been dimmed or disturbed —the sin- and the trespass-offering. Each of these four kinds of sacrifices will now have to be separately considered.

SYMBOLISM OF THE BURNT-OFFERING

I. *The burnt-offering—Olah,* or also *Chalil.* (Deut. 33:10; Ps. 51:19 literally rendered 'whole burnt-offering')—The derivation of the term Olah, as wholly 'ascending' unto God, indicates alike the mode of the sacrifice and its meaning. It symbolised the entire surrender unto God, whether of the individual or of the congregation, and His acceptance thereof. Hence, also, it could not be offered 'without shedding of blood.' Where other sacrifices were brought, it followed the sin- but preceded the peace-offering. In fact, it meant general acceptance on the ground of previous special acceptance, and it has rightly been called the *sacrificium latreuticum,* or sacrifice of devotion and service.[5] Thus day by day it formed the regular morning and evening service in the Temple, while on sabbaths, new moons, and festivals additional burnt-offerings followed the ordinary worship. There the covenant-people brought the covenant-sacrifice, and the multitude of offerings indicated, as it were, the fulness, richness, and joyousness of their self-surrender. Accordingly, although we can understand how this sacrifice might be said to 'make atonement' for an individual in the sense of assuring him of his acceptance, we cannot agree with the Rabbis that it was intended to atone for evil thoughts and purposes, and for breaches of positive commands, or of such negative as involved also a positive command.

The burnt-offering was always to be a male animal, as the more noble, and as indicating strength and energy. The blood was thrown on the angles of

Then there will be righteous sacrifices, whole burnt offerings to delight you; then bulls will be offered on your altar (Ps. 51:19).

---

[5]In the historical books the term *Olah* is, however, used in a more general sense to denote other sacrifices also.

the altar below the red line that ran round it. Then 'the sinew of the thigh' (Gen. 32:32),[6] the stomach and the entrails, etc., having been removed (in the case of birds also the feathers and the wings), and the sacrifice having been duly salted, it was wholly burned. The skins belonged to the ministering priests, who derived a considerable revenue from this source.[7] The burnt-offering was the only sacrifice which non-Israelites were allowed to bring.[8] The Emperor Augustus had a daily burnt-offering brought for him of two lambs and a bullock; and ever afterwards this sacrifice was regarded as indicating that the Jewish nation recognised the Roman emperor as their ruler. Hence at the commencement of the Jewish war Eleazar carried its rejection, and this became, as it were, the open mark of the rebellion.

Therefore to this day the Israelites do not eat the tendon attached to the socket of the hip, because the socket of Jacob's hip was touched near the tendon (Gen. 32:32).

...he also orders that the priests who minister the offering of the sacrifices, shall receive the skins of the whole burnt offerings (and they amount to an unspeakable number, this being no slight gift, but one of the most exceeding value and importance), from which circumstance it is plain, that although he has not given to the priesthood a portion of land as its inheritance, in the same manner that he has to others, he has yet assigned to them a more honourable and more untroubled share than any other tribe, granting them the first fruits of every description of sacrifice and offering (Philo, On the Special Laws I.151).

SYMBOLISM OF THE SIN-OFFERING

II. *The sin-offering*—This is the most important of all sacrifices. It made atonement for the *person* of the offender, whereas the trespass-offering only atoned for one special offence. Hence sin-offerings were brought on festive occasions for the whole people, but never trespass-offerings (comp. Num. 28, 29). In fact, the trespass-offering may be regarded as representing ransom for a special wrong, while the sin-offering symbolised general redemption. Both sacrifices applied only to sins 'through ignorance,' in opposition to those done 'presumptuously' (or 'with a high hand'). For the latter the law provided no atonement, but held out 'a certain fearful looking for of judgment and fiery indignation.' By sins 'through ignorance,' however, we are to understand, according to the Rabbis, not only such as were committed strictly through want of knowledge, but also those which had been unintentional, or through weakness, or where

---

[6]The 'sinew of the thigh' was neither allowed to be eaten nor to be sacrificed.

[7]Philo, *De Sacerd. Honor.* I.151 p. 833.

[8]If they brought a 'peace-offering,' it was to be treated as a burnt-offering, and that for the obvious reason that there was no one to eat the sacrificial meal. Of course, there was no imposition of hands in that case.

the offender at the time realised not his guilt. The fundamental difference between the two sacrifices appears also in this—that sin-offerings, having a retrospective effect on the worshippers, were brought at the various festivals, and also for purification in such defilements of the body as symbolically pointed to the sinfulness of our nature (sexual defilement, those connected with leprosy, and with death).[9] On the other hand, the animal brought for a trespass-offering was to be always a male (generally a ram, which was never used as a sin-offering); nor was it lawful, as in the sin-offering, to make substitution of something else in case of poverty. These two particulars indicate that the trespass-offering contemplated chiefly a wrong, for which decided satisfaction was to be made by offering a *male* animal, and for which a definite, unvarying ransom was to be given.[10]

IN ALL CASES REPENTANCE WAS NECESSARY

However, in reference both to sin- and to trespass-offerings, the Rabbinical principle must be kept in view—that they only atoned in case of real repentance. Indeed, their first effect would be 'a remembrance of sins' before God (Heb. 10:3). All sin-offerings were either *public* or *private* (congregational or individual). The former were always males; the latter always females, except the bullock for the high-priest's sin of ignorance (Lev. 4:3), and the kid for the same offence of a 'ruler' (Lev. 4:22). They were further divided into *fixed*, which were the same in the case of rich and poor, and *varying*, which 'ascended and descended' according to the circumstances of the offerer. 'Fixed' sacrifices were all those for sins 'through ignorance' against any of the prohibitory commands (of which the Rabbis enumerate 365);[11] for sins of deed, not of

Include one male goat as a sin offering to make atonement for you. These are in addition to the monthly and daily burnt offerings with their grain offerings and drink offerings as specified. They are offerings made to the LORD by fire— a pleasing aroma (Num. 29:5–6).

The LORD said to Moses: "When a person commits a violation and sins unintentionally in regard to any of the LORD's holy things, he is to bring to the LORD as a penalty a ram from the flock, one without defect and of the proper value in silver, according to the sanctuary shekel. It is a guilt offering" (Lev. 5:14–15).

---

[9]Oehler (in Herzog's *Encycl.* x, p. 643) applies the section Lev. 5:1–13 to *sin-offerings*, the word 'trespass' being taken in a general sense. The distinction between them and the ordinary trespass-offerings appears from ver. 14, etc.

[10]On the trespass-offering of the leper (Lev. 14:12), and of the Nazarite whose vow had been interrupted (Num. 6:12), see below.

[11]They also mention 248 affirmative precepts, or in all 613, according to the supposed number of members in the human body.

word; or else for such which, if they had been high-handed, would have carried the Divine punishment of being 'cut off' (of which the Rabbis enumerate 36). The 'varying' sacrifices were those for lepers (Lev. 14:21); for women after childbirth (of which concession to poverty Mary, the mother of Jesus, availed herself—Luke 2:24; Lev. 12:8); for having concealed a 'thing known' (Lev. 5:1); for having unwittingly sworn falsely; and for having either unwittingly eaten of what had been consecrated, or gone into the Temple in a state of defilement. Lastly, there were 'outer' and 'inner' sin-offerings, according as the blood was applied to the altar of burnt-offering or brought into the inner sanctuary. In the former case the flesh was to be eaten only by the officiating priests and within the sanctuary; the latter were to be wholly burnt without the camp or city.[12] In both cases, however, the 'inwards,' as enumerated in Lev. 4:8, were always first burned on the altar of burnt-offering. Neither oil nor frankincense were to be brought with a sin-offering. There was nothing joyous about it. It represented a terrible necessity, for which God, in His wondrous grace, had made provision.

Broad-tailed sheep of the Orient

If, however, he is poor and cannot afford these, he must take one male lamb as a guilt offering to be waved to make atonement for him, together with a tenth of an ephah of fine flour mixed with oil for a grain offering, a log of oil, and two doves or two young pigeons, which he can afford, one for a sin offering and the other for a burnt offering (Lev. 14:21–22).

If a person sins because he does not speak up when he hears a public charge to testify regarding something he has seen or learned about, he will be held responsible (Lev. 5:1).

THE SIN-OFFERING DIFFERED WITH THE RANK OF THE OFFERER

It only remains to explain in detail two peculiarities connected with the sin-offering. *First,* it differed according to the theocratic position of him who brought the sacrifice. For the high-priest on the Day of Atonement (Lev. 16:3), or when he had sinned, 'to the rendering guilty of the people' (Lev. 4:3), that is, in his official capacity as representing the people; or if the whole congregation had sinned through ignorance (Lev. 4:13);[13] and at the consecration of the priests and Levites a bullock was to be brought. This was the highest kind of sin-offering. Next in order was that of the 'kid of the goats,' offered for the people

---

[12]According to the Talmud, if doves were brought as a sin-offering, the carcases were not burned, but went to the priests.

[13]The Rabbis apply this to erroneous decisions on the part of the Sanhedrim.

on the Day of Atonement (Lev. 16:5), and on the other festivals and New Moons (Num. 28:15, etc.; 29:5, etc.); also for the ruler who had sinned through ignorance (Lev. 4:23); for the congregation if aught had been committed by any individual 'without the knowledge of the congregation' (Num. 15:24); and, lastly, at the consecration of the Tabernacle (Lev. 9:3, 15). The third kind of sin-offering consisted of a female kid of the goats[14] for individual Israelites (Lev. 4:28, etc.; 5:6), and of a ewe lamb for a Nazarite (Num. 6:14) and a leper (Lev. 14:10). The lowest grade of sin-offering was that of turtle-doves or young pigeons offered at certain purifications (Lev. 12:6; 15:14, 29; Num. 6:10); or else as a substitute for other sacrifices in case of poverty—in extreme cases something resembling to, or 'as a meat-offering' being even allowed (Lev. 5:11–13).

Wild goat of Sinai

THE BLOOD TO BE SPRINKLED

Secondly, the blood of the sin-offering was *sprinkled,* not thrown. In the case of a private Israelite, it was sprinkled, that is, either jerked or dropped successively on each of the four horns[15] of the altar of burnt-offering—beginning at the south-east, thence going to the north-east, then the north-west, and finishing at the south-west, where the rest of the blood was poured at the bottom of the altar through two funnels that conducted into the Kedron. On the other hand, when offering bullocks and goats, whose carcases were to be burned without the camp, the officiating priest stood in the Holy Place, between the golden altar and the candlestick, and sprinkled of the blood seven times[16] towards the Most Holy Place, to indicate that the covenant-relationship itself had been endangered and was to be re-established, and afterwards touched with it the horns of the altar of incense. The most solemn of all sacrifices were those

If the anointed priest sins, bringing guilt on the people, he must bring to the LORD a young bull without defect as a sin offering for the sin he has committed (Lev. 4:3).

This is the monthly burnt offering to be made at each new moon during the year. Besides the regular burnt offering with its drink offering, one male goat is to be presented to the LORD as a sin offering (Num. 28:14b–15).

---

[14]It is not very easy to understand why goats should have been chosen in preference for sin-offerings, unless it were that their flesh was the most unpalatable of meat.

[15]The 'horns' symbolised, as it were, the outstanding height and strength of the altar.

[16]Seven was the symbolical number of the covenant.

Altar of burnt offerings

Why didn't you eat the sin offering in the sanctuary area? It is most holy; it was given to you to take away the guilt of the community by making atonement for them before the LORD (Lev. 10:17).

The High Priest, arrayed in his linen garments, stood before the Lord himself within the Most Holy Place to make an atonement.

of the Day of Atonement, when the high-priest, arrayed in his linen garments, stood before the Lord Himself within the Most Holy Place to make an atonement. Every spot of blood from a sin-offering on a garment conveyed defilement, as being loaded with sin, and all vessels used for such sacrifices had either to be broken or scoured.

Quite another phase of symbolic meaning was intended to be conveyed by the sacrificial meal which the priests were to make of the flesh of such sin-offerings as were not wholly burnt without the camp. Unquestionably Philo[17] was right in suggesting, that one of the main objects of this meal was to carry to the offerer assurance of his acceptance, 'since God would never have allowed His servants to partake of it, had there not been a complete removal and forgetting of the sin' atoned for. This view entirely accords with the statement in Lev. 10:17, where the purpose of this meal by the priests is said to be 'to bear the iniquity of the congregation.' Hence, also, the flesh of all sacrifices, either for the high-priest, as representing the priesthood, or for the whole people, had to be burnt; because those who, as God's representatives, were alone allowed to eat the sacrificial meal were themselves among the offerers of the sacrifice.

SYMBOLISM OF THE TRESPASS-OFFERING

III. The *trespass-offering* was provided for certain transgressions committed through ignorance, or else, according to Jewish tradition, where a man afterwards voluntarily confessed himself guilty. The Rabbis arrange this class into those for *a doubtful* and for *a certain trespass.* The former were offered by the more scrupulous, when, uncertain whether they might not have committed an offence which, if done high-handed, would have implied being 'cut off,' or, if in ignorance, necessitated a sin-offering. Accordingly, the extreme party, or Chassidim, were wont to bring such a sacrifice every day! On the other hand, the offering for *certain* trespasses covered five distinct

---

[17] *De Vict.* 13.

cases,[18] which had all this in common, that they represented a wrong for which a special ransom was to be given. It forms no exception to this principle, that a trespass-offering was also prescribed in the case of a healed leper (Lev. 14:12), and in that of a Nazarite, whose vow had been interrupted by sudden defilement with the dead (Num. 6:10–12), since leprosy was also symbolically regarded as a wrong to the congregation as a whole,[19] while the interruption of the vow as a kind of wrong directly towards the Lord. But that this last was, at the same time, considered the lightest kind of trespass appears even from this—that, while ordinarily the flesh of the trespass-offering, after burning the inwards on the altar of burnt-offering (Lev. 7:3), was only to be eaten by the officiating priests within the Holy Place, the lamb offered for such a Nazarite might be eaten by others also, and anywhere within Jerusalem. The blood of the trespass-offering (like that of the burnt-offering) was thrown on the corners of the altar below the red line.

Against you, you only,
*   have I sinned*
*   and done what is evil in*
*   your sight,*
so that you are proved
*   right when you speak*
and justified when you
*   judge (Ps. 51:4).*

The sacrifices of God are a
*   broken spirit;*
a broken and contrite
*   heart,*
O God, you will not
*   despise (Ps. 51:17).*

THE PEACE-OFFERING

IV. The most joyous of all sacrifices was the *peace-offering*, or, as from its derivation it might also be rendered, the offering of completion.[20] This was, indeed, a season of happy fellowship with the Covenant God, in which he condescended to become Israel's Guest at the sacrificial meal, even as He was always their Host. Thus it symbolised the spiritual truth expressed in Rev. 3:20, 'Behold, I stand at the door, and knock: if any man hear My voice, and open the door, I will come in to him, and will sup with him, and he with Me.' In peace-offerings the sacrificial meal was the point of main importance. Hence the name 'Sevach,' by which it is designated in the

I will sacrifice a freewill
*   offering to you;*
I will praise your name,
*   O LORD,*
for it is good (Ps. 54:6).

---

[18]Lev. 5:15; 6:2; 19:20 (in these three cases the offering was a ram); and Lev. 14:12 and Num. 6:12 (where the offering was a he-lamb). The Word of God considers every wrong done to another, as also a wrong done against the Lord (Ps. 51:4), and hence, as needing a trespass-offering.

[19]Hence the leper was banished from the congregation.

[20]It always followed all the other sacrifices.

You may, however, present as a freewill offering an ox or a sheep that is deformed or stunted, but it will not be accepted in fulfillment of a vow (Lev. 22:23).

Anyone who brings a fellowship offering to the LORD is to bring part of it as his sacrifice to the LORD. With his own hands he is to bring the offering made to the LORD by fire; he is to bring the fat, together with the breast, and wave the breast before the LORD as a wave offering... You are to give the right thigh of your fellowship offerings to the priest as a contribution (Lev. 7:29b–30, 32).

Pentateuch, and which means 'slaying,' in reference to a meal. It is this sacrifice which is so frequently referred to in the Book of Psalms as the grateful homage of a soul justified and accepted before God (Ps. 51:17; 54:6; 56:12; 116:17, 18). If, on the one hand, then, the 'offering of completion' indicated that there was complete peace with God, on the other, it was also literally the offering of completeness. The peace-offerings were either *public* or *private*. The two lambs offered every year at Pentecost (Lev. 23:19) were a public peace-offering, and the only one which was regarded as 'most holy.' As such they were sacrificed at the north side of the altar, and their flesh eaten only by the officiating priests, and within the Holy Place. The other public peace-offerings were slain at the south side, and their 'inwards' burnt on the altar (Lev. 3:4, 5). Then, after the priests had received their due, the rest was to be eaten by the offerers themselves, either within the courts of the Temple or in Jerusalem (Deut. 27:7). On one occasion (1 Kgs. 8:63) no less than 22,000 oxen and 120,000 sheep were so offered. Private peace-offerings were of a threefold kind: 'sacrifices of thanksgiving,' 'vows,' and strictly 'voluntary offerings' (Lev. 7:11, 12, 16). The first were in general acknowledgment of mercies received; the last, the free gift of loving hearts, as even the use of the same term in Exod. 25:2, 35:29 implies. Exceptionally in this last case, an animal that had anything either 'defective' or 'superfluous' might be offered (Lev. 22:23).

WHAT CONSTITUTED PEACE-OFFERINGS

Peace-offerings were brought either of male or of female animals (chiefly of the former), but not of pigeons, the sacrifice being, of course, always accompanied by a meat- and a drink-offering (Lev. 7:11, etc.). As every other sacrifice, they needed imposition of hands, confession, and sprinkling of blood, the latter being done as in the burnt-offering. Then the 'inwards' were taken out and 'waved' before the Lord, along with 'the breast' and the 'right shoulder' (or, perhaps more correctly, the right leg). In reference to these two wave-offerings we remark, that the breast properly belonged to the Lord, and that He gave it to His priests (Lev. 7:30), while Israel gave the 'right shoulder' directly to the priests (Lev. 7:32). The ritual of waving has already been described,[21] the meaning of the movement being to present the sacrifice, as it were, to the Lord, and then to receive it back from Him. The Rabbinical suggestion, that there was a distinct rite of 'heaving' besides that of 'waving,' seems only to rest on a misunderstanding of such passages as Lev. 2:2, 9; 7:32; 10:15, etc.[22] The following were to be 'waved' before the Lord: the breast of the peace-offering (Lev. 7:30); the parts mentioned at the consecration of the priests (Lev. 8:25–29); the first *omer* at the Passover (Lev. 23:11); the jealousy-offering (Num. 5:25); the offering at the close of a Nazarite's vow (Num. 6:20); the offering of a cleansed leper (Lev. 14:12); and 'the two lambs' presented 'with the bread of the firstfruits,' at the Feast of Tabernacles (Lev. 23:20). The two last-mentioned offerings were 'waved' before being sacrificed. After the 'waving,' the 'inwards' (Lev. 3:3–5, etc.) were burnt on the altar of burnt-offering, and the rest eaten either by priests or worshippers, the longest term allowed in any case for the purpose of being two days and a night from the time of sacrifice. Of course, the guests, among whom were to be the Levites and the poor, must all be in a state of Levitical purity, symbolical of 'the wedding garment' needful at the better gospel-feast.

Meat-Offerings

We close with a few particulars about *meat-offerings*. These were either brought in conjunction with burnt- and peace-offerings (but never with sin- or with trespass-offerings) or else by themselves. The latter were either *public* or *private* meat-offerings. The three public meat-offerings were: the twelve loaves of

From the fellowship offering he is to bring a sacrifice made to the LORD by fire: all the fat that covers the inner parts or is connected to them, both kidneys with the fat on them near the loins, and the covering of the liver, which he will remove with the kidneys. Then Aaron's sons are to burn it on the altar on top of the burnt offering that is on the burning wood, as an offering made by fire, an aroma pleasing to the LORD (Lev. 3:3–5).

But when the king came in to see the guests, he noticed a man there who was not wearing wedding clothes. "Friend," he asked, "how did you get in here without wedding clothes?" The man was speechless.

Then the king told the attendants, "Tie him hand and foot, and throw him outside, into the darkness, where there will be weeping and gnashing of teeth."

For many are invited, but few are chosen (Matt. 22:11–14).

---

[21]The pieces were laid on the hands as follows: the feet, and then the breast, the right shoulder, the kidneys, the caul of the liver, and, in the case of a thank-offering, the bread upon it all.

[22]The 'heave' is, in reality, only the technical term for the priest's 'taking' his portion.

Table of shewbread

If you bring a grain offering baked in an oven, it is to consist of fine flour: cakes made without yeast and mixed with oil, or wafers made without yeast and spread with oil. If your grain offering is prepared on a griddle, it is to be made of fine flour mixed with oil, and without yeast. Crumble it and pour oil on it; it is a grain offering (Lev. 2:4–6).

shewbread, renewed every Sabbath, and afterwards eaten by the priests; the omer, or sheaf of the harvest, on the second day of the Passover; and the two wave-loaves at Pentecost. Four of the private meat-offerings were enjoined by the law, viz.: (1) the daily meat-offering of the high-priest, according to the Jewish interpretation of Lev. 6:20; (2) that at the consecration of priests (Lev. 6:20); (3) that in substitution for a sin-offering, in case of poverty (Lev. 5: 11, 12); and (4) that of jealousy (Num. 5:15). The following five were purely voluntary, viz. that of fine flour with oil, unbaken (Lev. 2:1); that 'baken in a pan;' 'in a frying-pan;' 'in the oven;' and the 'wafers' (Lev. 2:4–7). All these offerings were to consist of at least one omer of corn (which was the tenth part of an ephah—Exod. 16:36). But any larger number under 61 omers might be offered, the reason of the limitation being, that as the public meat-offerings enjoined on the Feast of Tabernacles amounted to 61,[23] all private offerings must be less than that number. In all baken meat-offerings, an 'omer' was always made into ten cakes—the symbolical number of completeness—except in that of the high-priest's daily meat-offering, of which twelve cakes were baken, as representative of Israel. Finally, as the Rabbis express it, every meat-offering prepared in a vessel had 'three pourings of oil'—first into the vessel, then to mingle with the flour, and lastly, after it was ready—the frankincense being then put upon it. The 'wafers' were 'anointed' with oil, after the form of the Hebrew letter *koph*, or the Greek letter *kappa*, as they explain, 'to run down in two parts.'[24]

---

[23]See Relandus, p. 353. This, however, only when the feast fell on a Sabbath.

[24]The subjoined Rabbinical table may be of use:

MEAT-OFFERINGS—

Requiring the addition of oil and frankincense: Of fine flour unbaken; baken in a pan; baken in a frying-pan; baken in the oven; the 'wafers;' the high-priest's daily and the priest's consecration offering; the flour from the 'sheaf' offered on the second day of the Passover. *Requiring oil without frankincense:* All meat-offerings, accompanying a burnt- or a peace-offering. *Requiring frankincense without oil:* The shewbread. *Requiring neither oil nor frankincense:* The two loaves at Pentecost; the jealousy-offering; and that in substitution for a sin-offering.

When presenting a meat-offering, the priest first brought it in the golden or silver dish in which it had been prepared, and then transferred it to a holy vessel, putting oil and frankincense upon it. Taking his stand at the south-eastern corner of the altar, he next took the 'handful' that was actually to be burnt, put it in another vessel, laid some of the frankincense on it, carried it to the top of the altar, salted it, and then placed it on the fire. The rest of the meat-offering belonged to the priests.[25] Every meat-offering was accompanied by a drink-offering of wine, which was poured at the base of the altar.

Vessels

Large Number of Priests Needed

So complicated a service, and one which enjoined such frequent sacrifices, must always have kept a large number of priests busy in the courts of the Temple. This was especially the case on the great festivals; and if the magnificent Temple could hold its 210,000 worshippers—if the liturgy, music, and ritual were equally gorgeous—we cannot wonder that it required multitudes of white-robed priests properly to discharge its ministry. Tradition has it, that on the Day of Atonement no less than five hundred priests were wont to assist in the services. On other feast-days even more must have been engaged, as it was a Rabbinical principle, 'that a man should bring all his offerings, that were either due from him or voluntarily dedicated, at the solemn festival that cometh next.' In other words, if a man incurred a sacrifice, or voluntarily promised one, he was to bring it when next he came to Jerusalem. But even this provision showed 'the weakness and unprofitableness thereof,' since in all ordinary cases a long time must have elapsed before the stain of guilt could be consciously removed by an atoning sacrifice, or a vow performed. Blessed be God, the reality in Christ Jesus in this, as in all other things, far out-distances the type! For we

When Christ came as high priest of the good things that are already here, he went through the greater and more perfect tabernacle that is not man–made, that is to say, not a part of this creation. He did not enter by means of the blood of goats and calves; but he entered the Most Holy Place once for all by his own blood, having obtained eternal redemption (Heb. 9:11–12).

---

[25] Except in the meat-offering of the high-priest, and of priests at their consecration; the exception in both cases for the obvious reason already referred to in explaining sacrificial meals. Similarly, the meat-offerings connected with burnt-sacrifices were wholly consumed on the altar.

have always 'liberty to enter into the Holiest by the blood of Jesus;' and 'if the blood of bulls and of goats, and the ashes of an heifer sprinkling the unclean, sanctifieth to the purifying of the flesh, how much more shall the blood of Christ, who through the Eternal Spirit offered Himself without spot to God, purge your conscience from dead works to serve the living God!'

7

AT NIGHT IN THE TEMPLE

✣

"Blessed is he who stays awake and keeps his clothes with him."—Revelation 16:15.

ALLUSIONS TO THE TEMPLE IN NEW TESTAMENT

There is a marked peculiarity and also a special charm about the allusions of the 'beloved disciple' to the 'Temple and its services.' The other New Testament writers refer to them in their narratives, or else explain their types, in such language as any well-informed worshipper at Jerusalem might have employed. But John writes not like an ordinary Israelite. He has eyes and ears for details which others would have left unnoticed. As, according to a Jewish tradition, the high-priest read the Divine answer of the Urim and Thummim by a heavenly light cast upon special letters in the names of the tribes graven upon his breast-plate, so to John the presence and the words of Jesus seem to render luminous the well-remembered services of the Temple. This, as we shall have frequent occasion to show, appears in his Gospel, but much more in the Book of Revelation. Indeed, the Apocalypse, as a whole, may be likened to the Temple services in its mingling of prophetic symbols with worship and praise. But it is specially remarkable, that the Temple-references with which the Book of Revelation abounds are generally to *minutiae*, which a writer who had not been as famil-iar with such details, as only personal contact and engagement with them could have rendered him,

...they are before the throne of God and serve him day and night in his temple; and he who sits on the throne will spread his tent over them (Rev. 7:15).

would scarcely have even noticed, certainly not employed as part of his imagery. They come in naturally, spontaneously, and so unexpectedly, that the reader is occasionally in danger of overlooking them altogether; and in language such as a professional man would employ, which would come to him from the previous exercise of his calling. Indeed, some of the most striking of these references could not have been understood at all without the professional treatises of the Rabbis on the Temple and its services. Only the studied minuteness of Rabbinical descriptions, derived from the tradition of eye-witnesses, does not leave the same impression as the unstudied illustrations of St. John.

Another angel, who had a golden censer, came and stood at the altar. He was given much incense to offer, with the prayers of all the saints, on the golden altar before the throne. The smoke of the incense, together with the prayers of the saints, went up before God from the angel's hand (Rev. 8:3–4).

FOURTH GOSPEL AND APOCALYPSE WRITTEN BEFORE TEMPLE SERVICES CEASED

These naturally suggest the twofold inference that the Book of Revelation and the Fourth Gospel must have been written before the Temple services had actually ceased, and by one who had not merely been intimately acquainted with, but probably at one time an actor in them.[1] The argument may be illustrated by an analogous case. Quite lately, they who have dug under the ruins of the Temple have discovered one of those tablets in the Court of the Temple which warned Gentiles, on pain of death, not to advance farther into the sanctuary. The tablet

---

[1] This is not the place for further critical discussions. Though the arguments in support of our view are only inferential, they seem to us none the less conclusive. It is not only that the name of John (given also to the son of the priest Zacharias) reappears among the kindred of the high-priest (Acts 4:6), nor that his priestly descent would account for that acquaintance with the high-priest (John 18:15, 16) which gave him access apparently into the council-chamber itself, while Peter, for whom he had gained admittance to the palace, was in 'the porch;' nor yet that, though residing in Galilee, the house of 'his own' to which he took the mother of Jesus (John 19:27) was probably at Jerusalem, like that of other priests—notably of the Levite family of Barnabas (Acts 12:12)—a supposition confirmed by his apparent entertainment of Peter, when Mary Magdalene found them together on the morning of the resurrection (John 20:2). But it seems highly improbable that a book so full of liturgical allusions as the Book of Revelation—and these, many of them, not to great or important points, but to *minutiae*—could have been written by any other than a priest, and one who had at one time been in actual service in the Temple itself, and thus become so intimately conversant with its details, that they came to him naturally, as part of the imagery he employed.

answers exactly to the description of Josephus, and its inscription is almost literally as he gives it.[2] This tablet seems like a witness suddenly appearing, after eighteen centuries, to bear testimony to the narrative of Josephus as that of a contemporary writer. Much of the same instantaneous conviction, only greatly stronger, is carried to our minds, when, in the midst of some dry account of what went on in the Temple, we suddenly come upon the very words which St. John had employed to describe heavenly realities. Perhaps one of the most striking instances of this kind is afforded by the words quoted at the head of this chapter—'Blessed is he that watcheth, and keepeth his garments.' They literally describe, as we learn from the Rabbis, the punishment awarded to the Temple-guards if found asleep at their posts; and the Rabbinical account of it is curiously confirmed by the somewhat *naïve* confession of one of their number,[3] that on a certain occasion his own maternal uncle had actually undergone the punishment of having his clothes set on fire by the captain of the Temple as he went his rounds at night.

Thus was the first enclosure. In the midst of which, and not far from it, was the second, to be gone up to by a few steps; this was encompassed by a stone wall for a partition, with an inscription, which forbade any foreigner to go in, under pain of death (Jos. Antiquities 15.417).

Behold, I come like a thief! Blessed is he who stays awake and keeps his clothes with him, so that he may not go naked and be shamefully exposed (Rev. 16:15).

NIGHT IN THE TEMPLE

For the service of the officiating ministers was not only by day, but also 'at night in the Temple.' From Scripture we know that the ordinary services of the sanctuary consisted of the morning and evening sacrifices. To these the Rabbis add another evening service, probably to account for their own transference of the evening service to a much later hour than that of the sacrifice.[4] There is, however, some difficulty about the exact time when each of the sacrifices

Every morning and evening they present burnt offerings and fragrant incense to the LORD (2 Chron. 13:11a).

---

[2]See the account of this remarkable discovery by M. Clermont-Ganneau in his letter to the *Athenaeum*, reprinted in the *Quarterly Statement of the Palestine Exploration Fund* for August, 1871, pp. 132, 133.

[3]Rabbi Elieser ben Jacob. See *Middoth*, i. 2.

[4]The Rabbinical statement about a correspondence between that service and 'the burning of the yet unconsumed fat and flesh' of the sacrifices (which must have lasted all night) is so far-fetched that we wonder to see it in Kitto's *Cyclopaedia*, third edition (art. Synagogue), while Grätz's assertion that it corresponded to the closing of the Temple gates (*Gesch.* vol. iii, p. 97) is quite unsupported.

Prepare one lamb in the morning and the other at twilight,…Prepare the second lamb at twilight, along with the same kind of grain offering and drink offering that you prepare in the morning. This is an offering made by fire, an aroma pleasing to the LORD (Num. 28:4, 8).

It is good to praise the LORD and make music to your name, O Most High, to proclaim your love in the morning and your faithfulness at night, to the music of the ten–stringed lyre and the melody of the harp (Ps. 92:1–3).

Praise the LORD, all you servants of the LORD who minister by night in the house of the LORD. Lift up your hands in the sanctuary and praise the LORD. May the LORD, the Maker of heaven and earth, bless you from Zion (Ps. 134).

was offered. According to general agreement, the morning sacrifice was brought at the 'third hour,' corresponding to our nine o'clock. But the preparations for it must have commenced more than two hours earlier. Few, if any, worshippers could have witnessed the actual slaying of the lamb, which took place immediately on opening the great Temple-gate. Possibly they may have gathered chiefly to join in the prayer 'at the time of incense' (Luke 1:10). In the modified sense, then, of understanding by the morning sacrifice the *whole service,* it no doubt coincided with the third hour of the day, or 9 A.M. This may explain how on the day of Pentecost such a multitude could so readily 'come together,' to hear in their various tongues 'the wonderful works of God'— seeing it was the third hour (Acts 2:15), when they would all be in the Temple. The evening sacrifice was fixed by the Law (Num. 28:4, 8) as 'between the evenings,' that is, between the darkness of the gloaming and that of the night.[5]

Such admonitions as 'to show forth thy faithfulness every night upon an instrument of ten strings and on the psaltery' (Ps. 92:2, 3), and the call to those who 'by night stand in the house of the Lord,' to 'lift up their hands in the sanctuary and bless the Lord' (Ps. 134), seem indeed to imply an evening service— an impression confirmed by the appointment of Levite singers for night service in 1 Chron. 9:33; 23:30. But at the time of our Lord the evening sacrifice certainly commenced much earlier. Josephus puts it down (*Ant.* 14.65) as at the ninth hour. According to the Rabbis the lamb was slain at the eighth hour and a-half, or about 2:30 P.M., and the pieces laid on the altar an hour later—about 3:30 P.M. Hence, when 'Peter and John went up together into the Temple at the hour of prayer, being the ninth hour' (Acts 3:1), it must have been for the evening sacrifice, or rather half an hour later, and, as the words indicate, for the 'prayer' that accompanied the offering of

---

[5]Sunset was calculated as on an average at 6 o'clock P.M. For a full discussion and many speculations on the whole subject, see Herzfeld, *Gesch. d. V. Is.* vol. iii, *Excurs.* xxiv, par. 2.

incense. The evening service was somewhat shorter than that of the morning, and would last, at any rate, about an hour and a-half, say till about four o'clock, thus well meeting the original requirement in Num. 28:4. After that no other offering might be brought except on the eve of the Passover, when the ordinary evening sacrifice took place two hours earlier, or at 12:30 P.M.[6]

CHANGE OF PRIESTS

We can conceive the laborious work of the day over, and the rest and solemnity of 'night in the Temple' begun. The last notes of the Temple music have died out, and the worshippers slowly retired, some after lingering for private prayer, or else tarrying in one of the marble porches. Already the short Eastern day is fading out of the west. Far over the mountains of Gibeon the sun is sinking in that ocean across which the better light is so soon to shine. The new company of priests and Levites who are to conduct the services of the morrow are coming up from Ophel under the leadership of their heads of houses, their elders. Those who have officiated during the day are preparing to leave by another gate. They have put off their priestly dress, depositing it in the appointed chambers, and resumed that of ordinary laymen, and their sandals. For such, although not shoes, might be worn in the Temple, the priests being barefoot only during their actual ministry. Nor did they otherwise wear any distinctive dress, not even the high-priest himself, nor yet those who performed in the Temple other than strictly sacrificial services.[7] As for the Levites, they had no clerical dress at all, but only wore

Sandals

All the Levites who were musicians—Asaph, Heman, Jeduthun and their sons and relatives—stood on the east side of the altar, dressed in fine linen and playing cymbals, harps and lyres. They were accompanied by 120 priests sounding trumpets (2 Chron. 5:12).

---

[6]Accordingly the Rabbis laid down the principle that evening prayers (of course, *out* of the Temple) might be lawfully said at any time after 12.30 P.M. This explains how 'Peter went up upon the house-top to pray about the sixth hour,' or about 12 o'clock (Acts 10:9)—or to what was really 'evening prayer.' Comp. Kitto's *Cycl.* iii, p. 904.

[7]Those who, being declared physically unfit, discharged only menial functions, wore not the priestly dress. They on whom no lot had fallen for daily ministration put off their priestly garments—all save the linen breeches—and also performed subordinate functions. But, according to some, it was lawful for priests while in the Temple to wear their peculiar dress—all but the girdle, worn always and only on sacrificial duty.

the white linen (2 Chron. 5:12), till they obtained from Agrippa II permission to wear priestly garments —as Josephus rightly remarks, 'contrary to the laws of our country' (*Ant.* 20.218).

THE FAREWELL ON THE SABBATH

The commanders of units of a hundred did just as Jehoiada the priest ordered. Each one took his men— those who were going on duty on the Sabbath and those who were going off duty—and came to Jehoiada the priest (2 Kgs. 11:9).

We know that on Sabbaths at least, when one company gave place to another, or, rather, as the out-going course left the Temple precincts, they parted from each other with a farewell, reminding us of St. Paul's to the Corinthians (2 Cor. 13:11), 'He that has caused His name to dwell in this house cause love, brotherhood, peace, and friendship to dwell among you.' Each of the twenty-four 'courses' into which not only the priests and Levites, but also all Israel, by means of representatives, were divided, served for one week, from Sabbath to Sabbath, distributing the *daily* service among their respective 'families' or 'houses.' For the Sabbath the new ministrants came earlier than on week-days.[8] As the 'family' whose daily 'ministration was accomplished' left the Temple, the massive gates were closed by priests or Levites, some requiring the united strength of twenty men. Then the Temple keys were hung up in a hollow square, under a marble slab in the 'fire-room' (Beth-ha-Moked), which may also be designated as the chief guard-room of the priests. Now, as the stars were shining out on the deep blue Eastern sky, the priests would gather for converse[9] or the evening meal.[10] Pieces of the sacrifices and the 'prepared' first-fruits (the Therumoth) supplied the needful refreshments.[11] Though the work of the day was over, certain arrangements had yet to be made. For the Levites in charge of collecting the tithes and other business

---

[8]Probably this had also been the arrangement in the first Temple. See 2 Kings 11:9; 2 Chron. 23:8. Herzfeld, *u.s.* p. 185.

[9]The question of evening prayers in the Temple is involved in some difficulty. The curious reader will find it discussed by Herzfeld with almost confusing minuteness.

[10]The partaking of sacred things by priests who had been ceremonially unclean is expressly stated by the Rabbis as 'when the stars shone out.'

[11]The Therumoth, such as oil, flour, etc., in opposition to those *au naturel*, such as corn, fruits, etc., called the Biccurim.

details were wont to purchase in large quantities what each who brought any sacrifice needed for meat- and drink-offerings, and to sell it to the offerers. This was a great accommodation to the worshipper, and a source of daily profit to the Temple. On payment of a price, fixed by tariff every month, the offerer received his proper counterfoil,[12] in exchange for which a Temple official gave him what he needed for his sacrifice. Now, the accounts of these transactions had to be made up and checked every evening.

The priests and the captain of the temple guard and the Sadducees came up to Peter and John while they were speaking to the people (Acts 4:1).

THE NIGHT-WATCHES

But already the night-watches had been set in the Temple. By day and night it was the duty of the Levites to keep guard at the gates, to prevent, so far as possible, the unclean from entering. To them the duties of the Temple police were also entrusted, under the command of an official known to us in the New Testament as the 'captain of the Temple' (Acts 4:1, etc.), but in Jewish writings chiefly as 'the man of the Temple Mount.' The office must have been of considerable responsibility, considering the multitude on feast-days, their keen national susceptibilities, and the close proximity of the hated Romans in Fort Antonia. At night guards were placed in twenty-four stations about the gates and courts. Of these twenty-one were occupied by Levites alone; the other inner-most three jointly by priests and Levites.[13] Each guard consisted of ten men; so that in all two hundred and forty Levites and thirty priests were on duty every night. The Temple guards were relieved by day, but not during the night, which the Romans divided into four, but the Jews, properly, into three watches, the fourth being really the morning watch (compare Matt. 14:25).[14] Hence, when the Lord saith, 'Blessed are those servants whom the lord when he cometh

---

[12]Of these there were four kinds, respectively bearing the words 'male,' when the sacrifice was a ram; 'sinner' when it was a sin-offering; and for others, 'calf,' or 'kid.'

[13]The watch at some of the gates seems at one time to have been hereditary in certain families. For this, see Herzfeld, vol. i, p. 419; ii, p. 57.

[14]See, however, the discussion in Jer. *Ber.* i. 1.

shall find watching,' He expressly refers to the second and third watches as those of deepest sleep (Luke 12:38).

THE ROUNDS OF THE CAPTAIN

It will be good for those servants whose master finds them ready, even if he comes in the second or third watch of the night (Luke 12:38).

Therefore keep watch because you do not know when the owner of the house will come back—whether in the evening, or at midnight, or when the rooster crows, or at dawn (Mark 13:35).

During the night the 'captain of the temple' made his rounds. On his approach the guards had to rise and salute him in a particular manner. Any guard found asleep when on duty was beaten, or his garments were set on fire—a punishment, as we know, actually awarded. Hence the admonition to us who, as it were, are here on Temple guard, 'Blessed is he that watcheth, and keepeth his garments' (Rev. 16:15). But, indeed, there could have been little inclination to sleep within the Temple, even had the deep emotion natural in the circumstances allowed it. True, the chief of the course and 'the heads of families' reclined on couches along that part of the Beth-Moked in which it was lawful to sit down,[15] and the older priests might lie on the floor, having wrapped their priestly garments beside them, while the younger men kept watch. But then the preparations for the service of the morning required each to be early astir. The priest whose duty it was to superintend the arrangements might any moment knock at the door and demand entrance. He came suddenly and unexpectedly, no one knew when. The Rabbis use almost the very words in which Scripture describes the unexpected coming of the Master (Mark 13:35), when they say, 'Sometimes he came at the cock-crowing, sometimes a little earlier, sometimes a little later. He came and knocked, and they opened to him. Then said he unto them, All ye who have washed, come and cast lots' (Mishnah, *Tamid.* i. 1, 2). For the customary bath required to have been taken before the superintending priest came round, since it was a principle that none might go into the court to serve, although he were clean, unless he had bathed. A subterranean passage, lit on both sides, led to the well-appointed bath-rooms where the priests immersed themselves. After that

---

[15]The part built out on the Chel; for it was not lawful for any but the king to sit down anywhere within the enclosure of the 'Priests' Court.'

they needed not[16] all that day to wash again, save their hands and feet, which they had to do each time, however often, they came for service into the Temple. It was, no doubt, to this that our Lord referred in His reply to Peter: 'He that is washed needeth not save to wash his feet, but is clean every whit' (John 13:10).[17]

CASTING LOTS FOR THE SERVICES

Those who were prepared now followed the superintending priest through a wicket into the court. Here they divided into two companies, each carrying a torch, except on the Sabbaths, when the Temple itself was lit up. One company passed eastwards, the other westwards, till, having made their circuit of inspection, they met at the chamber where the high-priest's daily meat-offering was prepared (Lev. 6:12–16),[18] and reported, 'It is well! All is well!' Thereupon those who were to prepare the high-priest's offering were set to their work, and the priests passed into the 'Hall of Polished Stones,'[19] to cast lots for the services of the day. This arrangement had been rendered necessary by certain painful scenes to which the eagerness of the priests for service had led. Altogether the lot was cast four times, though at different periods of the service. It was done in this manner. The priests stood in a circle around the president, who for a moment removed the head-gear of one of their number, to show that he would begin counting at him. Then all held up one, two, or more fingers—since it was not lawful in Israel to count persons—when the president named some number, say seventy, and began counting the fingers till he reached the number named, which marked that the lot had fallen on that priest. The first lot was for cleansing the altar and preparing it; the second, for

Aaron and his sons shall eat the rest of it, but it is to be eaten without yeast in a holy place; they are to eat it in the courtyard of the Tent of Meeting (Lev. 6:16).

---

[16]Except under one circumstance.

[17]The peculiarities of our Lord's washing the feet of the disciples are pointed out in Lightfoot, *Hor. Heb.* p. 1094.

[18]According to the Rabbinical interpretation of the law.

[19]Or Gazith, where also the Sanhedrim met. The sittings were, in that part, built out on the Chel.

*He was oppressed and
afflicted,
yet he did not open his
mouth;
he was led like a lamb to
the slaughter,
and as a sheep before her
shearers is silent,
so he did not open his
mouth (Isa. 53:7).*

those who were to offer the sacrifice, and for those who were to cleanse the candlestick and the altar of incense in the Holy Place. The *third* lot was the most important. It determined who was to offer the incense. If possible, none was to take part in it who had at any previous time officiated in the same capacity. The fourth lot, which followed close on the third, fixed those who were to burn the pieces of the sacrifice on the altar, and to perform the concluding portions of the service. The morning lot held good also for the same offices at the evening sacrifice, save that the lot was cast anew for the burning of the incense.

THE FIRST LOT

When the priests were gathered for 'the first lot' in the 'Hall of Polished Stones,' as yet only the earliest glow of morning light streaked the Eastern sky. Much had to be done before the lamb itself could be slain. It was a law that, as no sacrifice might be brought after that of the evening, nor after the sun had set, so, on the other hand, the morning sacrifice was only to be slain after the morning light had lit up 'the whole sky as far as Hebron,' yet before the sun had actually risen upon the horizon.[20] The only exception was on the great festivals, when the altar was cleansed much earlier,[21] to afford time for examining before actual sunrise the very numerous sacrifices which were to be brought during the day. Perhaps it was on this ground that, on the morning of the Passover, they who led Jesus from Caiaphas thronged so 'early' 'the judgment-hall of Pilate.' Thus, while some of them would be preparing in the Temple to offer the morning sacrifice, others were at the same moment unwittingly fulfilling the meaning of that very type, when He on whom was 'laid the iniquity of us all' was 'brought as a lamb to the slaughter' (Isa. 53:7).

---

[20]Maimonides, *Yad ha Chazakah*, the tractate on the daily sacrifice, i. 2.

[21]For the three great festivals, in the first watch; for the Day of Atonement, at midnight. See also Lightfoot, *Hor. Heb.* p. 1135.

8

THE MORNING AND
THE EVENING SACRIFICE[1]

Once when Zechariah's division was on duty and he was serving as priest before God, he was chosen by lot, according to the custom of the priesthood, to go into the temple of the Lord and burn incense. And when the time for the burning of incense came, all the assembled worshipers were praying outside.
—Luke 1:8-10.

PUBLIC PRAYER

Before proceeding to describe the 'morning sacrifice,' it is necessary to advert to a point of considerable interest and importance. There can be no doubt that, at the time of Christ, public prayer occupied a very prominent place in the ordinary daily services of the Temple. Yet the original institution in the law of Moses contains no mention of it; and such later instances as the prayer of Hannah, or that of Solomon at the dedication of the Temple, afford neither indication nor precedent as regards the ordinary public services. The confession of the high-priest over the scape-goat (Lev. 16:21) cannot be regarded as public prayer. Perhaps the nearest approach to it was on occasion of offering the first-fruits, especially in that concluding entreaty (Deut. 26:15): 'Look down from Thy holy habitation, from heaven, and bless Thy people Israel, and the land which Thou hast given us, as Thou swarest unto our fathers, a land that floweth with milk and honey.' But, after all, this was again private, not public prayer, and offered on a private

Then say to the LORD your God: "...I have not turned aside from your commands nor have I forgotten any of them" (Deut. 26:13).

---

[1] In Hebrew, *Tamid*, the *constant* sacrifice, *sacrificium juge.*

Hear the supplication of your servant and of your people Israel when they pray toward this place. Hear from heaven, your dwelling place, and when you hear, forgive (1 Kgs. 8:30).

When you spread out your hands in prayer, I will hide my eyes from you; even if you offer many prayers, I will not listen. Your hands are full of blood (Isa. 1:15).

One thing I ask of the LORD, this is what I seek: that I may dwell in the house of the LORD all the days of my life, to gaze upon the beauty of the LORD and to seek him in his temple (Ps. 27:4).

occasion, far different from the morning and evening sacrifices. The wording of King Solomon's prayer (1 Kgs. 8) implies indeed an act of united and congregational worship, but, strictly speaking, it conveys no more than that public supplication was wont to be offered in times of public necessity (1 Kgs. 8:30–52). Nor can anything definite be inferred from the allusions of Isaiah to the hypocrisy of his contemporaries (Isa. 1:15) in spreading forth their hands and making many prayers.[2]

REGULATIONS OF THE RABBIS

It was otherwise after the return from Babylon. With the institution and spread of synagogues— designed for the twofold purpose, that in every place Moses should be read every Sabbath day, and to provide a place 'where prayer was wont to be made' —the practice of public worship soon became general. In Neh. 11:17 we find already a special appointment 'to begin the thanksgiving in prayer.' Afterwards progress in this direction was rapid. The Apocrypha afford painful evidence how soon all degenerated into a mere form, and how prayer became a work of self-righteousness, by which merit might be obtained. This brings us to the Pharisees of the New Testament, with their ostentatious displays of devotion, and the hypocrisy of their endless prayers, full of needless repetitions and odious self-assertion. At the outset we here meet, as usual, at least seeming contradictions. On the one hand, the Rabbis define every attitude and gesture in prayer, fix the most rigid formulas, trace each of them up to one of the patriarchs,[3] and would have us believe that the pious have their nine hours of devotion, laying down this curious principle, suited to both worlds—'Prolix prayer protracts life.' On the other hand, they also tell us that prayer may be con-

---

[2]Such language as that of Ps. 27:4 seems also to point to the absence of any liturgy: 'to *behold* the beauty of the Lord.'

[3]The Rabbis ascribe the origin of the morning prayers to Abraham, that of the afternoon prayers to Isaac, and of the evening prayers to Jacob. In each case supposed Scriptural evidence for it is dragged in by some artificial mode of interpretation.

tracted within the narrowest limits, and that a mere summary of the prescribed formulas is sufficient; while some of their number go the length of strenuously contending for free prayer. In fact, free prayer, liturgical formulas, and special prayers taught by celebrated Rabbis, were alike in use. Free prayer would find its place in such private devotions as are described in the parable of the Publican and the Pharisee. It also mingled with the prescribed liturgical formulas. It may be questioned whether, even in reference to the latter, the words were always rigidly adhered to, perhaps even accurately remembered. Hence the Talmud lays it down (in the treatise *Berachoth*), that in such cases it sufficed to say the substance of the prescribed prayers.

Praise be to the LORD, the God of Israel, from everlasting to everlasting. Amen and Amen (Ps. 41:13).

Let everything that has breath praise the LORD. Praise the LORD (Ps. 150:6).

LITURGICAL FORMS

That liturgical formulas were used not only in the Temple, but in the daily private devotions, cannot be doubted. The first trace of them appears so early as in the arrangement of the Psalter, each of its first four books closing with a 'eulogy,' or benediction (Ps. 41; 72; 89; 106), and the fifth book with a psalm which may be designated as one grand doxology (Ps. 150). Although it is a task of no small difficulty to separate the ancient prayers of Temple-times from the later additions, which have gradually swelled into the present Jewish prayer-book, it has, in great measure, successfully been accomplished.[4] Besides such liturgical formulas, some prayers taught by celebrated Rabbis have been preserved. It was in accordance with this practice that John the Baptist seems to have given forms of prayer to his followers, and that the disciples asked the Saviour to teach them to pray (Luke 11:1).

One day Jesus was praying in a certain place. When he finished, one of his disciples said to him, "Lord, teach us to pray, just as John taught his disciples" (Luke 11:1).

THE LORD'S PRAYER

The prayer spoken by the Lord far transcended any that Jewish Rabbis ever conceived, even where its

---

[4]We here specially refer to the classical work of Zunz, *Die Gottesd. Vortr: d. Juden,* Berlin, 1832.

This, then, is how you should pray:
"Our Father in heaven, hallowed be your name, your kingdom come, your will be done
*   on earth as it is in heaven.*
Give us today our daily bread.
Forgive us our debts, as we also have forgiven our debtors.
And lead us not into temptation, but deliver us from the evil one"
(Matt. 6:9–13).

wording most nearly approaches theirs.[5] It is characteristic that two of its petitions find no real counterpart in the prayers of the Rabbis. These are: 'Forgive us our trespasses,' and 'Lead us not into temptation.' In the Temple the people never responded to the prayers by an *Amen,* but always with this benediction, 'Blessed be the name of the glory of His kingdom for ever!'[6] This formula was traced up to the patriarch Jacob, on his death-bed. In regard to 'the kingdom,' whatever the Rabbis understood by it, the feeling was so strong, that it was said: 'Any prayer which makes not mention of the kingdom, is not a prayer at all.'

ATTITUDE IN PRAYER

The attitude to be observed during prayer is very accurately defined by the Rabbis. The worshipper was to stand, turning towards the Holy Place; he was to compose his body and his clothes, to draw his feet close together, to cast down his eyes, at least at the beginning of his prayer, to cross his hands over his breast, and to 'stand as a servant before his master, with all reverence and fear.' Even the priests, while pronouncing the priestly blessing, were to look to the ground. In regard to the special manner of bowing before the Lord, a distinction was made between bending the knees, bending the head, and falling prostrate on the ground. The latter was not deemed 'fit for every man, but only for such as knew themselves righteous men, like Joshua.'[7]

THE TWO ELEMENTS IN PRAYER

In general the Rabbis distinguish two elements in prayer, on the ground of the two terms used by

---

[5]It must always be kept in mind that such expressions as 'Our Father,' 'Thy kingdom come,' and others like them, meant in the mouth of the Rabbis a predominance of the narrowest Judaism; in fact, the subjection of all the world to Rabbinical ordinances, and the carnal glory of Israel.

[6]Thus the words in our Authorised Version, Matt. 6:13, 'For Thine is the kingdom, and the power, and the glory, for ever. Amen,' which are wanting in all the most ancient MSS., are only the common Temple-formula of response, and as such may have found their way into the text. The word 'Amen' was in reality a solemn asseveration or a mode of oath.

[7]See Lightfoot, *De Minist. Templi,* ch. x, sect. 10.

Solomon (1 Kgs. 8:28)—thanksgiving and petition. To these correspond the two kinds of early Jewish prayer: the Eulogies and the Tephillah.[8] And thus far correctly, as the two Hebrew words for prayer indicate, the one adoration, the other supplication, or, rather, intercession.[9] Both kinds of prayer found expression in the Temple services. But only after the manifestation of Him, who in His person united the Divine with the human nature, could adoration and supplication be fully called out. Nay, the idea of supplication would only be properly realised after the outpouring of the Spirit of adoption, whereby the people of God also became the children of God. Hence it is not correct to designate sacrifices as 'prayers without words.'[10] The sacrifices were in no sense prayers, but rather the preparation for prayer. The Tabernacle was, as its Hebrew designation shows, the place 'of meeting'[11] between God and Israel; the sacrificial service, that which made such meeting possible; and the priest (as the root of the word implies), he who brought Israel near to God. Hence prayer could only follow after the sacrifice; and its appropriate symbol and time was burning of incense. This view is expressed in the words: 'Let my prayer be set forth before Thee as incense' (Ps. 141:2), and authoritatively confirmed in Rev. 5:8, where we read of the 'golden vials full of incense, which are the prayers of the saints.'

Bowing

Yet give attention to your servant's prayer and his plea for mercy, O LORD my God. Hear the cry and the prayer that your servant is praying in your presence this day (1 Kgs. 8:28).

May my prayer be set before you like incense; may the lifting up of my hands be like the evening sacrifice (Ps. 141:2).

BURNING THE INCENSE

It is this burning of incense which in the Gospel is alluded to in connection with the birth of John the Baptist (Luke 1:9). Zacharias had come up from the hill country of Judaea, from the neighbourhood of

---

[8]We regret not to enter more fully on the subject of prayer among the Hebrews or on an analysis of the remnants of prayers in Temple-times preserved to us. But this is not the place for such discussions. See, however, a note farther on in this chapter.

[9]Delitzsch, *Bibl. Com. über Is.* p. 45 note.

[10]Pressel, in Herzog's *Encycl.* vol. iv, p. 680.

[11]The *Ohel Moed.*, 'tabernacle of meeting'—*not* 'of the congregation,' as in our A.V. See Bähr's *Symbol.* vol. 1, and Keil's *Arch.* vol. 1, on this and kindred subjects.

*Priest with censer of
incense*

*Once when Zechariah's
division was on duty and
he was serving as priest
before God, he was chosen
by lot, according to the
custom of the priesthood,
to go into the temple of the
Lord and burn incense.
   And when the time for
the burning of incense
came, all the assembled
worshipers were praying
outside.
   Then an angel of the
Lord appeared to him,
standing at the right side
of the altar of incense
(Luke 1:8–11).*

priestly Hebron, to minister in the Temple.[12] His
course—that of Abia—was on duty for the week, and
the 'house of his fathers' for that special day. More
than that, the lot had fallen on Zacharias for the most
honourable service in the daily ministry—that of
burning the incense on the golden altar within the
Holy Place. For the first time in his life, and for the
last, would this service devolve on him. As the pious
old priest ministered within the Holy Place, he saw
with such distinctness that he could afterwards
describe the very spot, Gabriel standing, as if he had
just come out from the Most Holy Place, between the
altar and the table of shewbread, 'on the right side of
the altar.' So far as we know, this was the first and
only angelic appearance in the Temple. For we cannot
attach serious importance to the tradition that, during the forty years of his pontificate, an angel always
accompanied Simeon the Just, when on the Day of
Atonement he entered and left the Most Holy Place,
except the last year, when the angel left him in the
Sanctuary, to show that this was to be the end of his
ministry. What passed between Gabriel and Zacharias
is beside our present purpose. Suffice it to notice several details incidentally mentioned in this narrative,
such as that a special lot was cast for this ministry;
that the priest was alone in the Holy Place while burning the incense; and that 'the whole multitude of the
people were praying without at the time of incense.'

FILLING THE LAVER

The lot for burning the incense was, as we have
seen, the third by which the order of the ministry for
the day was determined. The *first* lot, which in reality
had been cast before the actual break of day, was that
to designate the various priests who were to cleanse
the altar and to prepare its fires. The *first* of the priests
on whom this lot had fallen immediately went out.
His brethren reminded him where the silver chafing-
dish was deposited, and not to touch any sacred vessel

---

[12]It has, however, been suggested that the correct reading of Luke 1:39 is not 'a city of
Judah,' but 'the city of Juttah.' Compare Josh. 21:16.

till he had washed his hands and feet. He took no light with him; the fire of the altar was sufficient for his office. Hands and feet were washed by laying the right hand on the right foot, and the left hand on the left.[13] The sound of the machinery, as it filled the laver with water, admonished the others to be in readiness. This machinery had been made by *Ben Catin,* who also altered the laver so that twelve priests could at the same time perform their ablutions. Otherwise the laver resembled that in the Temple of Solomon. It was of brass. All the vessels in the Sanctuary were of metal, the only exception being the altar of burnt-offering, which was solid, and wholly of stones taken from virgin soil, that had not been defiled by any tool of iron. The stones were fastened together by mortar, pitch, and molten lead. The measurement of the altar is differently given by Josephus and the Rabbis. It seems to have consisted of three sections, each narrower than the former: the base being thirty-two cubits wide, the middle twenty-eight, and the top, where the fire was laid (of course, not including the horns of the altar nor the space where the priests moved), only twenty-four cubits. With the exception of some parts of the altar, in which the cubit was calculated at five hand-breadths, the sacred cubit of the Temple was always reckoned at six hand-breadths. Lastly, as readers of the New Testament know, whatever touched the altar, or, indeed, any sacred vessel, was regarded as 'sanctified' (Matt. 23:19), but no vessel could be dedicated to the use of the Temple which had not been originally destined for it.[14]

One of the ten brazen lavers in Solomon's Temple, standing on its base or pedestal

Jesus answered, "A person who has had a bath needs only to wash his feet; his whole body is clean. And you are clean, though not every one of you" *(John 13:10).*

PREPARING THE ALTAR

But to return. While the assistant priests were waiting, the first priest had taken the silver chafing-dish, and scraped the fire on the altar, removing the

---

[13]Perhaps this might therefore be appropriately described as washing 'the feet only,' John 13:10.

[14]It is impossible in this place to enter into full details either about the laver, the altar of burnt-offering, or indeed any of the vessels of the ministry. These and similar topics belong to Biblical archaeology.

burnt coals, and depositing them at a little distance north of the altar. As he descended, the other priests quickly washed hands and feet, and took shovels and prongs, with which they moved aside what of the sacrifices had been left unburned from the previous evening, then cleaned out the ashes, laying part on the great heap in the middle of the altar, and the rest in a place whence it was afterwards carried out of the Temple. The next duty was to lay on the altar fresh wood, which, however, might be neither from the olive nor the vine. For the fire destined to feed the altar of incense the wood of the fig-tree was exclusively used, so as to secure good and sufficient charcoal. The hitherto unconsumed pieces of the sacrifice were now again laid upon the fire.

Fire on the altar

THE SECOND LOT

These preliminaries finished, the priests gathered once more for the *second* lot. The priest on whom it fell was designated, along with the twelve who stood nearest to him, for offering the sacrifice and cleansing the candlestick and the altar of incense. Immediately after casting this second lot, the president directed one to ascend some 'pinnacle,' and see whether it was time to kill the daily sacrifice. If the priest reported, 'The morning shineth already,' he was again asked, 'Is the sky lit up as far as Hebron?' If so, the president ordered the lamb to be brought from the chamber by the Beth-Moked, where it had been kept in readiness for four days. Others fetched the gold and silver vessels of service, of which the Rabbis enumerate ninety-three. The sacrificial lamb was now watered out of a golden bowl, and anew examined by torchlight, though its Levitical fitness had been already ascertained the evening before. Then the sacrificing priest, surrounded by his assistants, fastened the lamb to the second of the rings on the north side of the altar—in the morning in the western, in the evening in the eastern corner.[15] The sacrifice was held

---

[15]The sacrifice was always offered *against* the sun.

together[16] by its feet, the fore and hind feet of each side being tied together; its head was laid towards the south and fastened through a ring, and its face turned to the west, while the sacrificing priest stood on the east side. The elders who carried the keys now gave the order for opening the Temple gates. As the last great gate slowly moved on its hinges, the priests, on a signal given, blew three blasts on their silver trumpets, summoning the Levites and the 'representatives' of the people (the so-called 'stationary men') to their duties, and announcing to the city that the morning sacrifice was about to be offered. Immediately upon this the great gates which led into the Holy Place itself were opened to admit the priests who were to cleanse the candlestick and the altar of incense.

Egyptian stone knives, Assyrian bronze knives

THE SLAYING OF THE LAMB

The opening of these gates was the signal for actually slaying the sacrificial lamb. The sacrifice was offered in the following manner. One priest drew forward the windpipe and gullet of the sacrifice, and quickly thrust upwards the knife, while another caught the blood in a golden bowl. Standing at the east side of the altar, he sprinkled it, first at the north-east, and then at the south-west corner, below the red line which ran round the middle of the altar, in each case in such manner as to cover two sides of the altar, or, as it is described, in the form of the Greek letter Γ (gamma). The rest of the blood was poured out at the base of the altar. Ordinarily, the whole of this service would of course be performed by priests. But it was valid even if the sacrifice had been killed by a layman, or with an ordinary knife. Not so if the blood were caught up in any but a consecrated vessel, or sprinkled by other than the hands of a priest who at the time was Levitically fit for the service.

---

[16]This was a point in dispute between the orthodox and the heterodox. See Maimonides, *Yad ha Chaz,* Tr. *On the Daily Sacr.* Chap. i. 9.

THE ALTAR OF INCENSE AND THE CANDLESTICK

We proceed to describe the service of those whose duty it was to cleanse the altar of incense and to dress the golden candlestick in the Holy Place. A few particulars as to each of these will not be out of place. The triumphal Arch of Titus in Rome bears a representation of the golden mortars in which the incense was bruised, and of the golden candlestick, but not of the altar of incense. Still, we can form a sufficiently accurate idea of its appearance.[17] It was square, one cubit long and broad, and two cubits high, that is, half a cubit higher than the table of shewbread, but one cubit lower than the candlestick, and it had 'horns' at each of its four corners. It was probably hollow, and its top covered with a golden plate, and like an Eastern roof, surrounded by what resembled a balustrade, to prevent the coals and incense from falling off. Below this balustrade was a massive crown of gold. The incense burned upon this altar was prepared of the four ingredients mentioned in Exod. 30:34, with which, according to the Rabbis, seven others were mixed, besides a small quantity of 'Ambra,' and of a herb which gave out a dense smoke. To these thirteen substances (Jos. *Jewish War*, 5.218) salt was of course added. The mode of preparing the incense had been preserved in the family of *Abtinas*. The greatest care was taken to have the incense thoroughly bruised and mixed. Altogether 368 pounds were made for the year's consumption, about half a pound being used every morning and evening in the service. The censer for the Day of Atonement was different in size and appearance from that for ordinary days.[18] The golden candlestick was like that delineated in Exod. 25:31, etc., and is sufficiently known from its representation on the Arch of Titus.

Frankincense, which was pounded to make incense

Then the Lord said to Moses, "Take fragrant spices—gum resin, onycha and galbanum—and pure frankincense, all in equal amounts, and make a fragrant blend of incense, the work of a perfumer. It is to be salted and pure and sacred" (Exod. 30:34–35).

---

[17]See the notices in the Mishnah, and Maimonides, and the articles in the *Encycl.*, specially those of Herzog and Winer.

[18]Here also all details are beyond our present province. But it may be remarked that the expression in Heb. 9:4, rendered in our Authorised Version, 'which had the golden censer,' implies no more than that the censer *belonged* to the 'Holiest of all' ('having the golden censer'), not that the censer ordinarily stood in the Most Holy Place.

Now, while one set of priests were busy in the Court of the Priests offering the sacrifice, the two on whom it devolved to trim the lamps of the candlestick and to prepare the altar of incense had gone into the Holy Place. As nearly as possible while the lamb was being slain without, the first of these priests took with his hands the burnt coals and ashes from the golden altar, and put them into a golden vessel—called 'teni'—and withdrew, leaving it in the sanctuary. Similarly, as the blood of the lamb was being sprinkled on the altar of burnt-offering, the second priest ascended the three steps, hewn in stone, which led up to the candlestick. He trimmed and refilled the lamps that were still burning, removed the wick and old oil from those which had become extinguished, supplied fresh, and re-lit them from one of the other lamps. But the large central lamp, towards which all others bent, and which was called the western, because it inclined westward towards the Most Holy Place, might only be re-lit by fire from the altar itself. Only five, however, of the lamps were them trimmed; the other two were reserved to a later period of the service.

Candlestick

...*but the altar of incense, by its thirteen kinds of sweet–smelling spices with which the sea replenished it, signified that God is the possessor of all things that are both in the uninhabitable and habitable parts of the earth, and that they are all to be dedicated to his use (Jos. Jewish War 5.218).*

SALTING THE SACRIFICE

Meantime in the Court of the Priests the sacrifice had been hung on one of the hooks, flayed, cut up according to rules,[19] cleaned, and handed to the six priests who were successively to carry up the pieces to the rise of the altar, where they were salted and deposited. For 'every sacrifice must be salted with salt'—nay, everything that was laid on the altar, except the drink-offering.[20] At the same time, three other priests carried up to the rise of the altar the daily meat-offering, that of the high-priest, and the drink-offering. The skins of the sacrifices were salted, and on the eve of each Sabbath distributed among the 'course' of priests that had been on ministry.[21]

Make a lampstand of pure gold and hammer it out, base and shaft; its flower-like cups, buds and blossoms shall be of one piece with it (Exod. 25:31).

---

[19]These rules are so detailed that the priests, on any of whom the lot might at any time fall for this service, must have undergone very careful previous training.

[20]To this the Rabbis add somewhat needlessly: the blood of sprinkling and the wood for the fire!

[21]This in the case of burnt-, sin-, and trespass-offerings. The skins of the other offerings belonged to the offerers themselves.

PRAYER BEFORE THE THIRD LOT

And now the most solemn part of the service was about to begin. For the third time the priests assembled in the 'Hall of Polished Stones,' to draw the third and the fourth lots. But before doing so the president called on them to join in the prescribed prayers. Tradition has preserved these to us. Subjecting them to the severest criticism,[22] so as to eliminate all later details, the words used by the priests before the third and fourth lots were as follows:

High Priest

'With great love hast Thou loved us, O Lord our God, and with much overflowing pity hast Thou pitied us. Our Father and our King, for the sake of our fathers who trusted in Thee, and Thou taughtest them the statutes of life, have mercy on us, and enlighten our eyes[23] [in Thy law; cause our hearts to cleave to Thy commandments; unite our hearts to love and to fear Thy name, and we shall not be put to shame, world without end. For Thou art a God who preparest salvation, and us has Thou chosen from among all nations and tongues, and hast, in truth, brought us near to Thy great name, Selah, in order] that we in love may praise Thee and Thy Unity. Blessed be the Lord, who in love chose His people Israel.'

Hear, O Israel: The LORD our God, the LORD is one. Love the LORD your God with all your heart and with all your soul and with all your strength (Deut. 6:4–5).

After this prayer the ten commandments were (at one time) wont to be repeated, a practice discontinued, however, lest the Sadducees should declare them to be the only essential part of the law. Then all assembled said the so-called 'Shema'[24] (Hear, O Israel, etc., Deut. 6:4, etc.), which may be designated as a sort of 'credo' or 'belief.' It consisted of these three passages—Deut. 6:4–9; 11:13–21; and Num. 15:37–41.

---

[22]Compare the very full discussion of the subject in Zunz, *Gottesd. Vortr.* pp. 369 and following. Still, the matter is not quite clear of critical difficulties.

[23]The words here and afterwards within square brackets are regarded by Jost (*Gesch. d. Jud.*) as a later addition.

[24]So named from the first word, Shema, 'Hear,' viz. 'O Israel,' etc. By one of the strangest mistakes, Lightfoot confounds the contents of the 'Shema' with those of the phylacteries.

THE LOT FOR INCENSE

After this the lot was cast for burning the incense. No one might take part in it who had ministered in that office before, unless in the very rare case that all present had previously so officiated. Hence, while the other three lots held good for the evening service, that for the incense required to be repeated. He on whom this lot fell chose from among his friends his two assistants. Finally, the third was succeeded by the fourth lot, which designated those who were to lay on the altar the sacrifice and the meat-offerings, and to pour out the drink-offering.

OFFERING THE INCENSE

The incensing priest and his assistants now approached first the altar of burnt-offering. One filled with incense a golden censer held in a silver vessel, while another placed in a golden bowl burning coals from the altar. As they passed from the court into the Holy Place, they struck a large instrument (called the 'Magrephah'), at sound of which the priests hastened from all parts to worship, and the Levites to occupy their places in the service of song; while the chief of the 'stationary men' ranged at the Gate of Nicanor such of the people as were to be purified that day.[25] Slowly the incensing priest and his assistants ascended the steps to the Holy Place, preceded by the two priests who had formerly dressed the altar and the candlestick, and who now removed the vessels they had left behind, and, worshipping, withdrew. Next, one of the assistants reverently spread the coals on the golden altar; the other arranged the incense; and then the chief officiating priest was left alone within the Holy Place, to await the signal of the president before burning the incense. It was probably while thus expectant that the angel Gabriel appeared to Zacharias. As the president gave the word of command, which marked that 'the time of incense had come,' 'the whole multitude of the people without' withdrew from the

Censer

And when he had taken it, the four living creatures and the twenty-four elders fell down before the Lamb. Each one had a harp and they were holding golden bowls full of incense, which are the prayers of the saints (Rev. 5:8).

---

[25]The description of the daily sacrifice is given at length in the Mishnic tractate *Tamid*. See specially sect. v.

inner court, and fell down before the Lord, spreading their hands[26] in silent prayer.

IMAGERY IN THE APOCALYPSE

He heaped up the incense on the coals and the whole place became filled with smoke. He came out by the way he went in, and in the outer space he prayed a short prayer. But he did not prolong his prayer lest he put Israel in terror (Mishnah, Yoma v.1).

It is this most solemn period, when throughout the vast Temple buildings deep silence rested on the worshipping multitude, while within the sanctuary itself the priest laid the incense on the golden altar, and the cloud of 'odours' (Rev. 5:8)[27] rose up before the Lord, which serves as the image of heavenly things in this description (Rev. 8:1, 3, 4):[28] 'And when he had opened the seventh seal; there was silence in heaven about the space of half an hour....And another angel came and stood at the altar, having a golden censer; and there was given unto him much incense, that he should offer it with the prayers of all saints upon the golden altar which was before the throne. And the smoke of the incense, which came with the prayers of the saints, ascended up before God out of the angel's hand.'

PRAYERS WITH THE INCENSE

The prayers offered by priests and people at this part of the service are recorded by tradition as follows:[29] 'True it is that Thou art Jehovah our God,

---

[26]The practice of folding the hands together in prayer dates from the fifth century of our era, and is of purely Saxon origin. See Hölemann, *Bibel St.* i, p. 150, quoted by Delitzsch, *u.s.*

[27]It is a curious inconsistency on the part of Maimonides to assign this rationalistic object for the use of incense in the Temple—that it counteracted the effluvia from the sacrifices!

[28]According to *Tamid,* vi. 3, the incensing priest 'bowed down,' or prayed, on withdrawing backwards from the Holy Place.

[29]A few details for those who wish fuller information. Tradition has preserved two kinds of fragments from the ancient Jewish liturgy in the times of the Temple. The one is called the 'Tephillah,' or Prayer, the other the 'Eulogies,' or Benedictions. Of the latter there are eighteen, of which the three first and the three last are the oldest, though four, five, six, eight, and nine are also of considerable antiquity. Of the ancient Tephilloth four have been preserved—two used before and two (in the morning, one) after the Shema. The first morning and the last evening Tephillah are strictly morning and evening prayers. They were not used in the Temple service. The second Tephillah before the Shema was said by the priests in the 'Hall of Polished Stones,' and the first Tephillah after the Shema by priests and people during the burning of incense. This was followed by the three last of the eighteen Eulogies. Is it not a fair inference, then, that while the priests said their prayers in 'the hall,' the people repeated the three first Eulogies, which are of equal antiquity with the three last, which we know to have been repeated during the burning of incense?

and the God of our fathers; our King and the King of our fathers, our Saviour and the Saviour of our fathers; our Maker and the Rock of our salvation; our Help and our Deliverer. Thy name is from everlasting, and there is no God beside Thee. A new song did they that were delivered sing to Thy name by the seashore; together did all praise and own Thee as King, and say, Jehovah shall reign who saveth Israel.[30]

'Be graciously pleased, Jehovah our God, with Thy people Israel, and with their prayer. Restore the service to the oracle of Thy house; and the burnt-offerings of Israel and their prayer accept graciously and in love; and let the service of Thy people Israel be ever well-pleasing unto Thee.

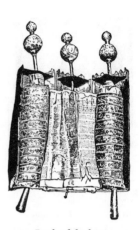

Book of the law

'We praise Thee, who art Jehovah our God, and the God of our fathers, the God of all flesh, our Creator, and the Creator from the beginning! Blessing and praise be to Thy great and holy name, that Thou hast preserved us in life and kept us. So preserve us and keep us, and gather the scattered ones into Thy holy courts, to keep Thy statutes, and to do Thy good pleasure, and to serve Thee with our whole heart, as this day we confess unto Thee. Blessed be the Lord, unto whom belongeth praise.

'Appoint peace, goodness, and blessing; grace, mercy, and compassion for us, and for all Israel Thy people. Bless us, O our Father, all of us as one, with the light of Thy countenance. For in the light of Thy countenance hast Thou, Jehovah, our God, given us the law of life, and loving mercy, and righteousness, and blessing, and compassion, and life, and peace. And may it please Thee to bless Thy people Israel at all times, and at every hour with Thy peace. [May we and all Thy people Israel be remembered and written before Thee in the book of life, with blessing and peace and support.] Blessed be Thou, Jehovah, who blessest Thy people Israel with peace.'

These prayers ended, he who had formerly trimmed the candlestick once more entered the Holy Place, to kindle the two lamps that had been left unlit;

---

[30]Now follow in the text the three last 'Eulogies.'

and then, in company with the incensing priest, took his stand on the top of the steps which led down to the Court of the Priests.[31] The other three who had also ministered within the Holy Place gathered beside him, still carrying the vessels of their ministry; while the rest of the priests grouped themselves on the steps beneath. Meanwhile he on whom the fourth lot had fallen had ascended to the altar. They whose duty it was handed to him, one by one, the pieces of the sacrifice. Upon each he pressed his hands, and next flung them confusedly upon the fire, that so the flesh of the sacrifice might be scattered as well as its blood sprinkled. After that he ranged them in order, to imitate as nearly as possible the natural shape of the animal. This part of the service was not unfrequently performed by the high-priest himself.

Priest

Meanwhile, the people were waiting for Zechariah and wondering why he stayed so long in the temple. When he came out, he could not speak to them. They realized he had seen a vision in the temple, for he kept making signs to them but remained unable to speak (Luke 1:21–22).

THE BLESSING

The priests, who were ranged on the steps to the Holy Place, now lifted their hands above their heads, spreading and joining their fingers in a peculiar mystical manner.[32] One of their number, probably the incensing priest, repeated in audible voice, followed by the others, the blessing in Num. 6:24–26: 'Jehovah bless thee, and keep thee: Jehovah make his face shine upon thee, and be gracious unto thee: Jehovah lift up His countenance upon thee, and give thee peace.' To this the people responded, 'Blessed be the Lord God, the God of Israel, from everlasting to everlasting.' In the modern synagogues the priestly blessing is divided into three parts; it is pronounced with a disguised voice and veiled faces, while the word 'Lord' is

---

[31]According to Maimonides, it was at this part of the service, and not before, that the sound of the Magrephah summoned the priests to worship, the Levites to their song, and the 'stationary men' to their duties.

[32]The high-priest lifted his hands no higher than the golden plate on his mitre. It is well known that, in pronouncing the priestly blessing in the synagogue, the priests join their two outspread hands, by making the tips of the first fingers touch each other. At the same time, the first and second, and the third and fourth fingers in each hand are knit together, while a division is made between those fingers by spreading them apart. A rude representation of this may be seen in Jewish cemeteries on the gravestones of priests.

substituted for the name of 'Jehovah.'[33] Of course all this was not the case in the Temple. But if it had been the duty of Zacharias, as incensing priest for the day, to lead in the priestly blessing, we can all the better understand the wonder of the people as 'he beckoned unto them, and remained speechless' (Luke 1:22), while they waited for his benediction.

After the priestly blessing the meat-offering was brought, and, as prescribed in the law, oil added to it. Having been salted, it was laid on the fire. Next the high-priest's daily meat-offering was presented, consisting of twelve cakes broken in halves—twelve half-cakes being presented in the morning, and the other twelve in the evening. Finally, the appropriate drink-offering was poured out upon the foundation of the altar.[34]

THE TEMPLE MUSIC

Upon this the Temple music began. It was the duty of the priests, who stood on the right and the left of the marble table on which the fat of the sacrifices was laid, at the proper time to blow the blasts on their silver trumpets. There might not be less than two nor more than 120 in this service; the former in accordance with the original institution (Num. 10:2), the latter not to exceed the number at the dedication of the first Temple (2 Chron. 5:12). The priests faced the people, looking eastwards, while the Levites, who crowded the fifteen steps which led from the Court of Israel to that of the Priests, turned westwards to the sanctuary. On a signal given by the president, the priests moved forward to each side of him who struck the cymbals. Immediately the choir of the Levites, accompanied by instrumental music, began the Psalm of the day. It was sustained by not less than twelve voices, with which mingled the delicious treble from selected voices of young sons of the Levites,

When he opened the fifth seal, I saw under the altar the souls of those who had been slain because of the word of God and the testimony they had maintained. They called out in a loud voice, "How long, Sovereign Lord, holy and true, until you judge the inhabitants of the earth and avenge our blood?" (Rev. 6:9–10).

Make two trumpets of hammered silver, and use them for calling the community together and for having the camps set out (Num. 10:2).

The earth is the LORD's, and everything in it, the world, and all who live in it; for he founded it upon the seas and established it upon the waters (Ps. 24:1–2).

Timbrel

---

[33]Dr. Geiger has an interesting argument to show that in olden times the pronunciation of the so-called ineffable name 'Jehovah,' which now is never spoken, was allowed even in ordinary life. See *Urschrift u. Uebers d. Bibel*, p. 259, etc.

[34]Perhaps there may be an allusion to this in Rev. 6:9, 10.

And God said, "Let there be light," and there was light....And God said, "Let there be an expanse between the waters to separate water from water."...And God said, "Let the water under the sky be gathered to one place, and let dry ground appear." And it was so....And God said, "Let there be lights in the expanse of the sky to separate the day from the night, and let them serve as signs to mark seasons and days and years,...And God said, "Let the water teem with living creatures, and let birds fly above the earth across the expanse of the sky."...And God said, "Let the land produce living creatures according to their kinds: livestock, creatures that move along the ground, and wild animals, each according to its kind." And it was so....Thus the heavens and the earth were completed in all their vast array (Gen. 1:3, 6, 9, 14, 20, 24; 2:1).

who, standing by their fathers, might take part in this service alone. The number of instrumental performers was not limited, nor yet confined to the Levites, some of the distinguished families which had intermarried with the priests being admitted to this service.[35] The Psalm of the day was always sung in three sections. At the close of each the priests drew three blasts from their silver trumpets, and the people bowed down and worshipped. This closed the morning service. It was immediately followed by the sacrifices and offerings which private Israelites might have to bring, and which would occasionally continue till near the time for evening service. The latter resembled in all respects that of the morning, except that the lot was only cast for the incense; that the incense was burned, *not*, as in the morning, *before*, but *after* the pieces of the sacrifice had been laid on the fire of the altar, and that the priestly blessing was generally omitted.

THE ORDER OF PSALMS

The following was the order of the Psalms in the daily service of the Temple.[36] On the first day of the week they sang Psalm 24, 'The earth is the Lord's,' etc., in commemoration of the first day of creation, when 'God possessed the world, and ruled in it.' On the second day they sang Psalm 48, 'Great is the Lord, and greatly to be praised,' etc., because on the second day of creation 'the Lord divided His works, and reigned over them.' On the third day they sang Psalm 82, 'God standeth in the congregation of the mighty,' etc., 'because on that day the earth appeared, on which are the Judge and the judged.' On the fourth day Psalm 94 was sung, 'O Lord God, to whom vengeance belongeth,' etc., 'because on the fourth day God made the sun, moon, and stars, and will be avenged on those that worship them.' On the fifth day they sang Psalm 81, 'Sing aloud unto God our strength,' etc., 'because of the variety of creatures

---

[35] It is a curious coincidence that of the two families named in the Talmud as admitted to this service, one—that of Tsippariah—should have been 'from Emmaus' (Luke 24:13).

[36] *Tamid*, sec. vii., and Maimonides in *Tamid*.

made that day to praise His name.' On the sixth day
Psalm 93 was sung, 'The Lord reigneth,' etc., 'because
on that day God finished His works and made man,
and the Lord ruled over all His works.' Lastly, on the
Sabbath day they sang Psalm 92, 'It is a good thing to
give thanks unto the Lord,' etc., 'because the Sabbath
was symbolical of the millennial kingdom at the end
of the six thousand years' dispensation, when the
Lord would reign over all, and His glory and service
fill the earth with thanksgiving.'

9

SABBATH IN THE TEMPLE

�֍

"The Sabbath was made for man, not man for the
Sabbath. So the Son of Man is Lord even of the
Sabbath."—Mark 2:27-28.

THE LAW NOT A BURDEN, BUT A GIFT

*For you make me glad by
your deeds, O LORD;
I sing for joy at the works
of your hands.
How great are your works,
O LORD,
how profound your
thoughts (Ps. 92:4–5)!*

It is a beautifully significant practice of the
modern Jews, that, before fulfilling any special observance directed in their Law, they always first bless
God for the giving of it. One might almost compare
the idea underlying this, and much else of a similar
character in the present religious life of Israel, to the
good fruits which the soil of Palestine bore even during the Sabbatical years, when it lay untilled. For it is
intended to express that the Law is felt not a burden,
but a gift of God in which to rejoice. And this holds
specially true of the Sabbath in its Divine institution, of
which it was distinctly said, 'I gave them My Sabbaths,
to be a sign between Me and them, that they might
know that I, Jehovah, sanctify them' (Ezek. 20:12). In
the same sense, the Sabbath is called 'a delight, the
holy of Jehovah, honourable' (Isa. 58:13); and the
great burden of the Sabbath-Psalm (Ps. 92)[1] is that of
joyous thanksgiving unto God.

---

[1] The Talmud discusses the question whether Ps. 92 bears reference to the Sabbath of
creation, or to that final Messianic Sabbath of the Kingdom—according to Rabbi Akibah, 'the
day which is wholly a Sabbath.' (See Delitzsch on the Psalm.) It is a curiously uncritical remark
of some Rabbis to ascribe the authorship of this Psalm to Adam, and its composition to the
beginning of the first Sabbath—Adam having fallen just before its commencement, and been
driven from Paradise, but not killed, because God would not execute the punishment of death
on the Sabbath.

The term Sabbath, 'resting,' points to the origin and meaning of the weekly festival. The Rabbis hold that it was not intended for the Gentiles, and most of them trace the obligation of its observance only to the legislation on Mount Sinai. Nor is another Rabbinical saying, that 'circumcision and the Sabbath preceded the law,' inconsistent with this. For even if the duty of Sabbath-observance had only commenced with the promulgation of the law on Mount Sinai, yet the Sabbath-law itself rested on the original 'hallowing' of the seventh day, when God rested from all His works (Gen. 2:3). But this was not the only rest to which the Sabbath pointed. There was also a rest of redemption, and the Sabbath was expressly connected with the deliverance of Israel from Egypt. 'Remember that thou wast a servant in the land of Egypt, and that Jehovah thy God brought thee out thence through a mighty hand and by a stretched out arm: therefore Jehovah thy God commanded thee to keep the Sabbath-day' (Deut. 5:15). At the close of the work-a-day week, holy rest in the Lord; at the end of the labour and sorrow of Egypt, redemption and rest; and both pointing forward to the better rest (Heb. 4:9), and ultimately to the eternal Sabbath of completed work, of completed redemption, and completed 'hallowing' (Rev. 11)—such was the meaning of the weekly Sabbath. It was because this idea of festive rest and sanctification was so closely connected with the weekly festival that the term Sabbath was also applied to the great festivals (as Lev. 23:15, 24, 32, 39). For a similar reason, the number seven, which was that of the weekly Sabbath (the first seven that had appeared in time), became in Scripture-symbolism the sacred or covenant number.[2]

And God blessed the seventh day and made it holy, because on it he rested from all the work of creating that he had done (Gen. 2:3).

There remains, then, a Sabbath-rest for the people of God (Heb. 4:9).

From the day after the Sabbath, the day you brought the sheaf of the wave offering, count off seven full weeks. Count off fifty days up to the day after the seventh Sabbath, and then present an offering of new grain to the LORD (Lev. 23:15–16).

LATER PERVERSION OF THE SABBATH

It is necessary to bear all this in remembrance when thinking of what the perverted ingenuity of the

---

[2]The term 'Sabbath' is also applied to 'a week,' as in Lev. 23:15; 25:8; and, for example, in Matt. 28:1; Mark 16:2; Luke 24:1; John 20:1. This seems to indicate that the Sabbath was not to be regarded as separate from, but as giving its character to the rest of the week, and to its secular engagements. So to speak, the week closes and is completed in the Sabbath.

Jesus asked the Pharisees and experts in the law, "Is it lawful to heal on the Sabbath or not?" But they remained silent. So taking hold of the man, he healed him and sent him away.

Then he asked them, "If one of you has a son or an ox that falls into a well on the Sabbath day, will you not immediately pull him out?" And they had nothing to say (Luke 14:3–6).

Then he said to them, "The Sabbath was made for man, not man for the Sabbath" (Mark 2:27).

Rabbis made the Sabbath at the time of Christ, and probably even more in the generations following. For there is evidence that the Sabbath-law has become stricter than it had been, since, for instance, the practice of taking an ox or an ass out of a pit, to which our Saviour alludes (Luke 14:5) as uncontroverted, would now no longer be lawful, unless, indeed, the animal were in actual danger of life; otherwise, it is to receive food and water in the pit. This 'actual danger to life,' whether to beast or to man (at any rate, to Israelites), determined the only cases in which a breach of the law of Sabbath-observance was allowed. At the outset, indeed, it must be admitted that the whole social Rabbinical legislation on the subject seems to rest on two sound underlying principles: negatively, the avoidance of all that might become work; and, positively, the doing of all which, in the opinion of the Rabbis, might tend to make the Sabbath 'a delight.' Hence, not only were fasting and mourning strictly prohibited, but food, dress, and every manner of enjoyment, not incompatible with abstinence from work, were prescribed to render the day pleasurable. 'All the days of the week,' the Rabbi says, 'has God paired, except the Sabbath, which is alone, that it may be wedded to Israel.' Israel was to welcome the Sabbath as a bride; its advent as that of a king. But in practice all this terribly degenerated. Readers of the New Testament know how entirely, and even cruelly, the spirit and object of the Sabbath were perverted by the traditions of 'the elders.' But those only who have studied the Jewish law on the subject can form any adequate conception of the state of matters. Not to speak of the folly of attempting to produce joy by prescribed means, nor of the incongruousness of those means, considering the sacred character of the day, the almost numberless directions about avoiding work must have made a due observance of the Sabbath-rest the greatest labour of all. All work was arranged under thirty-nine chief classes, or 'fathers,' each of them having ever so many 'descendants,' or subordinate divisions. Thus, 'reaping' was one of the 'fathers,' or chief classes, and 'plucking ears of corn' one of its descendants. So far did this punctiliousness go that it became necessary to devise ingenious means to render the ordinary intercourse of life possible, and to evade the inconvenient strictness of the law which regulated a 'Sabbath-day's journey.'[3]

THE SCHOOLS OF SHAMMAI AND HILLEL

The school of Shammai, the sect of the Essenes, and strange to say, the Samaritans, were the most stringent in their Sabbath-observance. The school of Shammai held that the duty of Sabbath-rest extended not only to men and to beasts, but even to inanimate objects, so that no process might be commenced on the Friday which would go on of itself during the Sabbath, such as laying out flax to dry, or putting wool into dye (*Shabb.* i. 5, 6, etc.). The school of Hillel excluded inanimate things from the Sabbath-rest, and also allowed work to be given on a Friday to Gentiles, irrespective of the question whether they could complete it before the Sabbath began. Both schools allowed the preparation of the passover-meal on the Sabbath, and also priests, while on their ministry in the Temple, to keep up the fire in the 'Beth Moked.' But this punctilious enforcement of the Sabbath-rest became occasionally dangerous to the nation. For at one time the Jews would not even defend themselves on the Sabbath against hostile attacks of armies, till the Maccabees laid down the principle, which ever afterwards continued in force (Jos. *Ant.* 12.275–277; 14.63), that defensive, though not offensive, warfare was lawful on the holy day. Even as thus modified, the principle involved peril, and during the last siege of Jerusalem it was not uniformly carried out.[4] Nor was it, so far as we can judge from analogy (Josh. 6:15, etc.), sanctioned by

The School of Shammai say: Ink, dyestuffs, or vetches may not be soaked [on a Friday] unless there is time for them to be [wholly] soaked the same day (Mishnah, Šabbat I.5).

There were about a thousand, with their wives and children, who were smothered and died in these caves; but many of those that escaped joined themselves to Mattathias, and appointed him to be their ruler, who taught them to fight even on the Sabbath day; and told them that unless they would do so, they would become their own enemies, by observing the law [so rigorously], while their adversaries would still assault them on this day, and they would not then defend themselves; and that nothing could then hinder but they must all perish without fighting (Jos. Antiquities 12.275–276).

---

[3]By depositing a meal of meat at the end of the Sabbath-day's journey to make it, by a legal fiction, a man's domicile, from which he might start on a fresh Sabbath-day's journey. The Mishnic tractate *Eruvin* treats of the connecting of houses, courts, etc., to render lawful the carrying out of food, etc. On the other hand, such an isolated expression occurs (*Mechilta*, ed. *Weiss*, p. 100a): 'The Sabbath is given to you, not you to the Sabbath.' If we might regard this as a current theological saying, it would give a fresh meaning to the words of our Lord, Mark 2:27.

[4]Compare *Jewish Wars*, 2.517, but, on the other hand, *Antiq.* 14.63.

There are six days when you may work, but the seventh day is a Sabbath of rest, a day of sacred assembly. You are not to do any work; wherever you live, it is a Sabbath to the LORD (Lev. 23:3).

Take fine flour and bake twelve loaves of bread, using two–tenths of an ephah for each loaf...This bread is to be set out before the LORD regularly, Sabbath after Sabbath, on behalf of the Israelites, as a lasting covenant (Lev. 24:5, 8).

Now it was the day of Preparation, and the next day was to be a special Sabbath. Because the Jews did not want the bodies left on the crosses during the Sabbath, they asked Pilate to have the legs broken and the bodies taken down (John 19:31).

Scripture precedent. But this is not the place further to explain either the Scripture or the Rabbinical law of Sabbath-observance,[5] as it affected the individual, the home, and the social life, nor yet to describe the Sabbath-worship in the ancient synagogues of Palestine. We confine our attention to what passed in the Temple itself.

SCRIPTURE RULES FOR THE SABBATH

The only directions given in Scripture for the celebration of the Sabbath in the sanctuary are those which enjoin 'a holy convocation,' or a sacred assembly (Lev. 23:3); the weekly renewal of the shewbread (Lev. 24:8; Num. 4:7); and an additional burnt-offering of two lambs, with the appropriate meat- and drink-offerings, 'beside the continual' (that is, the ordinary daily) 'burnt-offering and his drink-offering' (Num. 28:9, 10). But the ancient records of tradition enable us to form a very vivid conception of Sabbath-worship in the Temple at the time of Christ. Formally, the Sabbath commenced at sunset on Friday, the day being reckoned by the Hebrews from sunset to sunset. As no special hour for this was fixed, it must, of course, have varied not only at different seasons, but in different localities. Thus, the Rabbis mention that the inhabitants of a low-lying city, like Tiberias, commenced the observance of the Sabbath half an hour earlier, while those who lived on an eminence, such as at Sepphoris,[6] continued it half an hour later than their brethren. If the sun were not visible, sunset was to be reckoned from when the fowls went to roost. But long before that the preparations for the Sabbath had commenced. Accordingly, Friday is called by the Rabbis 'the eve of the Sabbath,' and in the Gospels 'the preparation' (Mark 15:42; John 19:31).[7] No fresh

---

[5]There is a special Mishnic tractate on the subject.

[6]Sepphoris, the Dio-Caesarea of the Romans, was near Nazareth. It is often referred to by Josephus, and, after the destruction of Jerusalem, became for a time the seat of the Sanhedrim. (See Robinson's *Researches in Pal.* vol. ii, p. 345.)

[7]The expression, Luke 6:1, rendered in our version 'the second Sabbath after the first,' really means, 'the first Sabbath after the second' day of the Passover, on which the first ripe sheaf was presented, the Jews calculating the weeks from that day to Pentecost.

business was then undertaken; no journey of any distance commenced; but everything purchased and made ready against the feast, the victuals being placed in a heated oven, and surrounded by dry substances to keep them warm.[8] Early on Friday afternoon, the new 'course' of priests, of Levites, and of the 'stationary men,' who were to be the representatives of all Israel, arrived in Jerusalem, and having prepared themselves for the festive season, went up to the Temple. The approach of the Sabbath, and then its actual commencement, were announced by threefold blasts from the priests' trumpets.[9] The first three blasts were drawn when 'one-third of the evening sacrifice service was over;' or, as we gather from the decree by which the Emperor Augustus set the Jews free from attendance in courts of law (Jos. *Ant.* 16.163), about the ninth hour, that is, about three P.M. on Friday. This, as we remember, was the hour when Jesus gave up the ghost (Matt. 27:45; Mark 15:34; Luke 23:44). When the priests for the first time sounded their trumpets, all business was to cease, and every kind of work to be stopped. Next, the Sabbath-lamp, of which even heathen writers knew,[10] was lit, and the festive garments put on. A second time the priests drew a threefold blast, to indicate that the Sabbath had actually begun. But the service of the new 'course' of priests had commenced before that. After the Friday evening service, the altar of burnt-offering was cleansed from its stains of blood.[11] Then the outgoing 'course' handed over to the incoming the keys of the sanctuary, the holy vessels, and all else of which they had had charge. Next the heads of the 'houses' or families of the incoming 'course' determined by lot which of the

With what may they cover up hot food and with what may they not cover it up? They may not cover it up with peat or dung or salt or lime or wet sand or dry, or straw or grape–skins or flocking, or herbs that are still wet (but they may do so if they are dried). They may cover up hot food with clothes or produce or feathers or sawdust or hackled flax (Mishnah, *Šabbat iv.1*).

From the sixth hour until the ninth hour darkness came over all the land. About the ninth hour Jesus cried out in a loud voice, "Eloi, Eloi, lama sabachthani?"—which means, "My God, my God, why have you forsaken me?" (Matt. 27:45–46).

---

[8]See the disquisition in Mishnah, *Shab.* iv, as to what substances are lawful for the purpose, and what not.

[9]Perhaps from the so-called 'tectum Sabbathi,' or 'Sabbath roof,' which Rhenferdius (*Op. Phil.* p. 770) identifies with the 'Sabbath covert,' 2 Kgs. 16: 18. See Geodwin, *Moses et Aaron* (ed. Hottinger), pp. 518, 519.

[10]Seneca, ep. 95.

[11]The altar was whitened twice a year, before the Passover and the Feast of Tabernacles. But no tool of iron was used in this.

families were to serve on each special day of their week of ministry, and also who were to discharge the various priestly functions on the Sabbath.

The Two Loaves were kneaded separately and baked separately. The [loaves of the] Shewbread were kneaded separately and baked in pairs. They were made ready in a mould; and when they were taken from the oven they were again put in a mould lest they suffer any hurt (Mishnah, Menaḥot xi.1).

Put the bread of the Presence on this table to be before me at all times (Exod. 25:30).

Over the table of the Presence they are to spread a blue cloth and put on it the plates, dishes and bowls, and the jars for drink offerings; the bread that is continually there is to remain on it (Num. 4:7).

The priests who serve the LORD are sons of Aaron, and the Levites assist them…They set out the bread on the ceremonially clean table and light the lamps on the gold lamp-stand every evening. We are observing the require-ments of the LORD our God (2 Chron. 13:10b–11).

THE SHEWBREAD

The first of these functions, immediately on the commencement of the Sabbath, was the renewal of the 'shewbread.' It had been prepared by the incoming course before the Sabbath itself, and—we might almost say, invariably—in one of the chambers of the Temple, though, in theory, it was held lawful to prepare it also at Bethpage (Mish. *Men.* xi. 2). For, although it was a principle that 'there is no Sabbath in the sanctuary,' yet no work was allowed which might have been done on any other day. Even circumcision, which, like the Temple services, according to the Rabbis, super-seded the Sabbath, was deferred by some to the close of the festive day.[12] Hence, also, if Friday, on the afternoon of which the shewbread was ordinarily prepared, fell on a feast day that required Sabbatical rest, the shewbread was prepared on the Thursday afternoon.[13] The Rabbis are at pains to explain the particular care with which it was made and baked, so that in appearance and colour the lower should be exactly the same as the upper part of it.

But this subject is too important to be thus briefly treated.[14] Our term 'shewbread' is a transla-tion of that used by Luther (*Schaubrod*), which, in turn, may have been taken from the Vulgate (*panes proepositionis*). The Scriptural name is 'Bread of the Face' (Exod. 25:30; 35:13; 39:36); that is, 'of the pres-ence of God,' just as the similar expression, 'Angel of the Face' (Isa. 63:9), means the 'Angel of His Presence.'[15] From its constant presence and disposi-tion in the sanctuary, it is also called 'perpetual bread'

---

[12] See Oehler in Herzog's *Real-Encycl.* xiii, p. 202.

[13] This must have been the case on the Thursday of Christ's betrayal.

[14] The articles of Kitto's *Cycl.* and in Smith's *Dict.* are meagre and unsatisfactory. Even Winer (*Real-Würterb.* ii, p. 401, etc.) is not so accurate as usual.

[15] The curious explanation of the Rabbis (Mish. *Men.* xi. 4) that it was called 'Bread of the Faces' because it was equally baked all round, as it were, all 'faces,' needs no refutation.

(Num. 4:7) and 'bread of laying out' (set in order), which latter most nearly corresponds to the term used in the New Testament (Matt. 12:4; Luke 6:4; Heb. 9:2). The placing and weekly renewal of the 'Bread of the Presence' was evidently among the principal Temple services (2 Chron. 13:10, 11). The 'table of shewbread' stood along the northern, or most sacred side of the Holy Place, being ranged lengthways of the Temple, as all its furniture was, except the Ark of the Covenant, which stood broadways.

THE TABLE ON THE ARCH OF TITUS

As described by the Rabbis, and represented on the triumphal Arch of Titus at Rome, the table of shewbread was two cubits long (two cubits = three feet), one cubit broad, and one and a half high.[16] It was made of pure gold, the feet being turned out and shaped to represent those of animals, and the legs connected, about the middle, by a golden plate, which was surrounded by a 'crown,' or wreath, while another wreath ran round the top of the table. Thus far its form was the same as that made at the first for the tabernacle (Exod. 25:23, etc.), which was of shittim-wood, overlaid with gold. The 'table' originally provided for the second Temple had been taken away by Antiochus Epiphanes (about 170 B.C.); but another was supplied by the Maccabees. Josephus tells a story (*Ant.* 12.60–63) about the gift of yet another and most splendid one by Ptolemy Philadelphus. But as its description does not tally with the delineations on the Arch of Titus, we infer that at the time of Christ the 'table' of the Maccabees stood in the Holy Place.[17]

THE VESSELS OF THE TABLE

Considerable doubt exists as to the precise meaning of the terms used in Scripture to describe

Make a table of acacia wood—two cubits long, a cubit wide and a cubit and a half high. Overlay it with pure gold and make a gold molding around it. Also make around it a rim a handbreadth wide and put a gold molding on the rim. Make four gold rings for the table and fasten them to the four corners, where the four legs are. The rings are to be close to the rim to hold the poles used in carrying the table. Make the poles of acacia wood, overlay them with gold and carry the table with them. And make its plates and dishes of pure gold, as well as its pitchers and bowls for the pouring out of offerings (Exod. 25:23–29).

---

[16]The table on the Arch of Titus seems only one cubit high. We know that it was placed by the victor in the Temple of Peace; was carried about the middle of the fifth century to Africa, by the Vandals under Genseric, and that Belisarius brought it back in 520 to Constantinople, whence it was sent to Jerusalem.

[17]Winer has, on other grounds, thrown doubt on the account of Josephus.

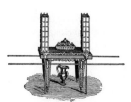

Table of shewbread

And the table, on which bread and salt are laid, was placed on the northern side, since it is the north which is the most productive of winds...(Philo, On the Life of Moses, II, 104).

the golden vessels connected with the 'table of shewbread' (Exod. 25:29). The 'dishes' are generally regarded as those on which the 'shewbread' was either carried or placed, the 'spoons' as destined for the incense, and the 'covers,' or rather 'flagons,' and the 'bowls' for the wine of the drink-offering. On the Arch of Titus there are also two urns. But all this does not prove, in the silence of Scripture, and against the unanimous testimony of tradition, that either flagons, or bowls, or urns were placed on the table of shewbread, nor that drink-offerings were ever brought into the 'Holy Place.'[18] On the other hand, the Rabbis regard the Hebrew terms, rendered 'covers' and 'bowls,' as referring to hollow golden tubes which were placed between the shewbread so as to allow the air to circulate between them; three of these tubes being always put under each, except the highest, under which there were only two, while the lowest rested on the table itself, or, rather, on a golden dish upon it. Thus they calculate that there were, in all, twenty-eight of these tubes to support the twelve loaves. The 'tubes' were drawn out each Friday, and again inserted between the new shewbread each Sunday, since the task of removing and reinserting them was not among those labours which made 'void the Sabbath.' Golden dishes, in which the shewbread was carried, and golden lateral plates, further to protect it on the stand, are also mentioned by the Rabbis.

THE SHEWBREAD ITSELF

The 'shewbread' was made of the finest wheaten flour, that had been passed through eleven sieves. There were twelve of these cakes, according to the number of the tribes of Israel, ranged in two piles, each of six cakes. Each cake was made of two omers of wheat (the omer = about five pints). Between the two rows, not upon them (as according to the Rabbis—*Menach.* xi. 5), two bowls with pure incense were

---

[18]We cannot here enter into the discussion, which the reader will find in Relandus, *Antiq.* pp. 39, 41.

placed, and, according to Egyptian tradition,[19] also salt. The cakes were anointed in the middle with oil, in the form of a cross. As described by Jewish tradition, they were each five handbreadths broad and ten handbreadths long, but turned up at either end, two handbreadths on each side, to resemble in outline the Ark of the Covenant. Thus, as each cake, after being 'turned up,' reached six handbreadths and was placed lengthwise on the breadth of the table, it would exactly cover it (the one cubit of the table being reckoned at six handbreadths); while, as the two rows of six cakes stood broadwise against each other (2 x 5 handbreadths), it would leave between them two handbreadths vacant on the length of the table (2 cubits = 12 handbreadths), on which the two bowls with the incense were placed.[20] The preparation of the shewbread seems to have been hereditarily preserved as a secret family tradition in 'the house of Garmu,' a family of the Kohathites (1 Chron. 9:32; *Mish. Shekal.* v. 1). The fresh cakes of shewbread were deposited in a golden dish on the marble table in the porch of the sanctuary, where they remained till the Sabbath actually commenced.

Some of their Kohathite brothers were in charge of preparing for every Sabbath the bread set out on the table (1 Chron. 9:32).

THE MODE OF CHANGING

The mode of changing the shewbread may be given in the words of the Mishnah (*Men.* xi. 7): 'Four priests enter (the Holy Place), two carrying, each, one of the piles (of six shewbread), the other two the two dishes (of incense). Four priests had preceded them —two to take off the two (old) piles of shewbread, and two the two (old) dishes of incense. Those who brought in (the bread and incense) stood at the north side (of the table), facing southwards; they who took away at the south side, facing north: these lifted off, and those replaced; the hands of these being right

---

[19]LXX Lev. 24:7; Philo ii. 151.

[20]We have been thus particular on account of the inaccuracies in so many articles on this subject. It ought to be stated that another Mishnic authority than that we have followed seems to have calculated the cubit at ten handbreadths, and accordingly gives different measurements for the 'shewbread;' but the result is substantially the same.

On the table of marble they laid the Shewbread when it was brought in, and on that of gold [they laid it] when it was brought out, since what is holy must be raised [in honour] and not brought down. And within was a table of gold whereon the Shewbread lay continually (Mishnah, Šeqalim vi.4).

over against the hands of those (so as to lift off and put on exactly at the same moment), as it is written: "Thou shalt set upon the table bread of the Presence before Me alway." ' The shewbread which had been taken off was then deposited on the golden table in the porch of the sanctuary, the incense burnt on that heap on the altar of burnt-offering from which the coals were taken for the altar of incense, after which the shewbread was distributed among the outgoing and the incoming course of priests.[21] The incoming priests stood at the north side, the outgoing at the south side, and each course gave to the high-priest half of their portion. The shewbread was eaten during the Sabbath, and in the Temple itself, but only such priests as were in a state of Levitical purity.

THE SYMBOLISM OF THE SHEWBREAD

The importance of the service which has just been described depended, of course, on its meaning. Ancient symbolism, both Jewish and Christian, regarded 'the bread of the Presence' as an emblem of the Messiah. This view is substantially, though not literally, correct. Jehovah, who dwelt in the *Most* Holy Place between the Cherubim, was the God manifest and worshipped in the Holy Place. There the mediatorial ministry, in the name of, and representing Israel, 'laid before' Him the bread of the Presence, kindled the seven-lamped candlestick, and burnt incense on the golden altar. The 'bread' 'laid before Him' in the northern or most sacred part of the Holy Place was that of His Presence, and meant that the Covenant-people owned 'His Presence' as their bread and their life; the candlestick, that He was their Lightgiver and Light; while between the table of shewbread and the candlestick burned the incense on the golden altar, to show that life and light are joined together, and come to us in fellowship with God and prayer. For a similar reason, pure incense was placed between the shewbread—for, the life which is in His Presence

---

[21]According to other authorities, however, the incense of the shewbread was burned along with the morning sacrifice on the Sabbath.

is one of praise; while the incense was burned before the shewbread was eaten by the priests, to indicate God's acceptance and ratification of Israel's dependence upon Him, as also to betoken praise to God while living upon His Presence. That this 'Presence' meant the special manifestation of God, as afterwards fully vouchsafed in Christ, 'the Angel of His Presence,' it is scarcely necessary to explain at length in this place.

THE COURSES ON THE SABBATH

But although the service of the incoming 'course' of priests had begun with the renewal of the 'shewbread,' that of the outgoing had not yet completely ceased. In point of fact, the outgoing 'course' of priests offered the morning sacrifice on the Sabbath, and the incoming the evening sacrifice, both spending the Sabbath in the sanctuary. The inspection of the Temple before the Sabbath morning service differed from that on ordinary days, inasmuch as the Temple itself was lit up, to obviate the necessity of the priests carrying torches on the holy day. The altar of burnt-offering was cleansed before the usual hour; but the morning service commenced later, so as to give an opportunity of attending to as many as possible. All appeared in their festive garments, and each carried in his hand some contribution for religious purposes. It was no doubt from this that the practice was derived of 'laying by in store upon the first day of the week,' which St. Paul recommended to the Corinthians (1 Cor. 16:1, 2). Similarly, the apostolic practice of partaking the Lord's Supper every Lord's-day may have been in imitation of the priests eating the shewbread every Sabbath. The Sabbath service was in every respect the same as on other days, except that at the close of the ordinary morning sacrifice the additional offering of two lambs, with its appropriate meat- and drink-offerings as brought (Num. 28:9, 10). When the drink-offering of the ordinary morning sacrifice was poured out, the Levites sang Ps. 92 in three sections, the priests drawing, at the close of each, three blasts from their trumpets, and the people worshipping. At the close of the additional Sabbath

He said, "Surely they are my people,
sons who will not be false to me";
and so he became their Savior.
In all their distress he too was distressed,
and the angel of his presence saved them.
In his love and mercy he redeemed them;
he lifted them up and carried them
all the days of old (Isa. 63:8–9).

Now about the collection for God's people: Do what I told the Galatian churches to do. On the first day of every week, each one of you should set aside a sum of money in keeping with his income, saving it up, so that when I come no collections will have to be made (1 Cor. 16:1–2).

On the Sabbath day, make an offering of two lambs a year old without defect, together with its drink offering and a grain offering of two-tenths of an ephah of fine flour mixed with oil. This is the burnt offering for every Sabbath, in addition to the regular burnt offering and its drink offering (Num. 28:9–10).

Listen, O heavens, and
I will speak;
hear, O earth, the words
of my mouth.
Let my teaching fall like
rain
and my words descend
like dew,
like showers on new grass,
like abundant rain on
tender plants
(Deut. 32:1–2).

The Spirit of the Sovereign
LORD is on me,
because the LORD has
anointed me
to preach good news to
the poor.
He has sent me to bind up
the brokenhearted,
to proclaim freedom for
the captives
and release from darkness
for the prisoners,
to proclaim the year of the
LORD's favor
and the day of vengeance
of our God,
to comfort all who mourn
(Isa. 61:1–2).

The land enjoyed its
sabbath rests; all the time
of its desolation it rested,
until the seventy years were
completed in fulfillment
of the word of the LORD
spoken by Jeremiah
(2 Chron. 36:21).

sacrifice, when its drink-offering as brought, the Levites sang the 'Song of Moses' in Deut. 32. This 'hymn' was divided into six portions, for as many Sabbaths (ver. 1–6; 7–12; 13–18; 19–28; 29–39; 40–end). Each portion was sung in three sections with three-fold blasts of the priests' trumpets, the people worshipping at each pause. If a Sabbath and a 'new moon' fell on the same day, the Sabbath hymn was sung in preference to that for the new moon; if a feast day fell on the Sabbath, the Sabbath sacrifice was offered before that prescribed for the day. At the evening sacrifice on the Sabbath the song of Moses in Exod. 15 was sung.

THE SABBATICAL YEAR

Though not strictly connected with the Temple services, it may be desirable briefly to refer to the observance of the Sabbatical year, as it was strictly enforced at the time of Christ. It was otherwise with the year of Jubilee. Strangely, there are traces of the latter during the period before the return from Babylon (1 Kgs. 21:3; Isa. 5:8; 37:30; 61:1–3; Ezek. 1:1; 7:12; Micah 2:2), while the Sabbatical year seems to have been systematically neglected. Hence Jewish tradition explains, in accordance with 2 Chron. 36:21, that the seventy years' captivity were intended to make up the neglected Sabbatical years—commencing the calculation, if it be taken literally, from about the accession of King Solomon. But while, after the return from Babylon, the year of Jubilee was no longer kept, at least, as a religious ordinance, the Sabbatical year was most strictly observed, not only by the Jews (Neh. 10:31; 1 Macc. 6:49, 53; Jos. *Antiq.* 13.234, 14.202, 15.7; *Jew. Wars,* 1.146), but also by the Samaritans (*Antiq.* 11.343). Jewish tradition has it, that as it took seven years for the first conquest, and another seven for the proper division of the Holy Land, 'tithes' were for the first time paid fourteen years after the entrance of Israel into Canaan; and the first Sabbatical year fell seven years later, or in the twenty-first year of their possession of Palestine. The Sabbatical law extended only to the soil of Palestine itself, which, however, included certain surrounding districts. The Rabbis add this curious proviso, that it was lawful to use (though not to store or sell) the spontaneous produce of the land throughout the extent originally possessed by Israel, but that even the use of these products was prohibited in such districts as having originally belonged to, were again occupied by Israel after their return from Babylon. But this, as other rules laid down by the Rabbis, had many exceptions (Mish. *Shev.* vi. 1).

SCRIPTURE REFERENCES TO IT

As Divinely enjoined, the soil was to be left uncultivated at the end of every period of six years, beginning, as the Jews argue, after the Passover for the barley, after Pentecost for the wheat, and after the Feast of Tabernacles for all fruit-trees. The Sabbatical year itself commenced, as most of them hold, on New Year's Day, which fell on the new moon of the tenth month, or Tishri.[22] Whatever grew of itself during the year was to belong to the poor (Exod. 23:10, 11), which, however, as Lev. 25:6 shows, did not exclude its use as 'meat,' only its storage and sale, by the family to which the land belonged. Yet a third Scriptural notice constitutes the Sabbatical year that of 'the Lord's release,' when no debt might be claimed from an Israelite (Deut. 15:1–6); while a fourth enjoins, that 'in the solemnity of the year of release, in the Feast of Tabernacles,' the law was to be read 'before all Israel in their hearing' (Deut. 31:10, 11).

THE 'PROSBUL'

It has been strangely overlooked that these four ordinances, instead of being separate and distinct, are in reality closely connected. As the assignment of what grew of itself did not exclude the usufruct by the owners, so it also followed of necessity that, in a year when all agricultural labour ceased, debts should not be claimed from an agricultural population. Similarly,

When the neighboring peoples bring merchandise or grain to sell on the Sabbath, we will not buy from them on the Sabbath or on any holy day. Every seventh year we will forgo working the land and will cancel all debts (Neh. 10:31).

For six years you are to sow your fields and harvest the crops, but during the seventh year let the land lie unplowed and unused. Then the poor among your people may get food from it, and the wild animals may eat what they leave. Do the same with your vineyard and your olive grove (Exod. 23:10–11).

At the end of every seven years you must cancel debts. This is how it is to be done: Every creditor shall cancel the loan he has made to his fellow Israelite. He shall not require payment from his fellow Israelite or brother, because the LORD's time for canceling debts has been proclaimed (Deut. 15:1–2).

---

[22]The year of Jubilee began on the 10th of Tishri, being the Day of Atonement.

If a fellow Hebrew, a man or a woman, sells himself to you and serves you six years, in the seventh year you must let him go free. And when you release him, do not send him away empty-handed. Supply him liberally from your flock, your threshing floor and your winepress. Give to him as the LORD your God has blessed you (Deut. 15:12–14).

it was quite in accordance with the idea of the Sabbath and the Sabbatical year that the law should be publicly read, to indicate that 'the rest' was not to be one of idleness, but of meditation on the Word of God.[23] It will be gathered that in this view the Divine law had not intended the absolute remission of debts, but only their 'release' during the Sabbatical year.[24] Jewish tradition, indeed, holds the opposite; but, by its ordinances, it rendered the law itself void. For, as explained by the Rabbis, the release from debt did not include debts for things purchased in a shop, nor judicial fines, nor yet money lent on a pledge. But, as the great Rabbi Hillel found that even these exceptions were not sufficient to insure the loan of money in view of the Sabbatical year, he devised a formula called 'Prosbul' (probably 'addition,' from a Greek word to the same effect), by which the rights of a creditor were fully secured. The 'Prosbul' ran thus: 'I, A. B., hand to you, the judges of C. D. (a declaration), to the effect that I may claim any debt due to me at whatever time I please.'

THE EFFECT OF IT

This 'Prosbul,' signed by the judges or by witnesses, enabled a creditor to claim money lent even in the Sabbatical year; and though professedly applying only to debts on real property, was so worded as to cover every case (Mish. *Shev.* sec. x). But even this was not all, and the following legal fiction was suggested as highly meritorious to all concerned. The debtor was to offer payment, and the creditor to reply, 'I remit;' upon which the debtor was to insist that 'nevertheless' the creditor was to accept the repayment. In general, money owing to Jewish proselytes was to be repaid to them, but not to their heirs, even though they also had turned Jews, as by becoming a

---

[23] Idleness is quite as much contrary to the Sabbath law as labour: 'not doing thine own ways, nor finding thine own pleasure, nor speaking thine own words' (Isa. 58:13).

[24] The manumission of Jewish slaves took place in the seventh year of their bondage, whenever that might be, and bears no reference to the Sabbatical year, with which, indeed, some of its provisions could not easily have been compatible (Deut. 15:14).

proselyte a man had separated himself from his kin, who therefore were no longer, strictly speaking, his natural heirs. Still, to make payment in such a case was deemed specially meritorious. The Rabbinical evasions of the law, which forbade the use of that which had grown spontaneously on the soil, are not so numerous nor so irrational. It was ruled that part of such products might be laid by in the house, provided sufficient of the same kind were left in the field for cattle and beasts to feed upon. Again, as much land might be tilled as was necessary to make payment of tribute or taxes. The omer (or 'wave-sheaf') at the Passover, and the two wave-loaves at Pentecost, were also to be made from the barley and wheat grown that year in the field. Lastly, Rabbinical ordinance fixed the following portions as being 'the law' which was to be publicly read in the Temple by the king or the high-priest at the Feast of Tabernacles in the Sabbatical year, viz., Deut. 1:1–6; 6:4–8; 11:13–22; 14:22; 15:23; 17:14; 26:12–19; 27; 28.[25] This service concluded with a benediction, which resembled that of the high-priest on the Day of Atonement, except that it referred not to the remission of sins.[26]

RABBINICAL PERVERSION OF THE SABBATICAL YEAR

The account just given proves that there was scarcely any Divine ordinance, which the Rabbis, by their traditions, rendered more fully void, and converted into 'a yoke which neither our fathers nor we were able to bear,' than the Sabbath law. On the other hand, the Gospels bring before us Christ more frequently on the Sabbath than on any other festive occasion. It seemed to be His special day for working the work of His Father. On the Sabbath He preached in the synagogues; He taught in the Temple; He

So if you faithfully obey the commands I am giving you today—to love the LORD your God and to serve him with all your heart and with all your soul—then I will send rain on your land in its season, both autumn and spring rains, so that you may gather in your grain, new wine and oil. I will provide grass in the fields for your cattle, and you will eat and be satisfied (Deut. 11:13–15).

Now then, why do you try to test God by putting on the necks of the disciples a yoke that neither we nor our fathers have been able to bear? No! We believe it is through the grace of our Lord Jesus that we are saved, just as they are (Acts 15:10–11).

---

[25]Mish. *Sotah,* vii. 8, where a curious story is also told, to show how deeply King Agrippa was affected when performing this service.

[26]Relandus suggests that the expression (Matt. 24:20), 'Pray that your flight be not on the Sabbath,' may apply to the Sabbatical year, as one in which the fugitives would find it difficult to secure needful support.

These all look to you to give them their food at the proper time (Ps. 104:27).

You open your hand and satisfy the desires of every living thing (Ps. 145:16).

healed the sick; He came to the joyous meal with which the Jews were wont to close the day (Luke 14:1). Yet their opposition broke out most fiercely in proportion as He exhibited the true meaning and object of the Sabbath. Never did the antagonism between the spirit and the letter more clearly appear. And if in their worship of the letter they crushed out the Spirit of the Sabbath law, we can scarcely wonder that they so overlaid with their ordinances the appointment of the Sabbatical year as well-nigh to extinguish its meaning.[27] That evidently was, that the earth, and all that is upon it, belongeth to the Lord; that the eyes of all wait upon Him, that He may 'give them their meat in due season' (Ps. 104:27; 145:16); that the land of Israel was His special possession; that man liveth not by bread alone, but by every word which proceedeth from the mouth of the Lord; and that He giveth us our daily bread, so that it is vain to rise up early, to sit up late, to eat the bread of sorrows (Ps. 127:2). Beyond it all, it pointed to the fact of sin and redemption: the whole creation which 'groaneth and travaileth in pain together until now,' waiting for and expecting that blessed Sabbath, when 'creation itself shall be delivered from the bondage of corruption into the glorious liberty of the children of God' (Rom. 8:21, 22). Thus, as the Sabbath itself, so the Sabbatical year pointed forward to the 'rest which remaineth to the people of God,' when, contest and labour completed, they sing, 'on the other side of the flood,' the song of Moses and of the Lamb (Rev. 15:3, 4): 'Great and marvellous are Thy works, Lord God Almighty; just and true are Thy ways, Thou King of saints. Who shall not fear Thee, O Lord, and glorify Thy name? for Thou only art holy: for all nations shall come and worship before Thee; for Thy judgments are made manifest.'[28]

---

[27]Compare also the remarks by Oehler in Herzog's *Encycl.* xii, p. 211.

[28]For an account of the Sabbatical years, mentioned by tradition, see Wieseler, *Chron. Synopse*, p. 204.

10
FESTIVE CYCLES AND
ARRANGEMENT OF THE CALENDAR

❈

They kept looking for Jesus, and as they stood in the temple area they asked one another, "What do you think? Isn't he coming to the Feast at all?"—John 11:56

THE NUMBER SEVEN

The symbolic character which is to be traced in all the institutions of the Old Testament, appears also in the arrangement of its festive calendar. Whatever classification of the festivals may be proposed, one general characteristic pervades the whole. Unquestionably, the number *seven* marks in Scripture the sacred measurement of time. The Sabbath is the seventh of days; seven weeks after the commencement of the ecclesiastical year is the Feast of Pentecost; the seventh month is more sacred than the rest, its 'firstborn' or 'New Moon' being not only devoted to the Lord like those of the other months, but specially celebrated as the 'Feast of Trumpets,' while three other festivals occur within its course—the Day of Atonement, the Feast of Tabernacles, and its Octave.[1] Similarly, each seventh year is Sabbatical, and after seven times seven years comes that of Jubilee. Nor is this all. *Seven* days in the year may be designated as the most festive, since in them alone 'no servile work' was to be done,[2] while on the so-called minor festivals (*Moed Katon*), that is, on the days following the first of the Passover

Even if you go and fight courageously in battle, God will overthrow you before the enemy, for God has the power to help or to overthrow (2 Chron. 25:8).

---

[1] Further particulars are given in the chapter on the Feast of Tabernacles.

[2] These are: the first and seventh days of the 'Feast of Unleavened Bread,' Pentecost, New Year's Day, the Day of Atonement, the first day of the Feast of Tabernacles, and its Octave.

week and of that of Tabernacles, the diminution of
festive observances and of restrictions on labour
marks their less sacred character.

THE THREE CYCLES

*It is a sabbath of rest for
you, and you must deny
yourselves. From the
evening of the ninth day
of the month until the
following evening you are
to observe your sabbath
(Lev. 23:32).*

Besides this general division of time by the
sacred number seven, certain general ideas probably
underlay the festive cycles. Thus we may mark two, or
else three, such cycles; the one commencing with the
Pascal sacrifice and ending on the Day of Pentecost,
to perpetuate the memory of Israel's calling and
wilderness life; the other, which occurs in the seventh
month (of rest), marking Israel's possession of the
land and grateful homage to Jehovah. From these two
cycles the Day of Atonement may have to be distinguished, as intermediate between, applying to both,
and yet possessing a character of its own, as Scripture
calls it, 'a Sabbath of Sabbatism,'[3] in which not only
'servile work,' but as on the weekly Sabbath, labour of
any kind was prohibited. In Hebrew two terms are
employed—the one, *Moed*, or appointed meeting,
applied to all festive seasons, including Sabbaths and
New Moons; the other, *Chag*, from a root which means
'to dance,' or 'to be joyous,' applying exclusively to the
three festivals of Easter, Pentecost, and Tabernacles,
in which all males were to appear before the Lord in
His sanctuary. If we might venture to render the
general term *Moadim* by 'trystings' of Jehovah with
His people, the other would be intended to express the
joyousness which was to be a leading characteristic
of the 'pilgrim-feasts.' Indeed, the Rabbis expressly
mention these three as marking the great festivals:
Reiyah, Chagigah, and *Simchah*; that is, *presence,* or
appearance at Jerusalem; the appointed *festive* offerings
of the worshippers, which are not to be confounded
with the public sacrifices offered on these occasions
in the name of the whole congregation; and *joyousness,* with which they connect the freewill offerings
that each brought, as the Lord had blessed him, and
which afterwards were shared with the poor, the

---

[3]The term is rendered in the Authorised Version, 'Sabbath of rest,' Lev. 16:31; 23:32.

desolate, and the Levite, in the joyous meal that followed the public services of the Temple. To these general characteristics of the three great feasts we ought, perhaps, to add in regard to all festive seasons, that each was to be a 'holy convocation,' or gathering for sacred purposes; the injunction of 'rest' from 'servile,' or else from all work; and, lastly, certain special sacrifices which were to be brought in the name of the whole congregation. Besides the Mosaic festivals, the Jews celebrated at the time of Christ two other feasts—that of Esther, or *Purim,* and that of the *Dedication of the Temple,* on its restoration by Judas the Maccabee. Certain minor observances, and the public fasts in memory of the great national calamities, will be noticed in the sequel. Private fasts would, of course, depend on individuals, but the strict Pharisees were wont to fast every Monday and Thursday[4] during the weeks intervening between the Passover and Pentecost, and again, between the Feast of Tabernacles and that of the Dedication of the Temple. It is to this practice that the Pharisee in the parable refers (Luke 18:12) when boasting: 'I fast twice in the week.'

He is to take some of the bull's blood and with his finger sprinkle it on the front of the atonement cover; then he shall sprinkle some of it with his finger seven times before the atonement cover.

He shall then slaughter the goat for the sin offering for the people and take its blood behind the curtain and do with it as he did with the bull's blood: He shall sprinkle it on the atonement cover and in front of it (Lev. 16:14–15).

THREE ANNUAL VISITS TO TEMPLE

The duty of appearing three times a year in the Temple applied to all male Israelites—bondsmen, the deaf, dumb, and lame, those whom sickness, infirmity, or age rendered incapable of going on foot up the mountain of the house, and, of course, all in a state of Levitical uncleanness, being excepted. In general, the duty of appearing before the Lord at the services of His house was deemed paramount. Here an important Rabbinical principle came in, which, although not expressed in Scripture, seems clearly founded upon it, that 'a sacrifice could not be offered for any one unless he himself were present,' to present and to lay his hand upon it (Lev. 1:3; 3:2, 8). It followed that, as the morning and evening sacrifices,

The Pharisee stood up and prayed about himself: "God, I thank you that I am not like other men— robbers, evildoers, adulterers —or even like this tax collector. I fast twice a week and give a tenth of all I get" (Luke 18:11–12).

---

[4]Because on a Thursday Moses had gone up to Mount Sinai, and came down on a Monday, when he received for the *second time* the Tables of the Law.

and those on feast-days were purchased with money contributed by all, and offered on behalf of the whole congregation, all Israel should have attended these services. This was manifestly impossible, but to represent the people twenty-four courses of lay attendants were appointed, corresponding to those of the priests

If the offering is a burnt offering from the herd, he is to offer a male without defect. He must present it at the entrance to the Tent of Meeting so that it will be acceptable to the LORD. He is to lay his hand on the head of the burnt offering, and it will be accepted on his behalf to make atonement for him (Lev. 1:3–4).

and the Levites. These were the 'stationary men,' or 'men of the station,' or 'standing men,' from 'their standing there in the Temple as Israel's representatives.' For clearness sake, we repeat that each of these 'courses' had its 'head,' and served for one week; those of the station on service, who did not appear in Jerusalem, meeting in a central synagogue of their district, and spending the time in fasting and prayer for their brethren. On the day before the Sabbath, on the Sabbath itself, and on the day following, they did not fast, on account of the joy of the Sabbath. Each day they read a portion of Scripture, the first and second chapters of Genesis being for this purpose arranged into sections for the week. This practice, which tradition traced up to Samuel and David (*Taan.* iv. 2), was of ancient date. But the 'men of the station' did *not* impose hands on either the morning or evening sacrifice, nor on any other public offering.[5] Their duty was twofold: to represent all Israel in the services of the sanctuary, and to act as a sort of guide to those who had business in the Temple. Thus, at a certain part of the service, the head of the course brought up those who had come to make an atonement on being cleansed from any impurity, and ranged them along the 'Gate of Nicanor,' in readiness for the ministry of the officiating priests. The 'men of the station' were dispensed from attendance in the Temple on all occasions when the '*Hallel*' was chanted,[6] possibly because the responses of the people when the hymn was sung showed that they needed no formal representatives.

When the time was come for a Course to go up, the priests and the levites thereof went up to Jerusalem, and the Israelites that were of the selfsame Course came together unto their own cities to read the story of Creation, and the men of the Maamad fasted four days in the week, from the second until the fifth day; and they did not fast on the eve of the Sabbath because of the honour due to the Sabbath, nor on the first day of the week, that they should not go forth from rest and pleasure to weariness and fasting, and so be like to die (Mishnah, Ta'anit iv.2).

---

[5] The only *public* offerings, with 'imposition of hands,' were the scapegoat on the Day of Atonement, and the bullock when the congregation had sinned through ignorance.

[6] This happened therefore on eighteen days of the year. These will be specified in a subsequent chapter.

HEBREW		GREEK		
Nîsān	נִיסָן	Xanthikos	Ξανθικός	March–April
'îyyār	אִיָּר	Artemisios	'Αρτεμίσιος	April–May
Sîwān	סִיוָן	Daisios	Δαίσιος	May–June
Tammûz	תַּמּוּז	Panemos	Πάνεμος	June–July
'āb	אָב	Lōos	Λῷος	July–August
ʾelûl	אֱלוּל	Gorpiaios	Γορπιαῖος	August–September
Tišrî	תִּשְׁרִי	Hyperberetaios	'Υπερβερεταῖος	September–October
Marḥešwān	מַרְחֶשְׁוָן	Dios	Δῖος	October–November
Kislēv	כִּסְלֵו	Apellaios	'Απελλαῖος	November–December
Ṭēbēṭ	טֵבֵת	Audynaios	Αὐδυναῖος	December–January
Šebāṭ	שְׁבָט	Peritios	Περίτιος	January–February
ʾadār	אֲדָר	Dystros	Δύστρος	February–March

Calendar of months used in the Postexilic Period

DIFFICULTIES OF THE CALENDAR

Hitherto we have not adverted to the difficulties which those who intended to appear in Jerusalem at the feasts would experience from the want of any fixed calendar. As the year of the Hebrews was *lunar,* not solar, it consisted of only 354 days 8 hours 48 minutes 38 seconds. This, distributed among twelve months, would in the course of years have completely disordered the months, so that the first month, or *Nisan* (corresponding to the end of March or the beginning of April), in the middle of which the first ripe barley was to be presented to the Lord, might have fallen in the middle of winter. Accordingly, the Sanhedrim appointed a Committee of three, of which the chief of the Sanhedrim was always president, and which, if not unanimous, might be increased to seven, when a majority of voices would suffice, to determine which year was to be made a leap-year by the insertion of a thirteenth month. Their resolution[7] was generally taken in the twelfth month (Adar), the additional, or thirteen month (Ve-Adar), being inserted between the twelfth and the first. A Sabbatical year could not be a leap-year, but that preceding it was always such. Sometimes two, but never three, leap-years succeeded

---

[7]Tradition has it, that neither high-priest nor king ever took part in these deliberations, the former because he might object to a leap-year as throwing the Day of Atonement later into the cold season; the king, because he might wish for thirteen months, in order to get thirteen months' revenue in one year!

each other. Commonly, every third year required the addition of a month. The mean duration of the Jewish month being 29 days 12 hours 44 minutes 3¹/₃ seconds, it required, during a period of nineteen years, the insertion of seven months to bring the lunar era in accordance with the Julian.

Now I am about to build a temple for the Name of the LORD my God and to dedicate it to him for burning fragrant incense before him, for setting out the consecrated bread regularly, and for making burnt offerings every morning and evening and on Sabbaths and New Moons and at the appointed feasts of the LORD our God. This is a lasting ordinance for Israel (2 Chron. 2:4).

THE NEW MOON

And this brings up yet another difficulty. The Jews calculated the month according to the phases of the moon, each month consisting of either twenty-nine or thirty days, and beginning with the appearance of the new moon. But this opened a fresh field of uncertainty. It is quite true that every one might observe for himself the appearance of a new moon. But this would again partly depend on the state of the weather. Besides, it left an authoritative declaration of the commencement of a month unsupplied. And yet not only was the first of every month to be observed as 'New Moon's Day,' but the feasts took place on the 10th, 15th, or other day of the month, which could not be accurately determined without a certain knowledge of its beginning. To supply this want the Sanhedrim sat in the 'Hall of Polished Stones' to receive the testimony of credible witnesses that they had seen the new moon. To encourage as many as possible to come forward on so important a testimony, these witnesses were handsomely entertained at the public expense. If the new moon had appeared at the commencement of the 30th day—which would correspond to our evening of the 29th, as the Jews reckoned the day from evening to evening—the Sanhedrim declared the previous month to have been one of twenty-nine days, or 'imperfect.'[8] Immediately thereon men were sent to a signal-station on the Mount of Olives, where beacon-fires were lit and torches waved, till a kindling flame on a hill in the distance indicated that the signal had been perceived. Thus the tidings, that this was the new moon, would be carried from hill to hill, far beyond the boundaries

---

[8]The formula used by the Sanhedrim upon declaring the new moon was, 'It is sacred!'

of Palestine, to those of the dispersion, 'beyond the river.' Again, if credible witnesses had not appeared to testify to the appearance of the new moon on the evening of the 29th, the next evening, or that of the 30th, according to *our* reckoning, was taken as the commencement of the new month, in which case the previous month was declared to have been one of thirty days, or *'full.'* It was ruled that a year should neither have less than four nor more than eight such full months of thirty days.

THE SEVEN MESSENGERS OF THE NEW MOON

But these early fire-signals opened the way for serious inconvenience. The enemies of the Jews lit beacons to deceive those at a distance, and it became necessary to send special messengers to announce the new moon. These were, however, despatched only seven times in the year, just in time for the various feasts—in *Nisan,* for the Passover on the 15th, and in the month following, *Iyar,* for the 'Second Passover,' kept by those who had been debarred from the first (Num. 9:9–11); in *Ab* (the fifth month), for the fast on the 9th, on account of the destruction of Jerusalem; in *Elul* (the sixth month), on account of the approaching solemnities of Tishri; in *Tishri* (the seventh month), for its festivals; in *Kislev* (the ninth month), for the Feast of the Dedication of the Temple; and in *Adar,* for *Purim.* Thus, practically, all difficulties were removed, except in reference to the month *Elul,* since, as the new moon of the following month, or Tishri, was the 'Feast of Trumpets,' it would be exceedingly important to know in time whether *Elul* had twenty-nine or thirty days. But here the Rabbis ruled that *Elul* should be regarded as a month of twenty-nine days, unless a message to the contrary were received—that, indeed, since the days of Ezra it had always been so, and that accordingly New Year's Day would be the day after the 29th of *Elul.* To make, however, assurance doubly sure, it soon became the practice to keep New Year's Day on *two* successive days, and this has since been extended into a duplication of all the great feast days (of course, with the exception of fasts), and

Tell the Israelites: "When any of you or your descendants are unclean because of a dead body or are away on a journey, they may still celebrate the LORD's Passover. They are to celebrate it on the fourteenth day of the second month at twilight. They are to eat the lamb, together with unleavened bread and bitter herbs" (Num. 9:10–11).

that continues, although the calendar has long been fixed, and error is therefore no more possible.

NAMES OF THE HEBREW MONTHS

The present Hebrew names of the month are variously supposed to be derived from the Chaldee, or from the Persian language. They certainly do not appear before the return from Babylon. Before that, the months were named only after their numbers, or else from the natural phenomena characteristic of the seasons, as *Abib,* 'sprouting,' 'green ears,' for the first (Exod. 13:4; 23:15; Deut. 16:1); *Ziv,* 'splendour,' 'flowering,' for the second (1 Kgs. 6:1); *Bul,* 'rain,' for the eighth (1 Kgs. 6:38); and *Ethanim,* 'flowing rivers,' for the seventh (1 Kgs. 8:2). The division of the year into *ecclesiastical,* which commenced with the month *Nisan* (the end of March or beginning of April), or about the spring equinox, and *civil,* which commenced with the seventh month, or *Tishri,* corresponding to the autumn equinox, has by many likewise been supposed to have only originated after the return from Babylon. But the analogy of the twofold arrangement of weights, measures, and money into civil and sacred, and other notices seem against this view, and it is more likely that from the first the Jews distinguished the civil year, which began in Tishri, from the ecclesiastical, which commenced in *Nisan,* from which month, as the first, all the others were counted. To this twofold division the Rabbis add, that for tithing the herds and flocks the year was reckoned from *Elul* to *Elul,* and for taxing fruits often from *Shebat* to *Shebat.*

THE ERAS USED BY THE JEWS

The earliest era adopted by the Jews was that which was reckoned to commence with the deliverance from Egypt. During the reigns of the Jewish kings, time was computed from the year of their accession to the throne. After their return from exile, the Jews dated their years according to the Seleucidic era, which began 312 B.C., or 3,450 from the creation of the world. For a short time after the war of indepen-

Observe the month of Abib and celebrate the Passover of the LORD your God, because in the month of Abib he brought you out of Egypt by night (Deut. 16:1).

The foundation of the temple of the LORD was laid in the fourth year, in the month of Ziv. In the eleventh year in the month of Bul, the eighth month, the temple was finished in all its details according to its specifications. He had spent seven years building it (1 Kgs. 6:37–38).

All the men of Israel came together to King Solomon at the time of the festival in the month of Ethanim, the seventh month (1 Kgs. 8:2).

dence, it became customary to reckon dates from the year of the liberation of Palestine. However, for a very long period after the destruction of Jerusalem (probably, till the twelfth century A.D.), the Seleucidic era remained in common use, when it finally gave place to the present mode of reckoning among the Jews, which dates from the creation of the world. To commute the Jewish year into that of our common era we have to add to the latter 3,761, always bearing in mind, however, that the common or civil Jewish year commences in the month of Tishri, *i.e.* in autumn.

Remember the Sabbath day by keeping it holy. Six days you shall labor and do all your work, but the seventh day is a Sabbath to the LORD your God (Exod. 20:8–10a).

THE WEEK

The week was divided into seven days, of which, however, only the seventh—the Sabbath—had a name assigned to it, the rest being merely noted by numerals. The day was computed from sunset to sunset, or rather to the appearance of the first three stars with which a new day commenced. Before the Babylonian captivity, it was divided into morning, mid-day, evening, and night; but during the residence in Babylon, the Hebrews adopted the division of the day into twelve hours, whose duration varied with the length of the day. The longest day consisted of fourteen hours and twelve minutes; the shortest, of nine hours forty-eight minutes; the difference between the two being thus more than four hours. On an average, the first hour of the day corresponded nearly to our 6 a.m.; the third hour (when, according to Matt. 20:3, the market-place was full), to our 9 A.M.; the close of the sixth hour, to our mid-day; while at the eleventh, the day neared its close. The Romans reckoned the hours from midnight, a fact which explains the apparent discrepancy between John 19:14, where, at the sixth hour (of Roman calculation), Pilate brings Jesus out to the Jews, while at the third hour of the Jewish, and hence the ninth of the Roman and of our calculation (Mark 15:25), He was led forth to be crucified. The night was divided by the Romans into four, by the Jews into three watches. The Jews subdivided the hour into 1,080 parts (chlakim), and again each part into seventy-six moments.

About the third hour he went out and saw others standing in the market-place doing nothing (Matt. 20:3).

It was the day of Preparation of Passover Week, about the sixth hour.
"Here is your king," Pilate said to the Jews (John 19:14).

For the convenience of the reader, we subjoin a calendar, showing the occurence of the various festive days—

I.—NISAN
Spring Equinox, end of March or beginning of April

DAYS
1 New Moon.
14 The preparation for the Passover and the Paschal Sacrifice.
15 First Day of the Feast of Unleavened Bread.
16 Waving of the first ripe Omer.
21 Close of the Passover.

II.—IVAR

DAYS
1 New Moon.
15 'Second' or 'little' Passover.
18 Lag-le-Omer, or the 33rd day in Omer, *i.e.* from the presentation of the first ripe sheaf offered on the 2nd day of the Passover, or the 15th of Nisan.

III.—SIVAN

DAYS
1 New Moon.
6 Feast of Pentecost, or of Weeks—7 weeks, or 50 days after the beginning of the Passover, when the two loaves of first ripe wheat were 'waved,' commemorative also of the giving of the Law on Mount Sinai.

IV.—THAMUS

DAYS
1 New Moon.
17 Fast; taking of Jerusalem on the 9th by Nebuchadnezzar (and on the 17th by Titus). If the 17th occur on a Sabbath, the Fast is kept on the day following.

V.—AB

DAYS
1 New Moon.
9 Fast—(threefold) destruction of the Temple.

VI.—ELUL

DAYS
1 New Moon.

VII.—TISHRI
Beginning of Civil Year
DAYS
1&2 New Year's Feast.
  3 Fast for the murder of Gedaliah.
10 Day of Atonement; Great Fast.
15 Feast of Tabernacles.
21 Close of the above.
22 Octave of the Feast of Tabernacles. (In the Synagogues, on the 23rd, Feast on the annual completion of the Reading of the Law.)

VIII.—MARCHESHVAN OR CHESHVAN
DAYS
  1 New Moon.

IX.—KISLEV
DAYS
  1 New Moon.
25 Feast of the Dedication of the Temple, or of Candles, lasting eight days, in remembrance of the Restoration of the Temple after the victory gained by Judas Maccabeus (B.C. 148) over the Syrians.

X.—TEBETH
DAYS
  1 New Moon.
10 Fast on account of the Siege of Jerusalem.

XI.—SHEBAT
DAYS
  1 New Moon.

XII.—ADAR[9]
DAYS
  1 New Moon.
13 Fast of Esther. If it falls on a Sabbath, kept on the Thursday preceding.
14 Purim, or Feast of Haman.
15 Purim Proper.

---

[9]The *Megillath Taanith* ('roll of fasts'), probably the oldest Aramean post-biblical record preserved (though containing later admixtures), enumerates thirty-five days in the year when fasting, and mostly also public mourning, are *not* allowed. One of these is the day of Herod's death! This interesting historical relic has been critically examined of late by such writers as Derenbourg and Grätz. After their exile the ten tribes, or at least their descendants, seem to have dated from that event (696 B.C.). This appears from inscriptions on tombstones of the Crimean Jews, who have been shown to have descended from the ten tribes. (Comp. Davidson in Kitto's *Cycl.* iii. 1173.)

11
THE PASSOVER

※

> Get rid of the old yeast that you may be a new batch without yeast—as you really are. For Christ, our Passover lamb, has been sacrificed.—1 Cor. 5:7

THE PASSOVER

The LORD's Passover begins at twilight on the fourteenth day of the first month. On the fifteenth day of that month the LORD's Feast of Unleavened Bread begins; for seven days you must eat bread made without yeast (Lev. 23:5–6).

The cycle of Temple-festivals appropriately opens with 'the Passover' and 'Feast of Unleavened Bread.' For, properly speaking, these two are quite distinct (Lev. 23:5, 6; Num. 28:16, 17; 2 Chron. 30:15, 21; Ezra 6:19, 22; Mark 14:1), the 'Passover' taking place on the 14th of Nisan, and the 'Feast of Unleavened Bread' commencing on the 15th, and lasting for seven days, to the 21st of the month (Exod. 12:15). But from their close connection they are generally treated as one, both in the Old and in the New Testament (Matt. 26:17; Mark 14:12; Luke 22:1); and Josephus, on one occasion, even describes it as 'a feast for eight days' (*Antiq.* 2.317; but comp. 3.249; 9.271).

For seven days you are to eat bread made without yeast. On the first day remove the yeast from your houses, for whoever eats anything with yeast in it from the first day through the seventh must be cut off from Israel (Exod. 12:15).

ITS PECULIARITIES

There are peculiarities about the Passover which mark it as the most important, and, indeed, take it out of the rank of the other festivals. It was the first of the three feasts on which all males in Israel were bound to appear before the Lord in the place which He would choose (the two others being the Feast of Weeks and that of Tabernacles—Exod. 23:14; 34:18–23; Lev. 23:4–22; Deut. 16:16). All the three great festivals bore a threefold reference. They pointed, *first*, to the season of the year, or rather to the enjoyment of the fruits of the good land which the Lord had given to His people in possession, but of which he claimed for Himself the real ownership (Lev. 25:23; Ps. 85:1; Isa. 8:8, 14:2; Hos. 9:3). This reference to nature is expressly stated in regard to the Feast of Weeks and that of Tabernacles (Exod. 23:14–16; 34:22), but, though not less distinct, it is omitted in connection with the feast of unleavened bread. On the other hand, great prominence is given to the *historical bearing* of the Passover, while it is not mentioned in the other two festivals, although it could not have been wholly wanting. But the feast of unleavened bread celebrated the one grand event which underlay the whole history of Israel, and marked alike their miraculous deliverance from destruction and from bondage, and the commencement of their existence as a nation. For in the night of the Passover the children of Israel, miraculously preserved and set free, for the first time became a people, and that by the direct interposition of God. The *third* bearing of all the festivals, but especially of the Passover, is typical. Every reader of the New Testament knows how frequent are such allusions to the Exodus, the Paschal Lamb, the Paschal Supper, and the feast of unleavened bread. And that this meaning was intended from the first, not only in reference to the Passover, but to all the feasts, appears from the whole design of the Old Testament, and from the exact correspondence between the types and the antitypes. Indeed, it is, so to speak, impressed upon the Old Testament by a law of internal necessity. For when God bound up the future of all nations in the history of Abraham and his seed (Gen. 12:3), He made that history prophetic; and each event and every rite became, as it were, a bud, destined to open in blossom and ripen into fruit on that tree under the shadow of which all nations were to be gathered.

SPECIAL NATURE OF THE PASSOVER

Thus *nature, history,* and *grace* combined to give a special meaning to the festivals, but chiefly to the Passover. It was the feast of spring; the springtime of nature, when, after the death of winter, the scattered

Three times a year all your men must appear before the LORD your God at the place he will choose: at the Feast of Unleavened Bread, the Feast of Weeks and the Feast of Tabernacles. No man should appear before the LORD empty-handed (Deut. 16:16).

Nations will take them and bring them to their own place. And the house of Israel will possess the nations as menservants and maidservants in the LORD's land. They will make captives of their captors and rule over their oppressors (Isa. 14:2).

Celebrate the Feast of Weeks with the firstfruits of the wheat harvest, and the Feast of Ingathering at the turn of the year (Exod. 34:22).

I will bless those who bless you, and whoever curses you I will curse; and all peoples on earth will be blessed through you (Gen. 12:3).

seeds were born into a new harvest, and the first ripe sheaf could be presented to the Lord; the spring-time of Israel's history, too, when each year the people celebrated anew their national birthday; and the spring-time of grace, their grand national deliverance pointing forward to the birth of the true Israel, and the Passover sacrifice to that 'Lamb of God which taketh away the sin of the world.' Accordingly, the month of the Passover, Abib, or as it was called in later times, Nisan,[1] was to be unto them 'the beginning of months'—the birth-month of the sacred, and at the same time the seventh in the civil, year. Here we mark again the significance of *seven* as the sacred or covenant number. On the other hand, the Feast of Tabernacles, which closed the festive cycle, took place on the 15th of the seventh month of the sacred, which was also the first in the civil, year. Nor is it less significant that both the Passover and the Feast of Tabernacles fell upon the 15th day of the month; that is, at full moon, or when the month had, so to speak, attained its full strength.

ORIGIN OF THE NAME

The name of the Passover, in Hebrew *Pesach*, and in Aramaean and Greek *Pascha,* is derived from a root which means to 'step over,' or to 'overleap,' and thus points back to the historical origin of the festival (Exod. 12). But the circumstances in which the people were placed necessarily rendered its first celebration, in some particulars, different from its later observance, which, so far as possible, was brought into harmony with the general Temple practice. Accordingly, Jewish authorities rightly distinguish between 'the Egyptian' and the 'Permanent Passover.' On its first institution it was ordained that the head of every house should, on the 10th of Nisan, select either a lamb or a kid of the goats, of the first year, and without blemish. Later Jewish ordinances, dating after the return from Babylon, limit it to a lamb; and it is explained that the four days previous to the slaying of the lamb referred

In the twelfth year of King Xerxes, in the first month, the month of Nisan, they cast the pur (that is, the lot) in the presence of Haman to select a day and month. And the lot fell on the twelfth month, the month of Adar (Esth. 3:7).

On that same night I will pass through Egypt and strike down every firstborn—both men and animals —and I will bring judgment on all the gods of Egypt. I am the LORD. The blood will be a sign for you on the houses where you are; and when I see the blood, I will pass over you. No destructive plague will touch you when I strike Egypt (Exod. 12:12–13).

---

[1]Abib is the month of 'sprouting' or of 'green ears.' Esth. 3:7; Neh. 2:1.

to the four generations that had passed after the children of Israel went down into Egypt. The lamb was to be killed on the eve of the 14th, or rather, as the phrase is, 'between the two evenings' (Exod. 12:6; Lev. 23:5; Num. 9:3, 5). According to the Samaritans, the Karaite Jews, and many modern interpreters, this means between actual sunset and complete darkness (or, say, between six and seven P.M.); but from the contemporary testimony of Josephus (*Jew. Wars*, 6.423), and from the Talmudic authorities, there cannot be a doubt that, at the time of our Lord, it was regarded as the interval between the sun's commencing to decline and his actual disappearance. This allows a sufficient period for the numerous lambs which had to be killed, and agrees with the traditional account that on the eve of the Passover the daily evening sacrifice was offered an hour, or, if it fell on a Friday, two hours, before the usual time.

Take care of them until the fourteenth day of the month, when all the people of the community of Israel must slaughter them at twilight (Exod. 12:6).

INSTITUTION OF THE PASSOVER

In the original institution the blood of the sacrifice was to be sprinkled with hyssop on the lintel and the two doorposts of the house, probably as being the most prominent place of entrance. Then the whole animal, without breaking a bone of it, was to be roasted, and eaten by each family—or, if the number of its members were too small, by two neighboring families—along with unleavened bread and bitter herbs, to symbolise the bitterness of their bondage and the haste of their deliverance, and also to point forward to the manner in which the true Israel were in all time to have fellowship in the Paschal Lamb (1 Cor. 5:7, 8). All who were circumcised were to partake of this meal, and that arrayed as for a journey; and whatsoever was not consumed was to be burnt on the spot. These ordinances in regard to the Passover were afterwards modified during the journey in the wilderness to the effect, that all males were to appear 'in the place which the Lord shall choose,' and there alike to sacrifice and to eat the lamb or kid, bringing at the same time also another offering with them (Exod. 34:18–20; Deut. 16:2, 16, 17). Lastly, it was also

Hyssop

ordered that if any man were unclean at the time of the regular Passover, or 'in a journey afar off,' he should celebrate it a month later (Num. 9:9–11).

DIRECTIONS IN THE MISHNAH

The *Mishnah* (*Pes.* ix. 5) contains the following, as the distinctions between the 'Egyptian' and the 'Permanent' Passover: 'The Egyptian Passover was selected on the 10th, and the blood was to be sprinkled with a sprig of hyssop on the lintel and the two door-posts, and it was to be eaten in haste in the first night; but the Permanent Passover is observed all the seven days; *i.e.* the use of unleavened cakes was, on its first observance, enjoined only for that one night, though, from Israel's haste, it must, for several days, have been the only available bread; while afterwards its exclusive use was ordered during the whole week. Similarly, also, the journey of the children of Israel commenced on the 15th of Nisan, while in after-times that day was observed as a festival like a Sabbath (Exod. 12:16; Lev. 23:7; Num. 28:18). To these distinctions the following are also added (*Tos. Pes.* viii): In Egypt the Passover was selected on the 10th, and killed on the 14th, and they did not, on account of the Passover, incur the penalty of 'cutting off,' as in later generations; of the Egyptian Passover it was said, 'Let him and his neighbour next unto his house take it,' while afterwards the Passover-companies might be indiscriminately chosen; in Egypt it was not ordered to sprinkle the blood and burn the fat on the altar, as afterwards; at the first Passover it was said, 'None of you shall go out of the door of his house until the morning,' which did not apply to later times; in Egypt it was slain by every one in his own house, while afterwards it was slain by all Israel in one place; lastly, formerly where they ate the Passover, there they lodged, but afterwards they might eat it in one, and lodge in another place.

SCRIPTURE RECORDS OF THE FEAST

Scripture records that the Passover was kept the second year after the Exodus (Num. 9:1–5), and then

---

Sacrifice as the Passover to the LORD your God an animal from your flock or herd at the place the LORD will choose as a dwelling for his Name (Deut. 16:2).

On the first day hold a sacred assembly, and another one on the seventh day. Do no work at all on these days, except to prepare food for everyone to eat—that is all you may do (Exod. 12:16).

not again till the Israelites actually reached the promised land (Josh. 5:10); but, as the Jewish commentators rightly observe, this intermission was directed by God Himself (Exod. 12:25; 13:5). After that, public celebrations of the Passover are only mentioned once during the reign of Solomon (2 Chron. 8:13), again under that of Hezekiah (2 Chron. 30:15), at the time of Josiah (2 Kgs. 23:21), and once more after the return from Babylon under Ezra (Ezra 6:19). On the other hand, a most significant allusion to the typical meaning of the Passover-blood, as securing immunity from destruction, occurs in the prophecies of Ezekiel (Ezek. 9:4–6), where 'the man clothed with linen' is directed to 'set a mark upon the foreheads' of the godly (like the first Passover-mark), so that they who were to 'slay utterly old and young' might not 'come near any' of them. The same symbolic reference and command occur in the Book of Revelation (Rev. 7:2, 3; 9:4), in regard to those who have been 'sealed as the servants of our God in their foreheads.'

LATER CELEBRATIONS

But the inference that the Passover was only celebrated on the occasions actually mentioned in Scripture seems the less warranted, that in later times it was so punctiliously and universally observed. We can form a sufficiently accurate idea of all the circumstances attending it at the time of our Lord. On the 14th of Nisan every Israelite who was physically able, not in a state of Levitical uncleanness, nor further distant from the city than fifteen miles, was to appear in Jerusalem. Though women were not legally obliged to go up, we know from Scripture (1 Sam. 1:3–7; Luke 2:41, 42), and from the rules laid down by Jewish authorities (Jos. *Wars*, 9.426; and *Mishnah Pes.* ix. 4, for ex.), that such was the common practice. Indeed, it was a joyous time for all Israel. From all parts of the land and from foreign countries the festive pilgrims had come up in bands, singing their pilgrim psalms, and bringing with them burnt- and peace-offerings, according as the Lord had blessed them; for none might appear empty before Him (Exod. 23:15; Deut.

On the evening of the fourteenth day of the month, while camped at Gilgal on the plains of Jericho, the Israelites celebrated the Passover (Josh. 5:10).

When you enter the land that the LORD will give you as he promised, observe this ceremony (Exod. 12:25).

"Go throughout the city of Jerusalem and put a mark on the foreheads of those who grieve and lament over all the detestable things that are done in it." As I listened, he said to the others, "Follow him through the city and kill, without showing pity or compassion. Slaughter old men, young men and maidens, women and children, but do not touch anyone who has the mark. Begin at my sanctuary." So they began with the elders who were in front of the temple (Ezek. 9:4–6).

Do not harm the land or the sea or the trees until we put a seal on the foreheads of the servants of our God (Rev. 7:3).

Every year his parents went to Jerusalem for the Feast of the Passover. When he was twelve years old, they went up to the Feast, according to the custom (Luke 2:41–42).

Celebrate the Feast of Unleavened Bread; for seven days eat bread made without yeast, as I commanded you. Do this at the appointed time in the month of Abib, for in that month you came out of Egypt.

No one is to appear before me empty-handed (Exod. 23:15).

16:16, 17). How large the number of worshippers was, may be gathered from Josephus, who records that, when Cestius requested the high-priest to make a census, in order to convince Nero of the importance of Jerusalem and of the Jewish nation, the number of lambs slain was found to be 256,500, which, at the lowest computation of ten persons to every sacrificial lamb, would give a population of 2,565,000, or, as Josephus himself puts it, 2,700,200 persons, while on an earlier occasion (A.D. 65) he computes the number present at not fewer than three millions (*Jew. Wars,* 6.425; 2.280).[2] Of course, many of these pilgrims must have camped outside the city walls.[3] Those who lodged within the walls were gratuitously accommodated, and in return left to their hosts the skins of the Passover lambs and the vessels which they had used in their sacred services. In such festive 'company' the parents of Jesus went to, and returned from this feast 'every year,' taking their 'holy child' with them, after He had attained the age of twelve—strictly in accordance with Rabbinical law (*Yoma,* 82a)—when He remained behind, 'sitting in the midst of the doctors,

Jesus at twelve years of age on his way to Jerusalem

[2]These computations, being derived from official documents, can scarcely have been much exaggerated. Indeed, Josephus expressly guards himself against this charge.

[3]It is deeply interesting that the Talmud (*Pes.* 53) specially mentions Bethphage and Bethany as celebrated for their hospitality towards the festive pilgrims.

both hearing them and asking them questions' (Luke 2:41–49). We know that the Lord Himself afterwards attended the Paschal feast, and that on the last occasion He was hospitably entertained in Jerusalem, apparently by a disciple (Matt. 26:18; Mark 14:12–16; Luke 22:7–13), although He seems to have intended spending the night outside the city walls (Matt. 26:30, 36; Mark 14:26, 32; Luke 22:39; John 18:1).

THE PREPARATIONS FOR THE PASSOVER

But the preparations for the Passover had begun long before the 14th of Nisan. Already a month previously (on the 15th of Adar), bridges and roads had been repaired for the use of the pilgrims. That was also the time for administering the testing draught to women suspected of adultery, for burning the red heifer, and for boring the ears of those who wished to remain in servitude—in short, for making all kinds of preliminary arrangements before the festive season began. One of these is specially interesting as recalling the words of the Saviour. In general, cemeteries were outside the cities; but any dead body found in the field was (according to an ordinance which tradition traces up to Joshua) to be buried on the spot where it had been discovered. Now, as the festive pilgrims might have contracted 'uncleanness' by unwitting contact with such graves, it was ordered that all 'sepulchres' should be 'whitened' a month before the Passover. It was, therefore, evidently in reference to what He actually saw going on around Him at the time He spoke, that Jesus compared the Pharisees 'unto whited sepulchres, which indeed appear beautiful outward, but are within full of dead men's bones, and of all uncleanness' (Matt. 23:27). Then, two weeks before Pesach, and at the corresponding time before the other two great festivals, the flocks and herds were to be tithed, and also the Temple treasury-chests publicly opened and emptied. Lastly, we know that 'many went out of the country up to Jerusalem before the Passover to purify themselves' (John 11:55). It is this practice which finds its spiritual application in regard to the better Passover, when, in the words of

Go into the city to a certain man and tell him, "The Teacher says: My appointed time is near. I am going to celebrate the Passover with my disciples at your house" (Matt. 26:18).

St. Paul (1 Cor. 11:27, 28), 'whosoever shall eat this bread, and drink this cup of the Lord, unworthily, shall be guilty of the body and blood of the Lord. But let a man examine himself, and so let him eat of that bread, and drink of that cup.'

Tell the whole community of Israel that on the tenth day of this month each man is to take a lamb for his family, one for each household (Exod. 12:3).

Then the Jews led Jesus from Caiaphas to the palace of the Roman governor. By now it was early morning, and to avoid ceremonial uncleanness the Jews did not enter the palace; they wanted to be able to eat the Passover (John 18:28).

The [freewill] festal-offering may be taken from the sheep or from the oxen, from the lambs or from the goats, from the males or from the females, and consumed during two days and one night (Mishnah, Pesaḥim vi.4).

THE CUSTOM OF MODERN DAYS

The modern synagogue designates the Sabbath before the Passover as 'the Great Sabbath,' and prescribes particular prayers and special instruction with a view to the coming festival. For, according to Jewish tradition, at the original institution of the Passover (Exod. 12:3), the 10th of Nisan, on which the sacrifice was to be selected, had fallen on a Sabbath. But there is no evidence that either the name or the observance of this 'Great Sabbath' had been in use at the time of our Lord, although it was enjoined to teach the people in the various synagogues about the Passover during the month which preceded the festival. There is also a significant tradition that some were wont to select their sacrificial lamb four days before the Passover, and to keep it tied in a prominent place within view, so as constantly to remind them of the coming service.

THE THREE THINGS

We have already explained that according to the Rabbis (*Chag.* ii. 1; vi. 2), three things were implied in the festive command to 'appear before the Lord'— 'Presence,' the 'Chagigah,' and 'Joyousness.' As specially applied to the Passover, the first of these terms meant, that every one was to come up to Jerusalem and to offer a burnt-offering, if possible on the first, or else on one of the other six days of the feast. This burnt-offering was to be taken only from 'Cholin' (or profane substance), that is, from such as did not otherwise belong to the Lord, either as tithes, firstlings, or things devoted, etc. The Chagigah, which was strictly a peace-offering, might be twofold. The first Chagigah was offered on the 14th of Nisan, the day of the Paschal sacrifice, and formed afterwards part of the Paschal Supper. The second Chagigah was offered on the 15th of Nisan, or the first day of the feast of unleavened bread. It is this second Chagigah which the Jews were afraid they might be unable to eat, if they contracted defilement in the judgment-hall of Pilate (John 18:28). In reference to the first Chagigah, the *Mishnah* lays down the rule, that it was only to be offered if the Paschal day fell on a week-day, not on a Sabbath, and if the Paschal lamb alone would not have been sufficient to give a satisfying supper to the company which gathered around it (*Pes.* vi. 4). As in the case of all other peace-offerings, part of this Chagigah might be kept, though not for longer than one night and two days from its sacrifice. Being a voluntary offering, it was lawful to bring it from sacred things (such as tithes of the flock). But the Chagigah for the 15th of Nisan was obligatory, and had therefore to be brought from 'Cholin.' The third duty incumbent on those who appeared at the feast was 'joyousness.' This expression, as we have seen, simply referred to the fact that, according to their means, all Israel were, during the course of this festival, with joyous heart to offer peace-offerings, which might be chosen from sacred things (Deut. 27:7). Thus the sacrifices which every Israelite was to offer at the Passover were, besides his share in the Paschal lamb, a burnt-offering, the Chagigah (one or two), and offerings of joyousness—all as God had blessed each household. As stated in a previous chapter, all the twenty-four courses, into which the priests were arranged, ministered in the Temple on this, as on the other great festivals, and they distributed among themselves alike what fell to them of the festive sacrifices and the shewbread. But the course which, in its proper order, was on duty for the week, alone offered all votive and voluntary, and the public sacrifices for the whole congregation, such as those of the morning and the evening (*Succah* v. 7).

The Course of priests whose time of service was determined [for that week] offered the Daily Whole-offerings, vow-offerings, freewill-offerings, and all other offerings of the congregation; it offered them all (Mishnah, Sukka v.7).

Special Preparations

The special preparations for the Passover commenced on the evening of the 13th of Nisan, with which, according to Jewish reckoning, the 14th began, the day being always computed from evening

*At that time I will search
Jerusalem with lamps
and punish those who are
complacent,
who are like wine left on
its dregs,
who think, "The Lord will
do nothing,
either good or bad"
(Zeph. 1:12).*

to evening.[4] Then the head of the house was to search with a lighted candle all places where leaven was usually kept, and to put what of it he found in the house in a safe place, whence no portion could be carried away by any accident. Before doing this, he prayed: 'Blessed art Thou, Jehovah, our God, King of the Universe, who hast sanctified us by Thy commandments, and commanded us to remove the leaven.' And after it he said: 'All the leaven that is in my possession, that which I have seen and that which I have not seen, be it null, be it accounted as the dust of the earth.' The search itself was to be accomplished in perfect silence and with a lighted candle. To this search the apostle may have referred in the admonition to 'purge out the old leaven' (1 Cor. 5:7). Jewish tradition sees a reference to this search with candles in Zeph. 1:12: 'And it shall come to pass at that time that I will search Jerusalem with candles.' If the leaven had not been removed on the evening of the 13th, it might still be done on the forenoon of the 14th of Nisan. The question what substances constituted leaven was thus solved. The unleavened cakes, which were to be the only bread using during the feast, might be made of these five kinds of grain—wheat, barley, spelt, oats, and rye—the cakes being prepared before fermentation had begun. Anything prepared of these five kinds of grains—but only of these—would come within range of the term 'leaven,' that is, if kneaded with water, but not if made with any other fluid, such as fruit-liquor, etc.

[4]The article in Kitto's *Cycl.* (3rd edition), vol. iii, p. 425, calls this day, 'the preparation for the Passover,' and confounds it with John 19:14. But from the evening of the 14th to that of the 15th is never called in Jewish writings 'the preparation for,' but 'the eve of, the Passover.' Moreover, the period described in John 19:14 was after, not before, the Passover. Dean Alford's notes on this passage, and on Matt. 26:17, suggest a number of needless difficulties, and contain inaccuracies, due to a want of sufficient knowledge of Hebrew authorities. In attempting an accurate chronology of these days, it must always be remembered that the Passover was sacrificed between the evenings of the 14th and 15th of Nisan; that is, before the close of the 14th and the beginning of the 15th. The Paschal Supper, however, took place on the 15th itself (that is, according to Jewish reckoning—the day beginning as the first stars become visible). 'The preparation' in John 19:14 means, as in verse 31, the preparation-day for the Sabbath, and the 'Passover,' as in 18:39, the whole Paschal week.

TIME OF ITS COMMENCEMENT

Early on the forenoon of the 14th of Nisan the feast of the Passover may be said to have begun. In Galilee, no work was done all that day; in Judaea it was continued till mid-day; the rule, however, being that no new work was to be commenced, though that which was in hand might be carried on. The only exception to this was in the case of tailors, barbers, and those engaged in the laundry. Even earlier than mid-day of the 14th it was no longer lawful to eat leaven. The strictest opinion fixes ten o'clock as the latest hour when leaven might be eaten, the more lax eleven. From that hour to twelve o'clock it was required to abstain from leaven, while at twelve it was to be solemnly destroyed, either by burning, immersing it in water, or scattering it to the winds. To secure strict obedience and uniformity, the exact time for abstaining from and for destroying the leaven was thus made known: 'They laid two desecrated cakes of a thank-offering on a bench in the porch (of the Temple). So long as they lay there, all the people might eat (leavened); when one of them was removed, they abstained from eating, but they did not burn (the leaven); when both were removed, all the people burnt (the leaven)' (*Pes.* i. 5).

Women grinding corn

CHOICE OF THE LAMB

The next care was to select a proper Paschal lamb, which, of course, must be free from all blemish, and neither less than eight days, nor more than exactly one year, old. Each Paschal lamb was to serve for a 'company,' which was to consist of not less than ten, nor more than twenty persons. The company at the 'Lord's Passover Supper' consisted of Himself and His disciples. Two of them, Peter and John, the Master had sent early forward to 'prepare the Passover,' that is, to see to all that was needful for the due observance of the Paschal Supper, especially the purchase and sacrifice of the Paschal lamb. Probably they may have purchased it in the Holy City, though not, as in the majority of cases, within the Temple-court itself, where a brisk and very profitable traffic in all such offerings

Jesus cleansing the Temple

Jesus entered the temple area and drove out all who were buying and selling there. He overturned the tables of the money changers and the benches of those selling doves. "It is written," he said to them, " 'My house will be called a house of prayer,' but you are making it a 'den of robbers' " (Matt. 21:12–13).

was carried on by the priests. For against this the Lord Jesus had inveighed only a few days before, when he 'cast out all them that sold and bought in the Temple, and overthrew the tables of the money-changers' (Matt. 21:12, 13), to the astonishment and indignation of those who would intensely resent His interference with their authority and gains (John 2:13–18).

SLAYING OF THE LAMB

While the Saviour still tarried with the other disciples outside the city, Peter and John were completing their preparations. They followed the motley crowd, all leading their sacrificial lambs up the Temple-mount. Here they were grouped into three divisions. Already the evening sacrifice had been offered. Ordinarily it was slain at 2.30 P.M., and offered at about 3.30. But on the eve of the Passover, as we have seen, it was killed an hour earlier; and if the 14th of Nisan fell on a Friday—or rather from Thursday at eve to Friday at eve—two hours earlier, so as to avoid any needless breach of the Sabbath. On the occasion to which we refer the evening sacrifice had been slain at 1.30, and offered at 2.30. But before the incense was burned or the lamps were trimmed, the Paschal sacrifice had to be offered.[5] It was done on this wise:—The first of the three festive divisions, with their Paschal lambs, was admitted within the Court of the Priests. Each division must consist of not less than thirty persons (3 x 10, the symbolic number of the Divine and of completeness). Immediately the massive gates were closed behind them. The priests drew a threefold blast from their silver trumpets when the Passover was slain. Altogether the scene was most impressive. All along the Court up to the altar of burnt-offering priests stood in two rows, the one holding golden, the other silver bowls. In these the blood of the Paschal lambs, which each Israelite slew for himself (as representative of his company at the Paschal Supper), was caught up by a priest, who handed it to his colleague, receiving back an empty bowl, and so the bowls with the blood were passed up to the priest at the altar, who jerked it in one jet at the base of the altar. While this was going on, a most solemn 'hymn' of praise was raised, the Levites leading in song, and the offerers either repeating after them or merely responding. Every first line of a Psalm was repeated by the people, while to each of the others they responded by a 'Hallelujah,' or 'Praise ye the Lord.' This service of song consisted of the so-called 'Hallel,' which comprised Psalm 113 to 118. Thus—

The Levites began: *'Hallelu Jah'* (Praise ye the Lord).

The people repeated: *'Hallelu Jah.'*

The Levites: 'Praise (*Hallelu*), O ye servants of Jehovah.'

The people responded: *'Hallelu Jah.'*

The Levites: 'Praise (*Hallelu*) the name of Jehovah.'

The people responded: *'Hallelu Jah.'*

Similarly, when Ps. 113 had been finished— Ps. 114.

Praise the LORD. *Praise, O servants of the* LORD, *praise the name of the* LORD. *Let the name of the* LORD *be praised, both now and forevermore. From the rising of the sun to the place where it sets, the name of the* LORD *is to be praised (Ps. 113:1–3).*

---

[5]According to the Talmud, 'the daily (evening) sacrifice precedes that of the Paschal lamb; the Paschal lamb the burning of the incense; the incense the trimming of the lamps' (for the night).

The Levites: 'When Israel went out of Egypt.'

The people repeated: 'When Israel went out of Egypt.'

The Levites: 'The house of Jacob from a people of strange language.'

The people responded: *'Hallelu Jah.'*

And in the same manner, repeating each first line and responding at the rest, till they came to Ps. 118, when, besides the first, these three lines were also repeated by the people (verses 25, 26):

'Save now, I beseech Thee, Jehovah.'

'O Jehovah, I beseech Thee, send now prosperity;' and

'Blessed be He that cometh in the name of Jehovah.'

May it not be that to this solemn and impressive 'hymn' corresponds the Alleluia song of the redeemed Church in heaven, as described in Rev. 19:1, 3, 4, 6?

THE 'HALLEL'

The singing of the 'Hallel' at the Passover dates from very remote antiquity. The Talmud dwells on its peculiar suitableness for the purpose, since it not only recorded the goodness of God towards Israel, but especially their deliverance from Egypt, and therefore appropriately opened (Ps. 113) with 'Praise ye Jehovah, ye servants of Jehovah'—and no longer of Pharaoh. Hence also this 'Hallel' is called the Egyptian, or 'the Common,' to distinguish it from the great 'Hallel', sung on very rare occasions, which comprised Psalms 120 to 136. According to the Talmud, the 'Hallel' recorded five things: 'The coming out of Egypt, the dividing of the sea, the giving out of the law, the resurrection of the dead, and the lot of the Messiah.' The Egyptian 'Hallel,' it may here be added, was altogether sung on eighteen days and on one night in the year. These eighteen days were, that of the Passover sacrifice, the Feast of Pentecost, and each of the eight days of the Feasts of Tabernacles and of the Dedication of the Temple. The only night in which it was recited was that of the Paschal Supper,

---

Give thanks to the LORD, for he is good; his love endures forever. Let Israel say: "His love endures forever." Let the house of Aaron say: "His love endures forever." Let those who fear the LORD say: "His love endures forever" (Ps. 118:1–4).

After this I heard what sounded like the roar of a great multitude in heaven shouting:
"Hallelujah!
Salvation and glory and power belong to our God" (Rev. 19:1).

when it was sung by every Paschal company in their houses, in a manner which will hereafter be explained.

COMPLETION OF THE SACRIFICE

If the 'Hallel' had been finished before the service of one division was completed, it was repeated a second and, if needful, even a third time. The *Mishnah* remarks, that as the Great Court was crowded by the first two divisions, it rarely happened that they got further than Ps. 116 before the services of the third division were completed. Next, the sacrifices were hung up on hooks along the Court, or laid on staves which rested on the shoulders of two men (on Sabbaths they were not laid on staves), then flayed, the entrails taken out and cleansed, and the inside fat separated, put in a dish, salted, and placed on the fire of the altar of burnt-offering. This completed the sacrifice. The first division of offerers being dismissed, the second entered, and finally the third, the service being in each case conducted in precisely the same manner. Then the whole service concluded by burning the incense and trimming the lamps for the night.

I call on the LORD in my distress, and he answers me. Save me, O LORD, from lying lips and from deceitful tongues (Ps. 120:1–2).

When all had been finished in the Temple, the priests washed the Great Court, in which so much sacrificial blood had been shed. But this was not done if the Passover had been slain on the Sabbath. In that case, also, the three divisions waited—the first in the Court of the Gentiles, the second on the Chel, and the third in the Great Court—so as not needlessly to carry their burdens on the Sabbath.

But, as a general rule, the religious services of the Passover, like all positive religious injunctions, 'made void the Sabbath.' In other respects the Passover, or rather the 15th of Nisan, was to be observed like a Sabbath, no manner of work being allowed. There was, however, one most important exception to this rule. It was permitted to prepare the necessary articles of food on the 15th of Nisan. This explains how the words of Jesus to Judas during the Paschal (not the Lord's) Supper could be misunderstood by the disciples as implying that Judas, 'who

Jerusalem in her glory

had the bag,' was to 'buy those things' that they had 'need of against the feast' (John 13:29).

Since Judas had charge of the money, some thought Jesus was telling him to buy what was needed for the Feast, or to give something to the poor (John 13:29).

OUR LORD'S CELEBRATION OF THE FEAST

It was probably as the sun was beginning to decline in the horizon that Jesus and the other ten disciples descended once more over the Mount of Olives into the Holy City. Before them lay Jerusalem in her festive attire. All around pilgrims were hastening towards it. White tents dotted the sward, gay with the bright flowers of early spring, or peered out from the gardens and the darker foliage of the olive plantations. From the gorgeous Temple buildings, dazzling in their snow-white marble and gold, on which the slanting rays of the sun were reflected, rose the smoke of the altar of burnt-offering. These courts were now crowded with eager worshippers, offering for the last time, in the real sense, their Paschal lambs. The streets must have been thronged with strangers, and the flat roofs covered with eager gazers, who either feasted their eyes with a first sight of the Sacred City for which they had so often longed, or else once more rejoiced in view of the well-remembered localities. It was the last day-view which the Lord had of the Holy City—till His resurrection! Only once more in the approaching night of His betrayal was He to look upon it in the pale light of the full moon. He was going forward to 'accomplish His death' in Jerusalem; to fulfil type and prophecy, and to offer Himself up as the true Passover Lamb—'the Lamb of God, which taketh away the sin of the world.' They who followed Him were busy with many thoughts. They knew that terrible events awaited them, and they had only a few days before being told that these glorious Temple-buildings, to which, with a national pride not unnatural, they had directed the attention of their Master, were to become desolate, not one stone being left upon the other. Among them, revolving his dark plans, and goaded on by the great Enemy, moved the betrayer. And now they were within the city. Its Temple, its royal bridge, its splendid palaces, its busy marts, its streets filled with festive pilgrims, were well known to them, as they made their way to the house where the guest-chamber had been prepared for them. Meanwhile the crowd came down from the Temple-mount, each bearing on his shoulders the sacrificial lamb, to make ready for the Paschal Supper.

The next day John saw Jesus coming toward him and said, "Look, the Lamb of God, who takes away the sin of the world!" (John 1:29).

12

THE PASCHAL FEAST AND
THE LORD'S SUPPER

While they were eating, Jesus took bread, gave thanks and broke it, and gave it to his disciples, saying, "Take and eat; this is my body." Then he took the cup, gave thanks and offered it to them, saying, "Drink from it, all of you. This is my blood of the covenant, which is poured out for many for the forgiveness of sins."—Matthew 26:26-28

As the sun was setting, Abram fell into a deep sleep, and a thick and dreadful darkness came over him...On that day the LORD made a covenant with Abram and said, "To your descendants I give this land..." (Gen 15:12, 18).

JEWISH TRADITIONS ABOUT THE PASSOVER

Jewish tradition has this curious conceit: that the most important events in Israel's history were connected with the Paschal season. Thus it is said to have been on the present Paschal night that, after his sacrifice, the 'horror of great darkness' fell upon Abraham when God revealed to him the future of his race (Gen. 15). Similarly, it is supposed to have been at Passover time that the patriarch entertained his heavenly guests, that Sodom was destroyed and Lot escaped, and that the walls of Jericho fell before the Lord. More than that—the 'cake of barley bread' seen in the dream, which led to the destruction of Midian's host, had been prepared from the Omer, presented on the second day of the feast of unleavened bread; just as at a later period alike the captains of Sennacherib and the King of Assyria, who tarried at Nob, were overtaken by the hand of God at the Passover season. It was at the Paschal time also that the mysterious handwriting appeared on the wall to declare Babylon's doom, and again at the Passover that Esther and the Jews fasted, and that wicked Haman perished. And so also in the last days it would

Gideon arrived just as a man was telling a friend his dream. "I had a dream," he was saying. "A round loaf of barley bread came tumbling into the Midianite camp. It struck the tent with such force that the tent overturned and collapsed" (Judg. 7:13).

be the Paschal night when the final judgments should
come upon 'Edom,' and the glorious deliverance of
Israel take place. Hence to this day, in every Jewish
home, at a certain part of the Paschal service—just
after the 'third cup,' or the 'cup of blessing,' has been
drunk—the door is opened to admit Elijah the
prophet as forerunner of the Messiah, while appropriate passages are at the same time read which fore-
tell the destruction of all heathen nations (Ps. 79:6;
69:25; Lam. 3:66). It is a remarkable coincidence that,
in instituting His own Supper, the Lord Jesus connected the symbol, not of judgment, but of His dying
love, with the 'third cup.' But, in general, it may be
interesting to know that no other service contains
within the same space the like ardent aspirations after
a return to Jerusalem and the rebuilding of the Temple,
nor so many allusions to the Messianic hope, as the
liturgy for the night of the Passover now in use among
the Jews.

*Pour out your wrath on
the nations
that do not acknowledge
you,
on the kingdoms
that do not call on your
name (Ps. 79:6).*

*Pursue them in anger and
destroy them
from under the heavens
of the LORD
(Lam. 3:66).*

If we could only believe that the prayers and
ceremonies which it embodies were the same as those
at the time of our Lord, we should have it in our
power to picture in minutest detail all that took place
when He instituted His own Supper. We should see
the Master as he presided among the festive company
of His disciples, know what prayers He uttered, and at
what special parts of the service, and be able to repro-
duce the arrangement of the Paschal table around
which they sat.

THE MODERN CEREMONIES

At present and for many centuries back the
Paschal Supper has been thus laid out: three large
unleavened cakes, wrapped in the folds of a napkin,
are placed on a salver, and on them the seven articles
necessary for the 'Passover Supper' are ranged in this
manner:

A roasted Egg.		*Roasted Shankbone of a Lamb.*
(Instead of the 14th day *Chagigah*.)		(Instead of the Paschal Lamb.)
Charoseth.	*Bitter Herbs.*	*Lettuce.*
(To represent the mortar of Egypt.)		
Salt Water.		*Chervil and Parsley.*

PRESENT RITUAL NOT THE SAME AS
THE NEW TESTAMENT TIMES

But, unfortunately, the analogy does not hold good. As the present Passover liturgy contains comparatively very few relics from New Testament times, so also the present arrangement of the Pascal table evidently dates from a time when sacrifices had ceased. On the other hand, however, by far the greater number of the usages observed in our own days are precisely the same as eighteen hundred years ago. A feeling, not of gratified curiosity, but of holy awe, comes over us, as thus we are able to pass back through those many centuries into the upper chamber where the Lord Jesus partook of that Passover which, with the loving desire of a Saviour's heart, He had desired to eat with His disciples. The leading incidents of the feast are all vividly before us—the handing of 'the sop dipped in the dish,' 'the breaking of bread,' 'the giving thanks,' 'the distributing of the cup,' and 'the concluding hymn.' Even the exact posture at the Supper is known to us. But the words associated with those sacred memories come with a strange sound when we find in Rabbinical writings the 'Passover lamb'[1] designated as 'His body,' or when our special attention is called to the cup known as 'the cup of blessing, which we bless;' nay, when the very term for the Passover liturgy itself, the 'Haggadah,'[2] which means 'showing forth,' is exactly the same as that used by St. Paul in describing the service of the Lord's Supper! (1 Cor. 11:23–29).

For I received from the Lord what I also passed on to you: The Lord Jesus, on the night he was betrayed, took bread, and when he had given thanks, he broke it and said, "This is my body, which is for you; do this in remembrance of me." In the same way, after supper he took the cup, saying, "This cup is the new covenant in my blood; do this, whenever you drink it, in remembrance of me." For whenever you eat this bread and drink this cup, you proclaim the Lord's death until he comes (1 Cor. 11:23–26).

THE ROASTING OF THE LAMB

Before proceeding further we may state that, according to Jewish ordinance, the Paschal lamb was roasted on a spit made of pomegranate wood, the spit passing right through from mouth to vent. Special care was to be taken that in roasting the lamb did not touch the oven, otherwise the part touched had to be

---

[1]The words of the *Mishnah* (*Pes.* x. 3) are: 'While the Sanctuary stood, they brought before him his body of (or for) the Passover.' The term 'body' also sometimes means 'substance.'

[2]The same root as employed in Exod. 13:8: 'And thou shalt show thy son in that day,' and from this the term 'Haggadah' has unquestionably been derived.

cut away. This can scarcely be regarded as an instance
of Rabbinical punctiliousness. It was intended to
carry out the idea that the lamb was to be undefiled
by any contact with foreign matter, which might otherwise have adhered to it. For everything here was
significant, and the slightest deviation would mar the
harmony of the whole. If it had been said, that not a
bone of the Paschal lamb was to be broken, that it was
not to be 'sodden at all with water, but roast with
fire[3]—his head with his legs, and with the purtenance
thereof,' and that none of it was to 'remain until the
morning,' all that had not been eaten being burnt
with fire (Exod. 12:8–10)—such ordinances had each a
typical object. Of all other sacrifices, even the most holy
(Lev. 6:21), it alone as not to be 'sodden,' because the
flesh must remain pure, without the admixture even
of water. Then, no bone of the lamb was to be broken:
it was to be served up entire—none of it was to be left
over; and those who gathered around it were to form
one family. All this was intended to express that it was
to be a complete and unbroken sacrifice, on the ground
of which there was complete and unbroken fellowship with the God who had passed by the blood-
sprinkled doors, and with those who together formed
but one family and one body. 'The cup of blessing
which we bless, is it not the communion of the blood
of Christ? The bread which we break, is it not the
communion of the body of Christ? For we, being
many, are one bread and one body; for we are all
partakers of that one bread' (1 Cor. 10:16, 17).

Do not eat the meat raw or cooked in water, but roast it over the fire—head, legs and inner parts. Do not leave any of it till morning; if some is left till morning, you must burn it (Exod. 12:9–10).

DISTINCT FROM ALL LEVITICAL SACRIFICES

Such views and feelings, which, no doubt, all
truly spiritual Israelites shared, gave its meaning to
the Paschal feast at which Jesus sat down with His
disciples, and which He transformed into the Lord's
Supper by linking it to His Person and Work. Every
sacrifice, indeed, had prefigured His Work; but none
other could so suitably commemorate His death, nor
yet the great deliverance connected with it, and the

---

[3]This could certainly have borne no reference to the haste of the Exodus.

Then he sent young Israelite men, and they offered burnt offerings and sacrificed young bulls as fellowship offerings to the LORD. Moses took half of the blood and put it in bowls, and the other half he sprinkled on the altar. Then he took the Book of the Covenant and read it to the people. They responded, "We will do everything the LORD has said; we will obey."

Moses then took the blood, sprinkled it on the people and said, "This is the blood of the covenant that the LORD has made with you in accordance with all these words" (Exod. 24:5–8).

great union and fellowship flowing from it. For other reasons also it was specially suited to be typical of Christ. It was a sacrifice, and yet quite out of the order of all Levitical sacrifices. For it had been instituted and observed before Levitical sacrifices existed; before the Law was given; nay, before the Covenant was ratified by blood (Exod. 24). In a sense, it may be said to have been the cause of all the later sacrifices of the Law, and of the Covenant itself. Lastly, it belonged neither to one nor to another class of sacrifices; it was neither exactly a sin-offering nor a peace-offering, but combined them both. And yet in many respects it quite differed from them. In short, just as the priesthood of Christ was a real Old Testament priesthood, yet not after the order of Aaron, but after the earlier, prophetic, and royal order of Melchisedek, so the sacrifice also of Christ was a real Old Testament sacrifice, yet not after the order of Levitical sacrifices, but after that of the earlier prophetic Passover sacrifice, by which Israel had become a royal nation.

GUESTS OF THE PASCHAL TABLE

As the guests[4] gathered around the Paschal table, they came no longer, as at the first celebration, with their 'loins girded,' with shoes on their feet, and a staff in their hand—that is, as travellers waiting to take their departure. On the contrary, they were arrayed in their best festive garments, joyous and at rest, as became the children of a king. To express this idea the Rabbis also insisted that the Paschal Supper—or at least part of it—must be eaten in that recumbent position with which we are familiar from the New Testament. 'For,' say they, 'they use this leaning posture, as free men do, in memorial of their freedom.' And, again, 'Because it is the manner of slaves to eat standing, therefore now they eat sitting and leaning, in order to show that they have been delivered from bondage into freedom.' And, finally: 'No, not the poorest in Israel may eat till he has sat down, leaning.' But, though it was deemed desirable

---

[4]The Karaites are alone in not admitting women to the Paschal Supper.

to 'sit leaning' during the whole Paschal Supper, it was only absolutely enjoined while partaking of the bread and the wine. This recumbent posture so far resembled that still common in the East, that the body rested on the feet. Hence, also, the penitent woman at the feast given by Simon is said to have 'stood at His feet, behind,' 'weeping' (Luke 7:38). At the same time, the left elbow was placed on the table, and the head rested on the hand, sufficient room being of course left between each guest for the free movements of the right hand. This explains in what sense John 'was leaning on Jesus' bosom,' and afterwards 'lying on Jesus' breast,' when he bent back to speak to Him (John 13:23, 25).

Wine bearers

THE USE OF WINE

The use of wine in the Paschal Supper,[5] though not mentioned in the Law, was strictly enjoined by tradition. According to the Jerusalem Talmud, it was intended to express Israel's joy on the Paschal night, and even the poorest must have 'at least four cups, though he were to receive the money for it from the poor's box' (*Pes.* x. 1). If he cannot otherwise obtain it, the Talmud adds, 'he must sell or pawn his coat, or hire himself out for these four cups of wine.' The same authority variously accounts for the number *four* as either corresponding to the four words used about Israel's redemption (bringing out, delivering, redeeming, taking), or to the fourfold mention of the cup in connection with the chief butler's dream (Gen. 40:9–15) or to the four cups of vengeance which God would in the future give the nations to drink (Jer. 25:15; 51:7; Ps. 75:8; 11:6), while four cups of consolation would be handed to Israel, as it is written: 'The Lord is the portion of my cup' (Ps. 16:5); 'My cup runneth over' (Ps. 23:5); 'I will take the cup of salvation' (Ps. 116:13), 'which,' it is added, 'was two'— perhaps from a second allusion to it in verse 17. In

One of them, the disciple whom Jesus loved, was reclining next to him. Simon Peter motioned to this disciple and said, "Ask him which one he means."
Leaning back against Jesus, he asked him, "Lord, who is it?"
(John 13:23–25).

---

[5]Every reader of the Bible knows how symbolically significant alike the vine and its fruit are throughout Scripture. Over the entrance to the Sanctuary a golden vine of immense proportions was suspended.

connection with this the following parabolic story from the Talmud may possess some interest: 'The holy and blessed God will make a feast for the righteous in the day that His mercy shall be shown to the seed of Israel. After they have eaten and drunk, they give the cup of blessing to Abraham our father. But he saith: I cannot bless it, because Ishmael came from me. Then he gives it to Isaac. But he saith: I cannot bless it, because Esau came from me. Then he hands it to Jacob. But he saith: I cannot take it, because I married two sisters, which is forbidden in the Law. He saith to Moses: Take it and bless it. But he replies: I cannot, because I was not counted worthy to come into the land of Israel, either alive or dead. He saith to Joshua: Take it and bless it. But he answers: I cannot, because I have no son. He saith to David: Take it and bless it. And he replies: I will bless it, and it is fit for me to do so, as it is written, "I will take the cup of salvation, and call upon the name of the Lord." '

This is what the LORD, the God of Israel, said to me: "Take from my hand this cup filled with the wine of my wrath and make all the nations to whom I send you drink it" (Jer. 25:15).

THE MISHNAH ACCOUNT

As detailed in the earliest Jewish record of ordinances—the *Mishnah*—the service of the Paschal Supper was exceedingly simple. Indeed, the impression left on the mind is, that, while all the observances were fixed, the prayers, with some exceptions preserved to us, were free. Rabbi Gamaliel, the teacher of St. Paul, said (*Pes.* x. 15): 'Whoever does not explain three things in the Passover has not fulfilled the duty incumbent on him. These three things are: the Passover lamb, the unleavened bread, and the bitter herbs. *The Passover lamb* means that God passed over the blood-sprinkled place on the houses of our fathers in Egypt; *the unleavened bread* means that our fathers were delivered out of Egypt (in haste); and *the bitter herbs* mean that the Egyptians made bitter the lives of our fathers in Egypt.' A few additional particulars are necessary to enable the reader to understand all the arrangements of the Paschal Supper. From the time of the evening-sacrifice nothing was to be eaten till the Paschal Supper, so that all might come to it with relish (*Pes.* x. 1). It is a moot point, whether at the time of our Lord two, or, as at present, three, large cakes of unleavened bread were used in the service. The *Mishnah* mentions (*Pes.* ii. 6) these five kinds as falling within the designation of 'bitter herbs,' viz. lettuce, endive, succory (garden endive?), what is called 'Charchavina' (*urtica,* beets?), and horehound (bitter coriander?). The 'bitter herbs' seem to have been twice partaken of during the service, once dipped in salt water or vinegar, and a second time with Charoseth, a compound of dates, raisins, etc., and vinegar, though the *Mishnah* expressly declares (*Pes.* x. 3) that Charoseth was not obligatory. Red wine alone was to be used at the Paschal Supper, and always mixed with water.[6] Each of the four cups must contain at least the fourth of a quarter of an hin (the hin equals one gallon two pints). Lastly, it was a principle that, after the Paschal meal, they had no *Aphikomen* (afterdish), an expression which may perhaps best be rendered by 'dessert.'

That same night they are to eat the meat roasted over the fire, along with bitter herbs, and bread made without yeast (Exod. 12:8).

Celebrate the Feast of Unleavened Bread, because it was on this very day that I brought your divisions out of Egypt. Celebrate this day as a lasting ordinance for the generations to come (Exod. 12:17).

THE 'GIVING THANKS'

The Paschal Supper itself commenced by the head of 'the company' taking the first cup of wine in his hand, and 'giving thanks' over it in these words: 'Blessed art Thou, Jehovah our God, who hast created the fruit of the vine! Blessed art Thou, Jehovah our God, King of the Universe, who hast chosen us from among all people, and exalted us from among all languages, and sanctified us with Thy commandments! And Thou hast given us, O Jehovah our God, in love, the solemn days for joy, and the festivals and appointed seasons for gladness; and this the day of the feast of unleavened bread, the season of our freedom, a holy convocation, the memorial of our departure from Egypt. For us hast Thou chosen; and us hast Thou sanctified from among all nations, and Thy holy festivals with joy and with gladness hast Thou caused us to inherit. Blessed art Thou, O Jehovah, who sanc-

---

[6]Of this there cannot be the slightest doubt. Indeed, the following quotation from the *Mishnah* (*Pes.* vii. 13) might even induce one to believe that *warm* water was mixed with the wine: 'If two companies eat (the Passover) in the same house, the one turns its face to one side, the other to the other, and the kettle (warming kettle) stands between them.'

tifiest Israel and the appointed seasons! Blessed art
Thou, Jehovah, King of the Universe, who hast preserved us alive and sustained us and brought us to
this season!'[7]

THE FIRST CUP

After that, he poured water into a basin and began to wash his disciples' feet, drying them with the towel that was wrapped around him (John 13:5).

The first cup of wine was then drunk, and each
washed his hands.[8] It was evidently at this time that
the Saviour in His self-humiliation proceeded also to
wash the disciples' feet (John 13:5). Our Authorised
Version wrongly translates verse 2 by, 'and supper
being ended,' instead of 'and when supper had come,'
or 'was begun.' Similarly, it was, in all probability, in
reference to the first cup that Luke gives the following
account (Luke 22:17): 'And He took the cup, and
gave thanks, and said, Take this, and divide it among
yourselves'—the 'cup of blessing,' which was the third,
and formed part of the new institution of the Lord's
Supper, being afterwards mentioned in verse 20. In
washing their hands this customary prayer was
repeated: 'Blessed are Thou, Jehovah our God, who
hast sanctified us with Thy commandments, and hast
enjoined us concerning the washing of our hands.'
Two different kinds of 'washing' were prescribed by
tradition—'dipping' and 'pouring.' At the Paschal
Supper the hands were to be 'dipped' in water.[9]

THE HERBS

These preliminaries ended, the Paschal table
was brought forward. The president of the feast first
took some of the herbs, dipped them in salt water, ate

---

[7]Such, according to the best criticism, were the words of this prayer at the time of Christ. But I must repeat that in regard to many of these prayers I cannot help suspecting that they rather indicate the spirit and direction of a prayer than embody the *ipsissima verba*.

[8]The modern practice of the Jews slightly differs from the ancient here, and in some other little matters of detail.

[9]The distinction is also interesting as explaining Mark 7:3. For when water was poured on the hands, they had to be lifted, yet so that the water should neither run up above the wrist, nor back again upon the hand; best, therefore, by doubling the fingers into a fist. Hence (as Lightfoot rightly remarks) Mark 7:3, which should be translated: 'For the Pharisees...except they wash their hands with the fist, eat not, holding the tradition of the elders.' The rendering of our Authorised Version, 'except they wash oft,' has evidently no meaning.

of them, and gave to the others. Immediately after it, all the dishes were removed from the table (as it was thought so strange a proceeding would tend to excite the more curiosity), and then the second cup was filled. A very interesting ceremony now took place. It had been enjoined in the law that at each Paschal Supper the father was to show his son the import of this festival. By way of carrying out this duty, the son (or else the youngest) was directed at this particular part of the service to make inquiry; and, if the child were too young or incapable, the father would do it for him.

THE SON'S QUESTION
The son asks: 'Why is this night distinguished from all other nights? For on all other nights we eat leavened or unleavened bread, but on this night only unleavened bread? On all other nights we eat any kind of herbs, but on this night only bitter herbs? On all other nights we eat meat roasted, stewed, or boiled, but on this night only roasted? On all other nights we dip (the herbs) only once, but on this night twice?' Thus far according to the earliest and most trustworthy tradition. It is added (*Mishnah, Pes.* x. 4): 'Then the father instructs his child according to the capacity of his knowledge, beginning with our disgrace and ending with our glory, and expounding to him from, 'A Syrian, ready to perish, was my father," till he has explained all through, to the end of the whole section' (Deut. 26:5–11). In other words, the head of the house was to relate the whole national history, commencing with Terah, Abraham's father, and telling of his idolatry, and continuing, in due order, the story of Israel up to their deliverance from Egypt and the giving of the Law; and the more fully he explained it all, the better.

THE DISHES
This done, the Paschal dishes were brought back on the table. The president now took up in succession the dish with the Passover lamb, that with the bitter herbs, and that with the unleavened bread, and

Then you shall declare before the LORD your God: "My father was a wandering Aramean, and he went down into Egypt with a few people and lived there and became a great nation, powerful and numerous. But the Egyptians mistreated us and made us suffer, putting us to hard labor. Then we cried out to the LORD, the God of our fathers, and the LORD heard our voice and saw our misery, toil and oppression. So the LORD brought us out of Egypt with a mighty hand and an outstretched arm, with great terror and with miraculous signs and wonders" (Deut. 26:5–8).

*On that day tell your son,
"I do this because of what
the LORD did for me when
I came out of Egypt." This
observance will be for you
like a sign on your hand
and a reminder on your
forehead that the law of
the LORD is to be on your
lips. For the LORD brought
you out of Egypt with his
mighty hand. You must
keep this ordinance at the
appointed time year after
year (Exod. 13:8–10).*

*While they were eating,
Jesus took bread, gave
thanks and broke it, and
gave it to his disciples, saying, "Take it; this is my
body" (Mark 14:22).*

briefly explained the import of each; for, according to
Rabbi Gamaliel: 'From generation to generation
every man is bound to look upon himself not otherwise than if he had himself come forth out of Egypt.
For so it is written (Exod. 13:8), "And thou shalt
show thy son in that day, saying, This is done because
of that which Jehovah did unto me when I came forth
out of Egypt." Therefore,' continues the *Mishnah*, giving the very words of the prayer used, 'we are bound to
thank, praise, laud, glorify, extol, honour, bless, exalt,
and reverence Him, because He hath wrought for our
fathers, and for us all these miracles. He brought us
forth from bondage into freedom, from sorrow into
joy, from mourning to a festival, from darkness to a
great light, and from slavery to redemption. Therefore
let us sing before Him: Hallelujah!' Then the first part
of the 'Hallel' was sung, comprising Psalms 113 and
114, with this brief thanksgiving at the close: 'Blessed
art Thou, Jehovah our God, King of the Universe,
who hast redeemed us and redeemed our fathers from
Egypt.' Upon this the second cup was drunk. Hands
were now washed a second time, with the same prayer
as before, and one of the two unleavened cakes broken
and 'thanks given.'

THE BREAKING OF THE BREAD

Rabbinical authorities distinctly state that this
thanksgiving was to follow, not to precede, the breaking of bread, because it was the bread of poverty, 'and
the poor have not whole cakes, but broken pieces.'
The distinction is important, as proving that since the
Lord in instituting His Supper, according to the uni-
form testimony of the three Gospels and of St. Paul
(Matt. 26:26; Mark 14:22; Luke 22:19; 1 Cor. 11:24),
first gave thanks and then brake the bread ('having
given thanks, He brake it'), it must have been at a later
period of the service.

Pieces of the broken cake with 'bitter herbs'
between them, and 'dipped' in the Charoseth, were
next handed to each in the company. This, in all
probability, was 'the sop' which, in answer to John's
inquiry about the betrayer, the Lord 'gave' to Judas

(John 13:25, etc; compare Matt. 26:21, etc.; Mark 14:18, etc.). The unleavened bread with bitter herbs constituted, in reality, the beginning of the Paschal Supper, to which the first part of the service had only served as a kind of introduction. But as Judas, after 'having received the sop, went immediately out,' he could not even have partaken of the Paschal lamb, far less of the Lord's Supper. The solemn discourses of the Lord recorded by St. John (John 13:31; 16) may therefore be regarded as His last 'table-talk,' and the intercessory prayer that followed (John 17) as His 'grace after meat.'

When he was gone, Jesus said, "Now is the Son of Man glorified and God is glorified in him. If God is glorified in him, God will glorify the Son in himself, and will glorify him at once" (John 13:31–32).

THE THREE ELEMENTS OF THE FEAST

The Paschal Supper itself consisted of the unleavened bread with bitter herbs, of the so-called Chagigah, or festive offering (when brought), and, lastly, of the Paschal lamb itself. After that nothing more was to be eaten, so that the flesh of the Paschal Sacrifice might be the last meat partaken of. But since the cessation of the Paschal Sacrifice the Jews conclude the Supper with a piece of unleavened cake, which they call the *Aphikomen,* or after-dish. Then, having again washed hands, the third cup is filled, and grace after meat said. Now, it is very remarkable that our Lord seems so far to have anticipated the present Jewish practice that He brake the bread 'when He had given thanks' (see 1 Cor. 11:24, and the Gospels), instead of adhering to the old injunction of not eating anything after the Passover lamb. And yet in so doing He only carried out the spirit of the Paschal feast. For, as we have already explained, it was commemorative and typical. It commemorated an event which pointed to and merged in another event—even the offering of the better Lamb, and the better freedom connected with that sacrifice. Hence, after the night of His betrayal, the Paschal lamb could have no further meaning, and it was right that the commemorative *Aphikomen* should take its place. The symbolical cord, if the figure may be allowed, had stretched to its goal—the offering up of the Lamb of God; and though again continued from that point onwards till

His second coming, yet it was, in a sense, as from a new beginning.

THE THIRD CUP

Immediately afterwards the third cup was drunk, a special blessing having been spoken over it.

Is not the cup of thanksgiving for which we give thanks a participation in the blood of Christ? And is not the bread that we break a participation in the body of Christ (1 Cor. 10:16)?

There cannot be any reasonable doubt that this was the cup which our Lord connected with His own Supper. It is called in Jewish writings, just as by St. Paul (1 Cor. 10:16), 'the cup of blessing,' partly because it and the first cup required a special 'blessing,' and partly because it followed on the 'grace after meat.' Indeed, such importance attached to it, that the Talmud (*Berac.* 51, 1) notes ten peculiarities, too minute indeed for our present consideration, but sufficient to show the special value set upon it.[10] The service concluded with the fourth cup, over which the second portion of the 'Hallel' was sung, consisting of Psalms 115, 116, 117, and 118, the whole ending with the so-called 'blessing of the song,' which comprised these two brief prayers: 'All Thy works shall praise Thee, Jehovah our God. And Thy saints, the righteous, who do Thy good pleasure, and all Thy people, the house of Israel, with joyous song let them praise, and bless, and magnify, and glorify, and exalt, and reverence, and sanctify, and ascribe the kingdom to Thy name, O our King! For it is good to praise Thee, and pleasure to sing praises unto Thy name, for from everlasting to everlasting Thou art God.'

*You are my God, and I will give you thanks;
you are my God, and I will exalt you.
Give thanks to the LORD,
for he is good;
his love endures forever
(Ps. 118:28–29).*

*I lift up my eyes to the hills—
where does my help come from?
My help comes from the LORD,
the Maker of heaven and earth (Ps. 121:1–2).*

'The breath of all that lives shall praise Thy name, Jehovah our God. And the spirit of all flesh shall continually glorify and exalt Thy memorial, O our King! For from everlasting to everlasting Thou art God, and besides Thee we have no King, Redeemer, or Saviour,' etc.[11]

---

[10]It is a curious circumstance that the *Mishnah* seems to contemplate the same painful case of drunkenness at the Paschal Supper, which, as we know, actually occurred in the church at Corinth, that so closely imitated the Jewish practice. The *Mishnah* does not, indeed, speak in so many words of drunkenness, but it lays down this rule: 'Does any one sleep at the Passover meal and wake again, he may not eat again after he is awaked.'

[11]Exceptionally a fifth cup was drunk, and over it 'the great Hallel' was said, comprising Ps. 120–137.

THE SUPPER IN OUR LORD'S TIME

In this manner was the Paschal Supper celebrated by the Jews at the time when our Lord for the last time sat down to it with His disciples. So important is it to have a clear understanding of all that passed on that occasion, that, at the risk of some repetition, we shall now attempt to piece together the notices in the various Gospels, adding to them again those explanations which have just been given in detail. At the outset we may dismiss, as unworthy of serious discussion, the theory, either that our Lord had observed the Paschal Supper at another than the regular time for it, or that St. John meant to intimate that He had partaken of it on the 13th instead of the 14th of Nisan.[12] To such violent hypotheses, which are wholly uncalled for, there is this one conclusive answer, that, except on the evening of the 14th of Nisan, no Paschal lamb could have been offered in the Temple, and therefore no Paschal Supper celebrated in Jerusalem. But abiding by the simple text of Scripture, we have the following narrative of events:—Early on the forenoon of the 14th of Nisan, the Lord Jesus having sent Peter and John before Him 'to prepare the Passover,' 'in the evening He cometh with the twelve' (Mark 14:17) to the 'guest-chamber,' the 'large upper room furnished' (Luke 22:11, 12) for the Supper, although He seems to have intended 'after Supper' to spend the night outside the city. Hence Judas and the band from the chief priests do not seek for Him where He had eaten the Passover, but go at once to 'the garden into which He had entered, and His disciples;' for Judas 'knew the place' (John 18:1, 2), and it was one to which 'Jesus ofttimes resorted with his disciples.' 'When the hour was come' for the commencement of the Paschal Supper, Jesus 'sat down, and the twelve apostles with Him,' all, as usual at the feast, 'leaning' (John 13:23), John on 'Jesus' bosom,' being placed next before Him, and Judas apparently next behind, while Simon Peter faced John, and was thus able to 'beckon unto

On the first day of the Feast of Unleavened Bread, when it was customary to sacrifice the Passover lamb, Jesus' disciples asked him, "Where do you want us to go and make preparations for you to eat the Passover?" (Mark 14:12).

---

[12]For the evidence that the 'Lord's Supper' took place on the Paschal night, see the Appendix.

I am telling you now before it happens, so that when it does happen you will believe that I am He. I tell you the truth, whoever accepts anyone I send accepts me; and whoever accepts me accepts the one who sent me (John 13:19–20).

See to it that no one misses the grace of God and that no bitter root grows up to cause trouble and defile many (Heb. 12:15).

him' when he wished inquiry to be made of the Lord. The disciples being thus ranged, the Lord Jesus 'took the cup and gave thanks, and said, Take this, and divide it among yourselves' (Luke 22:17). This was the first cup, over which the first prayer in the service was spoken. Next, as in duty bound, all washed their hands, only that the Lord here also gave meaning to the observance, when, expanding the service into Christian fellowship over His broken body, He 'riseth from Supper,' 'and began to wash the disciples' feet' (John 13:4, 5). It is thus we explain how this ministry, though calling forth Peter's resistance to the position which the Master took, did not evoke any question as to its singularity. As the service proceeded, the Lord mingled teaching for the present with the customary lessons of the past (John 13:12–20); for, as we have seen, considerable freedom was allowed, provided the instruction proper at the feast were given. The first part of the 'Hallel' had been sung, and in due order He had taken the 'bread of poverty' and the 'bitter herbs,' commemorative of the sorrow and the bitterness of Egypt, when 'He was troubled in spirit' about 'the root of bitterness' about to spring up among, and to 'trouble' them, by which 'many would be defiled.' The general concern of the disciples as to which of their number should betray Him, found expression in the gesture of Peter. His friend John understood its meaning, and 'lying back on Jesus' breast,' he put the whispered question, to which the Lord replied by giving 'the sop' of unleavened bread with bitter herbs, 'when He had dipped' it, to Judas Iscariot.

JUDAS ISCARIOT

'And after the sop Satan entered into him,' and he 'went out immediately.' It was an unusual time to leave the Paschal table, for with 'the sop dipped' into the 'Charoseth' the Paschal Supper itself had only just begun. But then 'some of them thought'—perhaps without fully considering it in their excitement—that Judas, who 'had the bag,' and on whom, therefore, the care of such things devolved, had only gone to see after 'those things that they had need of against the feast,' or to 'give something to the poor'—applying some of the common stock of money in helping to provide 'peace-offerings' for the poor. This would have been quite in accordance with the spirit of the ordinance, while neither supposition necessarily involved a breach of the law, since it was permitted to prepare all needful provision for the feast, and of course also for the Sabbath, which in this instance followed it. For, as we have seen, the festive observance of the 15th of Nisan differed in this from ordinary Sabbath-law, although there is evidence that even the latter was at that time by no means so strict as later Jewish tradition has made it. And then it was, after the regular Paschal meal, that the Lord instituted His own Supper, for the first time using the *Aphikomen* 'when He had given thanks' (after meat), to symbolise His body, and the third cup, or 'cup of blessing which we bless' (1 Cor. 10:16)—being 'the cup after supper' (Luke 22:20)— to symbolise His blood. 'And when they had sung an hymn' (Ps. 115–118), 'they went out into the mount of Olives' (Matt. 26:30).

In the same way, after the supper he took the cup, saying, "This cup is the new covenant in my blood, which is poured out for you" (Luke 22:20).

Then he returned to his disciples and found them sleeping. "Could you men not keep watch with me for one hour?" he asked Peter. "Watch and pray so that you will not fall into temptation. The spirit is willing, but the body is weak" (Matt. 26:40–41).

OUR LORD'S AGONY

Then it was that the Lord's great heaviness and loneliness came upon Him; when all around seemed to give way, as if crushed under the terrible burden about to be lifted; when His disciples could not watch with Him even one hour; when in the agony of His soul 'His sweat was as it were great drops of blood, falling down to the ground;' and when He 'prayed, saying: O my Father, if it be possible, let this cup pass from Me: nevertheless not as I will, but as Thou wilt.' But 'the cup which the Father' had given Him, He drank to the bitter dregs; and 'when He had offered up prayers and supplications with strong crying and tears unto Him that was able to save Him from death, and was heard in that He feared; though He were a Son, yet learned He obedience by the things which He suffered; and being made perfect, He became the author of eternal salvation unto all them that obey Him' (Heb. 5:7–9).

Thus the 'Lamb without blemish and without spot, who verily was foreordained before the foundation of the world' (1 Pet. 1:20)—and, indeed, 'slain from the foundation of the world' (Rev. 13:8)—was selected, ready, willing, and waiting. It only remained, that it should be actually offered up as 'the propitiation for our sins: and not for ours only, but also for the whole world' (1 John 2:2).

13

THE FEAST OF UNLEAVENED BREAD
AND THE DAY OF PENTECOST

❈

When the day of Pentecost came, they were all
together in one place.—Acts 2:1

THE FEAST OF UNLEAVENED BREAD

The 'Feast of Unleavened Bread' which commenced in the Paschal night itself and lasted for seven
days, derived its name from the *Mazzoth*, or unleavened cakes, which were the only bread allowed during
that week. This is called in Scripture 'the bread of
affliction' (Deut. 16:3), as is commonly supposed,
because its insipid and disagreeable taste symbolised
the hardship and affliction of Egypt. But this explanation must be erroneous. It would convert one of
the most joyous festivals into an annual season of
mourning. The idea intended to be conveyed by the
Scriptural term is quite different. For, just as we
should ever remember the death of our Saviour in
connection with His resurrection, so were Israel always
to remember their bondage in connection with their
deliverance. Besides, the bread of the Paschal night
was not that of affliction because it was unleavened; it
was unleavened because it had been that of affliction.
For it had been Israel's 'affliction,' and a mark of their
bondage and subjection to the Egyptians, to be driven
forth in such 'haste' (Deut. 16:3; Exod. 12:33, 39), as not
even to have time for leavening their bread. Hence also
the prophet, when predicting another and far more
glorious deliverance, represents Israel, in contrast to
the past, as too holy to seek enrichment by the possessions, and as too secure to be driven forth in haste

*Do not eat it with bread
made with yeast, but for
seven days eat unleavened
bread, the bread of affliction, because you left Egypt
in haste—so that all the
days of your life you may
remember the time of your
departure from Egypt
(Deut. 16:3).*

*With the dough they had
brought from Egypt, they
baked cakes of unleavened
bread. The dough was
without yeast because they
had been driven out of
Egypt and did not have
time to prepare food for
themselves (Exod. 12:39).*

by the fear of those who had held them captives:

'Depart ye, depart ye, go ye out from thence,—
   touch no unclean thing;
Go ye out of the midst of her; be ye clean that bear
   the vessels of Jehovah.
For ye shall not go out with haste,—nor go by flight:
For Jehovah will go before you; and the God of
   Israel will be your rereward.' (Isa. 52:11, 12)

Sacrifice fellowship offerings there, eating them and rejoicing in the presence of the LORD your God (Deut. 27:7).

The Passover, therefore was not so much the remembrance of Israel's bondage as of Israel's deliverance from that bondage, and the bread which had originally been that of affliction, because that of haste, now became, as it were, the bread of a new state of existence. None of Egypt's leaven was to pervade it; nay, all the old leaven, which served as the symbol of corruption and of death, was to be wholly banished from their homes. They were to be 'a new lump,' as they were 'unleavened' (1 Cor. 5:7). Thus what had originally been the necessity of one day, became the ordinance of a feast, bearing the sacred number of seven days. As the cross has become to us the tree of life; as death hath been abolished by death, and captivity been led captive by the voluntary servitude (Ps. 40:6, 7) of the Lord of glory, so to Israel the badge of former affliction became the symbol of a new and joyous life, in which they were to devote themselves and all that they had unto the Lord.

THE FIRST DAY OF THE FEAST

The same truth is fully symbolised in the sacrifices of this feast, and especially in the presentation of the first ripe sheaf on the second day of the Passover. The first day of 'unleavened bread,' or the 15th of Nisan, was a 'holy convocation,' when neither servile nor needless work was to be done, that only being allowed which was necessary for the joyous observance of the festival. After the regular morning sacrifice the public offerings were brought. These consisted, on each of the seven days of the festive week, of two young bullocks, one ram, and seven lambs for a burnt-offering, with their appropriate meat-offerings; and of 'one goat for a sin-offering, to make an atonement for you' (Num. 28:19–24). After these public sacrifices (for the whole congregation), the private offerings of each individual were brought, commonly on the first day of the feast (the 15th of Nisan), but if this had been neglected, on any of the other days. These sacrifices were a burnt-offering, of the value of at least one *meah* of silver[1] (= ¹/₃ denar, or about 2¹/₂ *d.*); then the 15th day Chagigah[2] (literally, festivity), of the value of least two meahs of silver (equals 5d.); and, lastly, the so-called 'sacrifices of joyousness' (Deut. 27:7), in which every one was left at liberty to offer, according to 'the blessing which the Lord had given' to each (Deut. 16:17). Both the Chagigah and the 'offerings of joyousness' were 'peace-offerings.' They required imposition of hands,[3] sprinkling of blood, burning of the inside fat and kidneys on the altar, and the proper setting aside of what went to the priest, viz. the breast as a wave- and the right shoulder as a heave-offering (Lev. 3:1–5; 7:29–34); the differ-ence, as we have seen, being, that the wave-offering belonged originally to Jehovah, who gave *His* portion to the priests, while the heave-offering came to them directly from the people. The rest was used by the offerers in their festive meals (but only during two days and one night from the time of sacrifice). Tradition allowed the poor, who might have many to share at their board, to spend even less than one meah on their burnt-offerings, if they added what had been saved to their peace-offerings. Things devoted to God, such as tithes, firstlings, etc., might be used for this purpose, and it was even lawful for priests to offer what had come to them as priestly dues (*Mishnah, Chag.* i. 3, 4). In short, it was not to be a heavy yoke of bondage,

Each of you must bring a gift in proportion to the way the LORD your God has blessed you (Deut. 16:17).

---

[1]In this, as in many other particulars, the teaching of Shammai differed from that of Hillel. We have followed Hillel, whose authority is generally recognised.

[2]It is strange that the differences between the Chagigah of the 14th and that of the 15th of Nisan should have been so entirely overlooked in Kitto's *Cycl.* iii, 428. They are well pointed out in Relandus' *Antiq.* pp. 404, 405. See also the very full statement of Saalschütz, *Mos. Recht*, pp. 414, 415.

[3]On this subject also Shammai and Hillel differed. See on the whole *Mishnah, Chag.* i. and ii.

(With the reward he got for his wickedness, Judas bought a field; there he fell headlong, his body burst open and all his intestines spilled out. Everyone in Jerusalem heard about this, so they called that field in their language Akeldama, that is, Field of Blood.) (Acts 1:18–19).

but a joyous festival. But on one point the law was quite explicit—the Chagigah might not be offered by any person who had contracted Levitical defilement (*Pes.* vi. 3). It was on this ground that, when the Jews led 'Jesus from Caiaphas unto the hall of judgment,' they themselves went not into the judgment-hall, lest they should be defiled, but that they might 'eat the Passover' (John 18:28). And this brings us once more to the history of the last real Passover.

THE DAY OF OUR LORD'S BETRAYAL

'It was early' on the 15th day of Nisan when the Lord was delivered into the hands of the Gentiles. In the previous night He and His disciples had partaken of the Paschal Supper. The betrayer alone was too busy with his plans to finish the meal. He had, so to speak, separated from the fellowship of Israel before he excommunicated himself from that of Christ. While the Paschal services in the 'guest-chamber' were prolonged by the teaching and the intercession of the Master, and when the concluding rites of that night merged in the institution of the Lord's Supper, Judas was completing, with the chief priests and elders, the betrayal of Jesus, and received the 'reward of iniquity' (Acts 1:18). Either the impetuosity of the traitor, or, more probably, the thought that such an opportunity might never come to them again, decided the elders, who, till then, had intended to delay the capture of Jesus till after the Feast, for 'fear of the multitude.' It was necessary to put aside, not only considerations of truth and of conscience, but to violate almost every fundamental principle of their own judicial administration. In such a cause, however, the end would sanctify any means.

THE ARREST OF OUR LORD

Some of their number hastily gathered the Temple guard under its captains. A detachment of Roman soldiers under an officer[4] would readily be granted from the neighbouring fortress, Antonia, when the avowed object was to secure a dangerous leader of rebellion and to prevent the possibility of a popular tumult in his favour. A number of trusty fanatics from the populace accompanied 'the band.' They were all armed with clubs and swords, 'as against a murderer;' and though the dazzling light of a full moon shone on the scene, they carried torches and lamps, in case He or His followers should hide in the recesses of the garden or escape observation. But far other than they had expected awaited them in 'the garden.' He whom they had come to take prisoner by violent means first overcame, and then willingly surrendered to them, only stipulating for the freedom of His followers. They led Him back into the city, to the Palace of the High Priest, on the slope of Mount Zion, almost opposite to the Temple. What passed there need not be further described, except to say, that, in their treatment of Jesus, the Sanhedrin violated not only the law of God, but grossly outraged every ordinance of their own traditions.[5] Possibly the consciousness of this, almost as much as political motives, may have influenced them in handing over the matter to Pilate. The mere fact that they possessed not the power of capital punishment would scarcely have restrained them from killing Jesus, as they afterwards stoned Stephen, and would have murdered Paul but for the intervention of the Roman garrison from Fort Antonia. On the other hand, if it was, at the same time, their object to secure a public condemnation and execution, and to awaken the susceptibilities of the civil power against the movement which Christ had initiated, it was necessary to carry the case to Pilate. And so in that grey morning light of the first day of unleavened bread the saddest and strangest scene in Jewish history was enacted. The chief priests and elders, and the most fanatical of the people were gathered in Fort Antonia. From where they stood outside the Praetorium they would, in all probability,

So Judas came to the grove, guiding a detachment of soldiers and some officials from the chief priests and Pharisees. They were carrying torches, lanterns and weapons.

Jesus, knowing all that was going to happen to him, went out and asked them, "Who is it you want?"

"Jesus of Nazareth," they replied.

"I am he," Jesus said. (And Judas the traitor was standing there with them.) When Jesus said, "I am he," they drew back and fell to the ground.

Again he asked them, "Who is it you want?"

And they said, "Jesus of Nazareth."

"I told you that I am he," Jesus answered. "If you are looking for me, then let these men go" (John 18:3–8).

---

[4]We derive our account from all the four Gospels. The language of St. John (18:3, 12) leaves no doubt that a detachment of Roman soldiers accompanied such of the elders and priests as went out with the Temple guard to take Jesus. There was no need to apply for Pilate's permission (as Lange supposes) before securing the aid of the soldiers.

[5]We cannot here enter on the evidence; the fact is generally admitted even by Jewish writers.

have a full view of the Temple buildings, just below the rocky fort; they could see the morning sacrifice offered, and the columns of sacrificial smoke and of incense rise from the great altar towards heaven. At any rate, even if they had not seen the multitude that thronged the sacred buildings, they could hear the Levites' song and the blasts of the priests' trumpets. And now the ordinary morning service was over, and the festive sacrifices were offered. It only remained to bring the private burnt-offerings, and to sacrifice the Chagigah,[6] which they must offer undefiled, if they were to bring it at all, or to share in the festive meal that would afterwards ensue. And so the strangest contradiction was enacted. They who had not hesitated to break every law of God's and of their own making, would not enter the Praetorium, lest they should be defiled and prevented from the Chagigah! Surely, the logic of inconsistency could go no further in punctiliously observing the letter and violating the spirit of the law.

A man is not a Jew if he is only one outwardly, nor is circumcision merely outward and physical. No, a man is a Jew if he is one inwardly; and circumcision is circumcision of the heart, by the Spirit, not by the written code. Such a man's praise is not from men, but from God (Rom. 2:28–29).

THE DARKNESS

That same afternoon of the first Passover day, 'when the sixth hour was come, there was darkness over the whole land until the ninth hour. And at the ninth hour Jesus cried with a loud voice, saying, Eloi, Eloi, lama sabachthani? which is, being interpreted, My God, my God, why hast Thou forsaken Me?... And Jesus cried with a loud voice, and gave up the ghost. And the veil of the Temple was rent in twain, from the top to the bottom.' This, just about the time when the evening sacrifice had been offered, so that the incensing priest standing in the Holy Place must have witnessed the awful sight.[7]

---

[6]The evidence that the expression in John 18:28, 'They went not into the judgment-hall...that they might eat the Passover,' refers *not* to the Paschal lamb, but to the Chagigah, is exceedingly strong, in fact, such as to have even convinced an eminent but impartial Jewish writer (Saalschütz, *Mos. Recht.* p. 414). It does seem strange that it should be either unknown to, or ignored by, 'Christian' writers.

[7]This would not necessarily disclose a view of the Most Holy Place if, as the Rabbis assert, there were *two* veils between the Holy and the Most Holy Place.

THE SHEAF OF FIRSTFRUITS

A little later on in the evening of that same day, just as it was growing dark, a noisy throng followed delegates from the Sanhedrim outside the city and across the brook Kedron. It was a very different procession, and for a very different purpose, from the small band of mourners which, just about the same time, carried the body of the dead Saviour from the cross to the rock-hewn tomb wherein no man had yet been laid. While the one turned into 'the garden' (John 20:15), perhaps to one side, the other emerged, amidst loud demonstrations, in a field across Kedron, which had been marked out for the purpose. They were to be engaged in a service most important to them. It was probably to this circumstance that Joseph of Arimathea owed their non-interference with his request for the body of Jesus, and Nicodemus and the women, that they could go undisturbed about the last sad offices of loving mourners. The law had it, 'Ye shall bring a sheaf [literally the omer] of the firstfruits of your harvest unto the priest; and he shall wave the omer before Jehovah, to be accepted for you: on the morrow after the Sabbath the priest shall wave it' (Lev. 23:10, 11). This Passover-sheaf, or rather omer, was to be accompanied by a burnt-offering, of a 'he lamb, without blemish, of the first year,' with its appropriate meat- and drink-offering, and after it had been brought, but not till then, fresh barley might be used and sold in the land. Now, this Passover-sheaf was reaped in public the evening before it was offered, and it was to witness this ceremony that the crowd gathered around 'the elders,' who took care that all was done according to traditional ordinance.

Later, Joseph of Arimathea asked Pilate for the body of Jesus. Now Joseph was a disciple of Jesus, but secretly because he feared the Jews. With Pilate's permission, he came and took the body away…At the place where Jesus was crucified, there was a garden, and in the garden a new tomb, in which no one had ever been laid. Because it was the Jewish day of Preparation and since the tomb was nearby, they laid Jesus there (John 19:38, 41–42).

You must not eat any bread, or roasted or new grain, until the very day you bring this offering to your God. This is to be a lasting ordinance for the generations to come, wherever you live (Lev. 23:14).

'THE MORROW AFTER THE SABBATH'

The expression, 'the morrow after the Sabbath' (Lev. 23:11), has sometimes been misunderstood as implying that the presentation of the so-called 'first sheaf' was to be always made on the day following the weekly Sabbath of the Passover-week. This view, adopted by the 'Boëthusians' and the Sadducees in the time of Christ, and by the Karaite Jews and certain

*In the month of Xanthicus,
which is by us called Nisan,
and is the beginning of our
year, on the fourteenth
day of the lunar month,
when the sun is in Aries
(for in this month it was
that we were delivered
from bondage under the
Egyptians) and law
ordained that we should
every year slay that sacrifice which I before told you
we slew when we came out
of Egypt, and which was
called the Passover; and
so we do celebrate this
passover in companies,
leaving nothing of what we
sacrifice till the day following (Jos. Antiquities 3.248).*

modern interpreters, rests on a misinterpretation of the word 'Sabbath' (Lev. 23:24, 32, 39). As in analogous allusions to other feasts in the same chapter, it means not the weekly Sabbath, but the day of the festival. The testimony of Josephus (*Antiq.* 3.248–249), of Philo (*Op.* ii. 294), and of Jewish tradition, leaves no room to doubt that in this instance we are to understand by the 'Sabbath' the 15th of Nisan, on whatever day of the week it might fall. Already, on the 14th of Nisan, the spot whence the first sheaf was to be reaped had been marked out by delegates from the Sanhedrim, by tying together in bundles, while still standing, the barley that was to be cut down. Though, for obvious reasons, it was customary to choose for this purpose the sheltered Ashes-valley across Kedron, there was no restriction on that point, provided the barley had grown in an ordinary field—of course in Palestine itself—and not in garden or orchard land, and that the soil had not been manured nor yet artificially watered.[8] When the time for cutting the sheaf had arrived, that is, on the evening of the 15th of Nisan (even though it were a Sabbath[9]), just as the sun went down, three men, each with a sickle and basket, formally set to work. But in order clearly to bring out all that was distinctive in the ceremony, they first asked the bystanders three times each of these questions: 'Has the sun gone down?' 'With this sickle?' 'Into this basket?' 'On this Sabbath (or the first Passover-day)?' —and, lastly, 'Shall I reap?' Having each time been answered in the affirmative, they cut down barley to the amount of one ephah, or ten omers, or three seahs, which is equal to about three pecks and three pints of our English measure. The ears were brought into the Court of the Temple, and thrashed out with canes or stalks, so as not to injure the corn; then 'parched' on

---

[8] *Mishnah, Menach.* viii. 1, 2. The field was to be ploughed in the autumn, and sowed seventy days before the Passover.

[9] There was a controversy on this point between the Pharisees and the Sadducees. The article in Kitto's *Cycl.* erroneously names the afternoon of the 16th of Nisan as that on which the sheaf was cut. It was really done after sunset on the 15th, which was the beginning of the 16th of Nisan.

a pan perforated with holes, so that each grain might be touched by the fire, and finally exposed to the wind. The corn thus prepared was ground in a barley-mill, which left the hulls whole. According to some, the flour was always successfully passed through thirteen sieves, each closer than the other. The statement of a rival authority, however, seems more rational—that it was only done till the flour was sufficiently fine (*Men.* vi. 6, 7), which was ascertained by one of the 'Gizbarim' (treasurers) plunging his hands into it, the sifting process being continued so long as any of the flour adhered to the hands (*Men.* viii. 2). Though one ephah, or ten omers, of barley was cut down, only one omer of flour, or about 5.1 pints of our measure, was offered in the Temple on the second Paschal, or 16th day of Nisan. The rest of the flour might be redeemed, and used for any purpose. The omer of flour was mixed with a 'log,' or very nearly three-fourths of a pint of oil, and a handful[10] of frankincense put upon it, then waved before the Lord, and a handful taken out and burned on the altar. The remainder belonged to the priest. This was what is popularly, thought not very correctly, called 'the presentation of the first or wave-sheaf' on the second day of the Passover-feast, or the 16th of Nisan.

They may not bring it from a manured field or from an irrigated field or from a tree–plantation. Yet if they did so it was valid. How was it made ready? In the first year a man would break up fresh ground and in the second sow it seventy days before Passover; thus it would bring forth fine flour in abundance (Mishnah, Menaḥot viii.2).

How was it tested? The [Temple–]treasurer used to thrust his hand into it; if dust came up therein it is invalid until it is sifted [afresh]. If it had become maggoty it is invalid (Mishnah, Menaḥot viii.2).

THE LAST DAY OF THE PASSOVER

Thus far the two first days. The last day of the Passover, as the first, was a 'holy convocation,' and observed like a Sabbath. The intervening days were 'minor festivals,' or Moed Katon. The *Mishnah* (Tract. *Moed Katon*) lays down precise rules as to the kind of work allowed on such days. As a general principle, all that was necessary either for the public interest or to prevent private loss was allowed; but no new work of any kind for private or public purposes might be begun. Thus you might irrigate dry soil, or repair works for irrigation, but not make new ones, nor dig

A man may bring in his produce for fear of thieves, or take his flax out of soak lest it perish, provided that he had not purposed to do his work during mid-festival. But in every like case if they had purposed to do their work during mid-festival it must be left to perish (Mishnah, Mo'ed Qaṭan ii.3).

---

[10]The term is difficult to define. The *Mishnah* (*Men.* ii. 2) says, 'He stretcheth the fingers over the flat of the hand.' I suppose, bending them inwards.

canals, etc.[11] It only remains to add, that any one prevented by Levitical defilement, disability, or distance from keeping the regular Passover, might observe what was called 'the second,' or 'the little Passover,' exactly a month later (Num. 9:9–12). The *Mishnah* has it (*Pes.* ix. 3) that the second differed from the first Passover in this—that leaven might be kept in the house along with the unleavened bread, that the Hallel was not sung at the Paschal Supper, and that no Chagigah was offered.

Wherein does the First Passover differ from the Second? To the first apply the prohibitions It shall not be seen and It shall not be found, whereas at the Second a man may have both unleavened bread and hametz with him in the house. At the eating of the First, the Hallel must be sung, but at the eating of the Second, the Hallel need not be sung (Mishnah, Pesahim ix.3).

When the day of Pentecost came...All of them were filled with the Holy Spirit and began to speak in other tongues as the Spirit enabled them (Acts 2:1a, 4).

PENTECOST

The 'Feast of the Unleavened Bread' may be said not to have quite passed till fifty days after its commencement, when it merged in that of Pentecost, or 'of Weeks.' According to unanimous Jewish tradition, which was universally received at the time of Christ, the day of Pentecost was the anniversary of the giving of the Law on Mount Sinai, which the Feast of Weeks was intended to commemorate. Thus, as the dedication of the harvest, commencing with the presentation of the first omer on the Passover, was completed in the thank-offering of the two wave-loaves at Pentecost, so that the memorial of Israel's deliverance appropriately terminated in that of the giving of the Law—just as, making the highest application of it, the Passover sacrifice of the Lord Jesus may be said to have been completed in the outpouring of the Holy Spirit on the day of Pentecost (Acts 2). Jewish tradition has it, that on the 2nd of the third month, or Sivan, Moses had ascended the Mount (Exod. 19:1–3), that he communicated with the people on the 3rd (Exod. 19:7), reascended the Mount on the 4th (Exod. 19:8), and that then the people sanctified themselves on the 4th, 5th, and 6th of Sivan, on which latter day the ten commandments were actually given them

---

[11]The assertion (Kitto's *Cycl.* iii, p.429), that on these days 'the lesser "Hallel" was recited, and not the great "Hallel," ' is incorrect. Indeed, it is inconsistent with the account of the 'Hallel,' given by the same writer in another part of the *Cycl.* The great 'Hallel' was never on ordinary occasions recited in the Temple at all, and 'the lesser (?) Hallel' certainly not during 'Moed Katon' of the Passover week.

(Exod. 19:10–16).[12] Accordingly the days before Pentecost were always reckoned as the first, second, third, etc., since the presentation of the omer. Thus Maimonides beautifully observes: 'Just as one who is expecting the most faithful of his friends is wont to count the days and hours to his arrival, so we also count from the omer of the day of our Exodus from Egypt to that of the giving of the law, which was the object of our Exodus, as it is said: "I bare you on eagle's wings, and brought you unto Myself." And because this great manifestation did not last more than one day, therefore we annually commemorate it only one day.'[13]

Full seven weeks after the Paschal day, counting from the presentation of the omer on the 16th of Nisan, or exactly on the fiftieth day (Lev. 23:15, 16), was the Feast of Weeks, or Pentecost, 'a holy convocation,' in which 'no servile work' was to be done (Lev. 23:21; Num. 28:26), when 'all males' were to 'appear before Jehovah' in His sanctuary (Exod. 23:14–17), and the appointed sacrifices and offerings to be brought. The names, 'Feast of Weeks' (Exod. 34:22; Deut. 16:10, 16; 2 Chron. 8:13), and 'Feast of the Fiftieth Day,' or 'Day of Pentecost' (Jos. *Jew. Wars*, 2.42; Acts 2:1; 20:16; 1 Cor. 16:8), bear reference to this interval from the Passover. Its character is expressed by the terms 'feast of harvest' (Exod. 23:16) and 'day of firstfruits (Num. 28:26), while Jewish tradition designates it as 'Chag ha Azereth,' or simply 'Azereth' (the 'feast of the conclusion,' or simply 'conclusion'), and the 'Season of the giving of our Law.'

The festive sacrifices for the day of Pentecost were, according to Num. 28:26–31, 'two young bullocks, one ram, and seven lambs of the first year' for a burnt-offering, along with their appropriate meat-offerings; and 'one kid of the goats' for a sin-offering —all these, of course, irrespective of the usual morn-

On the morning of the third day there was thunder and lightning, with a thick cloud over the mountain, and a very loud trumpet blast. Everyone in the camp trembled. Then Moses led the people out of the camp to meet with God, and they stood at the foot of the mountain. Mount Sinai was covered with smoke, because the LORD descended on it in fire. The smoke billowed up from it like smoke from a furnace, the whole mountain trembled violently, and the sound of the trumpet grew louder and louder. Then Moses spoke and the voice of God answered him (Exod. 19:16–19).

Now when that feast, which was observed after seven weeks, and which the Jews called Pentecost (i.e. the 50th day) was at hand, its name being taken from the number of the days [after the Passover], the people got together (Jos. Jewish Wars 2.42).

---

[12]Owing to the peculiarity of the Jewish calendar, Pentecost did not always take place exactly on the 6th Sivan. Care was taken that it should not occur on a Tuesday, Thursday, or Saturday. (Reland. p. 430.)

[13]*More Neb*, quoted in Kitto's *Cycl.* iii, p. 468.

But while there were daily skirmishes, the enemy waited for the coming of the multitude out of the country to Pentecost, a feast of ours so called; and when that day was come, many ten thousands of the people were gathered together about the temple... (Jos. Antiquities 14.337–338).

On the day of firstfruits, when you present to the LORD an offering of new grain during the Feast of Weeks, hold a sacred assembly and do no regular work (Num. 28:26).

ing sacrifice. But what gave to the feast its distinctive peculiarity was the presentation of the two loaves, and the sacrifices which accompanied them. Though the attendance of worshippers at the Temple may not have been so large as at the Passover, yet tens of thousands crowded to it (Jos. *Antiq.* 14.338; 17.254). From the narrative in Acts 2 we also infer that perhaps, more than at any of the other great festivals, Jews from distant countries came to Jerusalem, possibly from the great facilities for travelling which the season afforded. On the day before Pentecost the pilgrim bands entered the Holy City, which just then lay in the full glory of early summer. Most of the harvest all over the country had already been reaped,[14] and a period of rest and enjoyment seemed before them. As the stars shone out in the deep blue sky with the brilliancy peculiar to an Easter clime, the blasts of the priests' trumpets, announcing the commencement of the feast, sounded from the Temple mount through the delicious stillness of the summer night. Already in the first watch the great altar was cleansed, and immediately after midnight the Temple gates were thrown open. For before the morning sacrifice all burnt- and peace-offerings which the people proposed to bring at the feast had to be examined by the officiating priesthood. Great as their number was, it must have been a busy time, till the announcement that the morning glow extended to Hebron put an end to all such preparations, by giving the signal for the regular morning sacrifice. After the festive offerings prescribed in Num. 28:26–30 were brought—first, the sin-offering, with proper imposition of hands, confession of sin, and sprinkling of blood; and similarly the burnt-offerings, with their meat-offerings. The Levites were now chanting the 'Hallel' to the accompanying music of a single flute, which began and ended the song, so as to give it a sort of soft sweetness. The round, ringing treble of selected voices from the children of Levites, who stood below their fathers, gave richness

[14]The *completion* of the wheat harvest throughout the land is computed by the Rabbis at about a month later. See Relandus, *Antiq.* p. 428.

and melody to the hymn, while the people either repeated or responded, as on the evening of the Passover sacrifice.

THE TWO WAVE-LOAVES

Then came the peculiar offering of the day— that of the two wave-loaves, with their accompanying sacrifices. These consisted of seven lambs of the first year, without blemish, one young bullock, and two rams for a burnt-offering, with their appropriate meat offerings; and then 'one kid of the goats for a sin-offering, and two lambs of the first year for a sacrifice of peace-offerings' (Lev. 23:19).[15] As the omer for the 16th of Nisan was of barley, being the first ripe corn in the land, so the 'two wave-loaves' were prepared from wheat grown in the best district of the country —under conditions similar to those already noticed about the Passover-sheaf. Similarly, three *seahs*, or about three pecks and three pints of wheat, were cut down, brought to the Temple, thrashed like other meat-offerings, ground, and passed through twelve sieves.[16] From the flour thus obtained two omers (or double the quantity of that at the Passover) were used for 'the two loaves;' the rest might be redeemed and used for any purpose. Care was taken that the flour for each loaf should be taken separately from one and a half seah, that it should be separately kneaded with lukewarm water (like all thank-offerings), and separately baked—the latter in the Temple itself. The loaves were made the evening preceding the festival; or, if that fell on the Sabbath, two evenings before. In shape they were long and flat, and turned up, either at the edges or at the corners. According to the *Mishnah*, each loaf was four handbreadths wide, seven long, and four fingers high, and as it contained one omer of flour (5.1 pints, or rather less than four pounds' weight), the dough would weigh about five pounds

The remains of a glass oven

---

[15]This offering, accompanying the wave-loaves, has by some been confounded with the festive sacrifices of the day, as enumerated in Num. 28:27. But the two are manifestly quite distinct.

[16]In the case of the first omer it had been thirteen sieves; but both specifications may be regarded as Rabbinical fancifulness.

and three-quarters, yielding, say, five pounds and a quarter of bread, or ten and half for the two wave-loaves.'[17]

THE WAVE-LOAVES WERE LEAVENED

Contrary to the common rule of the Sanctuary, these loaves were leavened, which, as the *Mishnah* informs us (*Men.* v. 1), was the case in all thank-offerings. The common explanation—that the wave-loaves were leavened because they represented the ordinary food of the people—only partially accounts for this. No doubt these wave-loaves expressed the Old Testament acknowledgment of the truth which our Lord embodied in the prayer, 'Give us this day our daily bread.' But this is not all. Let it be remembered that these two loaves, with the two lambs that formed part of the same wave-offering, were the only public peace- and thank-offerings of Israel; that they were accompanied by burnt- and sin-offerings; and that, unlike ordinary peace-offerings, they were considered as 'most holy.' Hence they were leavened, because Israel's public thank-offerings, even the most holy, are leavened by imperfectness and sin, and they need a sin-offering. This idea of a public thank-offering was further borne out by all the services of the day. First, the two lambs were 'waved' while yet alive; that is, before being made ready for use. Then, after their sacrifice, the breast and shoulder, or principal parts of each, were laid beside the two loaves, and 'waved' (generally towards the east) forwards and backwards, and up and down.[18] After burning the fat, the flesh belonged, not to the offerers, but to the priests. As in the case of the most holy sacrifices, the sacrificial meal was to take place within the Temple itself, nor was any part of it to be kept beyond midnight. One of

All Meal–offerings were offered unleavened, excepting the leavened [cakes prescribed] for the Thank–offering and the Two Loaves, which were offered leavened (Mishnah, Menaḥot v.1).

---

[17]These numbers are sufficiently accurate for general computation. By actual experiment I find that a pint of flour weighs about three-quarters of a pound and two ounces, and that $3^3/4$ lbs. of flour, with half a teacup of barm and an ounce of salt, yield $5^3/4$ pounds of dough and $5^1/4$ lbs. of bread.

[18]The Rabbinical statement is, that the whole offering was to be waved together by a priest; but that if each loaf, with one breast and shoulder of lamb, was waved separately, it was valid. From the weight of the mass, this must have been the common practice.

the wave-loaves and of the lambs went to the high-priest; the other belonged to all the officiating priest-hood. Lastly, after the ceremony of the wave-loaves, the people brought their own freewill-offerings, each as the Lord had prospered him—the afternoon and evening being spent in the festive meal, to which the stranger, the poor, and the Levite were bidden as the Lord's welcome guests. On account of the number of such sacrifices, the Feast of Weeks was generally pro-tracted for the greater part of a week; and this the more readily that the offering of firstfruits also began at this time. Lastly, as the bringing of the omer at the Passover marked the period when new corn might be used in the land, so the presentation of the wave-loaves that when new flour might be brought for meat-offerings in the Sanctuary.

You show that you are a letter from Christ, the result of our ministry, written not with ink but with the Spirit of the living God, not on tablets of stone but on tablets of human hearts (2 Cor. 3:3).

THE LATER SIGNIFICANCE OF PENTECOST

If Jewish tradition connected the 'Feast of Firstfruits' with the 'Mount that might be touched,' and the 'voice of words which they that heard entreated that the word should not be spoken to them any more,' we have in this respect also 'come unto Mount Zion,' and to the better things of the New Covenant. To us the Day of Pentecost is, indeed, the 'feast of firstfruits,' and that of the giving of the better law, 'written not in tables of stone, but on the fleshy tables of the heart,' 'with the Spirit of the living God.' For, as the worshippers were in the Temple, probably just as they were offering the wave-lambs and the wave-bread, the multitude heard that 'sound from heaven, as of a mighty rushing wind,' which drew them to the house where the apostles were gathered, there to hear 'every man in his own language' 'the wonderful works of God.' And on that Pentecost day, from the harvest of firstfruits, not less than three thousand souls added to the Church were presented as a wave-offering to the Lord. The cloven tongues of fire and the apostolic gifts of that day of firstfruits have, indeed, long since disappeared. But the mighty rushing sound of the Presence and Power of the Holy Ghost has gone forth into all the world.

Peter replied, "Repent and be baptized, every one of you, in the name of Jesus Christ for the forgiveness of your sins. And you will receive the gift of the Holy Spirit."…Those who accepted his message were baptized, and about three thousand were added to their number that day (Acts 2:38, 41).

14

THE FEAST OF TABERNACLES

✤

> On the last and greatest day of the Feast, Jesus stood
> and said in a loud voice, "If anyone is thirsty, let
> him come to me and drink."—John 7:37

THE FEAST OF TABERNACLES

*On the fifteenth day of
the seventh month the
LORD's Feast of Tabernacles
begins, and it lasts for
seven days (Lev. 23:34).*

The most joyous of all festive seasons in Israel
was that of the 'Feast of Tabernacles.' It fell on a time
of year when the hearts of the people would naturally
be full of thankfulness, gladness, and expectancy. All
the crops had been long stored; and now all fruits
were also gathered, the vintage past, and the land only
awaited the softening and refreshment of the 'latter
rain,' to prepare it for a new crop. It was appropriate
that, when the commencement of the harvest had
been consecrated by offering the first ripe sheaf of
barley, and the full ingathering of the corn by the two
wave-loaves, there should now be a harvest feast of
thankfulness and of gladness unto the Lord. But that
was not all. As they looked around on the goodly
land, the fruits of which had just enriched them, they
must have remembered that by miraculous interposition the Lord their God had brought them to this
land and given it them, and that He ever claimed it as
peculiarly His own. For the land was strictly connected with the history of the people; and both the land
and the history were linked with the mission of Israel.
If the beginning of the harvest had pointed back to
the birth of Israel in their Exodus from Egypt, and
forward to the true Passover-sacrifice in the future; if
the corn-harvest was connected with the giving of the

law on Mount Sinai in the past, and the outpouring of the Holy Spirit on the Day of Pentecost; the harvest-thanksgiving of the Feast of Tabernacles reminded Israel, on the one hand, of their dwelling in booths in the wilderness, while, on the other hand, it pointed to the final harvest when Israel's mission should be completed, and all nations gathered unto the Lord. Thus the first of the three great annual feasts spoke, in the presentation of the first sheaf, of the founding of the Church; the second of its harvesting, when the Church in its present state should be presented as two leavened wave-loaves; while the third pointed forward to the full harvest in the end, when 'in this mountain shall the Lord of Hosts make unto all people a feast of fat things....And He will destroy in this mountain the face of the covering cast over all people, and the veil that is spread over all nations. He will swallow up death in victory; and the Lord God will wipe away tears from off all faces; and the rebuke of His people (Israel) shall He take away from all the earth' (Isa. 25:6–8; comp. Rev. 21:4, etc.).

Live in booths for seven days: All native-born Israelites are to live in booths so your descendants will know that I had the Israelites live in booths when I brought them out of Egypt. I am the LORD your God (Lev. 23:42–43).

He will wipe every tear from their eyes. There will be no more death or mourning or crying or pain, for the old order of things has passed away (Rev. 21:4).

THE NAMES OF THE FEAST

That these are not ideal comparisons, but the very design of the Feast of Tabernacles, appears not only from the language of the prophets and the peculiar services of the feast, but also from its position in the Calendar, and even from the names by which it is designated in Scripture. Thus in its reference to the harvest it is called 'the feast of ingathering' (Exod. 23:16; 34:22); in that to the history of Israel in the past, 'the Feast of Tabernacles' (Lev. 23:34; and specially ver. 43; Deut. 16:13, 16; 31:10; 2 Chron. 8:13; Ezra 3:4); while its symbolic bearing on the future is brought out in its designation as emphatically 'the feast' (1 Kgs. 8:2; 2 Chron. 5:3; 7:8, 9); and 'the Feast of Jehovah' (so, literally, in Lev. 23:39). In this sense also Josephus, Philo, and the Rabbis (in many passages of the *Mishnah*) single it out from all the other feasts. And quite decisive on the point is the description of the 'latter-day' glory at the close of the prophecies of Zechariah, where the conversion of all nations is

Celebrate the Feast of Harvest with the firstfruits of the crops you sow in your field.
Celebrate the Feast of Ingathering at the end of the year, when you gather in your crops from the field (Exod. 23:16).

distinctly connected with the 'Feast of Tabernacles' (Zech. 14:16–21). That this reference is by no means isolated will appear in the sequel.

Celebrate the Feast of Tabernacles for seven days after you have gathered the produce of your threshing floor and your winepress. Be joyful at your Feast— you, your sons and daughters, your menservants and maidservants, and the Levites, the aliens, the fatherless and the widows who live in your towns. For seven days celebrate the Feast to the LORD your God at the place the LORD will choose. For the LORD your God will bless you in all your harvest and in all the work of your hands, and your joy will be complete (Deut. 16:13–15).

Then the survivors from all the nations that have attacked Jerusalem will go up year after year to worship the King, the LORD Almighty, and to celebrate the Feast of Tabernacles (Zech. 14:16).

The first day is a sacred assembly; do no regular work. For seven days present offerings made to the LORD by fire, and on the eighth day hold a sacred assembly and present an offering made to the LORD by fire. It is the closing assembly; do no regular work (Lev. 23:35–36).

THE TIME OF THE FEAST

The Feast of Tabernacles was the third of the great annual festivals, at which every male in Israel was to appear before the Lord in the place which He should choose. It fell on the 15th of the seventh month, or Tishri (corresponding to September or the beginning of October), as the Passover had fallen on the 15th of the first month. The significance of these numbers in themselves and relatively will not escape attention, the more so that this feast closed the original festive calendar; for Purim and 'the feast of the dedication of the Temple,' which both occurred later in the season, were of post-Mosaic origin. The Feast of Tabernacles, or, rather (as it should be called), of 'booths,' lasted for seven days—from the 15th to the 21st Tishri—and was followed by an Octave on the 22nd Tishri. But this eighth day, though closely connected with the Feast of Tabernacles, formed no part of that feast, as clearly shown by the difference in the sacrifices and the ritual, and by the circumstance that the people no longer lived in 'booths.' The first day of the feast, and also its Octave, or Azereth (*clausura, conclusio*), were to be the days of 'holy convocation' (Lev. 23:35, 36), and each 'a Sabbath' (Lev. 23:39), not in the sense of the weekly Sabbath, but of festive rest in the Lord (Lev. 23:25, 32), when no servile work of any kind might be done.

IT FOLLOWED CLOSE UPON THE DAY OF ATONEMENT

There is yet another important point to be noticed. The 'Feast of Tabernacles' followed closely on the Day of Atonement. Both took place in the seventh month; the one on the 10th, the other on the 15th of Tishri. What the seventh day, or Sabbath, was in reference to the week, the seventh month seems to have been in reference to the year. It closed not only the sacred cycle, but also the agricultural or working year.

It also marked the change of seasons, the approach of rain and of the winter equinox, and determined alike the commencement and the close of a sabbatical year (Deut. 31:10). Coming on the 15th of this seventh month—that is, at full moon, when the 'sacred' month had, so to speak, attained its full strength—the Feast of Tabernacles appropriately followed five days after the Day of Atonement, in which the sin of Israel had been removed, and its covenant relation to God restored. Thus a sanctified nation could keep a holy feast of harvest joy unto the Lord, just as in the truest sense it will be 'in that day' (Zech. 14:20) when the meaning of the Feast of Tabernacles shall be really fulfilled.[1]

Then Moses commanded them: "At the end of every seven years, in the year for canceling debts, during the Feast of Tabernacles, when all Israel comes to appear before the LORD your God at the place he will choose, you shall read this law before them in their hearing" (Deut. 31:10–11).

THE THREE CHIEF FEATURES OF THE FEAST

Three things specially marked the Feast of Tabernacles: its joyous festivities, the dwelling in 'booths,' and the peculiar sacrifices and rites of the week. The first of these was simply characteristic of a 'feast of ingathering:' 'Because the Lord thy God shall bless thee in all thine increase, and in all the works of thine hands, therefore thou shalt surely rejoice—thou, and thy son, and thy daughter, and thy manservant, and thy maidservant, and the Levite, the stranger, and the fatherless, and the widow, that are within thy gates.' Nor were any in Israel to 'appear before the Lord empty: every man shall give as he is able, according to the blessing of the Lord thy God which He hath given thee' (Deut. 16:13–17). Votive, freewill, and peace-offerings would mark their gratitude to God, and at the meal which ensued the poor, the stranger, the Levite, and the homeless would be welcomed guests, for the Lord's sake. Moreover, when the people saw the treasury chests opened and emptied at this feast for the last time in the year, they would remember their brethren at a distance, in whose name, as well as their own, the daily and festive

On that day HOLY TO THE LORD will be inscribed on the bells of the horses, and the cooking pots in the LORD's house will be like the sacred bowls in front of the altar (Zech. 14:20).

---

[1]Quite another picture is drawn in Hos. 9, which seems also to refer to the Feast of Tabernacles (see specially verse 5). Indeed, it is remarkable how many allusions to this feast occur in the writings of the prophets, as if its types were the goal of all their desires.

sacrifices were offered. Thus their liberality would not only be stimulated, but all Israel, however widely dispersed, would feel itself anew one before the Lord their God and in the courts of His House. There was, besides, something about this feast which would peculiarly remind them, if not of their dispersion, yet of their being 'strangers and pilgrims in the earth.' For its *second characteristic* was, that during the seven days of its continuance 'all that are Israelites born shall dwell in booths; that your generations may know that I made the children of Israel to dwell in booths when I brought them out of the land of Egypt' (Lev. 23:42, 43).

On the first day you are to take choice fruit from the trees, and palm fronds, leafy branches and poplars, and rejoice before the LORD your God for seven days (Lev. 23:40).

THE BOOTHS

As usual, we are met at the outset by a controversy between the Pharisees and the Sadducees. The law had it (Lev. 23:40): 'Ye shall take you on the first day the fruit[2] of goodly trees, branches of palm trees, and the boughs of thick trees, and willows of the brook,' which the Sadducees understood (as do the modern Karaite Jews) to refer to the materials whence the booths were to be constructed, while the Pharisees applied it to what the worshippers were to carry in their hands. The latter interpretation is, in all likelihood, the correct one; it seems borne out by the account of the festival at the time of Nehemiah (Neh. 8:15, 18), when the booths were constructed of branches of other trees than those mentioned in Leviticus 23; and it was universally adopted in practice at the time of Christ. The *Mishnah* gives most minute details as to the height and construction of these 'booths,' the main object being to prevent any invasion of the law. Thus it must be a real booth, and constructed of boughs of living trees, and solely for the purposes of this festival. Hence it must be high enough, yet not too high—at least ten handbreadths, but not more than thirty feet; three of its walls must be boughs; it must be fairly covered with boughs, yet not so shaded as not to admit sunshine, nor yet so

They found written in the Law, which the LORD had commanded through Moses, that the Israelites were to live in booths during the feast of the seventh month and that they should proclaim this word and spread it throughout their towns and in Jerusalem: "Go out into the hill country and bring back branches from olive and wild olive trees, and from myrtles, palms and shade trees, to make booths"—as it is written (Neh. 8:14–15).

---

[2]So correctly in the margin.

open as to have not sufficient shade, the object in each case being neither sunshine nor shade, but that it should be a real booth of boughs of trees. It is needless to enter into further details, except to say that these booths, and not their houses, were to be the regular dwelling of all in Israel during the week, and that, except in very heavy rain, they were to eat, sleep, pray, study—in short, entirely to live in them. The only exceptions were in favour of those absent on some pious duty, the sick, and their attendants (*Succ.* ii. 4), women, slaves, and infants who were still depending on their mothers (*Succ.* ii. 8). Finally, the rule was that 'whatever might contract Levitical defilement (such as boards, cloth, etc.), or whatever did not grow out of the earth, might not be used' in constructing the 'booths' (*Succ.* i. 4).

THE FRUIT AND PALM BRANCHES

It has already been noticed that, according to the view universally prevalent at the time of Christ, the direction on the first day of the feast to 'take the fruit of goodly trees, branches of palm trees, and the boughs of thick trees, and willows of the brook,' was applied to what the worshippers were to carry in their hands. The Rabbis ruled, that 'the fruit of the goodly trees' meant the *aethrog,* or citron, and 'the boughs of thick trees' the myrtle, provided it had 'not more berries than leaves.' The *aethrogs* must be without blemish or deficiency of any kind; the palm branches at least three handbreadths high, and fit to be shaken; and each branch fresh, entire, unpolluted, and not taken from any idolatrous grove. Every worshipper carried the *aethrog* in his left hand, and in his right the *lulav,* or palm, with myrtle and willow branch on either side of it, tied together on the outside with its own kind, though in the inside it might be fastened even with gold thread (*Succ.* iii. 8). There can be no doubt that the *lulav* was intended to remind Israel of the different stages of their wilderness journey, as represented by the different vegetation—the palm branches recalling the valleys and plains, the 'boughs of thick trees,' the bushes on the mountain heights,

Myrtle

This is the general rule: What is susceptible to uncleanness or does not grow from the soil may not serve as Sukkah–roofing; but what is not susceptible to uncleanness and grows from the soil may serve as Sukkah–roofing (Mishnah, Sukka i.4).

and the willows those brooks from which God had given His people drink;[3] while the *aethrog* was to remind them of the fruits of the good land which the Lord had given them. The *lulav* was used in the Temple on each of the seven festive days, even children, if they were able to shake it, being bound to carry one. If the first day of the feast fell on a Sabbath, the people brought their *lulavs* on the previous day into the synagogue on the Temple Mount, and fetched them in the morning, so as not needlessly to break the Sabbath rest.

So beginning with the fifteenth day of the seventh month, after you have gathered the crops of the land, celebrate the festival to the LORD for seven days; the first day is a day of rest, and the eighth day also is a day of rest (Lev. 23:39).

With each lamb for the burnt offering or the sacrifice, prepare a quarter of a hin of wine as a drink offering.
  With a ram prepare a grain offering of two-tenths of an ephah of fine flour mixed with a third of a hin of oil, and a third of a hin of wine as a drink offering. Offer it as an aroma pleasing to the LORD (Num. 15:5–7).

Present an offering made by fire as an aroma pleasing to the LORD, a burnt offering of thirteen young bulls, two rams and fourteen male lambs a year old, all without defect. With each of the thirteen bulls prepare a grain offering of three-tenths of an ephah of fine flour mixed with oil; with each of the two rams, two-tenths; and with each of the fourteen lambs, one-tenth (Num. 29:13–15).

THE OFFERINGS

The *third characteristic* of the Feast of Tabernacles was its offerings. These were altogether peculiar. The sin-offering for each of the seven days was 'one kid of the goats.' The burnt-offerings consisted of bullocks, rams, and lambs, with their appropriate meat- and drink-offerings. But, whereas the number of the rams and lambs remained the same on each day of the festival, that of the bullocks decreased every day by one—from thirteen on the first to seven bullocks on the last day, 'that great day of the feast.' And no special injunctions are given about the drink-offering, we infer that it was, as usually (Num. 15:1–10), $1/4$ of a hin of wine for each lamb, $1/3$ for each ram, and $1/2$ for each bullock (the hin = 1 gallon 2 pints). The 'meat-offering' is expressly fixed (Num. 29:12, etc.) at $1/10$ of an ephah of flour, mixed with $1/4$ of a hin of oil, for each lamb; $2/10$ of an ephah, with $1/3$ hin of oil, for each ram; and $3/10$ of an ephah, with $1/2$ hin of oil, for each bullock. Three things are remarkable about these burnt-offerings. First, they are evidently the characteristic sacrifice of the Feast of Tabernacles. As compared with the Feast of Unleavened Bread, the number of the rams and lambs is double, while that of the bullocks is fivefold (14 during the Passover week, 5 x 14 during that of Tabernacles.) Secondly, the number of the burnt-sacrifices, whether taking each kind by itself or all of them together, is always

[3]See the Art. by Pressel in Herzog's *Real.-Encycl.* vol. viii.

divisible by the sacred number *seven*. We have for the week 70 bullocks, 14 rams, and 98 lambs, or altogether 182 sacrifices (26 x 7), to which must be added 336 (48 x 7) tenths of ephahs of flour for the meat-offering. We will not pursue the tempting subject of this symbolism of numbers further than to point out that, whereas the sacred number 7 appeared at the Feast of Unleavened Bread only in the number of its days, and at Pentecost in the period of its observance (7 x 7 days after Passover), the Feast of Tabernacles lasted seven days, took place when the seventh month was at its full height, and had the number 7 impressed on its characteristic sacrifices. It is not so easy to account for the third peculiarity of these sacrifices—that of the daily diminution in the number of bullocks offered. The common explanation, that it was intended to indicate the decreasing sanctity of each successive day of the feast, while the sacred number 7 was still to be reserved for the last day, is not more satisfactory than the view propounded in the Talmud, that these sacrifices were offered, not for Israel, but for the nations of the world: 'There were seventy bullocks, to correspond to the number of the seventy nations in the world.' But did the Rabbis understand the prophetic character of this feast? An attentive consideration of its peculiar ceremonial will convince that it must have been exceedingly difficult to ignore it entirely.

On the day before the Feast of Tabernacles—the 14th Tishri—the festive pilgrims had all arrived in Jerusalem. The 'booths' on the roofs, in the court-yards, in streets and squares, as well as roads and gardens, within a Sabbath day's journey, must have given the city and neighbourhood an unusually pic-turesque appearance. The preparation of all that was needed for the festival—purification, the care of the offerings that each would bring, and friendly com-munications between those who were to be invited to the sacrificial meal—no doubt sufficiently occupied their time. When the early autumn evening set in, the blasts of the priests' trumpets on the Temple Mount announced to Israel the advent of the feast.

The Feast of Tabernacles happened to fall at the same time, which was kept by the Hebrews as a most holy and most eminent feast (Jos. Antiquities 8.100).

SPECIAL SERVICE AT THE TEMPLE

As at the Passover and at Pentecost, the altar of burnt-offering was cleansed during the first night-watch, and the gates of the Temple were thrown open immediately after midnight. The time till the beginning of the ordinary morning sacrifice was occupied in examining the various sacrifices and offerings that were to be brought during the day. While the morning sacrifice was being prepared, a priest, accompanied by a joyous procession with music, went down to the Pool of Siloam, whence he drew water into a golden pitcher, capable of holding three log (rather more than two pints). But on the Sabbaths they fetched the water from a golden vessel in the Temple itself, into which it had been carried from Siloam on the preceding day. At the same time that the procession started for Siloam, another went to a place in the Kedron valley, close by, called Motza, whence they brought willow branches, which, amidst the blasts of the priests' trumpets, they stuck on either side of the altar of burnt-offering, bending them over towards it, so as to form a kind of leafy canopy. Then the ordinary sacrifice proceeded, the priest who had gone to Siloam so timing it, that he returned just as his brethren carried up the pieces of the sacrifice to lay them on the altar. As he entered by the 'Watergate,' which obtained its name from this ceremony, he was received by a threefold blast from the priests' trumpets. The priests then went up the rise of the altar and turned to the left, where there were two silver basins with narrow holes—the eastern a little wider for the wine, and the western somewhat narrower for the water. Into these the wine of the drink-offering was poured, and at the same time the water from Siloam, the people shouting to the priest, 'Raise thy hand,' to show that he really poured the water into the basin which led to the base of the altar. For, sharing the objections of the Sadducees, Alexander Jannaeus, the Maccabean king-priest (about 95 B.C.), had shown his contempt for the Pharisees by pouring the water at this feast upon the ground, on which the people pelted him with their *aethrogs*, and would have mur-

As to Alexander, his own people were seditious against him; for at a festival which was then celebrated, when he stood upon the altar, and was going to sacrifice, the nation rose upon him and pelted with citrons…(Jos. Antiquities 13.372).

dered him, if his foreign body-guard had not interfered, on which occasion no less than six thousand
Jews were killed in the Temple.

THE MUSIC OF THE FEAST

As soon as the wine and the water were being
poured out, the Temple music began, and the 'Hallel'
(Ps. 113–118) was sung in the manner previously
prescribed, and to the accompaniment of flutes,
except on the Sabbath and on the first day of the feast,
when flute-playing was not allowed, on account of
the sanctity of the days. When the choir came to these
words (Ps. 118:1), 'O give thanks to the Lord,' and
again when they sang (Ps. 118:25), 'O work then
now salvation, Jehovah;' and once more at the close
(Ps. 118:29), 'O give thanks unto the Lord,' all the
worshippers shook their *lulavs* towards the altar.
When, therefore, the multitudes from Jerusalem, on
meeting Jesus, 'cut down branches from the trees,
and strewed them in the way, and…cried, saying, O
then, work now salvation to the Son of David!' (Matt.
21:8, 9; John 12:12, 13), they applied, in reference to
Christ, what was regarded as one of the chief ceremonies of the Feast of Tabernacles, praying that God
would now from 'the highest' heavens manifest and
send that salvation in connection with the Son of
David, which was symbolised by the pouring out of
water. For though the ceremony was considered by
the Rabbis as bearing a subordinate reference to the
dispensation of the rain, the annual fall of which they
imagined was determined by God at that feast, its
main and real application was to the future outpouring of the Holy Spirit, as predicted—probably in
allusion to this very rite—by Isaiah the prophet.[4]
Thus the Talmud says distinctly: 'Why is the name of

The next day the great crowd that had come for the Feast heard that Jesus was on his way to Jerusalem. They took palm branches and went out to meet him, shouting,
"Hosanna!"
"Blessed is he who comes in the name of the Lord!"
"Blessed is the King of Israel!"
(John 12:12–13).

[4]Isaiah 12:3. Of course, one or other of these two views is open, either, that the words of Isaiah were based on the ceremony of water-pouring, or that this ceremony was derived from the words of Isaiah. In either case, however, our inference from it holds good. It is only fair to add, that by some the expression 'water' in Isa. 12:3 is applied to the 'law.' But this in no way vitiates our conclusion, as the Jews expected the general conversion of the Gentiles to be a conversion to Judaism.

it called, The drawing out of water? Because of the pouring out of the Holy Spirit, according to what is said: "With joy shall ye draw water out of the wells of salvation." ' Hence, also, the feast and the peculiar joyousness of it are alike designated as those of 'the drawing out of water;' for, according to the same Rabbinical authorities, the Holy Spirit dwells in man only through joy.

On the last and greatest day of the Feast, Jesus stood and said in a loud voice, "If anyone is thirsty, let him come to me and drink. Whoever believes in me, as the Scripture has said, streams of living water will flow from within him" (John 7:37–38).

THE DAILY CIRCUIT OF THE ALTAR

A similar symbolism was expressed by another ceremony which took place at the close, not of the daily, but of the festive sacrifices. On every one of the seven days the priests formed in procession, and made the circuit of the altar, singing: 'O then, now work salvation, Jehovah! O Jehovah, give prosperity!' (Ps. 118:25). But on the seventh, 'that great day of the feast,' they made the circuit of the altar seven times, remembering how the walls of Jericho had fallen in similar circumstances, and anticipating how, by the direct interposition of God, the walls of heathenism would fall before Jehovah, and the land lie open for His people to go in and possess it.

THE REFERENCES IN JOHN 7:37

We can now in some measure realise the event recorded in John 7:37. The festivities of the Week of Tabernacles were drawing to a close. 'It was the last day, that great day of the feast.' It obtained this name, although it was not one of 'holy convocation,' partly because it closed the feast, and partly from the circumstances which procured it in Rabbinical writings the designations of 'Day of the Great Hosannah,' on account of the sevenfold circuit of the altar with 'Hosannah;' and 'Day of Willows,' and 'Day of Beating the Branches,' because all the leaves were shaken off the willow boughs, and the palm branches beaten in pieces by the side of the altar. It was on that day, after the priest had returned from Siloam with his golden pitcher, and for the last time poured its contents to the base of the altar; after the 'Hallel' had been sung to the sound of the flute, the people responding and worshipping as the priests three times drew the three-fold blasts from their silver trumpets—just when the interest of the people had been raised to its highest pitch, that, from amidst the mass of worshippers, who were waving towards the altar quite a forest of leafy branches as the last words of Ps. 118 were chanted—a voice was raised which resounded through the Temple, startled the multitude, and carried fear and hatred to the hearts of their leaders. It was Jesus, who 'stood and cried, saying, If any man thirst, let him come unto Me, and drink.' Then by faith in Him should each one truly become like the Pool of Siloam, and from his inmost being 'rivers of living water flow' (John 7:38). 'This spake He of the Spirit, which they that believe on Him should receive.' Thus the significance of the rite, in which they had just taken part, was not only fully explained, but the mode of its fulfillment pointed out. The effect was instantaneous. It could not but be, that in that vast assembly, so suddenly roused by being brought face to face with Him in whom every type and prophecy is fulfilled, there would be many who, 'when they heard this saying, said, Of a truth this is the Prophet. Others said, This is the Christ.' Even the Temple-guard, whose duty it would have been in such circumstances to arrest one who had so interrupted the services of the day, and presented himself to the people in such a light, owned the spell of His words, and dared not to lay hands on Him. 'Never man spake like this man,' was the only account they could give of their unusual weakness, in answer to the reproaches of the chief priests and Pharisees. The rebuke of the Jewish authorities, which followed, is too characteristic to require comment. One only of their number had been deeply moved by the scene just witnessed in the Temple. Yet, timid as usually, Nicodemus only laid hold of this one point, that the Pharisees had traced the popular confession of Jesus to their ignorance of the law, to which he replied, in the genuine Rabbinical manner of arguing, without meeting one's opponent face to face: 'Doth our law judge any man before it hear him, and know what he doeth?'

On hearing his words, some of the people said, "Surely this man is the Prophet."
Others said, "He is the Christ."
Still others asked, "How can the Christ come from Galilee? Does not the Scripture say that the Christ will come from David's family and from Bethlehem, the town where David lived?" Thus the people were divided because of Jesus. Some wanted to seize him, but no one laid a hand on him (John 7:40–44).

Nicodemus, who had gone to Jesus earlier and who was one of their own number, asked, "Does our law condemn anyone without first hearing him to find out what he is doing?" (John 7:50–51).

The Golden Candlestick

When Jesus spoke again to the people, he said, "I am the light of the world. Whoever follows me will never walk in darkness, but will have the light of life" (John 8:12).

THE MAN BORN BLIND

But matters were not to end with the wrangling of priests and Pharisees. The proof which Nicodemus had invited them to seek from the teaching and the miracles of Christ was about to be displayed both before the people and their rulers in the healing of the blind man. Here also it was in allusion to the ceremonial of the Feast of Tabernacles that Jesus, when He saw the 'man blind from his birth,' said (John 9:5): 'As long as I am in the world, I am the light of the world;' having 'anointed the eyes of the blind man with the clay,' just as He told him, 'Go, wash in the Pool of Siloam (which is, by interpretation, Sent).' For the words, 'I am the light of the world,' are the same which He had just spoken in the Temple (John 8:12), and they had in all probability been intended to point to another very peculiar ceremony which took place at the Feast of Tabernacles. In the words of the *Mishnah* (*Succah* v. 2, 3, 4), the order of the services for that feast was as follows: 'They went first to offer the daily sacrifice in the morning, then the additional sacrifices; after that the votive and freewill-offerings; from thence to the festive meal; from thence to the study of the law; and after that to offer the evening sacrifice; and from thence they went to the joy of the pouring out of the water.' It is this 'joy of the pouring out of the water' which we are about to describe.

THE CEREMONIES IN THE COURT OF THE WOMEN

At the close of the first day of the feast the worshippers descended to the Court of the Women, where great preparations had been made. Four golden candelabras were there, each with four golden bowls, and against them rested four ladders; and four youths of priestly descent held, each a pitcher of oil, capable of holding one hundred and twenty log, from which they filled each bowl. The old, worn breeches and girdles of the priests served for wicks to these lamps. There was not a court in Jerusalem that was not lit up by the light of 'the house of water-pouring.' The 'Chassidim' and 'the men of Deed' danced before the

Straight trumpets

people with flaming torches in their hands, and sang
before them hymns and songs of praise; and the Levites,
with harps, and lutes, and cymbals, and trumpets,
and instruments of music without number, stood
upon the fifteen steps which led down from the Court
of Israel to that of the Women, according to the number of the fifteen Songs of Degrees in the Book of
Psalms. They stood with their instruments of music,
and sang hymns. Two priests, with trumpets in their
hands, were at the upper gate (that of Nicanor),
which led from the Court of Israel to that of the
Women. At cock-crowing they drew a threefold blast.
As they reached the tenth step, they drew another
threefold blast; as they entered the court itself, they
drew yet another threefold blast; and so they blew as
they advanced, till they reached the gate which opens
upon the east (the Beautiful Gate). As they came to
the eastern gate, they turned round towards the west
(to face the Holy Place), and said: 'Our fathers who
were in this place, they turned their back upon the
Sanctuary of Jehovah, and their faces towards the east,
and they worshipped towards the rising sun; but as
for us, our eyes are towards the Lord.'

A fragment of one of the hymns sung that night
has been preserved. It was sung by the 'Chassidim'
and 'men of Deed,' and by those who did penance in
their old age for the sins of their youth:

The Chassidim and Men of Deed
'Oh joy, that our youth, devoted, sage,
Doth bring no shame upon our old age!'

The Penitents
'Oh joy, we can in our old age
Repair the sins of youth not sage!'

The people walking in darkness have seen a great light; on those living in the land of the shadow of death a light has dawned (Isa. 9:2).

Both in unison
'Yes, happy he on whom no early guilt doth rest,
And he who, having sinned, is now with pardon blest.

SIGNIFICANCE OF THE ILLUMINATION

Arise, shine, for your light has come, and the glory of the LORD rises upon you. See, darkness covers the earth and thick darkness is over the peoples, but the LORD rises upon you and his glory appears over you. Nations will come to your light, and kings to the brightness of your dawn (Isa. 60:1–3).

It seems clear that this illumination of the Temple was regarded as forming part of, and having the same symbolical meaning as, 'the pouring out of water.' The light shining out of the Temple into the darkness around, and lighting up every court in Jerusalem, must have been intended as a symbol not only of the Shechinah which once filled the Temple, but of that 'great light' which 'the people that walked in darkness' were to see, and which was to shine 'upon them that dwell in the land of the shadow of death' (Isa. 9:2). May it not be, that such prophecies as Isa. 9 and 60 were connected with this symbolism? At any rate, it seems most probable that Jesus had referred to this ceremony in the words spoken by Him in the Temple at that very Feast of Tabernacles: 'I am the light of the world; he that followeth Me shall not walk in darkness, but shall have the light of life' (John 8:12).

THE SIX MINOR DAYS

Only the first of the seven days of this feast was 'a holy convocation;' the other six were 'minor festivals.' On each day, besides the ordinary morning and evening sacrifices, the festive offerings prescribed in Num. 29:12–38 were brought. The Psalms sung at the drink-offering after the festive sacrifices (or *Musaph,* as they are called), were, for the first day of the feast, Ps. 105; for the second, Ps. 29; for the third, Ps. 50, from ver. 16; for the fourth, Ps. 94, from ver. 16; for the fifth, Ps. 94, from ver. 8; for the sixth, Ps. 81, from ver. 6; for the last day of the feast, Ps. 82, from ver. 5. As the people retired from the altar at the close of each day's service, they exclaimed, 'How beautiful art thou, O altar!'—or, according to a later version, 'We give thanks to Jehovah and to thee, O altar!' All the four-and-twenty orders of the priesthood were engaged in the festive offerings, which were apportioned among them according to definite rules, which also fixed how the priestly dues were to be divided among them. Lastly, on every sabbatical year the Law was to be publicly read on the first day of the feast (Deut. 31:10–13).[5]

On the afternoon of the seventh day of the feast the people began to remove from the 'booths.' For at the Octave, on the 22nd of Tishri, they lived no longer in booths, nor did they use the *lulav*. But it was observed as 'a holy convocation;' and the festive sacrifices prescribed in Num. 29:36–38 were offered, although no more by all the twenty-four courses of priests, and finally the 'Hallel' sung at the drink-offering.

Give thanks to the LORD, call on his name; make known among the nations what he has done. Sing to him, sing praise to him; tell of all his wonderful acts (Ps. 105:1–2).

When the priests withdrew from the Holy Place, the cloud filled the temple of the LORD. And the priests could not perform their service because of the cloud, for the glory of the LORD filled his temple (1 Kgs. 8:10–11).

THE POURING AND LIGHTING POST-MOSAIC

It will have been observed that the two most important ceremonies of the Feast of Tabernacles— the pouring out of water and the illumination of the Temple—were of post-Mosaic origin. According to Jewish tradition, the pillar of cloud by day and of fire by night had first appeared to Israel on the 15th of Tishri, the first day of the feast. On that day also Moses was said to have come down from the Mount, and announced to the people that the Tabernacle of God was to be reared among them. We know that the dedication of Solomon's Temple and the descent of the Shechinah took place at this feast (1 Kgs. 8; 2 Chron. 7). Nor can we greatly err in finding an allusion to it in this description of heavenly things: 'After this I beheld, and, lo, a great multitude, which no man could number, of all nations, and kindreds, and

---

[5]In later times only certain portions were read, the law as a whole being sufficiently known from the weekly prelections in the synagogues.

people, and tongues, stood before the throne, and before the Lamb, clothed with white robes, and palms in their hands; and cried with a loud voice, saying, Salvation to our God, which sitteth upon the throne, and unto the Lamb' (Rev. 7:9, 10).

Whether or not our suggestions be adopted as to the typical meaning of the two great ceremonies of the 'pouring out of the water' and the Temple Illumination, the fact remains, that the Feast of Tabernacles is the one and only type in the Old Testament which has not yet been fulfilled.

15
THE NEW MOONS:
THE FEAST OF THE SEVENTH NEW MOON,
OR OF TRUMPETS, OR NEW YEAR'S DAY

Therefore do not let anyone judge you by what you
eat or drink, or with regard to a religious festival, a
New Moon celebration or a Sabbath day. These are
a shadow of the things that were to come; the reality,
however, is found in Christ.—Col. 2:16–17

THE NEW MOONS

Scarcely any other festive season could have left so continuous an impress on the religious life of Israel as the 'New Moons.' Recurring at the beginning of every month, and marking it, the solemn proclamation of the day, by—'It is sanctified,' was intended to give a hallowed character to each month, while the blowing of the priests' trumpets and the special sacrifices brought, would summon, as it were, the Lord's host to offer their tribute unto their exalted King, and thus bring themselves into 'remembrance' before Him. Besides, it was also a popular feast, when families, like that of David, might celebrate their special annual sacrifice (1 Sam. 20:6, 29); when the king gave a state-banquet (1 Sam. 20:5, 24); and those who sought for instruction and edification resorted to religious meetings, such as Elisha seems to have held (2 Kgs. 4:23). And so we trace its observance onwards through the history of Israel; marking in Scripture a special Psalm for the New Moon (in Tishri—Ps. 81:3); noting how from month to month the day was kept as an outward ordinance, even in the decay of religious life (Isa. 1:13; Hos. 2:11), apparently all the more rigidly, with abstinence from work, not enjoined in the law, that its spirit was no longer understood (Amos 8:5);

So David said, "Look, tomorrow is the New Moon festival, and I am supposed to dine with the king; but let me go and hide in the field until the evening of the day after tomorrow. If your father misses me at all, tell him, 'David earnestly asked my permission to hurry to Bethlehem, his hometown, because an annual sacrifice is being made there for his whole clan' " (1 Sam. 20:5–6).

Stop bringing meaningless offerings! Your incense is detestable to me. New Moons, Sabbaths and convocations— I cannot bear your evil assemblies (Isa. 1:13).

Therefore do not let anyone judge you by what you eat or drink, or with regard to a religious festival, a New Moon celebration or a Sabbath day. These are a shadow of the things that were to come; the reality, however, is found in Christ (Col. 2:16–17).

and finally learning from the prophecies of Isaiah and Ezekiel that it also had a higher meaning, and was destined to find a better fulfillment in another dispensation, when the New Moon trumpet should summon 'all flesh to worship before Jehovah' (Isa. 66:23), and the closed eastern gate to the inner court of the new Temple be opened once more to believing Israel (Ezek. 46:1). And in New Testament times we still find the 'New Moon' kept as an outward observance by Jews and Judaising Christians, yet expressly characterised as 'a shadow of things to come; but the body is of Christ' (Col. 2:16, 17).

THE DETERMINATION OF THE NEW MOON

We have already shown of what importance the right determination of the new moon was in fixing the various festivals of the year, and with what care and anxiety its appearance was ascertained from witnesses who had actually seen it; also how the tidings were afterwards communicated to those at a distance. For the new moon was reckoned by actual personal observation, not by astronomical calculation, with which, however, as we know, many of the Rabbis must have been familiar, since we read of astronomical pictures, by which they were wont to test the veracity of witnesses. So important was it deemed to have faithful witnesses, that they were even allowed, in order to reach Jerusalem in time, to travel on the Sabbath, and, if necessary, to make use of horse or mule (*Mish. Rosh ha Sh.* i. 9; iii. 2). While strict rules determined who were not to be admitted as witnesses (*Mish. Rosh ha Sh.* i. 8), every encouragement was given to trustworthy persons, and the Sanhedrim provided for them a banquet in a large building specially destined for that purpose, and known as the *Beth Yaazek* (*Mish. Rosh ha Sh.* ii. 5).

THE BLOWING OF TRUMPETS

In the law of God only these two things are enjoined in the observance of the 'New Moon'—the 'blowing of trumpets' (Num. 10:10) and special festive sacrifices (Num. 28:11–15). Of old the 'blowing of trumpets' had been the signal for Israel's host on their march through the wilderness, as it afterwards summoned them to warfare, and proclaimed or marked days of public rejoicing, and feasts, as well as the 'beginnings of their months' (Num. 10:1–10). The object of it is expressly stated to have been 'for a memorial,' that they might 'be remembered before Jehovah,' it being specially added: 'I am Jehovah your God.' It was, so to speak, the host of God assembled, waiting for their Leader; the people of God united to proclaim their King. At the blast of the priests' trumpets they ranged themselves, as it were, under His banner and before His throne, and this symbolical confession and proclamation of Him as 'Jehovah their God,' brought them before Him to be 'remembered' and 'saved.' And so every season of 'blowing the trumpets,' whether at New Moons, at the Feast of Trumpets or New Year's Day, at other festivals, in the Sabbatical and Year of Jubilee, or in the time of war, was a public acknowledgment of Jehovah as King. Accordingly we find the same symbols adopted in the figurative language of the New Testament. As of old the sound of the trumpet summoned the congregation before the Lord at the door of the Tabernacle, so 'His elect' shall be summoned by the sound of the trumpet in the day of Christ's coming (Matt. 24:31), and not only the living, but those also who had 'slept' (1 Cor. 15:52)—'the dead in Christ' (1 Thess. 4:16). Similarly, the heavenly hosts are marshalled to the war of successive judgments (Rev. 8:2; 10:7), till, as 'the seventh angel sounded,' Christ is proclaimed King Universal: 'The kingdoms of this world are become the kingdoms of our Lord, and of His Christ, and He shall reign for ever and ever' (Rev. 11:15).

Also at your times of rejoicing—your appointed feasts and New Moon festivals—you are to sound the trumpets over your burnt offerings and fellowship offerings, and they will be a memorial for you before your God. I am the LORD your God (Num. 10:10).

On the first of every month, present to the LORD a burnt offering of two young bulls, one ram and seven male lambs a year old, all without defect (Num. 28:11).

And he will send his angels with a loud trumpet call, and they will gather his elect from the four winds, from one end of the heavens to the other (Matt. 24:31).

But in the days when the seventh angel is about to sound his trumpet, the mystery of God will be accomplished, just as he announced to his servants the prophets (Rev. 10:7).

THE SACRIFICES OF THE NEW MOON

Besides the 'blowing of trumpets,' certain festive sacrifices were ordered to be offered on the New Moon (Num. 28:11–15). These most appropriately mark 'the beginning of months' (Num. 28:11). For it is a universal principle in the Old Testament, that 'the first' always stands for the whole—the firstfruits for the whole harvest, the firstborn and the firstlings for all the rest; and that 'if the firstfruit be holy, the lump is also holy.' And so the burnt-offerings and the sin-offering at 'the beginning' of each month consecrated the whole. These festive sacrifices consisted of two young bullocks, one ram, and seven lambs of the first year for a burnt-offering, with their appropriate meat- and drink-offerings, and also of 'one kid of the goats for a sin-offering unto Jehovah.'[1]

Whether [the New Moon] was manifestly visible or not, they may profane the Sabbath because of it. R. Jose says: If it was manifestly visible they may not profane the Sabbath because of it (Mishnah, Roš Hašana i.5).

When we pass from these simple Scriptural directions to what tradition records of the actual observance of 'New Moons' in the Temple, our difficulties increase. For this and New Year's Day are just such feasts, in connection with which superstition would most readily grow up, from the notions which the Rabbis had, that at changes of seasons Divine judgments were initiated, modified, or finally fixed.

NECESSITY FOR DISTINGUISHING THE TEMPLE AND SYNAGOGUE USE

Modern critics have not been sufficiently careful in distinguishing what had been done in the Temple from what was introduced into the synagogue, gradually and at much later periods. Thus, prayers which date long after the destruction of Jerusalem have been represented as offered in the Temple, and the custom of chanting the 'Hallel' (Ps. 113–118) on New Moons in the synagogue has been erroneously traced to Biblical times.[2] So far as we can gather, the following was the order of service on New Moon's Day. The

---

[1] There is a curious and somewhat blasphemous *Haggadah*, or story, in the Talmud on this subject. It appears that at first the sun and moon had been created of equal size, but that when the moon wished to be sole 'ruler' to the exclusion of the sun, her jealousy was punished by diminution. In reply to her arguments and importunity, God had then tried to comfort the moon, that the three righteous men, Jacob, Samuel, and David, were likewise to be small—and when even thus the moon had the better of the reasoning, God had directed that a 'sin-offering' should be brought on the new moon, because He had made the moon smaller and less important than the sun!

[2] This even by Buxtorf, in his *Lex. Rabb.* and also by Dr. Ginsburg in Kitto's *Cycl.* vol. iii. In general, articles on the 'New Moon' and 'New Year,' notwithstanding their ability, do not display sufficient critical discernment on the part of their author. That the 'Hallel' was *not* sung in the Temple on New Moons is shown by Jost., *Gesch. d. Judenth.* i, 184.

Council sat from early morning to just before the evening sacrifice, to determine the appearance of the new moon. The proclamation of the Council—'It is sanctified!'—and not the actual appearance of the new moon, determined the commencement of the feast. Immediately afterwards, the priests blew the trumpets which marked the feast. After the ordinary morning sacrifice, the prescribed festive offerings were brought, the blood of the burnt-offerings being thrown round the base of the altar below the red line, and the rest poured out into the channel at the south side of the altar; while the blood of the sin-offering was sprinkled or dropped from the finger on the horns of the altar of burnt-offering, beginning from the east, the rest being poured out, as that of the burnt-offerings. The two bullocks of the burnt-offerings were hung up and flayed on the uppermost of the three rows of hooks in the court, the rams on the middle, and the lambs on the lowest hooks. In all no less than 107 priests officiated at this burnt-offering—20 with every bullock, 11 with every ram, and 8 with every lamb, including, of course, those who carried the appropriate meat- and drink-offerings. At the offering of these sacrifices the trumpets were again blown. All of them were slain at the north side of the altar, while the peace- and freewill-offerings, which private Israelites were wont at such seasons to bring, were sacrificed at the south side. The flesh of the sin-offering and what of the meat-offering came to them, was eaten by the priests in the Temple itself; their portion of the private thank-offerings might be taken by them to their homes in Jerusalem, and there eaten with their households.

Before this temple stood the altar, fifteen cubits high, and equal both in length and breadth; each of which dimensions was fifty cubits. The figure it was built in was a square, and it had corners like horns; and the passage up to it was by an insensible acclivity (Jos. Jewish Wars 5.225).

A PRAYER OF THE THIRD CENTURY, A.D.

If any special prayers were said in the Temple on New Moons' Days, tradition has not preserved them, the only formula dating from that period being that used on first seeing the moon—'Blessed be He who reneweth the months.' To this the synagogue, towards the close of the third century, added the following: 'Blessed be He by whose word the heavens were created, and by the breath of whose mouth all the hosts thereof were formed! He appointed them a law and time, that they should not overstep their course. They rejoice and are glad to perform the will of their Creator, Author of truth; their operations are truth! He spoke to the moon, Be thou renewed, and be the beautiful diadem (*i.e.* the hope) of man (*i.e.* Israel), who shall one day be quickened again like the moon (*i.e.* at the coming of the Messiah), and praise their Creator for His glorious kingdom. Blessed be He who reneweth the moons.'[3] At a yet much later period, a very superstitious prayer was next inserted, its repetition being accompanied by leaping towards the moon! New Moon's Day, though apparently observed in the time of Amos as a day of rest (Amos 8:5), is not so kept by the Jews in our days, nor, indeed, was abstinence from work enjoined in the Divine Law.[4]

When will the New Moon be over that we may sell grain, and the Sabbath be ended that we may market wheat (Amos 8:5a)?

On the first day of the seventh month you are to have a day of rest, a sacred assembly commemorated with trumpet blasts (Lev. 23:24).

On the first day of the seventh month hold a sacred assembly and do no regular work. It is a day for you to sound the trumpets (Num. 29:1).

THE MOON OF THE SEVENTH MONTH

Quite distinct from the other new moons, and more sacred than they, was that of the *seventh* month, or *Tishri,* partly on account of the symbolical meaning of the seventh or sabbatical month, in which the great feasts of the Day of Atonement and of Tabernacles occurred, and partly, perhaps, because it also marked the commencement of the civil year, always supposing that, as Josephus and most Jewish writers maintain, the distinction between the sacred and civil year dates from the time of Moses.[5] In Scripture this feast is designated as the 'memorial

---

[3] The article 'New Moon' in Kitto's *Cycl.* erroneously states that not only this prayer, but even the much later superstitious addition was 'during the period of the second Temple offered up by every Israelite.' But comp. Jost. *Gesch. d. Judenth.* ii. 265, 266, where the time of their origin is traced.

[4] The Talmud has this curious story in explanation of the custom that women abstain from work on New Moons—that the women had refused to give their earrings for the golden calf, while the men gave theirs, whereas, on the other hand, the Jewish females contributed their ornaments for the Tabernacles.

[5] In another place we have adopted the common, modern view, that this distinction only dates from the return from Babylon. But it must be admitted that the weight of authority is all on the other side. The Jews hold that the world was created in the month Tishri.

blowing' (Lev. 23:24), or 'the day of blowing' (Num. 29:1), because on that day the trumpets, or rather, as we shall see, the horns were blown all day long in Jerusalem. It was to be observed as 'a Sabbath,' and 'a holy convocation,' in which 'no servile work' might be done. The prescribed offerings for the day consisted, besides the ordinary morning and evening sacrifices, first, of the burnt-offerings, *but not the sin-offering*, of ordinary new moons, with their meat- and drink-offerings, and after that, of another festive burnt-offering of one young bullock, one ram, and seven lambs, with their appropriate meat- and drink-offerings, together with 'one kid of the goats for a sin-offering, to make an atonement for you.' While the drink-offering of the festive sacrifice was poured out, the priests and Levites chanted Psalm 81, and if the feast fell on a Thursday, for which that Psalm was, at any rate, prescribed, it was sung twice, beginning the second time at verse 7 in the Hebrew text, or verse 6 of our Authorized Version. At the evening sacrifice Psalm 29 was sung. For reasons previously explained,[6] it became early common to observe the New Year's Feast on two successive days, and the practice may have been introduced in Temple times.

THE MISHNAH ON NEW YEAR'S DAY

The *Mishnah*, which devotes a special tractate to this feast, remarks that a year may be arranged according to four different periods; the first, beginning with the 1st of Nisan, being for 'kings' (to compute taxation) and for computing the feasts; the second, on the 1st of Elul (the sixth month), for tithing flocks and herds, any animal born after that not being reckoned within the previous year; the third, on the 1st of Tishri (the seventh month), for the Civil, the Sabbatical, and the Jubilee year, also for trees and herbs; and lastly, that on the 1st of Shebat (the eleventh month), for all fruits of trees. Similarly, continues the *Mishnah*, there are four seasons when judgment is pronounced upon the world: at the

Ascribe to the LORD, O mighty ones, ascribe to the LORD glory and strength. Ascribe to the LORD the glory due his name; worship the LORD in the splendor of his holiness (Ps. 29:1–2).

There are four 'New Year' days: on the 1st of Nisan is the New Year for kings and feasts; on the 1st of Elul is the New Year for the Tithe of Cattle...on the 1st of Tishri is the New Year for [the reckoning of] the years [of foreign kings], of the Years of Release and Jubilee years, for the planting [of trees] and for vegetables; and the 1st of Shebat is the New Year for [fruit–]trees...(Mishnah, Roš Hašana i.1).

---

[6]Chiefly to prevent possible mistakes.

Passover, in regard to the harvest; at Pentecost, in regard to the fruits of trees; on the Feast of Tabernacles, in regard to the dispensation of rain; while on 'New Year's Day all the children of men pass before Him like lambs (when they are counted for the tithing), as it is written (Ps. 33:15), "He fashioneth their hearts alike; He considereth all their works." '

THE TALMUD ON THE NEW YEAR

To this we may add, as a comment of the Talmud, that on New Year's Day *three* books were opened—that of life, for those whose works had been good; another of death, for those who had been thoroughly evil; and a third, intermediate, for those whose case was to be decided on the Day of Atonement (ten days after New Year), the delay being granted for repentance, or otherwise, after which their names would be finally entered, either in the book of life, or in that of death. By these terms, however, eternal life or death are not necessarily meant; rather earthly well-being, and, perhaps, temporal life, or the opposite. It is not necessary to explain at length on what Scriptural passages this curious view about the *three* books is supposed to rest.[7] But so deep and earnest are the feelings of the Rabbis on this matter, that by universal consent the ten days intervening between New Year and the Day of Atonement are regarded as 'days of repentance.' Indeed, from a misunderstanding of a passage in the *Mishnah* (*Sheb.* i. 4, 5), a similar superstition attaches to every new moon, the day preceding it being kept by rigid Jews as one of fasting and repentance, and called the 'Lesser Day of Atonement.' In accordance with this, the Rabbis hold that the blowing of the trumpets is intended, first, to bring Israel, or rather the merits of the patriarchs and God's covenant with them, in remembrance before the Lord; secondly, to be a means of confounding Satan,

The shofar [blown in the Temple] at the New Year was [made from the horn] of the wild goat, straight, with its mouthpiece overlaid with gold. And at the sides [of them that blew the shofar] were two [that blew upon] trumpets. The shofar blew a long note and the trumpets a short note, since the duty of the day fell on the shofar (Mishnah, Roš Hašana iii.3).

That if you confess with your mouth, "Jesus is Lord," and believe in your heart that God raised him from the dead, you will be saved. For it is with your heart that you believe and are justified, and it is with your mouth that you confess and are saved (Rom. 10:9–10).

---

[7]The two principal passages are Psa. 69:28, and Exod. 32:32; the former is thus explained: 'Let them be blotted out of the book,' which means the book of the wicked, while the expression, 'of the living' refers to that of the righteous, so that the next clause, 'and not be written with the righteous,' is supposed to indicate the existence of a third or intermediate book!

who appears on that day specially to accuse Israel; and lastly, as a call to repentance—as it were, a blast to wake men from their sleep of sin.[8]

NEW YEAR'S DAY IN JERUSALEM

During the whole of New Year's Day, trumpets and horns were blown in Jerusalem from morning to evening. In the Temple it was done, even on a Sabbath, but not outside its walls. Since the destruction of Jerusalem this restriction has been removed, and the horn is blown in every synagogue, even though the feast fall upon a Sabbath. It has already been hinted that the instruments used were not the ordinary priests' trumpets, but *horns*. The *Mishnah* holds that any kind of horns may be blown except those of oxen or calves, in order not to remind God of the sin of the golden calf! The *Mishnah*, however, specially mentions the straight horn of the antelope and the bent horn of the ram; the latter with special allusion to the sacrifice in substitution of Isaac, it being a tradition that New Year's Day was that in which Abraham, despite Satan's wiles to prevent or retard him, had offered up his son Isaac on Mount Moriah. The mouthpieces of the horns for New Year's Day were fitted with gold—those used on fast days with silver. Another distinction was this—on New Year's Day those who blew the horn were placed between others who blew the trumpets, and the sound of the horn was prolonged beyond that of the trumpets; but on fast days those who sounded the trumpets stood in the middle, and their blast was prolonged beyond that of the horns. For the proper observance of these solemn seasons, it was deemed necessary not only to hear but to listen to the sound of the horn, since, as the *Mishnah* adds, everything

Trumpets on a coin from Bar-Cochba

---

[8]Maimonides, *Moreh Nev.* iii. 43. In opposition to this, Luther annotates as follows: 'They were to blow with the horn in order to call God and His wondrous works to remembrance; how He had redeemed them—as it were to preach about it, and to thank Him for it, just as among us Christ and His redemption is remembered and preached by the Gospel;' to which the *Weimar Glossary* adds: 'Instead of the horn and trumpets we have bells.' See Lundius, *Jüd. Heiligth.* p. 1024, col. ii. Buxtorf applies Amos 3:16 to the blowing of the horn.

Just as Moses lifted up the snake in the desert, so the Son of Man must be lifted up, that everyone who believes in him may have eternal life (John 3:14–15).

depends on the intent of the heart, not on the mere outward deed, just as it was not Moses lifting up his hands that gave Israel the victory, nor yet the lifting up of the brazen serpent which healed, but the upturning of the heart of Israel to 'their Father who is in heaven'—or faith (*Rosh ha Sh.* iii. 8). We quote the remark, not only as one of the comparatively few passages in the *Mishnah* which turn on the essence of religion, but as giving an insight into the most ancient views of the Rabbis on these types, and as reminding us of the memorable teaching of our Lord to one of those very Rabbis (John 3:14, 15).

THE NEW YEAR'S BLESSINGS

The *Mishnah* (*Rosh ha Sh.* iv. 5, etc.) mentions various 'Berachoth' or 'benedictions' as having been repeated on New Year's Day. These, with many others of later date, still form part of the liturgy in the synagogue for that day. But there is internal evidence that the prayers, at any rate in their present form, could not have been used, at least, in the Temple.[9] Besides, the Rabbis themselves differ as to their exact amount and contents, and finally satisfy themselves by indicating that the titles of these benedictions are rather intended as *headings*, to show their contents, and what special direction their prayers had taken. One set of them bore on 'the kingdom' of God, and is accordingly called *Malchiyoth;* another, the *Sichronoth*, referred to the various kinds of 'remembrance' on the part of God; while a third, called *Shopharoth*, consisted of benedictions, connected with the 'blowing of the horn.' It is said that any one who simply repeated ten passages from Scripture—according to another authority, three—bearing on 'the kingdom of God,' 'the remembrance of God,' and 'the blowing of horns,' had fulfilled his duty in regard to these 'benedictions.'

[9]From the text of *Rosh ha Sh.* iv. 7, it distinctly appears that they were intended to be used in the synagogues. Of course, this leaves the question open, whether or not something like them was also said in the Temple. The *Mishnah* mentions altogether nine of these 'benedictions.'

THE FIRST DAY OF THE SEVENTH MONTH

From Scripture we know with what solemnity the first day of the seventh month was observed at the time of Ezra, and how deeply moved the people were by the public reading and explanation of the law, which to so many of them came like a strange sound, all the more solemn, that after so long a period they heard it again on that soil which, as it were, bore witness to its truth (Neh. 8:1–12). In the New Testament there is no reference to our Lord having ever attended this feast in Jerusalem. Nor was this necessary, as it was equally celebrated in all the synagogues of Israel.[10] Yet there seems some allusion to the blowing of the horn in the writings of St. Paul. We have already stated that, according to Maimonides,[11] one of its main purposes was to rouse men to repentance. In fact, the commentator of Maimonides makes use of the following words to denote the meaning of the blowing of trumpets: 'Rouse ye, rouse ye from your slumber; awake, awake from your sleep, you who mind vanity, for slumber most heavy has fallen upon you. Take it to heart, before Whom you are to give an account in the judgment.' May not some such formula also have been anciently used in the synagogue;[12] and may not the remembrance of it have been present to the mind of the apostle, when he wrote (Eph. 5:14): 'Wherefore it is said, Awake thou that sleepest, and arise from the dead, and Christ shall give thee light!' If so, we may possibly find an allusion to the appearance of the new moon, specially to that of the seventh month, in these words of one of the preceding verses (Eph. 5:8): 'For ye were sometimes darkness, but now are ye light in the Lord: walk as children of light!'

...all the people assembled as one man in the square before the Water Gate. They told Ezra the scribe to bring out the Book of the Law of Moses, which the LORD *had commanded for Israel....*

Then Nehemiah the governor, Ezra the priest and scribe, and the Levites who were instructing the people said to them all, "This day is sacred to the LORD *your God. Do not mourn or weep." For all the people had been weeping as they listened to the words of the Law (Neh. 8:1, 9).*

---

[10]But in the synagogues out of Jerusalem, the *horn,* not trumpets, was blown on New Year's Day.

[11]*Moreh Nev.* iii. c. 43.

[12]Comp. Goodwin, *Moses et Aaron* (ed. Hottinger), p. 601.

16
THE DAY OF ATONEMENT

※

But only the high priest entered the inner room, and that only once a year, and never without blood, which he offered for himself and for the sins the people had committed in ignorance....When Christ came as high priest of the good things that are already here...he entered the Most Holy Place once for all by his own blood, having obtained eternal redemption.—Heb. 9:7, 11, 12

WEAKNESS OF THE LAW

It may sound strange, and yet it is true, that the clearest testimony to 'the weakness and unprofitableness' 'of the commandment' is that given by 'the commandment' itself. The Levitical arrangements for the removal of sin bear on their forefront, as it were, this inscription: 'The law made nothing perfect'— having neither a perfect mediatorship in the priesthood, nor a perfect 'atonement' in the sacrifices, nor yet a perfect forgiveness as the result of both. 'For the law having a shadow of good things to come, and not the very image of the things, can never with those sacrifices which they offered year by year continually make the comers thereunto perfect' (Heb. 10:1). And this appears, *first,* from the continual recurrence and the multiplicity of these sacrifices, which are intended the one to supplement the other, and yet always leave something to be still supplemented; and, *secondly,* from the broad fact that, in general, 'it is not possible that the blood of bulls and of goats should take away sins' (Heb. 10:4). It is therefore evident that the Levitical dispensation, being stamped with imperfectness alike in the means which it employed for the 'taking away' of sin, and in the results which it obtained by these means, declared itself, like John the Baptist, only a 'forerunner,' the breaker up and pre-parer of the way—not the satisfying, but, on the contrary, the calling forth and 'the bringing in of a better hope' (Heb. 7:19; see marginal rendering).

The former regulation is set aside because it was weak and useless (for the law made nothing perfect), and a better hope is introduced, by which we draw near to God (Heb. 7:18–19).

THE DAY OF ATONEMENT

As might have been expected, this 'weakness and unprofitableness of the commandment' became most apparent in the services of the day in which the Old Testament provision for pardon and accep-tance attained, so to speak, its *climax*. On the Day of Atonement, not ordinary priests, but the high-priest *alone* officiated, and that not in his ordinary dress, nor yet in that of the ordinary priesthood, but in one peculiar to the day, and peculiarly expressive of purity. The worshippers also appeared in circumstances dif-ferent from those on any other occasion, since they were to fast and to 'afflict their souls;' the day itself was to be 'a Sabbath of Sabbatism,'[1] while its central services consisted of a series of grand expiatory sacri-fices, unique in their character, purpose, and results, as described in these words: 'He shall make an atone-ment for the holy sanctuary, and he shall make an atonement for the tabernacle of the congregation, and for the altar, and he shall make an atonement for the priests, and for all the people of the congregation (Lev. 16:33). But even the need of such a Day of Atonement, after the daily offerings, the various festive sacrifices, and the private and public sin-offerings all the year round, showed the insufficiency of all such sacrifices, while the very offerings of the Day of Atonement proclaimed themselves to be only temporary and provisional, 'imposed until the time of reformation.' We specially allude here to the mysterious appearance of the so-called 'scapegoat,' of which we shall, in the sequel, have to give an account differing from that of previous writers.

---

[1]Rendered 'Sabbath of rest' in Authorised Version.

ITS NAMES

The names 'Day of Atonement,' or in the Talmud, which devotes to it a special tractate, simply '*the* day,' (perhaps also in Heb. 7:27[2]), and in the Book of Acts 'the fast' (Acts 27:9), sufficiently designate its general object. It took place on the tenth day of the seventh month (*Tishri*), that is, symbolically, when the sacred or Sabbath of months had just attained its completeness. Nor must we overlook the position of that day relatively to the other festivals. The seventh or sabbatical month closed the festive cycle, the Feast of Tabernacles on the 15th of that month being the last in the year. But, as already stated, before that grand festival of harvesting and thanksgiving Israel must, as a nation, be reconciled unto God, for only a people at peace with God might rejoice before Him in the blessing with which He had crowned the year.[3] And the import of the Day of Atonement, as preceding the Feast of Tabernacles, becomes only more striking, when we remember how that feast of harvesting prefigured the final ingathering of all nations. In connection with this point it may also be well to remember that the Jubilee Year was always proclaimed on the Day of Atonement (Lev. 25:9).[4]

THE TEACHING OF SCRIPTURE ABOUT THE DAY

In briefly reviewing the Divine ordinances about this day (Lev. 16; 23:26–32; Num. 29:11), we find that only on that one day in every year the high-priest was allowed to go into the Most Holy Place, and then arrayed in a peculiar white dress, which differed from that of the ordinary priests, in that its girdle also was white, and not of the Temple colours, while 'the bonnet' was of the same shape, though not the same material as 'the mitre,' which the high-priest

Unlike the other high priests, he does not need to offer sacrifices day after day, first for his own sins, and then for the sins of the people. He sacrificed for their sins once for all when he offered himself (Heb. 7:27).

Much time had been lost, and sailing had already become dangerous because by now it was after the Fast (Acts 27:9).

Then have the trumpet sounded everywhere on the tenth day of the seventh month; on the Day of Atonement sound the trumpet throughout your land (Lev. 25:9).

---

[2]In that case we should translate Heb. 7:27, 'Who needeth not on each day (viz. of atonement), as those high-priests, to offer up his sacrifices,' etc.

[3]See ch. 14. So also Keil, Oehler, Kurtz, Hupfeld, and almost all writers on the subject.

[4]According to the Jewish view, it was also the day on which Adam had both sinned and repented; that on which Abraham was circumcised; and that on which Moses returned from the mount and made atonement for the sin of the golden calf.

ordinarily wore.[5] The simple white of his array, in distinction to the 'golden garments' which he otherwise wore, pointed to the fact that on that day the high-priest appeared, not 'as the bridegroom of Jehovah,' but as bearing in his official capacity the emblem of that perfect purity which was sought by the expiations of that day.[6] Thus, in the prophecies of Zechariah the removal of Joshua's 'filthy garments' and the clothing him with 'change of raiment,' symbolically denoted—'I have caused thine iniquity to pass from thee' (Zech. 3:3, 4). Similarly those who stand nearest to God are always described as arrayed 'in white' (see Ezek. 9:2, etc.; Dan. 10:5; 12:6). And because these were emphatically 'the holy garments,' 'therefore' the high-priest had to 'wash his flesh in water, and so put them on' (Lev. 16:4), that is, he was not merely to wash his hands and feet, as before ordinary ministrations, but to bathe his whole body.

And I saw six men coming from the direction of the upper gate, which faces north, each with a deadly weapon in his hand. With them was a man clothed in linen who had a writing kit at his side. They came in and stood beside the bronze altar (Ezek. 9:2).

He is to put on the sacred linen tunic, with linen undergarments next to his body; he is to tie the linen sash around him and put on the linen turban. These are sacred garments; so he must bathe himself with water before he puts them on (Lev. 16:4).

NUMBERS 29:7–11

From Numbers 29:7–11 it appears that the offerings on the Day of Atonement were really of a three-fold kind—'the continual burnt-offering,' that is, the daily morning and evening sacrifices, with their meat- and drink-offerings; the festive sacrifices of the day, consisting for the high-priest and the priesthood, of 'a ram for a burnt-offering' (Lev. 16:3), and for the people of one young bullock, one ram, and seven lambs of the first year (with their meat-offerings) for a burnt-sacrifice, and one kid of the goats for a sin-offering; and, thirdly, and chiefly, the peculiar expiatory sacrifices of the day, which were a young bullock as a *sin-offering* for the high-priest, his house, and the sons of Aaron, and another *sin-offering* for the people, consisting of two goats, one of which was to be killed and its blood sprinkled, as directed, while the other was to be sent away into the

---

[5]This appears from the Hebrew terms.

[6]According to *Yoma*, iii.7, the High Priest wore in the morning white raiments of *Pelusian*, and 'between the evenings' of *Indian* stuff—respectively valued (no doubt, extravagantly) at about £118 and £79.

On the tenth day of this seventh month hold a sacred assembly. You must deny yourselves and do no work. Present as an aroma pleasing to the LORD a burnt offering of one young bull, one ram and seven male lambs a year old, all without defect. With the bull prepare a grain offering of three-tenths of an ephah of fine flour mixed with oil; with the ram, two-tenths; and with each of the seven lambs, one-tenth. Include one male goat as a sin offering, in addition to the sin offering for atonement and the regular burnt offering with its grain offering, and their drink offerings (Num. 29:7–11).

High Priest in his robes
on the Day of
Expiation/Atonement

wilderness, bearing 'all the iniquities of the children of Israel, and all their transgressions in all their sins' which had been confessed 'over him,' and laid upon him by the high-priest. Before proceeding further, we note the following as the *order* of these sacrifices— first, the ordinary morning sacrifice; next the expiatory sacrifices for the high-priest, the priesthood, and the people (one bullock, and one of the two goats, the other being so-called scapegoat); then the festive burnt-offerings of the priests and the people (Num. 29:7–11), and with them another sin-offering; and, lastly, the ordinary evening sacrifice, being, as Maimonides observes, in all fifteen sacrificial animals. According to Jewish tradition,[7] the whole of the services of that day were performed by the high-priest himself, of course with the assistance of others, for which purpose more than 500 priests were said to have been employed.[8] Of course, if the Day of Atonement fell on a Sabbath, besides all these, the ordinary Sabbath sacrifices were also offered. On a principle previously explained, the high-priest purchased from his own funds the sacrifices brought for himself and his house, the priesthood, however, contributing, in order to make them sharers in the offering, while the public sacrifices for the whole people were paid for from the Temple treasury. Only while officiating in the distinctly expiatory services of the day did the high-priest wear his 'linen garments;' in all the others he was arrayed in his 'golden vestments.' This necessitated a frequent change of dress, and before each he bathed his whole body. All this will be best understood by a more detailed account of the order of service, as given in the Scriptures and by tradition.[9]

---

[7]Special references would here be too numerous, and we must in general refer to *Mish. Yoma,* and to the tractates of Maimonides on the order of that service, which latter we follow very closely.

[8]Comp. Jost. *Gesch. d. Judenth.* vol. i, p. 164.

[9]The reader will readily distinguish what is derived from Scripture and what merely from tradition.

THE DUTIES OF THE HIGH-PRIEST

Seven days before the Day of Atonement the high-priest left his own house in Jerusalem, and took up his abode in his chambers in the Temple. A substitute was appointed for him, in case he should die or become Levitically unfit for his duties. Rabbinical punctiliousness went so far as to have him twice sprinkled with the ashes of the red heifer—on the 3rd and the 7th day of his week of separation—in case he had, unwittingly to himself, been defiled by a dead body (Num. 19:13).[10] During the whole of that week, also, he had to practise the various priestly rites, such as sprinkling the blood, burning the incense, lighting the lamp, offering the daily sacrifice, etc. For, as already stated, every part of that day's services devolved on the high-priest, and he must not commit any mistake. Some of the elders of the Sanhedrim were appointed to see it, that the high-priest fully understood, and knew the meaning of the service, otherwise they were to instruct him in it. On the eve of the Day of Atonement the various sacrifices were brought before him, that there might be nothing strange about the services of the morrow. Finally, they bound him by a solemn oath not to change anything in the rites of the day. This was chiefly for fear of the Sadducean notion, that the incense should be lighted *before* the high-priest actually entered into the Most Holy Place; while the Pharisees held that this was to be done only within the Most Holy Place itself.[11] The evening meal of the high-priest before the great day was to be scanty. All night long he was to be hearing and expounding the Holy Scriptures, or otherwise kept employed, so that he might not fall asleep.[12] At midnight the lot was cast for removing the ashes and

Whoever touches the dead body of anyone and fails to purify himself defiles the LORD's tabernacle. That person must be cut off from Israel. Because the water of cleansing has not been sprinkled on him, he is unclean; his uncleanness remains on him (Num. 19:13).

---

[10]May not the 'sprinkling of the ashes of an heifer' in Heb. 9:13 refer to this? The whole section bears on the Day of Atonement.

[11]The only interesting point here is the Scriptural argument on which the Sadducees based their view. They appealed to Lev. 16:2, and explained the expression, 'I will appear in the cloud upon the mercy-seat,' in a rationalistic sense as applying to the cloud of incense, not to that of the Divine Presence, while the Pharisees appealed to verse 13.

[12]For special Levitical reasons.

preparing the altar; and to distinguish the Day of Atonement from all others, *four,* instead of the usual three, fires were arranged on the great altar of burnt-offering.

THE MORNING SERVICE

He shall bathe himself with water in a holy place and put on his regular garments. Then he shall come out and sacrifice the burnt offering for himself and the burnt offering for the people, to make atonement for himself and for the people (Lev. 16:24).

The services of the day began with the first streak of morning light. Already the people had been admitted into the sanctuary. So jealous were they of any innovation or alteration, that only a linen cloth excluded the high-priest from public view, when, each time before changing his garments, he bathed— not in the ordinary place of the priests, but in one specially set apart for his use. Altogether he changed his raiments and washed his whole body *five* times on that day,[13] and his hands and feet *ten* times.[14] When the first dawn of morning was announced in the usual manner, the high-priest put off his ordinary (layman's) dress, bathed, put on his golden vestments, washed his hands and feet, and proceeded to perform all the principal parts of the ordinary morning service. Tradition has it, that immediately after that, he offered certain parts of the burnt-sacrifices for the day, viz. the bullock and the seven lambs, reserving his own ram and that of the people, as well as the sin-offering of a kid of the goats (Num. 29:8–11), till after the special expiatory sacrifices of the day had been brought. But the text of Lev. 16:24 is entirely against this view, and shows that the *whole* of the burnt offerings and the festive sin-offering were brought *after* the expiatory services. Considering the relation between these services and sacrifices, this might, at any rate, have been expected, since a burnt-offering could only be acceptable *after,* not before, expiation.

---

[13]In case of age or infirmity, the bath was allowed to be heated, either by adding warm water, or by putting hot irons into it.

[14]The high-priest did not on that day wash in the ordinary laver, but in a golden vessel specially provided for the purpose.

THE SIN-OFFERING

The morning service finished, the high-priest washed his hands and feet, put off his golden vestments, bathed, put on his 'linen garments,' again washed his hands and feet, and proceeded to the peculiar part of the day's services. The bullock for his sin-offering stood between the Temple-porch and the altar. It was placed towards the south, but the high-priest, who stood facing the east (that is, the worshippers), turned the head of the sacrifice towards the west (that is, to face the sanctuary). He then laid both his hands upon the head of the bullock, and confessed as follows:– 'Ah, JEHOVAH! I have committed iniquity; I have transgressed; I have sinned—I and my house. Oh, then, JEHOVAH, I entreat Thee, cover over (atone for, let there be atonement for) the iniquities, the transgressions, and the sins which I have committed, transgressed, and sinned before Thee, I and my house—even as it is written in the law of Moses, Thy servant: "For, on that day will He cover over (atone) for you to make you clean; from all your transgressions before JEHOVAH ye shall be cleansed." ' It will be noticed that in this solemn confession the name JEHOVAH occurred three times. Other three times was it pronounced in the confession which the high-priest made over the same bullock for the priesthood; a seventh time was it uttered when he cast the lot as to which of the two goats as to be 'for JEHOVAH;' and once again he spoke it three times in the confession over the so-called 'scape-goat' which bore the sins of the people. All these *ten* times the high-priest pronounced the very name of JEHOVAH, and, as he spoke it, those who stood near cast themselves with their faces on the ground, while the multitude responded: 'Blessed be the Name; the glory of His kingdom is for ever and ever.'[15] Formerly it had been the practice to pronounce the so-called 'Ineffable Name' distinctly, but afterwards, when some attempted to make use of it for magical purposes, it was spoken with bated

...on this day atonement will be made for you, to cleanse you. Then, before the LORD, you will be clean from all your sins (Lev. 16:30).

---

[15]In support of this benediction, reference is made to Deut. 32:3.

breath, and, as one relates[16] who has stood among the priests in the Temple and listened with rapt attention to catch the mysterious name, it was lost amidst the sound of the priests' instruments, as they accompanied the benediction of the people.

Aaron is to offer the bull for his own sin offering to make atonement for himself and his household. Then he is to take the two goats and present them before the LORD at the entrance to the Tent of Meeting. He is to cast lots for the two goats—one lot for the LORD and the other for the scapegoat....But the goat chosen by lot as the scapegoat shall be presented alive before the LORD to be used for making atonement by sending it into the desert as a scapegoat (Lev. 16:6–8, 10).

CHOOSING THE SCAPE-GOAT

The first part of the expiatory service—that for the priesthood—had taken place close to the Holy Place, between the porch and the altar. The next was performed close to the worshipping people. In the eastern part of the Court of Priests, that is, close to the worshippers, and on the north side of it, stood an urn, called *Calpi*, in which were two lots of the same shape, size, and material—in the second Temple they were of gold; the one bearing the inscription 'la-JEHOVAH,' for Jehovah, the other 'la-Azazel,' for Azazel, leaving the expression (Lev. 16:8, 10, 26—rendered 'scape-goat' in the Authorised Version) for the present untranslated. These two goats had been placed with their backs to the people and their faces towards the sanctuary (westwards). The high-priest now faced the people, as, standing between his substitute (at his right hand), and the head of the course on ministry (on his left hand), he shook the urn, thrust his two hands into it, and at the same time drew the two lots, laying one on the head of each goat. Popularly it was deemed of good augury if the right-hand lot had fallen 'for Jehovah.' The two goats, however, must be altogether alike in look, size, and value; indeed, so earnestly was it sought to carry out the idea that these two formed parts of one and the same sacrifice, that it was arranged they should, if possible, even be purchased at the same time. The importance of this view will afterwards be explained.

---

[16]Rabbi Tryphon in the *Jerus. Talm.* Possibly some readers may not know that the Jews never pronounce the word *Jehovah*, but always substitute for it 'Lord' (printed in capitals in the Authorised Version). Indeed, the right pronunciation of the word has been lost, and is matter of dispute, all that we have in the Hebrew being the letters *I.H.V.H.*—forming the so-called *tetragrammaton*, or 'four-lettered word.'

THE GOAT SHOWN TO THE PEOPLE

The lot having designated each of the two goats, the high-priest tied a tongue-shaped piece of scarlet cloth to the horn of the goat for Azazel—the so-called 'scape-goat'—and another round the throat of the goat for Jehovah, which was to be slain. The goat that was to be sent forth was now turned round towards the people, and stood facing them, waiting, as it were, till their sins should be laid on him, and he would carry them forth into 'a land not inhabited.' Assuredly a more marked type of Christ could not be conceived, as He was brought forth by Pilate and stood before the people, just as He was about to be led forth, bearing the iniquity of the people. And, as if to add to the significance of the rite, tradition has it that when the sacrifice was fully accepted the scarlet mark which the scape-goat had borne became white, to symbolise the gracious promise in Isa. 1:18; but it adds that this miracle did not take place for forty years before the destruction of the Temple!

Egyptian censers

"Do you want me to release to you the king of the Jews?" asked Pilate, knowing it was out of envy that the chief priests had handed Jesus over to him. But the chief priests stirred up the crowd to have Pilate release Barabbas instead (Mark 15:9–11).

THE CONFESSION OF SIN AND THE SACRIFICE

With this presentation of the scape-goat before the people commenced the third and most solemn part of the expiatory services of the day. The high-priest now once more returned towards the sanctuary, and a second time laid his two hands on the bullock, which still stood between the porch and the altar, to confess over him, not only as before, his own and his household's sins, but also those of the priesthood. The formula used was precisely the same as before, with the addition of the words, 'the seed of Aaron, Thy holy people,' both in the confession and in the petition for atonement. Then the high-priest killed the bullock, caught up his blood in a vessel, and gave it to an attendant to keep it stirring, lest it should coagulate. Advancing to the altar of burnt-offering, he next filled the censer with burning coals, and then ranged a handful of frankincense in the dish destined to hold it. Ordinarily, everything brought in actual ministry unto God must be carried in the right hand—hence the incense in the right and the censer in the left. But on this occasion, as the censer for the Day of Atonement was larger and heavier than usual, the high-priest was allowed to reverse the common order. Every eye was strained towards the sanctuary as, slowly bearing the censer and the incense, the figure of the white-robed high-priest was seen to disappear within the Holy Place. After that nothing further could be seen in his movements.

THE MERCY-SEAT

Ark of the Covenant with the mercy seat

The curtain of the Most Holy Place was folded back, and the high-priest stood alone and separated from all the people in the awful gloom of the Holiest of All, only lit up by the red glow of the coals in the priest's censer. In the first Temple the ark of God had stood there with the 'mercy-seat' overshadowing it; above it, the visible presence of Jehovah in the cloud of the *Shechinah,* and on either side the outspread wings of the cherubim; and the high-priest had placed the censer between the staves of the ark. But in the Temple of Herod there was neither *Shechinah* nor ark—all was empty; and the high-priest rested his censer on a large stone, called the 'foundation-stone.'[17] He now most carefully emptied the incense into his hand, and threw it on the coals of the censer, as far from himself as possible, and so waited till the smoke had filled the Most Holy Place. Then, retreating backwards, he prayed outside the veil as follows:[18] 'May it please Thee, O Lord our God, and the God of our fathers, that neither this day nor during this year any captivity come upon us. Yet, if captivity befall us this day or this year, let it be to a place where the law is cultivated. May it please Thee, O Lord our God, and the God of our fathers, that want come not upon us, either this day or this year. But if want visit us this day or this year, let it be due to the liberality of our char-

---

[17]There is no need for here entering on the legends connected with this so-called 'foundation-stone.'

[18]We give the prayer in its simplest form from the Talmud. But we cannot help feeling that its *form* savours of later than Temple-times. Probably only its substance dates from those days, and each high-priest may have been at liberty to formulate it according to his own views.

itable deeds. May it please Thee, O Lord our God, and the God of our fathers, that this year may be a year of cheapness, of fulness, of intercourse and trade; a year with abundance of rain, of sunshine, and of dew; one in which Thy people Israel shall not require assistance one from another. And listen not to the prayers of those who are about to set out on a journey.[19] And as to Thy people Israel, may no enemy exalt himself against them. May it please Thee, O Lord our God, and the God of our fathers, that the houses of the men of Saron may not become their graves.'[20] The high-priest was not to prolong this prayer, lest his protracted absence might fill the people with fears for his safety.

Bowl/laver

THE SPRINKLING OF THE BLOOD

While the incense was offering in the Most Holy Place the people withdrew from proximity to it, and worshipped in silence. At last the people saw the high-priest emerging from the sanctuary, and they knew that the service had been accepted. Rapidly he took from the attendant, who had kept it stirring, the blood of the bullock. Once more he entered into the Most Holy Place, and sprinkled with his finger once upwards, towards where the mercy-seat had been, and seven times downwards, counting as he did so: 'Once' (upwards), 'once and once' (downwards), 'once and twice' and so on to 'once and seven times,' always repeating the word 'once,' which referred to the upwards sprinkling, so as to prevent any mistake. Coming out from the Most Holy Place, the high-priest now deposited the bowl with the blood before the veil. Then he killed the goat set apart for Jehovah, and, entering the Most Holy Place a third time, sprinkled as before, once upwards and seven times downwards, and again deposited the bowl with the blood of the goat on a second golden stand before the veil. Taking

---

[19]Who might pray against the fall of rain. It must be remembered that the autumn rains, on which the fruitfulness of the land depended, were just due.

[20]This on account of the situation of that valley, which was threatened either by sudden floods or by dangerous landslips.

Tabernacle uncovered (A. The Holy Place—B. The Holy of Holies)

up the bowl with the bullock's blood, he next sprinkled once upwards and seven times downwards towards the veil, outside the Most Holy Place, and then did the same with the blood of the goat. Finally, pouring the blood of the bullock into the bowl which contained that of the goat, and again the mixture of the two into that which had held the blood of the bullock, so as thoroughly to commingle the two, he sprinkled each of the horns of the altar of incense, and then, making a clear place on the altar, seven times the top of the altar of incense. Thus he had sprinkled forty-three times with the expiatory blood, taking care that his own dress should never be spotted with the sin-laden blood. What was left of the blood the high-priest poured out on the west side of the base of the altar of burnt-offering.

THE CLEANSING COMPLETED

By these expiatory sprinkings the high-priest had cleansed the sanctuary in all its parts from the defilement of the preisthood and the worshippers. The Most Holy Place, the veil, the Holy Place, the altar of incense, and the altar of burnt-offering were now clean alike, so far as the priesthood and as the people were concerned; and in their relationship to the sanctuary both priests and worshippers were atoned for. So far as the law could give it, there was now again free access for all; or, to put it otherwise, the continuance of typical sacrificial communion with God was once more restored and secured. Had it not been for these services, it would have become impossible for priests and people to offer sacrifices, and so to obtain the forgiveness of sins, or to have fellowship with God. But the *consciences* were not yet free from a sense of personal guilt and sin. That remained to be done through the 'scape-goat.' All this seems clearly implied in the distinctions made in Lev. 16:33: 'And he shall make an atonement for the holy sanctuary, and he shall make an atonement for the tabernacle of the congregation, and for the altar, and he shall make an atonement for the priests, and for all the people of the congregation.'

When Aaron has finished making atonement for the Most Holy Place, the Tent of Meeting and the altar, he shall bring forward the live goat. He is to lay both hands on the head of the live goat and confess over it all the wickedness and rebellion of the Israelites— all their sins—and put them on the goat's head (Lev. 16:20–21a).

THE SCAPE-GOAT

Most solemn as the services had hitherto been, the worshippers would chiefly think with awe of the high-priest going into the immediate presence of God, coming out thence alive, and securing for them by the blood the continuance of the Old Testament privileges of sacrifices and of access unto God through them. What now took place concerned them, if possible, even more nearly. Their own personal guilt and sins were now to be removed from them, and that in a symoblical rite, at one and the same time the most mysterious and the most significant of all. All the while the 'scape-goat,' with the 'scarlet-tongue,' telling of the guilt it was to bear, had stood looking eastwards, confronting the people, and waiting for the terrible load which it was to carry away 'unto a land not inhabited.' Laying both his hands on the head of this goat, the high-priest now confessed and pleaded: 'Ah, JEHOVAH! they have committed iniqutiy; they have transgressed; they have sinned— Thy people, the house of Israel. Oh, then, JEHOVAH! cover over (atone for), I intreat Thee, upon their iniquities, their transgressions, and their sins, which they have wickedly committed, transgressed, and sinned before Thee—Thy people, the house of Israel. As it is written in the law of Moses, Thy servant, saying: "For on that day shall it be covered over (atoned) for you, to make you clean from all your sins before JEHOVAH ye shall be cleansed." ' And while the prostrate multitude worshipped at the name of Jehovah, the high-priest turned his face towards them as he uttered the last words, '*Ye shall be cleansed!*' as if to declare to them the absolution and remission of their sins.

He shall send the goat away into the desert in the care of a man appointed for the task. The goat will carry on itself all their sins to a solitary place; and the man shall release it in the desert (Lev. 16:21b–22).

THE GOAT SENT INTO THE WILDERNESS

Then a strange scene would be witnessed. The priests led the sin-burdened goat out through 'Solomon's Porch,' and, as tradition has it, through the eastern gate, which opened upon the Mount of Olives.[21] Here an arched bridge spanned the intervening valley, and over it they brought the goat to the Mount of Olives, where one, specially appointed for the purpose, took him in charge. Tradition enjoins that he should be a stranger, a non-Israelite, as if to make still more striking the type of Him who was delivered over by Israel unto the Gentiles! Scripture tells us no more of the destiny of the goat that bore upon him all the iniquities of the children of Israel, than that they 'shall send him away by the hand of a fit man into the wilderness,' and that 'he shall let go the goat in the wilderness' (Lev. 16:22). But tradition supplements this information. The distance between Jerusalem and the beginning of 'the wilderness' is computed at ninety *stadia*, making precisely ten intervals, each half a Sabbath-day's journey from the other. At the end of each of these intervals there was a station, occupied by one or more persons, detailed for the purpose, who offered refreshment to the man leading the goat, and then accompanied him to the next station. By this arrangement two results were secured: some trusted persons accompanied the goat all along his journey, and yet none of them walked more than a Sabbath-day's journey—that is, half a

---

[21] The Talmud has it, that the foreign Jews present used to burst into words and deeds of impatience, that the 'sin-bearer' might be gone.

journey going and the other half returning. At last they reached the edge of the wilderness. Here they halted, viewing afar off, while the man led forward the goat, tore off half the 'scarlet-tongue,' and stuck it on a projecting cliff; then, leading the animal backwards, he pushed it over the projecting ledge of rock. There was a moment's pause, and the man, now defiled by contact with the sin-bearer, retraced his steps to the last of the ten stations, where he spent the rest of the day and the night. But the arrival of the goat in the wilderness was immediately telegraphed, by the waving of flags, from station to station, till, a few minutes after its occurrence, it was known in the Temple, and whispered from ear to ear, that 'the goat had borne upon him all their iniquities into a land not inhabited.'

Then the priest shall order that one of the birds be killed over fresh water in a clay pot. He is then to take the live bird and dip it, together with the cedar wood, the scarlet yarn and the hyssop, into the blood of the bird that was killed over the fresh water. Seven times he shall sprinkle the one to be cleansed of the infectious disease and pronounce him clean. Then he is to release the live bird in the open fields (Lev. 14:5–7).

THE MEANING OF THE RITE

What then was the meaning of a rite on which such momentous issues depended? Everything about it seems strange and mysterious—the lot that designated it, and that 'to Azazel;' the fact, that though the highest of all sin-offerings, it was neither sacrificed nor its blood sprinkled in the Temple; and the circumstance that it really was only *part* of a sacrifice— the two goats together forming one sacrifice, one of them being killed, and the other 'let go,' there being no other analogous case of the kind except at the purification of a leper, when one bird was killed and the other dipped in its blood, and let go free. Thus these two sacrifices—one in the removal of what symbolically represented indwelling sin, the other contracted guilt—agreed in requiring two animals, of whom one was killed, the other 'let go.' This is not the place to discuss the various views entertained of the import of the scape-goat.[22] But it is destructive of one and all of the received interpretations, that the sins of the people were confessed not on the goat which was killed, but on that which was 'let go in the wilderness,' and that it was this goat—not the other—which 'bore

---

[22]For a full discussion, we must refer to works on *Biblical Antiquities* and on the *Types of the Old Testament.*

upon him all the iniquities' of the people. So far as the conscience was concerned, this goat was real and the only sin-offering 'for all the iniquities of the children of Israel, and all their transgressions in all their sins,' for upon it the high-priest laid the sins of the people, after he had by the blood of the bullock and of the other goat 'made an end of reconciling the Holy Place, and the tabernacle of the congregation, and the altar' (Lev. 16:20). The blood sprinkled had effected this; but it had done no more, and it could do no more, for it 'could not make him that did the service perfect, as pertaining to the conscience' (Heb. 9:9). The symbolical representation of *this* perfecting was by the live goat, which, laden with the confessed sins of the people, carried them away into 'the wilderness' to 'a land not inhabited.' The only meaning of which this seems really capable, is that though confessed guilt was removed from the people to the head of the goat, as the symbolical substitute, yet as the goat was not killed, only sent far away, into 'a land not inhabited,' so, under the Old Covenant, sin was not really blotted out, only put away from the people, and put aside till Christ came, not only to take upon Himself the burden of transgression, but to *blot it out and to purge it away*.[23]

This is an illustration for the present time, indicating that the gifts and sacrifices being offered were not able to clear the conscience of the worshiper (Heb. 9:9).

First he said, "Sacrifices and offerings, burnt offerings and sin offerings you did not desire, nor were you pleased with them" (although the law required them to be made). Then he said, "Here I am, I have come to do your will." He sets aside the first to establish the second. And by that will, we have been made holy through the sacrifice of the body of Jesus Christ once for all (Heb. 10:8–10).

THE TEACHING OF SCRIPTURE

Thus viewed, not only the text of Lev. 16, but the language of Heb. 9 and 10, which chiefly refer to the Day of Atonement, becomes plain. The 'blood,' both of the bullock and of the goat which the high-priest carried 'once a year' within 'the sacred veil,' was 'offered for himself (including the priesthood) and for the errors (or rather ignorances) of the people.' In the language of Lev. 16:20, it reconciled 'the Holy Place, and the tabernacle of the congregation, and the altar,' that is, as already explained, it rendered on the part of priests and people the continuance of sacrificial worship possible. But this live scape-goat 'let go' in the wilderness, over which, in the exhaustive

---

[23]May there be here also a reference to the doctrine of Christ's descent into *Hades?*

language of Lev. 16:21, the high-priest had confessed and on which he had laid 'all the iniquities of the children of Israel, and all their transgressions in all their sins,' meant something quite different. It meant the inherent 'weakness and unprofitableness of the commandment;' it meant, that 'the law made nothing perfect, but was the bringing in of a better hope;' that in the covenant mercy of God guilt and sin were indeed removed from the people, that they were 'covered up,' and in that sense atoned for, or rather that they were both 'covered up' and removed, but that they were not really *taken away and destroyed* till Christ came; that they were only taken into a land not inhabited, till He should blot it out by His own blood; that the provision which the Old Testament made was only preparatory and temporary, until the 'time of the reformation;' and that hence real and true forgiveness of sins, and with it the spirit of adoption, could only be finally obtained after the death and resurrection of 'the Lamb of God which taketh away the sin of the world.' Thus in the fullest sense it was true of the 'fathers,' that 'these all...*received* not the promise: God having provided some better thing for us, that they without us should not be made perfect.' For 'the law having a shadow of the good things to come,' could not 'make the comers thereunto perfect;' nor yet was it possible 'that the blood of bulls and of goats should take away sins.' The live goat 'let go' was every year a remover of sins which yet were never really removed in the sense of being blotted out— only deposited, as it were, and reserved till He came 'whom God hath set forth as a propitiation....because of the passing over of the former sins, in the forbearance of God' (Rom. 3:25).[24] 'And for this cause He is the mediator of a new covenant, in order that, death having taken place for the propitiation of the transgressions under the first covenant, they which have been called may receive the promise of the eternal inheritance' (Heb. 9:15).

God presented him as a sacrifice of atonement, through faith in his blood. He did this to demonstrate his justice, because in his forbearance he had left the sins committed beforehand unpunished (Rom. 3:25).

---

[24]We have generally adopted the rendering of Dean Alford, where the reader will perceive any divergence from the Authorised Version.

This is not the place for following the argument further. Once understood, many passages will recur which manifest how the Old Testament removal of sin was shown in the law itself to have been complete indeed, so far as the individual was concerned, but not really and in reference to God, till He came to Whom as the reality these types pointed, and Who 'now once at the end of the world hath been manifested to put away sin by the sacrifice of Himself' (Heb. 9:26). And thus did the types themselves prove their own inadequacy and insufficiency, showing that they had only 'a shadow of the good things to come, and not the very image of the things themselves' (Heb. 10:1). With this also agree the terms by which in the Old Testament atonement is designated as a 'covering up' by a substitute, and the mercy-seat as 'the place of covering over.'

The law is only a shadow of the good things that are coming—not the realities themselves. For this reason it can never, by the same sacrifices repeated endlessly year after year, make perfect those who draw near to worship (Heb. 10:1).

THE TERM 'LA-AZAZEL'

After this it is comparatively of secondary importance to discuss, so far as we can in these pages, the question of the meaning of the term 'la-Azazel' (Lev. 16:8, 10, 26). Both the interpretation which makes it a designation of the goat itself (as 'scape-goat' in our Authorised Version), and that which would refer it to a certain locality in the wilderness,[25] being, on many grounds, wholly untenable, two other views remain, one of which regards *Azazel* as a person, and denoting *Satan;* while the other would render the term by 'complete removal.' The insurmountable difficulties connected with the first of these notions lie on the surface. In reference to the second, it may be said that it not only does violence to Hebrew grammar, but implies that the goat which was to be for 'complete removal' as not even to be sacrificed, but actually 'let go!' Besides, what in that case could be the object of the first goat which *was* killed, and whose blood was sprinkled in the Most Holy Place? We may here at once state, that the later Jewish practice of pushing the goat over a rocky precipice was

---

[25]Thus the book *Sifra* paraphrases it: 'a rough place in the mountains.'

undoubtedly an *innovation*, in no wise sanctioned by the law of Moses, and not even introduced at the time the Septuagint translation was made, as its rendering of Lev. 16:26 shows. The *law* simply ordained that the goat, once arrived in 'the land not inhabited,' was to be 'let go' free, and the Jewish ordinance of having it pushed over the rocks is signally characteristic of the Rabbinical perversion of its spiritual type. The word *Azazel,* which only occurs in Lev. 16, is by universal consent derived from a root which means 'wholly to put aside,' or, 'wholly to go away.' Whether, therefore, we render 'la-Azazel' by 'for him who is wholly put aside,' that is, the sin-bearing Christ, or 'for being wholly separated,' or 'put wholly aside or away,' the truth is still the same, as pointing through the temporary and provisional removal of sin by the goat 'let go' in 'the land not inhabited,' to the final, real, and complete removal of sin by the Lord Jesus Christ, as we read it in Isa. 53:6: 'Jehovah hath made the iniquities of us all to meet on Him.'

The man who releases the goat as a scapegoat must wash his clothes and bathe himself with water; afterward he may come into the camp (Lev. 16:26).

THE CARCASSES BURNT 'OUTSIDE THE CITY'

While the scape-goat was being led into the wilderness, the high-priest proceeded to cut up the bullock and the goat with whose blood he had previously 'made atonement,' put the 'inwards' in a vessel which he committed to an attendant,[26] and sent the carcasses to be burnt 'outside the city,' in the place where the Temple ashes were usually deposited. Then, according to tradition, the high-priest, still wearing the linen garments,[27] went into the 'Court of the Women,' and read the passages of Scripture bearing on the Day of Atonement, viz. Lev. 16; 23:27–32; also repeating by heart[28] Num. 29:7–11. A series of prayers accompanied this reading of the Scriptures. The most interesting of these supplications may be thus

---

[26]Lightfoot (*De Minist. Templi*) erroneously states that the high-priest immediately burnt them.

[27]But this was not strictly necessary; he might in this part of the service have even officiated in his ordinary layman's dress.

[28]Maimonides gives a curious Rabbinical reason for this.

Do no work on that day, because it is the Day of Atonement, when atonement is made for you before the LORD your God. Anyone who does not deny himself on that day must be cut off from his people. I will destroy from among his people anyone who does any work on that day. You shall do no work at all. This is to be a lasting ordinance for the generations to come, wherever you live. (Lev. 23:28–31).

summed up:—Confession of sin with prayer for forgiveness, closing with the words, *'Praise be to Thee, O Lord, Who in Thy mercy forgivest the sins of Thy people Israel;'* prayer for the permanence of the Temple, and that the Divine Majesty might shine in it, closing with—*'Praise be to Thee, O Lord, Who inhabitest Zion;'* prayer for the establishment and safety of Israel, and the continuance of a king among them, closing—*'Thanks be to Thee, O Lord, Who hast chosen Israel;'* prayer for the priesthood, that all their doings, but especially their sacred services, might be acceptable unto God, and He be gracious unto them, closing with—*'Thanks be to Thee, O Lord, Who hast sanctified the priesthood;'* and, finally (in the language of Maimonides), prayers, entreaties, hymns, and petitions of the high-priest's own, closing with the words: *'Give help, O Lord, to Thy people Israel, for Thy people needeth help; thanks be unto Thee, O Lord, Who hearest prayer.'*[29]

THE HIGH-PRIEST IN GOLDEN GARMENTS

These prayers ended, the high-priest washed his hands and feet, put off his 'linen,' and put on his 'golden vestments,' and once more washed hands and feet before proceeding to the next ministry. He now appeared again before the people as the Lord's anointed in the golden garments of the bride-chamber. Before he offered the festive burnt-offerings of the day, he sacrificed 'one kid of the goats for a sin-offering' (Num. 29:16), probably with special reference to these festive services, which, like everything else, required atoning blood for their acceptance. The flesh of this sin-offering was eaten at night by the priests within the sanctuary. Next, he sacrificed the burnt-offerings for the people and that for himself (one ram, Lev. 16:3), and finally burned the 'inwards' of the expiatory offerings, whose blood had formerly been sprinkled in the Most Holy Place. This, properly

---

[29]In regard to these prayers we refer the reader to our remarks in a previous chapter. The view there expressed about the wording of the prayers holds also good in regard to those on the Day of Atonement.

speaking, finished the services of the day. But the high-priest had yet to offer the ordinary evening sacrifice, after which he washed his hands and his feet, once more put off his 'golden' and put on his 'linen garments,' and again washed his hands and feet. This before entering the Most Holy Place a fourth time on that day (Heb. 9:7),[30] to fetch from it the censer and incense-dish which he had left there. On his return he washed once more hands and feet, put off his linen garments, which were never to be used again, put on his golden vestments, washed hands and feet, burned the evening incense on the golden altar, lit the lamps on the candlestick for the night, washed his hands and feet, put on his ordinary layman's dress, and was escorted by the people in procession to his own house in Jerusalem. The evening closed with a feast.

This is how Aaron is to enter the sanctuary area: with a young bull for a sin offering and a ram for a burnt offering (Lev. 16:3).

THE MISHNAH

If this ending of the Day of Atonement seems incongruous, the *Mishnah* records (*Taan.* iv. 8) something yet more strange in connection with the day itself. It is said that on the afternoon of the 15th of Ab, when the collection of wood for the sanctuary was completed, and on that Day of Atonement, the maidens of Jerusalem went in white garments, specially lent them for the purpose, so that rich and poor might be on an equality, into the vineyards close to the city, where they danced and sung. The following fragment of one of their songs has been preserved:[31]

'Around in circle gay, the Hebrew maidens see;
From them our happy youths their partners choose.
Remember! Beauty soon its charm must lose—
And seek to win a maid of fair degree.

When fading grace and beauty low are laid,
Then praise shall her who fears the Lord await;
God does bless her handiwork—and, in the gate,
"Her works do follow her," it shall be said.'

---

[30]States that the high-priest went 'once in every year,' that is, on one day in every year, *not* on one occasion during that day.

[31]The Talmud repeatedly states the fact and gives the song. Nevertheless we have some doubt on the subject, though the reporter in the *Mishnah* is said to be none other than Rabbi Simeon, the son of Gamaliel, Paul's teacher.

THE DAY OF ATONEMENT IN THE
MODERN SYNAGOGUE

We will not here undertake the melancholy task of describing what the modern synagogue has made the Day of Atonement, nor how it observes the occasion—chiefly in view of their gloomy thoughts, that on that day man's fate for the year, if not his life or death, is finally fixed. But even the *Mishnah* already contains similar perverted notions of how the day should be kept, and what may be expected from its right observance (*Mish. Yoma,* viii.). Rigorous rest and rigorous fasting are enjoined from sundown of one day to the appearance of the first stars on the next. Neither food nor drink of any kind may be tasted; a man may not even wash, nor anoint himself, nor put on his sandals.[32] The sole exception made is in favour of the sick and of children, who are only bound to the full fast—girls at the age of twelve years and one day, and boys at that of thirteen years and one day, though it is recommended to train them earlier to it.[33] In return for all this 'affliction' Israel may expect that *death along with the Day of Atonement* will finally blot out all sins! That is all—the Day of Atonement and our own death! Such are Israel's highest hopes of expiation! It is unspeakably saddening to follow this subject further through the *minutiae* of Rabbinical ingenuity—how much exactly the Day of Atonement will do for a man; what proportion of his sins it will remit, and what merely suspend; how much is left over for after-chastisements, and how much for final extinction at death. The law knows nothing of such miserable petty misrepresentations of the free pardon of God. In the expiatory sacrifices of the Day of Atonement every kind[34] of transgres-

On the Day of Atonement, eating, drinking, washing, anointing, putting on sandals, and marital intercourse are forbidden. A king or a bride may wash their faces and a woman after childbirth may put on sandals (Mishnah, Yoma viii.1).

The Sin-offering and the unconditional Guilt-offering effect atonement; death and the Day of Atonement effect atonement if there is repentance. Repentance effects atonement for lesser transgressions against both positive and negative commands in the Law; while for graver transgressions it suspends punishment until the Day of Atonement comes and effects atonement (Mishnah, Yoma viii.8).

---

[32]Only woollen socks are to be used—the only exception is, where there is fear of serpents or scorpions.

[33]Kings and brides within thirty days of their wedding are allowed to wash their faces; the use of a towel which has been dipped the *previous* day in water is also conceded.

[34]For high-handed, purposed sins, the law provided no sacrifice (Heb. 10:26), and it is even doubtful whether they are included in the declaration of Lev. 16:21, wide as it is. Thank God, we know that 'the blood of Jesus Christ His Son cleanseth from *all* sin,' without exception.

sion, trespass, and sin is to be removed from the people of God. Yet annually anew, and each time confessedly only provisionally, not really and finally, till the gracious promise (Jer. 31:34) should be fulfilled: 'I will forgive their iniquity, and I will remember their sin no more.' Accordingly it is very marked, how in the prophetic, or it may be symbolical, description of Ezekiel's Temple (Ezek. 40–46) all mention of the Day of Atonement is omitted; for Christ has come 'an high-priest of good things to come,' and 'entered in once into the Holy Place,' to *put away* sin by the sacrifice of Himself' (Heb. 9:11, 12, 26).

17
Post-Mosaic Festivals

Then came the Feast of Dedication at Jerusalem. It was winter, and Jesus was in the temple area walking in Solomon's Colonnade.—John 10:22–23

Post-Mosaic Festivals

Besides the festivals mentioned in the Law of Moses, other festive seasons were also observed at the time of our Lord, to perpetuate the memory either of great national deliverances or of great national calamities. The former were popular feasts, the latter public fasts. Though most, if not all of them, are alluded to in the Canonical Scriptures, it is extremely difficult to form a clear idea of how they were kept in the *Temple.* Many of the practices connected with them, as described in Jewish writings, or customary at present, are of much later date than Temple times, or else apply rather to the festive observances in the various synagogues of the land than to those in the central sanctuary. And the reason of this is evident. Though those who were at leisure might like to go to Jerusalem for every feast, yet the vast majority of the people would, except on great festivals, naturally gather in the synagogues of their towns and villages. Moreover, these feasts and fasts were rather *national* than typical—they commemorated a past event instead of pointing forward to a great and world-important fact yet to be realised. Lastly, being of later, and indeed, of human, not Divine institution, the authorities at Jerusalem did not venture to prescribe for them special rites and sacrifices, which, as we have seen, constituted the essence of Temple worship.

THE FEAST OF PURIM

Arranging these various feasts and fasts in the order of their institution and importance, we have:—

1. The Feast of *Purim,* that is 'of lots,' or the Feast of Esther, also called in 2 Maccab. 15:36 'the day of *Mordecai,*' which was observed in memory of the preservation of the Jewish nation at the time of Esther. The name '*Purim*' is derived from 'the lot' which Haman cast in connection with his wicked desire (Esth. 3:7; 9:24). It was proposed by Mordecai to perpetuate the anniversary of this great deliverance on the 14th and the 15th of Adar (about the beginning of March), and universally agreed to by the Jews of his time (Esth. 9:17–24). Nevertheless, according to the Jerusalem Talmud, its general introduction after the return from Babylon formed a subject of grave doubt and deliberation among the 'eighty-five elders'—a number which, according to tradition, included upwards of thirty prophets (*Jer. Megillah,* 70*b*).[1] Even this shows that *Purim* was never more than a popular festival. As such it was kept with great merriment and rejoicing, when friends and relations were wont to send presents to each other. There seems little doubt that this was the 'feast of the Jews,' to which the Saviour 'went up to Jerusalem' (John 5:1), when He healed the 'impotent man' at the Pool of Bethesda. For no other feast could have intervened between December (John 4:35) and the Passover (John 6:4), except that of the 'Dedication of the Temple,' and that is specially designated as such (John 10:22), and not simply as 'a feast of the Jews.'

This happened on the thirteenth day of the month of Adar, and on the fourteenth they rested and made it a day of feasting and joy (Esth. 9:17).

Some time later, Jesus went up to Jerusalem for a feast of the Jews (John 5:1).

CEREMONIES OF THE FEAST

So far as we can gather, the religious observances of *Purim* commenced with a *fast*—'the Fast of

---

[1] The learned Jost (*Gesch. d. Judenth.,* i, 42, note 1) suggests that these '85 elders' were really the commencement of 'the great synagogue,' to which so many of the Jewish ordinances were traced in later times. The number was afterwards, as Jost thinks, arbitrarily increased to 120, which is that assigned by tradition to 'the great synagogue.' 'The great synagogue' may be regarded as the 'constituent' Jewish authority on all questions of ritual after the return from Babylon. Lastly, Jost suggests that the original 85 were the signatories to 'the covenant,' named in Neh. 10:1–27.

Scroll

Esther'—on the 13th of Adar. But if *Purim* fell on a Sabbath or a Friday, the fast was relegated to the previous *Thursday,* as it was not lawful to fast either on a Sabbath or the day preceding it. But even so, there were afterwards disputes between the Jews in Palestine and the much larger and more influential community that still resided in Babylon as to this fast,[2] which seem to throw doubt on its very early observance. On the evening of the 13th of Adar, or rather on the beginning of the 14th, the Book of Esther, or the *Megillah* ('the roll,' as it is called *par excellence*), was publicly read, as also on the forenoon of the 14th day, except in ancient walled cities, where it was read on the 15th. In Jerusalem, therefore, it would be read on the evening of the 13th, and on the 15th—always provided the day fell not on a Sabbath, on which the *Megillah* was not allowed to be read.[3] In the later Jewish calendar arrangements care was taken that the first day of *Purim* should fall on the first, the third, the fifth, or the sixth day of the week. Country people, who went into their market towns every week on the Monday and Thursday, were not required to come up again specially for *Purim,* and in such synagogues the *Megillah,* or at least the principal portions of it, was read on the previous Thursday. It was also allowed to read the Book of Esther in any language other than the Hebrew, if spoken by the Jews resident in the district, and any person, except he were deaf, an idiot or a minor, might perform this service. The prayers for the occasion now used in the synagogue, as also the practice of springing rattles and other noisy demonstrations of anger, contempt, and scorn, with which the name of Haman, where it occurs in the *Megillah,* is always greeted by young and old, are, of course, of much later date. Indeed, so far from prescribing any fixed form of prayer, the *Mishnah* (*Megill.* iv. 1) expressly leaves it an open question, to be determined according to the usage of a place,

---

[2] See Jost, vol. i, p. 265.

[3] We have chiefly quoted from the Mishnic tractate *Megillah,* which, however, is more discursive even than the rest, and alludes to many subjects besides the feast of *Purim.*

whether or not to accompany the reading of the *Megillah* with prayer. According to the testimony of Josephus (*Antiq.* 11.292), in his time 'all the Jews that are in the habitable earth' kept 'these days festivals,' and sent 'portions to one another.' In our own days, though the synagogue has prescribed for them special prayers and portions of Scripture, they are chiefly marked by boisterous and uproarious merrymaking, even beyond the limits of propriety.

In like manner the Jews that were in Shushan gathered themselves together, and feasted on the fourteenth day, and that which followed it; whence it is, that even now all the Jews that are in the habitable earth keep these days festivals, and send portions to one another (Jos. Antiquities 11.292).

THE FEAST OF THE DEDICATION OF THE TEMPLE

2. The Feast of the Dedication of the Temple, *Chanuchah* ('the dedication'), called in 1 Maccab. 4:52–59 'the dedication of the altar,' and by Josephus (*Antiq.* 12.324–325) 'the Feast of Lights,' was another popular and joyous festival. It was instituted by Judas Maccabaeus in 164 B.C., when, after the recovery of Jewish independence from the Syro-Grecian domination, the Temple of Jerusalem was solemnly purified, the old polluted altar removed, its stones put in a separate place on the Temple-mount, and the worship of the Lord restored. The feast commenced on the 25th of Chislev (December), and lasted for *eight days.* On each of them the 'Hallel' was sung, the people appeared carrying palm and other branches, and there was a grand illumination of the Temple and of all private houses. These three observances bear so striking a resemblance to what we know about the Feast of Tabernacles, that it is difficult to resist the impression of some intended connection between the two, in consequence of which the daily singing of the 'Hallel,' and the carrying of palm branches was adopted during the Feast of the Dedication, while the practice of Temple-illumination was similarly introduced into the Feast of Tabernacles.[4] All this becomes the more interesting, when we remember, on the one hand, the typical meaning of the Feast of Tabernacles,

Nay, they were so very glad at the revival of their customs, when after a long time of intermission, they unexpectedly had regained the freedom of their worship, that they made it a law for their posterity, that they should keep a festival, on account of the restoration of their temple worship, for eight days. And from that time to this we celebrate this festival, and call it Lights (Jos. Antiquities 12.324–325).

---

[4]In point of fact, the three are so compared in 2 Macc. 10:6, and even the same name applied to them, 1:9, 18. Geiger (*Urschr. u. Uebers,* p. 227) has attempted an ingenious but unsatisfactory explanation of the latter circumstance.

and on the other that the date of the Feast of the Dedication—the 25th of Chislev—seems to have been adopted by the ancient Church as that of the birth of our blessed Lord—Christmas—the Dedication of the true Temple, which was the body of Jesus (John 2:19).[5]

I suppose the reason was, because this liberty beyond our hopes appeared to us; and that thence was the name [Lights] given to that festival (Jos. Antiquities 12.325).

When Solomon finished praying, fire came down from heaven and consumed the burnt offering and the sacrifices, and the glory of the LORD filled the temple (2 Chron. 7:1).

THE ORIGIN OF THIS FESTIVAL

From the hesitating language of Josephus (*Antiq.* 12.325), we infer that even in his time the real origin of the practice of illuminating the Temple was unknown. Tradition, indeed, has it that when in the restored Temple the sacred candlestick[6] was to be lit, only one flagon of oil, sealed with the signet of the high-priest, was found to feed the lamps. This, then, was *pure* oil, but the supply was barely sufficient for one day—when, lo, by a miracle, the oil increased, and the flagon remained filled for eight days, in memory of which it was ordered to illuminate for the same space of time the Temple and private houses. A learned Jewish writer, Dr. Herzfeld,[7] suggests, that to commemorate the descent of fire from heaven upon the altar in the Temple of Solomon (2 Chron. 7:1), 'the feast of lights' was instituted when the sacred fire was relit on the purified altar of the second Temple. But even so the practice varied in its details. Either the head of a house might light one candle for all the members of his family, or else a candle for each inmate, or if very religious he would increase the number of candles for each individual every evening, so that if a family of ten had begun the first evening with ten candles they would increase them the next evening to twenty, and so on, till on the eighth night eighty candles were lit. But here also there was a difference between the schools of Hillel and Shammai—the former observing the practice as just described, the latter burning the largest number of candles the first evening, and so on decreasingly to the last day of

---

[5]See 'Christmas a Festival of Jewish Origin,' in the *Leisure Hour* for Dec., 1873.

[6]According to tradition, the first candlestick in that Temple was of iron, tinned over; the second of silver, and then only a golden one was procured.

[7]*Gesch. d. Volkes Isr.*, vol. ii, p. 271.

the feast. On the Feast of the Dedication, as at Purim and New Moons, no public fast was to be kept (*Taan.* ii. 10), though private mourning was allowed (*Moed Katon*, iii. 9).[8]

The forms of prayer at present in use by the Jews are of comparatively late date, and indeed the Karaites, who in many respects represent the more ancient traditions of Israel, do not observe the festival at all. But there cannot be a doubt that our blessed Lord Himself attended this festival at Jerusalem (John 10:22), on which occasion He told them plainly: "I and My Father are one." This gives it a far deeper significance than the rekindling of the fire on the altar, or even the connection of this feast with that of Tabernacles.

Now the next day was the festival of Xylophory; upon which the custom was for every one to bring wood for the altar (that there might never be a want of fuel for that fire which was unquenchable and always burning) (Jos. Jewish Wars 2.425).

THE FEAST OF WOOD-OFFERING

3. *The Feast of Wood-offering* (*Mish. Taan.* iv.; Jos. *Jew. Wars*, 2.425) took place on the 15th Ab[9] (August), being the last of the *nine* occasions on which offerings of wood were brought for the use of the Temple. For the other eight occasions the Talmud names certain families as specially possessing this privilege, which they had probably originally received "by lot" at the time of Nehemiah (Neh. 10:34; 13:31). At any rate, the names mentioned in the *Mishnah* are exactly the same as those in the Book of Ezra.[10] But on the 15th of Ab, along with certain families, *all* the people—even proselytes, slaves, Nethinim, and bastards, but notably the priests and Levites, were allowed to bring up wood, whence also the day is called 'the time of wood for the priests.' The other eight seasons were the 20th of Elul (September), the 1st of Tebeth (January), the 1st of Nisan (end of March or April), the 20th of Thammus (save, 'for the family of David'), the 5th, the 7th, the 10th, and the 20th of Ab. It will be observed that five of these

We—the priests, the Levites and the people— have cast lots to determine when each of our families is to bring to the house of our God at set times each year a contribution of wood to burn on the altar of the LORD our God, as it is written in the Law (Neh. 10:34).

---

[8]Accordingly, the statement in Kitto's *Encycl.* i, p. 653, that 'mourning' for any 'bereavement' was not permitted, must be corrected, or at least modified.

[9]By a mistake, our copies of Josephus make him fix the 14th as the date of this feast.

[10]Ezra 2; see Herzfeld, vol. i, 469; ii, 144.

seasons fall in the month of Ab, probably because the wood was then thought to be in best condition. The Rabbinical explanations of this are confused and contradictory, and do not account for the 15th of Ab being called, as it was, 'the day on which the axe is broken,' unless it were that after that date till spring no wood might be *felled* for the altar, although what had been previously cut might be brought up. The 15th of the month was fixed for the feast, probably because at full moon the month was regarded as at its maturity. Tradition, of course, had its own story to account for it. According to one version it was Jereboam, the wicked King of Israel, to whom so much evil is always traced; according to another, a Syro-Grecian monarch—Antiochus Epiphanes; and according to yet a third, some unnamed monarch who had prohibited the carrying of wood and of the firstfruits of Jerusalem, when certain devoted families braved the danger, and on that day secretly introduced wood into the Temple, in acknowledgment whereof the privilege was for ever afterwards conceded to their descendants.

Axes for cutting wood

THE WOOD USED IN THE FESTIVALS

The wood was first deposited in an outer chamber, where that which was worm-eaten or otherwise unfit for the altar was picked out by priests who were disqualified from other ministry. The rest was handed over to the priests who were Levitically qualified for their service, and by them stored in 'the wood chamber.' The 15th of Ab was observed as a popular and joyous festival. On this occasion (as on the Day of Atonement) the maidens went dressed in white, to dance and sing in the vineyards around Jerusalem, when an opportunity was offered to young men to select their companions for life. We may venture on a suggestion to account for this curious practice. According to the Talmud, the 15th of Ab was the day on which the prohibition was removed which prevented heiresses from marrying out of their own tribes.[11] If there is any historical foundation for this,

---

[11]Comp. Herzfeld, vol. ii, p. 144, note 33.

it would be very significant, that when all Israel, without any distinction of tribes or families, appeared to make their offerings at Jerusalem, they should be at liberty similarly to select their partners in life without the usual restrictions.

FASTS

4. *Fasts.*—These may be arranged into *public* and *private*, the latter on occasions of personal calamity or felt need. The former alone can here claim our attention. Properly speaking, there was only one Divinely-ordained public fast, that of the Day of Atonement. But it was quite in accordance with the will of God, and the spirit of the Old Testament dispensation, that when great national calamities had overtaken Israel, or great national wants arose, or great national sins were to be confessed, a day of public fasting and humiliation should be proclaimed.[12] To these the Jews added, during the Babylonian captivity, what may be called *memorial-fasts*, on the anniversaries of great national calamities. Evidently this was an unhealthy religious movement. What were idly bewailed as national calamities were really Divine judgments, caused by national sins, and should have been acknowledged as righteous, the people turning from their sins in true repentance unto God. This, if we rightly understand it, was the meaning of Zechariah's reply (Zech. 7, 8) to those who inquired whether the fasts of the fourth, the fifth, the seventh, and the tenth months, were to be continued after the return of the exiles from Babylon.

THE FOUR GREAT FASTS

At the same time, the inquiry shows, that the *four* great Jewish fasts, which, besides the Day of Atonement and the Fast of Esther, are still kept, were observed so early as the Babylonian captivity (Zech. 8:19). 'The fast of the fourth month' took place on the 17th Thammus (about June or July), in memory of

Then the Israelites, all the people, went up to Bethel, and there they sat weeping before the LORD. They fasted that day until evening and presented burnt offerings and fellowship offerings to the LORD (Judg. 20:26).

Ask all the people of the land and the priests, "When you fasted and mourned in the fifth and seventh months for the past seventy years, was it really for me that you fasted? And when you were eating and drinking, were you not just feasting for yourselves?" (Zech. 7:5–6).

This is what the LORD Almighty says: "The fasts of the fourth, fifth, seventh and tenth months will become joyful and glad occasions and happy festivals for Judah. Therefore love truth and peace" (Zech. 8:19).

---

[12]See for example, Judg. 20:26; 1 Sam. 7:6; 1 Kgs. 21:27; 2 Chron. 20:3.

the taking of Jerusalem by Nebuchadnezzar and the interruption of the daily sacrifice. To this tradition adds, that it was also the anniversary of making the golden calf, and of Moses breaking the Tables of the Law. 'The fast of the fifth month,' on the 9th of Ab, was kept on account of the destruction of the first

Zion will be plowed like a field, Jerusalem will become a heap of rubble, the temple hill a mound overgrown with thickets (Jer. 26:18b).

(and afterwards of the second) Temple. It is significant that the second Temple (that of Herod) was destroyed on the *first day* of the week. Tradition has it, that on that day God had pronounced judgment that the carcasses of all who had come out of Egypt should fall in the wilderness, and also, that again it was fated much later to witness the fulfilment of Jer. 26:18–23, when a Roman centurion had the ploughshare drawn over the site of Zion and of the Temple. 'The fast of the seventh month,' on the 2nd of Tishri, is said by tradition to be in memory of the slaughter of Gedaliah and his associates at Mizpah (Jer. 41:1). 'The fast of the tenth month' was on the 10th of Tebeth, when the siege of Jerusalem by Nebuchadnezzar commenced.

OTHER FASTS

Besides these four, the Day of Atonement, and the Fast of Esther, the Jewish calendar at present contains other twenty-two fast-days. But that is not all. It was customary to fast *twice a week* (Luke 18:12), between the Paschal week and Pentecost, and between the Feast of Tabernacles and that of the Dedication of the Temple. The days appointed for this purpose were the Monday and Thursday of every week—because, according to tradition, Moses went up Mount Sinai the second time to receive the Tables of the Law on a Thursday, and came down again on a Monday. On public fasts, the practice was (see *Taanith*, ii. 1–6) to bring the ark which contained the rolls of the law from the synagogue into the streets, and to strew ashes upon it. The people all appeared covered with sackcloth and ashes. Ashes were publically strewn on the heads of the elders and judges. Then one more venerable than the rest would address the people, his sermon being based on such admonition as this: 'My brethren, it is not said of the men of Nineveh, that God has respect to their sackcloth or their fasting, but that "God saw their works, that they turned from their evil way" (Jonah 3:10). Similarly, it is written in the "traditions" (of the prophets: "Rend your heart, and not your garments, and turn unto Jehovah your God" ' (Joel 2:13). An aged man, whose heart and home 'God had emptied,' that he might give himself wholly to prayer, was chosen to lead the devotions. Confession of sin and prayer mingled with the penitential Psalms (Psalms 102; 120; 121; 130).[13] In Jerusalem they gathered at the eastern gate, and seven times[14] as the voice of prayer ceased, they bade the priests 'blow!' and they blew with horns and their priests' trumpets. In other towns, they only blew horns. After prayer, the people retired to the cemeteries to mourn and weep. In order to be a proper fast, it must be continued from one sundown till after the next, when the stars appeared, and for about twenty-six hours the most rigid abstinence from all food and drink was enjoined. Most solemn as some of these ordinances sound, the reader of the New Testament knows how sadly all degenerated into mere formalism (Matt. 9:14; Mark 2:18; Luke 5:33); how frequent fasting became mere work- and self-righteousness, instead of being the expression of true humiliation (Luke 18:12); and how the very appearance of the penitent, unwashed and with ashes on his head, was even made matter of boasting and religious show (Matt. 6:16). So true is it that all attempts at penitence, amendment, and religion, without the Holy Spirit of God and a change of heart, only tend to

When God saw what they did and how they turned from their evil ways, he had compassion and did not bring upon them the destruction he had threatened (Jonah 3:10).

Hear my prayer, O LORD; let my cry for help come to you.
Do not hide your face from me when I am in distress.
Turn your ear to me; when I call, answer me quickly (Ps. 102:1–2).

Now John's disciples and the Pharisees were fasting. Some people came and asked Jesus, "How is it that John's disciples and the disciples of the Pharisees are fasting, but yours are not?" (Mark 2:18).

---

[13]Our account is based on the *Mishnah* (*Taan.* ii.). But we have not given the Psalms in the order there mentioned, nor yet reproduced the prayers and 'benedictions,' because they seem mostly, if not entirely, to be of later date. In general, each of the latter bases the hope of being heard on some Scriptural example of deliverance in answer to prayer, such as that of Abraham on Mount Moriah, of Israel when passing through the Red Sea, of Joshua at Gilgal, of Samuel at Mizpah, of Elijah on Mount Carmel, of Jonah in the whale's belly, and of David and Solomon in Jerusalem. Certain relaxations of the fast were allowed to the priests when actually on their ministry.

[14]See the very interesting description of details in *Taan.* ii. 5.

When you fast, do not look somber as the hypocrites do, for they disfigure their faces to show men they are fasting. I tell you the truth, they have received their reward in full (Matt. 6:16).

entangle man in the snare of self-deception, to fill him with spiritual pride, and still further to increase his real alienation from God.[15]

[15]Of the three sects or schools of Pharisees were here the strictest, being in this also at the opposite pole from the Sadducees. The fasts of the Essenes were indeed even more stringent, and almost constant, but they were intended not to procure *merit*, but to set the soul free from the bondage of the body, which was regarded as the seat of all sin. Besides the above-mentioned fast, and one of all the firstborn on the eve of every Passover, such of the 'men of the station' as went not up to Jerusalem with their company fasted on the Monday, Tuesday, Wednesday, and Thursday, in their respective synagogues, and prayed for a blessing on their brethren and on the people. They connected their fasts and prayers with the section in Gen. 1, which they read on those days—praying on the Monday (Gen. 1:9) for those at sea; on the Tuesday (vers. 11, 12) for all on a journey; on the Wednesday (ver. 14) on account of the supposed dangerous influences of sun and moon, against diseases of children; and on the Thursday (ver. 20) for women labouring with child and for infants.

Further particulars would lead us from a description of the Temple-services to those of the synagogue. But it is interesting to note how closely the Roman Church has adopted the practices of the synagogue. In imitation of the four Jewish fasts mentioned in Zech. 8:19, the year was divided into four seasons—Quatember—each marked by a fast—three of these being traced by tradition to Bishop Callistus (223), and the fourth to Pope Leo 1 (440). In 1095, Urban II fixed these four fasts on the Wednesdays after Ash-Wednesday, Whit-Sunday, the Exaltation of the Cross, and the Feast of S. *Lucia* (13th December) according to this monkish distich:—

'Post Luciam, cineres, post sanctum pneuma, crucemque
Tempora dat quatuor feria quarta sequens.'

The early Church substituted for the two weekly Jewish fast-days—Monday and Thursday—the so-called 'dies stationum,' 'guard or watch-days' of the Christian soldier, or Christian fast-days—Wednesday and Friday, on which the Saviour had been respectively betrayed and crucified. See the article '*Fasten,*' in Herzog's *Encycl.* vol. iii, pp. 334–339.

18
ON PURIFICATIONS

❦

THE BURNING OF THE RED HEIFER—
THE CLEANSING OF THE HEALED LEPER—
THE TRIAL OF THE WOMAN SUSPECTED
OF ADULTERY

Then Jesus said to him, "See that you don't tell anyone. But go, show yourself to the priest and offer the
gift Moses commanded, as a testimony to them."
—Matthew 8:4

Festive seasons were not only occasions which
brought worshippers to Jerusalem. Every trespass and
sin, every special vow and offering, and every defilement called them to the Temple. All the rites then
enjoined are full of deep meaning. Selecting from
them those on which the practice of the Jews at the
time of Christ casts a special light, our attention is
first called to a service, distinguished from the rest by
its unique character.

THE RED HEIFER
1. *The purification from the defilement of death
by the ashes of the red heifer* (Num. 19). In the worship
of the Old Testament, where everything was *symbolical,* that is, where spiritual realities were conveyed
through outward signs, every physical defilement
would point to, and carry with it, as it were, a spiritual counterpart. But especially was this the case with
reference to birth and death, which were so closely
connected with sin and the second death, with redemption and the second birth. Hence, all connected
with the origin of life and with death, implied defile-

*The LORD said to Moses
and Aaron: "This is a
requirement of the law that
the LORD has commanded:
Tell the Israelites to bring
you a red heifer without
defect or blemish and that
has never been under a
yoke" (Num. 19:1–2).*

ment, and required Levitical purification. But here there was considerable difference. Passing over the minor defilements attaching to what is connected with the origin of life, the woman who had given birth to a child was Levitically unclean for forty or for eighty days, according as she had become the mother of a son or a daughter (Lev. 12). After that she was to offer for her purification a lamb for a burnt-, and a turtledove, or young pigeon, for a sin-offering; in case of poverty, altogether only two turtledoves or two young pigeons. We remember that the mother of Jesus availed herself of that provision for the poor, when at the same time she presented in the Temple the Royal Babe, her firstborn son (Luke 2:22).

When the time of their purification according to the Law of Moses had been completed, Joseph and Mary took him to Jerusalem to present him to the Lord (Luke 2:22).

THE OFFERING FOR THE FIRST-BORN

On bringing her offering, she would enter the Temple through 'the gate of the first-born,' and stand in waiting at the Gate of Nicanor, from the time that the incense was kindled on the golden altar. Behind her, in the Court of the Women, was the crowd of worshippers, while she herself, at the top of the Levites' steps, which led up to the great court, would witness all that passed in the sanctuary. At last one of the officiating priests would come to her at the Gate of Nicanor, and take from her hand the 'poor's offering,'[1] which she had brought. The morning sacrifice was ended; and but few would linger behind while the offering for her purification was actually made. She who brought it mingled prayer and thanksgiving with the service. And now the priest once more approached her, and, sprinkling her with the sacrificial blood, declared her cleansed. Her 'first-born' was next redeemed at the hand of the priest, with five shekels of silver;[2] two benedictions being at the same time pronounced, one for the happy event which had

---

[1] So it is literally called in the Talmud.
[2] According to the Mishnah (*Beehor.* viii. 7) 'of Tyrian weight' = 10 to 12 shillings of our money. The Rabbis lay it down that redemption-money was only paid for a son who was the firstborn of his mother, and who was 'suitable for the priesthood,' that is, had no disqualifying bodily blemishes.

enriched the family with a first-born, the other for the law of redemption.[3] And when, with grateful heart, and solemnised in spirit, she descended those fifteen steps where the Levites were wont to sing the 'Hallel,' a sudden light of heavenly joy filled the heart of one who had long been in waiting 'for the consolation of Israel.' If the Holy Spirit had revealed it to just and devout *Simeon,* that he 'should not see death before he had seen the Lord's Christ,' who should vanquish death, it was the same Spirit, who had led him up into the Temple 'when the parents brought in the child Jesus, to do for Him after the custom of the law.' Then the aged believer took the Divine Babe from His mother's into his own arms. He felt that the faithful Lord had truly fulfilled His word. Content now to depart in peace, he blessed God from the fulness of a grateful heart, for his eyes had seen His salvation—'a light to lighten the Gentiles,' and the 'glory of His people Israel.' But Joseph and Mary listened, wondering, to the words which fell from Simeon's lips.

Simeon took him in his arms and praised God, saying:
"Sovereign Lord, as you have promised,
you now dismiss your servant in peace.
For my eyes have seen your salvation,
which you have prepared in the sight of all people,
a light for revelation to the Gentiles
and for glory to your people Israel"
(Luke 2:28–32).

PURIFICATION FOR THE DEAD

Such was the service of purification connected with the origin of life. Yet it was not nearly so solemn or important as that for the removal of defilement from contact with death. A stain attached indeed to the spring of life; but death, which cast its icy shadow from the gates of Paradise to those of Hades, pointed to the second death, under whose ban every one lay, and which, if unremoved, would exercise eternal sway. Hence defilement by the dead was symbolically treated as the greatest of all. It lasted seven days; it required a special kind of purification; and it extended not only to those who had touched the dead, but even to the house or tent where the body had lain, and all open vessels therein. More than that, to enter such a house; to come into contact with the smallest bone, or with a grave;[4] even to partake of a feast for

Whoever touches the dead body of anyone will be unclean for seven days. He must purify himself with the water on the third day and on the seventh day; then he will be clean. But if he does not purify himself on the third and seventh days, he will not be clean (Num. 19:11–12).

---

[3]See Jost, vol. ii, p. 264.
[4]According to Jewish tradition, a dead body, however deeply buried, communicated defilement all the way up to the surface, unless indeed it were vaulted in, or vaulted over, to cut off contact with the earth above.

the dead (Hos. 9:4), rendered ceremonially unclean for seven days (Num. 19:11–16, 18; 31:19). Nay, he who was thus defiled in turn rendered everything unclean which he touched (Num. 19:22; comp. Hag. 2:13). For priests and Nazarites the law was even more stringent (Lev. 21, etc.; comp. Ezek. 44:25, etc.; Num. 6:7, etc.). The former were not to defile themselves by touching any dead body, except those of their nearest of kin; the high-priest was not to approach even those of his own parents.

THE SIX DEGREES OF DEFILEMENT

In general, Jewish writers distinguish *six* degrees, which they respectively term, according to their intensity, the 'father of fathers,' the 'fathers,' and the 'first,' 'second,' 'third,' and 'fourth children of defilement.' They enumerate in all twenty-nine 'fathers of defilement,' arising from various causes, and of these no less than eleven arise from some contact with a dead body. Hence also the law made here exceptional provision for purification. 'A red heifer without spot,' that is, without any white or black hair on its hide, without 'blemish, and on which never yoke came,' was to be sacrificed as a *sin-offering* (Num. 19:9, 17), and that outside the camp, not in the sanctuary, and by the son of, or by the presumptive successor to the high-priest. The blood of this sacrifice was to be sprinkled seven times with the finger, not on the altar, but towards the sanctuary; then the whole animal— skin, flesh, blood, and dung—burned, the priest casting into the midst of the burning 'cedarwood, and hyssop, and scarlet.' The ashes of this sacrifice were to be gathered by 'a man that is clean,' and laid up 'without the camp in a clean place.' But the priest, he that burned the red heifer, and who gathered her ashes, were to be 'unclean until the even,' to wash their clothes, and the two former also to 'bathe,' their 'flesh in water' (Num. 19:7, 8). When required for purification, a clean person was to take of those ashes, put them in a vessel, pour upon them 'living water,' then dip hyssop in it, and on the third and seventh days sprinkle him who was to be purified; after which he

Anything that an unclean person touches becomes unclean, and anyone who touches it becomes unclean till evening (Num. 19:22).

A man who is clean shall gather up the ashes of the heifer and put them in a ceremonially clean place outside the camp. They shall be kept by the Israelite community for use in the water of cleansing; it is for purification from sin (Num. 19:9).

had to wash his clothes and bathe his flesh, when he became 'clean' on the evening of the seventh day. The tent or house, and all the vessels in it, were to be similarly purified. Lastly, he that touched 'the water of separation,' 'of avoidance,' or 'of uncleanness,'[5] was to be unclean until even, and he that sprinkled it to wash his clothes (Num. 19:21).

DEATH THE GREATEST DEFILEMENT

From all these provisions it is evident that as death carried with it the greatest defilement, so the sin-offering for its purification was in itself and in its consequences the most marked. And its application must have been so frequently necessary in every family and circle of acquaintances that the great truths connected with it were constantly kept in view of the people. In general, it may here be stated, that the laws in regard to defilement were primarily intended as symbols of spiritual truths, and not for social, nor yet sanitary purposes, though such results would also flow from them. Sin had rendered fellowship with God impossible; sin was death, and had wrought death, and the dead body as well as the spiritually dead soul were the evidence of its sway.

Then the elders of the town nearest the body shall take a heifer that has never been worked and has never worn a yoke...Then all the elders of the town nearest the body shall wash their hands over the heifer whose neck was broken in the valley, and they shall declare: "Our hands did not shed this blood, nor did our eyes see it done" (Deut. 21:3, 6–7).

LEVITICAL DEFILEMENT TRACEABLE TO DEATH

It has been well pointed out,[6] that all classes of Levitical defilement can ultimately be traced back to death, with its two great outward symptoms, the corruption which appears in the skin on the surface of the body, and to which leprosy may be regarded as akin, and the fluxes from the dead body, which have their counterpart in the morbid fluxes of the living body. As the direct manifestation of sin which separates man from God, defilement by the dead required a *sin-offering,* and the ashes of the red heifer are expressly so designated in the words: 'It *is a sin-*

---

[5]The expression is fully discussed in Saalschütz, *Mos. Recht.* pp. 341, 342.
[6]By Sommers, in his *Bibl. Abh.* vol. i, p. 201, etc.

offering' (Num. 9:17).[7] But it differs from all other sin-offerings. The sacrifice was to be of pure red colour; one 'upon which never came yoke;'[8] and a female, all other sin-offerings for the congregation being males (Lev. 4:14). These particulars symbolically point to life in its freshness, fulness, and fruitfulness—that is, the fullest life and the spring of life. But what distinguished it even more from all others was, that it was a sacrifice offered once for all (at least so long as its ashes lasted); that its blood was sprinkled, not on the altar, but outside the camp towards the sanctuary; and that it was *wholly* burnt, along with cedarwood, as the symbol of imperishable existence, hyssop, as that of purification from corruption, and 'scarlet,' which from its colour was the emblem of life. Thus the sacrifice of highest life, brought as a sin-offering, and, so far as possible, once for all, was in its turn accompanied by the symbols of imperishable existence, freedom from corruption, and fulness of life, so as yet more to intensify its significance. But even this is not all. The gathered ashes with running water were sprinkled on the third and seventh days on that which was to be purified. Assuredly, if death meant 'the wages of sin,' this purification pointed, in all its details, to 'the gift of God,' which is 'eternal life,' through the sacrifice of Him in whom is the fulness of life.

THE SCAPEGOAT, THE RED HEIFER, AND THE LIVING BIRD DIPPED IN BLOOD

And here there is a remarkable analogy between three sacrifices, which, indeed, form a separate group. The scape-goat, which was to remove the personal guilt of the Israelites—not their theocratic alienation from the sanctuary; the red heifer, which was to take away the defilement of death, as that which stood between God and man; and the 'living bird,' dipped

When they become aware of the sin they committed, the assembly must bring a young bull as a sin offering and present it before the Tent of Meeting (Lev. 4:14).

For the wages of sin is death, but the gift of God is eternal life in Christ Jesus our Lord (Rom. 6:23).

---

[7]The Authorised Version translates, without any reason: 'It is a purification for sin.' It seems strange indeed, that Professor Fairbairn should have reproduced this rendering without note or comment in his *Typology,* vol. ii, p. 376.

[8]The only other instance in which this is enjoined is Deut. 21:3, though we read of it again in 1 Sam. 6: 7.

in 'the water and the blood,' and then 'let loose in the field at the purification from leprosy, which symbolised the living death of personal sinfulness, were all, either wholly offered, or in their essentials completed *outside the sanctuary.* In other words, the Old Testament dispensation had confessedly within its sanctuary no real provision for the spiritual wants to which they symbolically pointed; their removal lay outside its sanctuary and beyond its symbols. Spiritual death, as the consequence of the fall, personal sinfulness, and personal guilt lay beyond the reach of the Temple-provision, and pointed directly to Him who was to come. Every death, every case of leprosy, every Day of Atonement, was a call for His advent, as the eye, enlightened by faith, would follow the goat into the wilderness, or watch the living bird as, bearing the mingled blood and water, he winged his flight into liberty, or read in the ashes sprung from the burning of the red heifer the emblem of purification from spiritual death. Hence, also, the manifest internal connection between these rites. In the sacrifices of the Day of Atonement and of the purified leper, the offering was twofold, one being slain, the other sent away alive, while the purification from leprosy and from death had also many traits in common.

Hyssop

But the hide of the bull and all its flesh, as well as the head and legs, the inner parts and offal—that is, all the rest of the bull—he must take outside the camp to a place ceremonially clean, where the ashes are thrown, and burn it in a wood fire on the ash heap (Lev. 4:11–12).

THESE SACRIFICES DEFILED THOSE WHO TOOK PART IN THEM

Lastly, all these sacrifices equally defiled those who took part in their offering,[9] except in the case of leprosy, where the application would necessarily only be *personal.* Thus, also, we understand why the red heifer as, so to speak, the most intense of sin-offerings, was *wholly* burnt outside the camp, and other sin-offerings only partially so (Lev. 4:11, 12, 20, etc.). For this burning signified that 'in the theocracy there was no one, who, by his own holiness, could bear or take away the sin imputed to these sin-offerings, so that it was needful, as the wages of sin, to burn the sacrifice which

---

[9]Hence the high-priest was prohibited from offering the red heifer.

had been made sin.'[10] The ashes of this sin-offering, mixed with living water and sprinkled with hyssop, symbolised purification from that death which separates between God and man. This parallelism between the blood of Christ and the ashes of an heifer, on the one hand, and on the other between the purification of the flesh by these means, and that of the conscience from dead works, is thus expressed in Heb. 9:13, 14: 'If the blood of bulls and of goats, and the ashes of an heifer sprinkling the defiled, sanctifieth to the purifying of the flesh: how much more shall the blood of Christ, who through the eternal Spirit offered Himself without spot to God, purify your conscience from dead works to serve the living God?' And that this spiritual meaning of the types was clearly apprehended under the Old Testament appears, for example, from the reference to it in this prayer of David (Ps. 51:7): 'Purge me from sin[11] (purify me) with hyssop, and I shall be clean: wash me, and I shall be whiter than snow;' which is again further applied in what the prophet Isaiah says about the forgiveness of sin (Isa. 1:18).

"Come now, let us reason together,"
says the LORD.
"Though your sins are like scarlet,
they shall be as white as snow;
though they are red as crimson,
they shall be like wool"
(Isa. 1:18).

SIGNIFICANCE OF THE RED HEIFER

This is not the place more fully to vindicate the views here propounded. Without some deeper symbolical meaning attaching to them, the peculiarities of the sin-offering of the red heifer would indeed be well-nigh unintelligible.[12] This must be substantially the purport of a Jewish tradition to the effect that King Solomon, who knew the meaning of all God's ordinances, was unable to understand that of the red heifer. A 'Haggadah' maintains that the wisest of men had in Eccl. 7:23 thus described his experience in this

---

[10]Keil, *Bibl. Archaeol.* vol. i, p. 283.

[11]The Hebrew (*Piel*) form for 'purge from sin' has no English equivalent, unless we were to coin the word 'unsin' or 'unguilt' me—remove my sin.

[12]It is impossible here fully to explain our views. All the more we bespeak for them a calm and candid examination. Christian writers in this country, whether theological or popular, have either passed over the subject, or (like Fairbairn, *Typology,* vol. ii, p. 376) taken too superficial a view to require special notice.

respect: 'All this have I proved by wisdom,' that is, all other matters; 'I said, I will be wise,' that is, in reference to the meaning of the red heifer; 'but it was far from me.' But if Jewish traditionalism was thus conscious of its spiritual ignorance in regard to this type, it was none the less zealous in prescribing, with even more than usual precision, its ceremonial. The first object was to obtain a proper 'red heifer' for the sacrifice. The *Mishnah* (*Parah,* i., ii.) states the needful age of such a *red heifer* as from two to four, and even five years; the colour of its hide, two white or black hairs springing from the *same follicle* disqualifying it; and how, if she had been put to any use, though only a cloth had been laid on her, she would no longer answer the requirement that upon her 'never came yoke.'

THE SACRIFICE OF THE RED HEIFER

Even more particular are the Rabbis to secure that the sacrifice be properly offered (*Parah,* iii., iv.). Seven days before, the priest destined for the service was separated and kept in the Temple—in 'the House of Stoves'—where he was daily sprinkled with the ashes—as the Rabbis fable—of all the red heifers ever offered. When bringing the sacrifice, he was to wear his white priestly raiments. According to their tradition, there was an arched roadway leading from the east gate of the Temple out upon the Mount of Olives— double arched, that is, arched also over the supporting pillars, for fear of any possible pollution through the ground upwards. Over this the procession passed. On the Mount of Olives the elders of Israel were already in waiting. First, the priest immersed his whole body, then he approached the pile of cedar-, pine-, and fig-wood which was heaped like a pyramid, but having an opening in the middle, looking towards the west. Into this the red heifer was thrust, and bound, with its head towards the south and its face looking to the west, the priest standing east of the sacrifice, his face, of course, also turned westwards. Slaying the sacrifice with his right hand, he caught up the blood in his left. Seven times he dipped his finger in it, sprinkling it towards the Most Holy Place,

R. Jose the Galilean says: Bullocks must be [not more than] two years old, for it is written, And 'a second [year]' bullock of the herd shalt thou take for a Sin–offering. But the Sages say: They may even be three years old. R. Meir says: Even if they are four years old or five they are valid; but they do not offer them that are old out of reverence [towards the Altar] (Mishnah, Para i.2).

There were five gates to the Temple Mount: the two Huldah Gates on the south…the Kiponus Gate on the west…the Tadi Gate on the north…the Eastern Gate on which was portrayed the Palace of Shushan. Through this the High Priest that burned the [Red] Heifer, and the heifer, and all that aided him went forth to the Mount of Olives (Mishnah, Middot i.3).

*There were courtyards in
Jerusalem built over the
rock, and beneath them the
rock was hollowed for fear
of any grave down in the
depths; and they used to
bring women while they
were pregnant and there
they bore their children
and reared them
(Mishnah, Para iii.2).*

which he was supposed to have in full view over the
Porch of Solomon or through the eastern gate. Then,
immediately descending, he kindled the fire. As soon
as the flames burst forth, the priest, standing outside
the pit in which the pile was built up, took cedar-
wood, hyssop, and 'scarlet' wool, asking three times
as he held up each: 'Is this cedarwood? Is this hyssop?
Is this scarlet?' so as to call to the memory of every
one the Divine ordinance. Then tying them together
with the scarlet wool, he threw the bundle upon the
burning heifer. The burnt remains were beaten into
ashes by sticks or stone mallets and passed through
coarse sieves; then divided into three parts—one of
which was kept in the Temple-terrace (the *Chel*), the
other on the Mount of Olives, and the third distributed among the priesthood throughout the land.

*Take your lord's servants
with you and set Solomon
my son on my own mule
and take him down to
Gihon. There have Zadok
the priest and Nathan the
prophet anoint him king
over Israel. Blow the
trumpet and shout, "Long
live King Solomon!"
(1 Kgs. 1:33–34).*

CHILDREN USED IN THE OFFERING

The next care was to find one to whom no
suspicion of possible defilement could attach, who
might administer purification to such as needed it.
For this purpose a priest was not required; but any
one—even a child—was fit for the service. In point of
fact, according to Jewish tradition, children were
exclusively employed in this ministry. If we are to
believe the *Mishnah* (*Parah*, iii. 2–5), there were at
Jerusalem certain dwellings built upon rocks, that
were hollowed beneath, so as to render impossible
pollution from unknown graves beneath. Here the
children destined for this ministry were to be born,
and here they were reared and kept till fit for their
service. Peculiar precautions were adopted in leading
them out to their work. The child was to ride on a
bullock, and to mount and descend it by boards. He
was first to proceed to the Pool of *Siloam*,[13] and to fill
a stone cup with its water, and thence to ride to the
Temple Mount, which, with all its courts, was also
supposed to be free from possible pollutions by being
hollowed beneath. Dismounting, he would approach

---

[13]Or *Gihon*. According to Jewish tradition, the kings were always anointed at Siloam
(1 Kings 1:33, 38).

the 'Beautiful Gate,' where the vessel with the ashes of the red heifer was kept. Next a goat would be brought out, and a rope, with a stick attached to it, tied between its horns. The stick was put into the vessel with the ashes, the goat driven backwards, and of the ashes thereby spilt the child would take for use in the sacred service so much as to be visible upon the water. It is only fair to add, that one of the Mishnic sages, deprecating a statement which might be turned into ridicule by the Sadducees, declares that any clean person might take with his hand from the vessel so much of the ashes as was required for the service. The purification was made by sprinkling with hyssop. According to the Rabbis (*Parah,* xi. 9), three separate stalks, each with a blossom on it, were tied together, and the tip of these blossoms dipped into the water of separation, the hyssop itself being grasped while sprinkling the unclean. The same authorities make the most incredible assertion that altogether, from the time of Moses to the final destruction of the Temple, only seven, or else nine, such red heifers had been offered: the first by Moses, the second by Ezra, and the other five, or else seven, between the time of Ezra and that of the taking of Jerusalem by the Romans. We only add that the cost of this sacrifice, which was always great, since a pure red heifer was very rare,[14] was defrayed from the Temple treasury, as being offered for the whole people.[15] Those who lived in the country would, for purification from defilement by the dead, come up to Jerusalem seven days before the great festivals, and, as part of the ashes were distributed among the priesthood, there could never be any difficulty in purifying houses or vessels.

The [bunch of] hyssop should be made up from three stalks having [in all] three buds. R. Judah says: Three to each (Mishnah, Para xi.9).

---

[14]It might be purchased even from non-Israelites, and the Talmud relates a curious story, showing at the same time the reward of filial piety, and the *fabulous* amount which it is *supposed* such a red heifer might fetch.

[15]Philo erroneously states that the high-priest was sprinkled with it each time before ministering at the altar. The truth is, he was only so sprinkled in preparation for the Day of Atonement, *in case* he might have been unwittingly defiled. Is the Romish use of 'holy water' derived from Jewish purifications, or from Greek heathen practice of sprinkling on entering a temple?

PURIFICATION OF THE LEPER

2. After what has already been explained, it is not necessary to enter into details about *the purification of the leper,* for which this, indeed, is not the place. Leprosy was not merely the emblem of sin, but of death, to which, so to speak, it stood related, as does our actual sinfulness to our state of sin and death before God. Even a Rabbinical saying ranks lepers with those who may be regarded as dead.[16] They were excluded from 'the camp of Israel,' by which, in later times, the Talmudists understood all cities walled since the days of Joshua, who was supposed to have sanctified them. Lepers were not allowed to go beyond their proper bounds, on pain of forty stripes. For every place which a leper entered was supposed to be defiled. They were, however, admitted to the synagogues, where a place was railed off for them, ten handbreadths high and four cubits wide, on condition of their entering the house of worship before the rest of the congregation, and leaving it after them (*Negaim,* xiii. 12). It was but natural that they should consort together. This is borne out by such passages as Luke 17:12, which at the same time show how even this living death vanished at the word or the touch of the Saviour.

As he was going into a village, ten men who had leprosy met him. They stood at a distance and called out in a loud voice, "Jesus, Master, have pity on us!"

When he saw them, he said, "Go, show yourselves to the priests." And as they went, they were cleansed (Luke 17:12–14).

EXAMINATION OF THE LEPER

The Mishnic tractate, *Negaim,* enters into most wearisome details on the subject of leprosy, as affecting persons or things. It closes by describing the ceremonial at its purification. The actual *judgment* as to the existence of leprosy always belonged to the *priest,* though he might consult any one who had knowledge of the matter. Care was to be taken that no part of the examination fell on the Sabbath, nor was any on whom the taint appeared to be disturbed either during his marriage week, or on feast days (*Negaim,* i. 4; iii. 2). Great precautions were taken to render the examination thorough. It was not to be proceeded

---

[16]The other three classes are the blind, the poor, and those who have no children.

with early in the morning, nor 'between the evenings,' nor inside the house, nor on a cloudy day, nor yet during the glare of midday, but from 9 A.M. to 12 o'clock noon, and from 1 P.M. to 3 P.M.; according to Rabbi Jehudah, only at 10 or 11 o'clock A.M., and at 2 and 3 o'clock P.M. The examining priest must neither be blind of an eye, nor impaired in sight, nor might he pronounce as to the leprosy of his own kindred (*Negaim*, ii. 2, 3, 5). For further caution, judgment was not to be pronounced at the same time about two suspicious spots, whether on the same or different persons (*Negaim*, iii. 1).

> *A man may examine any leprosy-signs excepting his own leprosy-signs. R. Meir says: Excepting also those in his near of kin (Mishnah, Nega'im ii.5).*

RIGHT MEANING OF LEV. 13:12, 13

A very curious mistake by writers on typology here requires passing notice. It is commonly supposed[17] that Lev. 13:12, 13 refers to cases of true leprosy, so that if a person had presented himself covered with leprosy over 'all his flesh,' 'from his head even to his foot, wheresoever the priest looketh,' the priest was to pronounce: 'He is clean.' If this interpretation were correct, the priest would have had to declare what was *simply untrue!* And, mark, it is not a question about *cleansing* one who had been a leper, but about declaring such an one clean, that is, not a leper at all, while yet the malady covered his whole body from head to foot! Nor does even the doctrinal analogy, for the sake of which this strange view must have been adopted, hold good. For to confess oneself, or even to present oneself as wholly covered by the leprosy of sin, is not yet to be cleansed—that requires purification by the blood of Christ. Moreover, the Old Testament type speaks of being *clean*, not of cleansing; of being non-leprous, not of being purified from leprosy! The correct interpretation of Lev. 13:12, 13 evidently is, that an eruption having the symptoms there described is not that

> *If the disease breaks out all over his skin and, so far as the priest can see, it covers all the skin of the infected person from head to foot, the priest is to examine him, and if the disease has covered his whole body, he shall pronounce that person clean. Since it has all turned white, he is clean (Lev. 13:12–13).*

---

[17]All popular writers on typology have fallen into this error. Even the learned Lightfoot has committed it. It is also adopted by Mr. Poole in Smith's *Dict. of the Bible* (ii, p. 94), and curiously accounted for by the altogether unfounded hypothesis that the law 'imposed segregation' only 'while the disease manifested activity'!

of true leprosy at all.[18] But where, in the Divine mercy, one really leprous had been restored, the law (Lev. 14) defined what was to be done for his 'purification.' The rites are, in fact, twofold—the first (Lev. 14:1–9), to restore him to fellowship with the congregation; the other to introduce him anew to communion with God (Lev. 14:10–20). In both respects he had been dead, and was alive again; and the new life, so consecrated, was one higher than the old could ever have been.

THE MISHNAH

This will appear from an attentive study of the ceremonial of purification, as described in the *Mishnah*.[19] The priest having pronounced the former leper clean, a quarter of a log (the log rather less than a pint) of 'living water' was poured into an earthenware dish. Then two 'clean birds' were taken—the Rabbis say two sparrows[20]—of whom one was killed over 'the living water,' so that the blood might drop into it, after which the carcass was buried. Next, cedar-wood, hyssop, and scarlet wool were taken and tied together (as at the burning of the red heifer), and dipped, along with the living bird, which was seized by the tips of his wings and of his tail, into the blood-stained water, when the person to be purified was sprinkled seven times on the back of his hand, or, according to others, on his forehead. Upon this the living bird was set free, neither towards the sea, nor towards the city, nor towards the wilderness, but towards the fields. Finally, the leper had all the hair on his body shorn with a razor, after which he washed his clothes, and bathed, when he was clean, though still interdicted his house[21] for seven days.

These are the regulations for the diseased person at the time of his ceremonial cleansing, when he is brought to the priest... Then the priest is to sacrifice the sin offering and make atonement for the one to be cleansed from his uncleanness. After that, the priest shall slaughter the burnt offering and offer it on the altar, together with the grain offering, and make atonement for him, and he will be clean (Lev. 14:2, 19–20).

---

[18]Even the modified view of Keil, which is substantially adopted in Kitto's *Encycl.* (3rd edit.), p. 812, that the state described in Lev. 13:12, 13, 'was regarded as indicative of the crisis, as the whole evil matter thus brought to the surface formed itself into a scale, which dried and peeled off,' does not meet the requirements of the text.

[19]*Negaim*, xiii.

[20]May not our Saviour refer to this when He speaks of 'sparrows' as of marketable value: 'Are not two sparrows sold for one farthing' (Matt. 10:29)?

[21]The *Mishnah* and all commentators apply this to conjugal intercourse.

THE SECOND STAGE

The first stage of purification had now been completed, and the seven days' seclusion served as preparation for the second stage. The former might take place anywhere, but the latter required the attendance of the purified leper in the sanctuary. It began on the seventh day itself, when the purified leper had again all his hair shorn, as at the first, washed his clothes, and bathed. The *Mishnah* remarks (*Negaim,* xiv. 4) that three classes required this legal tonsure of all hair—lepers, Nazarites, and the Levites at their consecration—a parallel this between the purified lepers and the Levites, which appears even more clearly in their being anointed on the head with oil (Lev. 14:29), and which was intended to mark that their new life was higher than the old, and that, like Levi, they were to be specially dedicated to God.[22] Though not of any special importance, we may add that, according to the *Mishnah,* as in the analogous case of the two goats for the Day of Atonement, the two birds for the leper were to be of precisely the same colour, size, and value, and, if possible, bought on the same day—to mark that the two formed integral parts of one and the same service; the cedar-wood was to be one cubit long and 'the quarter of a bedpost' thick; the hyssop of the common kind, that is, not such as had any other bye-name, as Grecian, Roman, ornamental, or wild; while the scarlet wool was to be a shekel's weight. The rest of the ceremonial we give in the words of the *Mishnah* itself (*Negaim,* xiv. 7, etc.): —'On the eighth day the leper brings three sacrifices —a sin-, a trespass-, and a burnt-offering, and the poor brings a sin- and a burnt-offering of a bird. He stands before the trespass-offering, lays his hands upon it, and kills it. Two priests catch up the blood— one in a vessel, the other in his hand. He who catches it up in the vessels goes and throws it on the side of the altar, and he who catches it in his hand goes and stands before the leper. And the leper, who had previously bathed in the court of the lepers, goes and

The rest of the oil in his palm the priest shall put on the head of the one to be cleansed, to make atonement for him before the LORD *(Lev. 14:29).*

On the eighth day he brought three beasts: a Sin-offering, a Guilt-offering and a Whole-offering. If he was poor, he brought a Sin-offering of a bird and a Whole-offering of a bird (Mishnah, Nega'im xiv.7).

---

[22]The significance of anointing the head with oil is sufficiently known.

This, then, is the law of jealousy when a woman goes astray and defiles herself while married to her husband, or when feelings of jealousy come over a man because he suspects his wife. The priest is to have her stand before the LORD *and is to apply this entire law to her. The husband will be innocent of any wrongdoing, but the woman will bear the consequences of her sin (Num. 5:29–31).*

stands in the Gate of Nicanor. Rabbi Jehudah says:— He needs not to bathe. He thrusts in his head (viz. into the great court which he may not yet enter), and the priest puts of the blood upon the tip of his ear; he thrusts in his hand, and he puts it upon the thumb of his hand; he thrusts in his foot, and he puts it upon the great toe of his foot. Rabbi Jehudah says:—He thrusts in the three at the same time. If he have lost his thumb, great toe, or right ear, he cannot ever be cleansed. Rabbi Eliezer says:—The priest puts it on the spot where it had been. Rabbi Simeon says:—If it be applied on the corresponding left side of the leper's body, it sufficeth. The priest now takes from the log of oil and pours it into the palm of his colleague— though if he poured it into his own it were valid. He dips his finger and sprinkles seven times towards the Holy of Holies, dipping each time he sprinkles. He goes before the leper; and on the spot where he had put the blood he puts the oil, as it is written, "upon the blood of the trespass-offering." And the remnant of the oil that is in the priest's hand, he pours on the head of him that is to be cleansed, for an atonement; if he so puts it, he is atoned for, but if not, he is not atoned for. So Rabbi Akiba. Rabbi Jochanan, the son of Nuri, saith:—This is only the remnant of the ordinance—whether it is done or not, the atonement is made; but they impute it to him (the priest?) as if he had not made atonement.'

PURIFICATION FROM SUSPICION OF ADULTERY

3. It still remains to describe the peculiar ceremonial connected with *the purification of a wife from the suspicion of adultery.* Strictly speaking, there was no *real* offering connected with this. The rites (Num. 5:11–31) consisted of two parts, in the first of which the woman in her wave-offering solemnly commended her ways to the Holy Lord God of Israel, thus professing innocence; while in the second, she intimated her readiness to abide the consequences of her profession and appeal to God. Both acts were symbolical, nor did either of them imply anything like an *ordeal.* The meat-offering which she brought in her hand

symbolised her works, the fruit of her life. But owing to the fact that her life was open to suspicion, it was brought, not of wheat, as on other occasions, but of barley-flour, which constituted the poorest fare, while, for the same reason, the customary addition of oil and frankincense was omitted. Before this offering was waved and part of it burned on the altar, the priest had to warn the woman of the terrible consequences of a false profession before the Lord, and to exhibit what he spoke in a symbolical act. He wrote the words of the curse upon a roll; then, taking water out of the laver, in which the daily impurities of the priests were, so to speak, symbolically cleansed, and putting into it dust of the sanctuary, he washed in this mixture the writing of the curses, which were denounced upon the special sin of which she was suspected. And the woman, having by a repeated *Amen* testified that she had quite apprehended the meaning of the whole, and that she made her solemn appeal to God, was then in a symbolical act to do two things. First, she presented in her meat-offering, which the priest waved, her life to the heart-searching God, and then, prepared for the consequences of her appeal, she drank the bitter mixture of the threatened curses, assured that it could do no harm to her who was innocent, whereas, if guilty, she had appealed to God, judgment would certainly at some time overtake her, and that in a manner corresponding to the sin which she had committed.

REGULATIONS AS GIVEN IN THE MISHNAH

According to the *Mishnah*, which devotes to this subject a special tractate (*Sotah*), a wife could not be brought to this solemn trial unless her husband have previously warned her, in presence of two witnesses, against intercourse with one whom he suspected, and also two witnesses had reported that she had contravened his injunction. The Rabbis, moreover, insist that the command must have been express, that it only applied to intercourse out of reach of public view, and that the husband's charge to his wife before witnesses should be preceded by private and loving

"But if you have gone astray while married to your husband and you have defiled yourself by sleeping with a man other than your husband"—here the priest is to put the woman under this curse of the oath—"may the LORD cause your people to curse and denounce you when he causes your thigh to waste away and your abdomen to swell. May this water that brings a curse enter your body so that your abdomen swells and your thigh wastes away."

Then the woman is to say, "Amen. So be it" (Num. 5:20–22).

If a man would warn his wife, R. Eliezer says: He must warn her before two witnesses, and he may [then] make her drink on the evidence of one witness or on his own evidence. R. Joshua says: He must warn her before two witnesses, and he may make her drink [only] on the evidence of two witnesses (Mishnah, Soṭa i.1).

"See, it stands written
before me:
I will not keep silent but
will pay back in full;
I will pay it back into
their laps—
both your sins and the sins
of your fathers,"
says the LORD.
"Because they burned
sacrifices on the
mountains
and defied me on the hills,
I will measure into
their laps
the full payment for their
former deeds"
(Isa. 65:6–7).

If she was an Israelite's
daughter married to a
priest, her Meal–offering
must be burnt; and if she
was a priest's daughter
married to an Israelite, her
Meal–offering is consumed
[by the priests] (Mishnah,
Soṭa iii.7).

admonition.[23] But if, after all this, she had left such warning unheeded, her husband had first to bring her before the *Sanhedrim* of his own place, who would dispatch two of their scholars with the couple to Jerusalem, where they were to appear before the Great Sanhedrim. The first endeavor of that tribunal was to bring the accused by any means to make confession. If she did so, she only lost what her husband had settled upon her, but retained her own portion.[24] If she persisted in her innocence, she was brought through the eastern gate of the Temple, and placed at the Gate of Nicanor, where the priest tore off her dress to her bosom, and dishevelled her hair. If she wore a white dress, she was covered with black; if she had ornaments, they were taken from her, and a rope put round her neck. Thus she stood, exposed to the gaze of all, except her own parents. All this to symbolise the Scriptural warning (Isa. 65:7): 'Therefore I will measure their former work into their bosom;' for in what had been her pride and her temptation she was now exposed to shame. The priest was to write, *in ink*, Num. 5:19–22, of course leaving out the introductory clauses in verses 19 and 21, and the concluding 'Amen.' The woman's double response of *Amen* bore reference first to her innocence, and secondly to the threatened curse.

The waving of the woman's offering was done in the usual manner, but opinions differ whether she had to drink 'the bitter water' before or after part of her offering had been burned on the altar. If before the writing was washed into the water she refused to take the test, her offering was scattered among the ashes; similarly, if she confessed herself guilty. But if she insisted on her innocence after the writing was washed, she was forced to drink the water. The Divine

---

[23]The tractate *Sotah* enters into every possible detail, with prurient casuistry—the tendency, as always in Jewish criminal law, being in favour of the accused.

[24]According to Rabbinical law adulteresses only suffered death if they persisted in the actual crime *after* having been warned of the consequences by two witnesses. It is evident that this canon must have rendered the infliction of the death penalty the rarest exception—indeed, almost inconceivable.

judgment was supposed to overtake the guilty sooner or later, as some thought, according to their other works. The wave-offering belonged to the priest, except where the suspected woman was the wife of a priest, in which case the offering was burned.[25] If a husband were deaf or insane, or in prison, the magistrates of the place would act in his stead in insisting on a woman clearing herself of just suspicion. An adulteress was prohibited from living with her seducer. It is beside our purpose further to enter into the various legal determinations of the *Mishnah*. But it is stated that, with the decline of morals in Palestine, the trial by the 'water of jealousy' gradually ceased (in accordance with what we read in Hos. 4:14), till it was finally abolished by Rabbi Jochanan, the son of Zacchai, some time after the death of our Lord.[26] While recording this fact the *Mishnah* (*Sotah*, ix. 9–15) traces, in bitter language, the decay and loss of what had been good and precious to Israel in their worship, Temple, wisdom, and virtues, pointing forward to the yet greater sorrow of 'the last day,' 'shortly before the coming of Messiah,' when all authority, obedience, and fear of God would decline in the earth, and 'our only hope and trust' could spring from looking up to our Heavenly Father. Yet beyond it stands out, in the closing words of this tractate in the *Mishnah*, the final hope of a revival, of the gift of the Holy Spirit, and of the blessed resurrection, all connected with the long-expected ministry of Elijah!

> *I will not punish your daughters*
> *when they turn to prostitution,*
> *nor your daughters-in-law when they commit adultery,*
> *because the men themselves consort with harlots*
> *and sacrifice with shrine prostitutes—*
> *a people without understanding will come to ruin*
> *(Hos. 4:14)!*

> *R. Simeon b. Eleazar says: [When] purity [ceased in Israel it] took away the flavour and the fragrance; [when] the Tithes [ceased they] took away the fatness of the corn; and, the Sages say, fornication and sorceries have made an end of them altogether ((Mishnah, Soṭa ix.13).*

---

[25]The *Mishnah* defines particularly the cases in which the trial by bitter waters was inapplicable.

[26]Not, as Dr. Farrar states (*The Life of Christ*, ii, 65), long before it. He regards the decay of morals at the time of Christ as so universal and great, that among the accusers of the woman taken in adultery there was not one 'free from the taint of this class of sins.' I am thankful to say, that so sweeping a charge is not in anywise borne out by historical evidence.

19
On Vows

THE NAZARITE'S VOW—THE OFFERING OF FIRSTFRUITS IN THE TEMPLE

But Christ has indeed been raised from the dead, the firstfruits of those who have fallen asleep....They were purchased from among men and offered as firstfruits to God and the Lamb.—1 Cor. 15:20; Rev. 14:4

Moses said to the heads of the tribes of Israel: "This is what the LORD commands: When a man makes a vow to the LORD or takes an oath to obligate himself by a pledge, he must not break his word but must do everything he said" (Num. 30:1–2).

Vows

'If a man vow a vow unto Jehovah, or swear an oath to bind his soul with a bond, he shall not profane his word; he shall do according to all that hath proceeded out of his mouth' (Num. 30:2). These words establish the lawfulness of vows, define their character, and declare their inviolableness. At the outset a distinction is here made between a positive and a negative vow, an undertaking and a renunciation, a *Neder* and an *Issar.* In the former 'a man vowed a vow unto Jehovah'—that is, he consecrated unto Him some one or more persons or things, which he expressly designated; in the latter he 'swore an oath to bind his soul with a bond'—that is, he renounced the use of certain things binding himself to abstinence from them. The renunciation of the fruit of the vine would seem to place the Nazarite's vow in the class termed *Issar.* But, on the other hand, there was, as in the case of Samson and Samuel, also such positive dedication to the Lord, and such other provisions as seem to make the Nazarite's the vow of vows—that is, the full carrying out of the idea of a vow, alike in its positive and negative aspects—being, in fact, a voluntary and entire surrender unto Jehovah, such as, in its more general bearing, the Aaronic priesthood had been intended to express.

MAN CAN ONLY VOW HIS OWN THINGS

It lies on the surface, that all vows were limited by higher obligations. A man could not have vowed anything that was not fairly his own; hence, according to the *Mishnah*, neither what of his fortune he owed to others, nor his widow's portion, nor yet what already of right belonged unto the Lord (Num. 30); nor might he profane the Temple by bringing to the altar the reward of sin or of unnatural crime.[1] Similarly, the Rabbinical law declared any vow of abstinence *ipso facto* invalid, if it interfered with the preservation of life or similar obligations, and it allowed divorce to a woman if her husband's vow curtailed her liberty or her rights. On this ground it was that Christ showed the profaneness of the traditional law, which virtually sanctioned transgression of the command to honour father and mother, by pronouncing over that by which they might have been profited the magic word *Corban*, which dedicated it to the Temple (Mark 7:11–13). In general, the Rabbinical ordinances convey the impression, on the one hand, of a desire to limit the obligation of vows, and, on the other, of extreme strictness where a vow had really been made. Thus a vow required to have been expressly spoken; yet if the words used had been even intentionally so chosen as afterwards to open a way of escape, or were such as connected themselves with the common form of a vow, they conveyed its obligations. In all such cases goods might be distrained to secure the performance of the vow; the law, however, providing that the recusant was to be allowed to retain food for a month, a year's clothing, his beds and bedding, and, if an artisan, his necessary tools. In the case of women, a father or husband had the right to annul a vow, provided he did so *immediately* on

You must not bring the earnings of a female prostitute or of a male prostitute into the house of the LORD your God to pay any vow, because the LORD your God detests them both (Deut. 23:18).

But you say that if a man says to his father or mother: "Whatever help you might otherwise have received from me is Corban" (that is, a gift devoted to God), then you no longer let him do anything for his father or mother. Thus you nullify the word of God by your tradition that you have handed down. And you do many things like that (Mark 7:11–13).

---

[1] This is undoubtedly the meaning of the expression 'price of a dog' in Deut. 23:18.

If anyone making the vow is too poor to pay the specified amount, he is to present the person to the priest, who will set the value for him according to what the man making the vow can afford (Lev. 27:8).

It is a trap for a man to dedicate something rashly and only later to consider his vows (Prov. 20:25).

Then Jacob made a vow, saying, "If God will be with me and will watch over me on this journey I am taking and will give me food to eat and clothes to wear so that I return safely to my father's house, then the LORD will be my God and this stone that I have set up as a pillar will be God's house, and of all that you give me I will give you a tenth" (Gen. 28:20–22).

hearing it (Num. 30:3–8). All *persons* vowed unto the Lord had to be redeemed according to a certain scale; which, the case of the poor, was to be so lowered as to bring it within reach of their means (Lev. 27:2–8).[2] Such 'beasts' 'whereof men bring an offering,' went to the altar; all others, as well as any other thing dedicated, were to be valued by the priest, and might be redeemed on payment of the price, together with one-fifth additional, or else were sold for behoof of the Temple treasury (Lev. 27:11–27). How carefully the law guarded against all profanity, or from the attempt to make merit out of what should have been the free outgoing of believing hearts, appears from Deut. 23:22–24, Lev. 27:9, 10, and such statements as Prov. 20:25. As Scriptural instances of vows, we may mention that of Jacob (Gen. 28:20), the rash vow of Jephthah (Judges 11:30, 31), the vow of Hannah (1 Sam. 1:11), the pretended vow of Absalom (2 Sam. 15:7, 8) and the vows of the sailors who cast Jonah overboard (Jon. 1:16). On the other hand, it will be understood how readily, in times of religious declension, vows might be turned from their proper object to purposes contrary to the Divine mind.[3]

CARELESSNESS IN LATER TIMES

In the latter times of the Temple such vows, made either thoughtlessly, or from Pharisaical motives, became painfully frequent, and called forth protests on the part of those who viewed them in a more reverent and earnest spirit. Thus it is said,[4] that the high-priest, *Simeon the Just*—to whom tradition ascribes so much that is good and noble—declared

---

[2]The *Mishnah* declares that this scale was only applicable, if express reference had been made to it in the vow; otherwise the price of redemption was, what the person would have fetched if sold in the market as a slave.

[3]In general the later legislation of the Rabbis was intended to discourage vows, on account of their frequent abuse (*Nedar.* i., iii., ix.). It was declared that only evil-doers bound themselves in this manner, while the pious gave of their own free-will. Where a vow affected the interests of others, every endeavour was to be made, to get him who had made it to seek absolution from its obligations, which might be had from one 'sage,' or from three persons, in the presence of him who had been affected by the vow. Further particulars are beyond our present scope.

[4]See the Talmudical story in Jost, vol. i, pp. 171, 172.

that he had uniformly refused, except in one instance, to partake of the trespass-offering of Nazarites, since such vows were so often made rashly, and the sacrifice was afterwards offered reluctantly, not with pious intent. A fair youth, with beautiful hair, had presented himself for such a vow, with whom the high-priest had expostulated: 'My son, what could have induced thee to destroy such splendid hair?' To which the youth replied: 'I fed my father's flock, and as I was about to draw water for it from a brook, I saw my wraith, and the evil spirit seized and would have destroyed me (probably by vanity). Then I exclaimed: Miserable fool, why boastest thou in a possession which does not belong to thee, who art so soon to be the portion of maggots and worms? By the Temple! I cut off my hair, to devote it to God.' 'Upon this,' said *Simeon*, 'I rose and kissed him on the forehead, saying, Oh that many in Israel were like thee! Thou hast truly, and in the spirit of the Law, made this vow according to the will of God.'

That great abuses crept in appears even from the large numbers who took them. Thus the Talmud records that, in the days of King Jannai no fewer than 300 Nazarites presented themselves before Simeon, the son of Shetach. Moreover, a sort of traffic in good works, like that in the Romish Church before the Reformation, was carried on. It was considered meritorious to 'be at charges' for poor Nazarites, and to defray the expenses of their sacrifices. King Agrippa, on arriving at Jerusalem, seems to have done this to conciliate popular favour (Jos. *Antiq.* 19.294). A far holier motive than this influenced St. Paul (Acts 21:23, etc.), when, to remove the prejudices of Jewish Christians, he was 'at charges' for four poor Christian Nazarites, and joined them, as it were, in their vow by taking upon himself some of its obligations, as, indeed, he was allowed to do by the traditional law.

If a man or woman wants to make a special vow, a vow of separation to the LORD as a Nazirite, he must abstain from wine and other fermented drink and must not drink vinegar made from wine or from other fermented drink. He must not drink grape juice or eat grapes or raisins...

During the entire period of his vow of separation no razor may be used on his head. He must be holy until the period of his separation to the LORD is over; he must let the hair of his head grow long. Throughout the period of his separation to the LORD he must not go near a dead body.... Throughout the period of his separation he is consecrated to the LORD (Num. 6:2–3, 5–6, 8).

THE NAZARITE VOW

1. The law concerning the Nazarite vow (Num. 6) seems to imply, that it had been an institution already existing at the time of Moses, which was only

further defined and regulated by him. The name, as well as its special obligations, indicate its higher bearing. For the term *Nazir* is evidently derived from *nazar, to separate,* and 'the vow of a Nazarite' was to separate himself unto Jehovah (Num. 6:2). Hence the Nazarite was 'holy unto Jehovah' (Num. 6:8). In the sense of separation the term *Nazir* was applied to Joseph (Gen. 49:26; comp. Deut. 32:16), and so the root is frequently used. But, besides separation and holiness, we have also here the idea of *royal priesthood,* since the word *Nezer* is applied to 'the holy *crown* upon the mitre' of the high-priest (Exod. 29:6; 39:30; Lev. 8:9), and 'the *crown* of the anointing oil' (Lev. 21:12), as also, in a secondary sense, to the royal crown (2 Sam. 1:10; 2 Kgs. 11:12; Zech. 9:16).[5] We have, therefore, in the Nazarite, the three ideas of separation, holiness, and the crown of the royal priesthood, all closely connected. With this agree the threefold obligations incumbent on a Nazarite. He was to be not only a priest, but one in a higher and more intense sense, since he became such by personal consecration instead of by mere bodily descent. If the priest was to abstain from wine during his actual ministration in the sanctuary, the Nazarite must during the whole period of his vow refrain from all that belongs to the fruit of the vine, 'from the kernels even to the husk' (Num. 6:3, 4). A priest was to avoid all defilement from the dead, except in the case of his nearest relatives, but the Nazarite, like the high-priest (Lev. 21:11), was to ignore in that respect even father and mother, brother and sister (Num. 6:7). Nay more, if unwittingly he had become so defiled, the time of his vow which had already elapsed was to count for nothing; after the usual seven days' purifi-

He must not enter a place where there is a dead body. He must not make himself unclean, even for his father or mother (Lev. 21:11).

---

[5]The learned writer of the article 'Nazarite' in Kitto's *Encycl.* regards the meaning 'diadem' as the fundamental one, following in this the somewhat unsafe critical guidance of Saalschütz, *Mos. Recht.* p. 158. In proof, he appeals to the circumstance that the 'undressed vine' of the Sabbatical and the Jubilee year is designated by the term 'Nazir' in Lev. 25:5, 11. But evidently the uncut, untrimmed vine of those years derived its designation from the Nazarite with his untrimmed hair, and not *vice versa.* Some of the Rabbis have imagined that the vine had grown in Paradise, and that somehow the Nazarite's abstinence from its fruit was connected with the paradisiacal state, and with our fall.

cation (Num. 19:11, 12), he was to cut off his hair, which, in that case, was buried, not burnt, and on the eighth day to bring two turtle-doves, or two young pigeons, the one for a sin-, the other for a burnt-offering, with a lamb of the first year for a trespass-offering; after which he had to commence his Nazarite vow anew. Lastly, if the high-priest wore 'the holy *Nezer* upon the mitre,' the Nazarite was not to cut his hair, which was 'the *Nezer* of his God upon his head' (Num. 6:7). And this use of the word *Nezer*, as applied to the high-priest's crown, as well as to the separation unto holiness of the Nazarite, casts additional light alike upon the object of the priesthood and the character of the Nazarite vow.

THE MISHNAH REGULATIONS

According to the *Mishnah*,[6] all epithets of, or allusions to, the Nazarite vow, carried its obligation. Thus if one said, 'I will be it! or, I will be a beautiful one!'—with reference to the long hair—or made any similar allusion, he had legally taken upon him the vow. If taken for an indefinite period, or without express declaration of the time, the vow lasted for thirty days, which was the shortest possible time for a Nazarite. There were, however, 'perpetual Nazarites,' the *Mishnah* distinguishing between an ordinary 'perpetual Nazarite' and a 'Samson-Nazarite.' Both were 'for life,' but the former was allowed occasionally to shorten his hair, after which he brought the three sacrifices. He could also be defiled by the dead, in which case he had to undergo the prescribed purification. But as Samson had not been allowed under any circumstances to poll his hair, and as he evidently had come into contact with death without afterwards undergoing any ceremonial (Judg. 14:8; 15:15), so the Samson-Nazarite might neither shorten his hair, nor could he be defiled by the dead. However, practically such a question probably never

Any substitute for [the form of words used to utter] a Nazirite-vow is as binding as the Nazirite-vow itself. If a man said, 'I will be [such]', he becomes a Nazirite; [if he said,] 'I will be "comely"', he becomes a Nazirite (Mishnah, Nazir i.1).

No razor may be used on his head, because the boy is to be a Nazirite, set apart to God from birth, and he will begin the deliverance of Israel from the hands of the Philistines (Judg. 13:5b).

---

[6]Tractate *Nazir*. We again omit such details, which, though important as legal determinations, would not advance our knowledge as to the mode in which the Nazarite was discharged of his vow in the Temple.

arose, and the distinction was no doubt merely made to meet an exegetical necessity to the Jews,—that of vindicating the conduct of Samson! As already stated, another might undertake part or the whole of the charges of a Nazarite, and thus share in his vow (*Naz.* ii. 5, 6). A father, but not a mother, might make a Nazarite vow for a son, while he was under the legal age of thirteen. The *Mishnah* (*Naz.* vi.) discusses at great length the three things interdicted to a Nazarite: 'defilement, cutting the hair, and whatever proceedeth from the vine.' Any wilful trespass in these respects, provided the Nazarite had been expressly warned, carried the punishment of stripes, and that for every individual act of which he had been so warned.

A Nazirite may rub or scratch his hair but he may not comb it. R. Ishmael says: He may not rub it with earth since it makes the hair fall out (Mishnah, Nazir vi.3).

Gentiles may not vow the Nazirite-vow. Women and slaves may vow the Nazirite-vow. Greater stringency applies to women than to slaves, since one may compel his slave [to break the vow], but he cannot compel his wife (Mishnah, Nazir ix.1).

RABBINICAL REGULATIONS

To prevent even the accidental removal of hair, the Rabbis forbade the use of a comb (*Naz.* vi. 3). According to the Law, defilement from death annulled the previous time of the vow, and necessitated certain offerings. To this the *Mishnah* adds, that if anyhow the hair were cut, it annulled the previous time of a vow up to thirty days (the period of an indefinite vow), while it is curiously determined that the use of anything coming from the vine did *not* interrupt the vow. Another Rabbinical contravention of the spirit of the law was to allow Nazarites the use of all intoxicating liquors other than what came from the vine (such as palm-wine, etc.). Lastly, the *Mishnah* determines (*Naz.* 9:1) that a master could not annul the Nazarite vow of his slave; and that, if he prevented him from observing it, the slave was bound to renew it on attaining his liberty. The offerings of a Nazarite on the completion of his vow are explicitly described in Num. 6:13–21. Along with the 'ram without blemish for peace-offerings,' he had to bring 'a basket of unleavened bread, cakes of fine flour mingled with oil, and wafers of unleavened bread anointed with oil,' as well as the ordinary 'meat-offering and their drink-offerings' (Num. 6:14, 15). The Rabbis explain, that the 'unleavened bread,' to accompany 'the peace-offerings,' was to be made of six-tenth deals and two-thirds of a tenth deal of flour, which were to be baked into ten unleavened cakes and ten unleavened wafers, all anointed with the fourth part of a log of oil; and that all this 'bread' was to be offered in *one* vessel, or 'basket'.[7] The sin-offering was the first brought, then the burnt-, and last of all the peace-offering. In the Court of the Women there was a special Nazarite's chamber. After the various sacrifices had been offered by the priest, the Nazarite retired to this chamber, where he boiled the flesh of his peace-offerings, cut off his hair, and threw it in the fire under the caldron. If he had already cut off his hair before coming to Jerusalem, he must still bring it with him, and cast it in the fire under the caldron; so that whether or not we understand Acts 18:18 as stating that Paul himself had taken a vow, he *might* have cut off his hair at Cenchrea (Acts 18:18), and brought it with him to Jerusalem. After that the priest waved the offering, as detailed in Num. 6:19, 20,[8] and the fat was salted, and burned upon the altar. The breast, the fore-leg, the boiled shoulder, and the waved cake and wafer, belonged to the priests—the remaining bread and meat were eaten by the Nazarite. Lastly, the expression, 'besides that that his hand shall get,' after mention of the other offerings (Num. 6:21), seems to imply that the Nazarites were also wont to bring free-will offerings.

Scripture mentions three Nazarites for life: Samson, Samuel, and John the Baptist, to which Christian tradition adds the name of James the Just, 'the brother of the Lord,' who presided over the Church at Jerusalem when Paul joined in the Nazarite-offering.[9] In this respect it is noteworthy that, among those who urged upon Paul to 'be at charges' with the four Christian Nazarites, James himself is not specially mentioned (Acts 21:20–25).

Paul stayed on in Corinth for some time. Then he left the brothers and sailed for Syria, accompanied by Priscilla and Aquila. Before he sailed, he had his hair cut off at Cenchrea because of a vow he had taken (Acts 18:18).

So he told her everything. "No razor has ever been used on my head," he said, "because I have been a Nazirite set apart to God since birth. If my head were shaved, my strength would leave me, and I would become as weak as any other man" (Judg. 16:17).

---

[7]Comp. the quotations from Maimonides in the article, 'Nazarite,' in Kitto's *Cycl.*
[8]This part of the service was the same as the consecration of the priests (Lev. 8:26).
[9]Eusebius, *Eccl. Hist.* ii. 23. 3.

OFFERING THE FIRSTFRUITS

2. Properly speaking, *the offering of the firstfruits* belonged to the class of religious and charitable contributions, and falls within our present scope only in so far as certain of them had to be presented in the Temple at Jerusalem. Two of these firstfruit offerings were *public* and *national;* viz. the first *omer,* on the second day of the Passover, and the wave-loaves at Pentecost. The other two kinds of 'firstfruits'—or *Reshith,* 'the first, the beginning,'—were offered on the part of each family and of every individual who had possession in Israel, according to the Divine directions in Exod. 22:29; 23:19; 34:26; Num. 15:20, 21; 18:12, 13; Deut. 18:4; and Deut. 26:2–11, where the ceremonial to be observed in the Sanctuary is also described. Authorities distinguish between the *Biccurim* (*primitiva*), or firstfruits offered in their natural state, and the *Terumoth* (*primitiae*), brought not as raw products, but in a prepared state,—as flour, oil, wine, etc.[10] The distinction is convenient, but not strictly correct, since the *Terumoth* also included vegetables and garden produce. (*Ter.* ii. 5; iii. 1; x. 5.) Still less accurate is the statement of modern writers that the Greek term *Protogennemata* corresponds to *Biccurim,* and *Aparchai* to *Terumoth,* an assertion not even supported by the use of those words in the version of the Septuagint, which is so deeply tinged with traditionalism.

Bring the best of the firstfruits of your soil to the house of the LORD your God (Exod. 23:19a).

When you have entered the land the LORD your God is giving you as an inheritance and have taken possession of it and settled in it, take some of the firstfruits of all that you produce from the soil of the land the LORD your God is giving you and put them in a basket. Then go to the place the LORD your God will choose as a dwelling for his Name and say to the priest in office at the time, "I declare today to the LORD your God that I have come to the land the LORD swore to our forefathers to give us" (Deut. 26:1–3).

THE BICCURIM AND TERUMOTH

Adopting, however, the distinction of the terms, for convenience sake, we find that the *Biccurim* (*primitiva*) were only to be brought while there was a national Sanctuary (Exod. 23:19; Deut. 26:2; Neh. 10:35). Similarly, they must be the produce of the Holy Land itself, in which, according to tradition, were included the ancient territories of Og and Sihon, as well as that part of Syria which David had subjugated. On the

---

[10]In our Authorised Version 'Terumah' is generally rendered by 'heave-offering,' as in Exod. 29:27; Lev. 7:14, 32, 34; Num. 15:19; 18:8, 11; 31:41; and sometimes simply by 'offering,' as in Exod. 25:2; 30:13; 35:5; 36:3, 6; Lev. 22:12; Num. 5:9.

other hand, both the tithes[11] and the *Terumoth* were also obligatory on Jews in Egypt, Babylon, Ammon, and Moab. The *Biccurim* were only presented in the Temple, and belonged to the priesthood there officiating at the time, while the *Terumoth* might be given to any priest in any part of the land. The *Mishnah* holds that, as according to Deut. 8:8 only the following seven were to be regarded as the produce of the Holy Land, from them alone *Biccurim* were due: viz. wheat, barley, grapes, figs, pomegranates, olives, and dates.[12] If the distance of the offerer from Jerusalem was too great, the figs and grapes might be brought in a dried state.

Pomegranate

The amount of the *Biccurim* was not fixed in the Divine Law, any more than of the wheat which was to be left in the corners of the fields in order to be gleaned by the poor.[13] But according to the Rabbis in both these cases one-sixtieth was to be considered as the *minimum*. From Exod. 23:16 and Lev. 23:16, 17, it was argued that the *Biccurim* were not to be brought to Jerusalem before Pentecost; nor yet were they offered later than the Feast of the Dedication of the Temple. If given at any other time than between Pentecost and the 25th Kislev, the regular service was not gone through at their presentation. Before describing this, we add a few particulars about the *Terumoth*. In regard to them it was said that 'a fine eye' (a liberal man) 'gives one-fortieth,' 'an evil eye' (a covetous person) 'one-sixtieth,' while the average rate of contribution—'a middling eye'—was to give

R. Jose the Galilean says: They may not bring First-fruits from beyond Jordan since that is not a land flowing with milk and honey (Mishnah, *Bikkurim i.10*).

For the LORD your God is bringing you into a good land...a land with wheat and barley, vines and fig trees, pomegranates, olive oil and honey (Deut. *8:7a, 8*).

---

[11] The *Mishnah* (*Bicc.* i. 10) expressly mentions 'the olive-trees beyond Jordan,' although R. Joses declared that Biccurim were not brought from east of Jordan, since it was not a land flowing with milk and honey (Deut. 26:15)!

[12] The expression 'honey' in Deut. 8:8 must refer to the produce of the date-palm.

[13] The *Mishnah* enumerates five things of which the amount is not fixed in the Law (*Peah.* i. 1): the corners of the field for the poor; the *Biccurim*; the sacrifices on coming up to the feasts; pious works, on which, however, not more than one-fifth of one's property was to be spent; and the study of the Law (Josh. 1:8). Similarly, 'these are the things of which a man eats the fruit in this world, but their possession passes into the next world (literally, 'the capital continueth for the next,' as in this world we only enjoy the interest): to honour father and mother, pious works, peacemaking between a man and his neighbour, and the study of the Law, which is equivalent to them all.' In *Shab.* 127, *a*, six such things are mentioned.

one-fiftieth, or two per cent. The same proportion we may probably also set down as that of the *Biccurim*. Indeed, the Rabbis have derived from this the word *Terumah*, as it were *Terei Mimeah* 'two out of a hundred.'

In the class *Terumoth* we may also include the *Reshith* or 'first of the fleece' (Deut. 18:11); which, according to the *Mishnah* (*Chol.* xi. 1, 2), had to be given by every one who possessed at least five sheep, and amounted, without dust or dirt, as a *minimum*, to five Judaean, or ten Galilean, shekel weight of pure wool (one Judaean, or sacred shekel = to under two hundred and seventy-four Parisian grains); and, further, the *Reshith Challah*, or 'first of the dough' (Num. 15:18–21),[14] which, if the dough was used for private consumption, was fixed by the Rabbis at one-twenty-fourth, if for sale at one-forty-eighth, while if it were made for non-Israelites, it was not taxed at all. The Rabbis have it that the 'first of the dough' was only due from wheat, barley, casmin, oats, and rye, but not if the dough has been made of other esculents, such as rice, etc.

Of course, neither tithes, nor *Biccurim*, nor *Terumoth*, were to be given of what already belonged to the Lord, nor of what was not fairly the propety of a person. Thus if only the trees, but not the land in which they grew, belonged to a man, he would not give firstfruits. If proselytes, stewards, women, or slaves brought firstfruits, the regular service was not gone through, since such could not have truthfully said either one or other of these verses (Deut. 26:3, 10): 'I am come to the country which the Lord sware to our fathers to give us;' or, 'I have brought the firstfruits of the land which Thou, O Lord, hast given me.' According to Lev. 19:23–25, for three years the fruits of a newly-planted tree were to remain unused, while in the fourth year they were, according to the Rabbis, to be eaten in Jerusalem.

Biccurim, *Terumoth*, and what was to be left in the 'corners' of the fields for the poor were always set

---

[14]The *Mishnah* lays down varying rules as to the amount of the *Challah* in different places outside Palestine (*Chal.* iv. 8).

apart *before* the tithing was made. If the offering of 'firstfruits' had been neglected, one-fifth was to be added when they were brought. Thus the *prescribed* religious contributions of every Jewish layman at the time of the second Temple were as follows: *Biccurim* and *Terumoth,* say *two* per cent.; from the 'first of the fleece,' at least five shekels' weight; from the 'first of the dough,' say *four* per cent.; 'corners of the fields' for the poor, say *two* per cent; the first, or Levitical tithe, *ten* per cent.; the *second,* or festival tithe, to be used at the feasts in Jerusalem, and in the third and sixth years to be the 'poor's tithe,' *ten* per cent.; the firstlings of all animals, either in kind or money-value; five shekels for every first-born son, provided he were the first child of his mother, and free of blemish; and the half-shekel of the Temple-tribute. Together, these amounted to certainly more than the fourth of the return which an agricultural population would have. And it is remarkable, that the Law seems to regard Israel as intended to be only an agricultural people— no contribution being provided for from trade or merchandise. Besides these prescribed, there were, of course, all manner of *voluntary* offerings, pious works, and, above all, the various sacrifices which each, according to his circumstances or piety, would bring in the Temple at Jerusalem.

How do they take up the First–fruits [to Jerusalem]? [The men of] all the smaller towns that belonged to the Maamad gathered together in the town of the Maamad and spent the night in the open place of the town and came not into the houses; and early in the morning the officer [of the Maamad] said, Arise ye and let us go up to Zion unto the Lord our God (Mishnah, *Bikkurim iii.2*).

BICCURIM IN THE TEMPLE

Having thus explained the nature of the various religious contributions, it only remains to describe the mode in which the *Biccurim* or 'firstfruits,' were ordinarily set apart, and the ceremonial with which they were brought to Jerusalem, and offered in the Temple.[15] Strictly speaking, the presentation of the firstfruits was an act of family religion. As in the first *omer* at the Passover, and by the Pentecostal loaves, Israel as a nation owned their God and King, so each family, and every individual separately acknowledged, by the yearly presentation of the firstfruits, a

---

[15]See the *Mishnah,* Tract. *Biccurim* and the *Gemaras,* also Maimonides. The rites have also been described by Jost (vol. i, pp. 172, 173), Saalschütz (*Mos. Recht*), and in other similar works.

How do they set apart the First–fruits? When a man goes down to his field and sees [for the first time] a ripe fig or a ripe cluster of grapes or a ripe pomegranate, he binds it round with reed–grass and says, 'Lo, these are First–fruits' (Mishnah, Bikkurim iii.1).

living relationship between them and God, in virtue of which they gratefully received at His hands all they had or enjoyed, and solemnly dedicated both it and themselves to the Lord. They owned Him as the Giver and real Lord of all, and themselves as the recipients of His bounty, and dependants on His blessing, and the stewards of His property. Their daily bread they would seek and receive only at His hand, use it with thanksgiving, and employ it in His service; and this, their dependence upon God, was their joyous freedom, in which Israel declared itself the redeemed people of the Lord.

As a family feast the presentation of the first-fruits would enter more than any other rite into family religion and family life. Not a child in Israel—at least of those who inhabited the Holy Land—could have been ignorant of all connected with this service, and that even though it had never been taken to the beautiful 'city of the Great King,' nor gazed with marvel and awe at the Temple of Jehovah. For scarcely had a brief Eastern spring merged into early summer, when with the first appearance of ripening fruit, whether on the ground or on trees, each household would prepare for this service. The head of the family —if we may follow the sketch in the harvest-picture of the household of the Shunammite—accompanied by his child, would go into his field and mark off certain portions from among the most promising of the crop. For only *the best* might be presented to the Lord, and it was set apart before it was yet ripe, the solemn dedication being, however, afterwards renewed, when it was actually cut. Thus, each time any one would go into the field, he would be reminded of the ownership of Jehovah, till the reapers cut down the golden harvest. So, also, the head of the house would go into his vineyards, his groves of broad-leaved fig-trees, of splendid pomegranates, rich olives and stately palms, and, stopping short at each best tree, carefully select what seemed the most promising fruit, tie a rush round the stem, and say: 'Lo, these are the firstfruits.' Thus he renewed his covenant-relationship to God each year as 'the winter was past, the rain over and gone, the flowers appeared on the earth, the time of the singing of birds was come, and the voice of the turtle was heard in the land, the fig-tree put forth his green figs, and the vines with the tender grapes gave a good smell.' And as these fruits gradually ripened, the ceremonies connected first with setting them apart, and then with actually offering them, must have continued in every Israelitish household during the greater portion of the year, from early spring till winter, when the latest presentation might be made in the Temple on the 25th Kislev (corresponding to our December).

SONGS OF ASCENT

Of course every family could not always have sent its representatives to Jerusalem. But this difficulty was provided for. It will be remembered that as the priests and the Levites, so all Israel, were divided into twenty-four courses, who were represented in the Sanctuary by the so-called 'standing-men,' or 'men of the station.' This implied a corresponding division of the land into twenty-four districts or circuits. In the capital of each district assembled those who were to go up with the firstfruits to the Temple. Though all Israel were brethren, and especially at such times would have been welcomed with the warmest hospitality each home could offer, yet none might at that season avail himself of it. For they must camp at night in the open air, and not spend it in any house, lest some accidental defilement from the dead, or otherwise, might render them unfit for service, or their oblation unclean. The journey was always to be made slowly, for the pilgrimage was to be a joy and a privilege, not a toil or weariness. In the morning, as the golden sunlight tipped the mountains of Moab, the stationary man of the district, who was the leader, summoned the ranks of the procession in the words of Jeremiah 31:6: 'Arise ye, and let us go up to Zion, and unto Jehovah our God.' To which the people replied, as they formed and moved onwards, in the appropriate language of Ps. 122: 'I was glad when they said unto me, Let us go into the house of Jehovah.'

Before them went the ox, having its horns overlaid with gold and a wreath of olive–leaves on its head. The flute was played before them until they drew nigh to Jerusalem. When they had drawn nigh to Jerusalem they sent messengers before them and bedecked their Firstfruits. The rulers and the prefects and the treasurers of the Temple went forth to meet them. According to the honour due to them that came in used they to go forth. And all the craftsmen in Jerusalem used to rise up before them and greet them, saying, 'Brethren, men of such-and-such a place, ye are welcome!' (Mishnah, Bikkurim iii.3).

Ancient Egyptian baskets

The rich brought their First-fruits in baskets overlaid with silver and gold, while the poor brought them in wicker baskets of peeled willow-branches, and baskets and First–fruits were given to the priests (Mishnah, Bikkurim iii.8).

First went one who played the pipe; then followed a sacrificial bullock, destined for a peace-offering, his horns gilt and garlanded with olive-branches; next came the multitude, some carrying the baskets with the firstfruits, others singing the Psalms, which many writers suppose to have been specially destined for that service, and hence to have been called 'the Songs of Ascent;' in our Authorised Version 'the Psalms of Degrees.' The poorer brought their gifts in wicker baskets, which afterwards belonged to the officiating priests; the richer theirs in baskets of silver or of gold, which were given to the Temple treasury. In each basket was arranged, with vine-leaves between them, first the barley, then the wheat, then the olives; next the dates, then the pomegranates, then the figs; while above them all clustered, in luscious beauty, the rich swelling grapes.

And so they passed through the length and breadth of the land, everywhere wakening the echoes of praise. As they entered the city, they sang Ps. 122:2: 'Our feet stand within thy gates, O Jerusalem.' A messenger had preceded them to announce their approach, and a deputation from the Temple, consisting of priests, Levites, and treasurers, varying in numbers according to the importance of the place from which the procession came, had gone out to receive them. In the streets of Jerusalem each one came out to welcome them, with shouts of, 'Brethren of such a place' (naming it), 'ye come to peace; welcome! Ye come in peace, ye bring peace, and peace be upon you!'

As they reach the Temple Mount, each one, whatever his rank or condition, took one of the baskets on his shoulder, and they ascended, singing that appropriate hymn (Ps. 150), 'Praise ye Jehovah! praise God in His sanctuary: praise Him in the firmament of His power,' etc. As they entered the courts of the Temple itself, the Levites intoned Ps. 30: 'I will extol Thee, O Jehovah; for Thou hast lifted me up, and hast not made my foes to rejoice over me,' etc. Then the young pigeons and turtle-doves which hung from the baskets were presented for burnt-offerings.

After that, each one, as he presented his gifts, repeated this solemn confession (Deut. 26:3): 'I profess this day unto Jehovah thy God, that I am come unto the country that Jehovah sware unto our fathers for to give us.' At these words, he took the basket from his shoulder, and the priest put his hands under it and waved it, the offering continuing: 'A Syrian ready to perish was my father, and he went down into Egypt, and sojourned there with a few, and became there a nation—great, mighty, and populous.' Then reciting in the words of inspiration the narrative of the Lord's marvellous dealings, he closed with the dedicatory language of verse 10: 'And now, behold, I have brought the firstfruits of the land which Thou, O Jehovah, hast given me.' So saying, he placed the basket at the side of the altar, cast himself on his face to worship, and departed. The contents of the baskets belonged to the officiating priests, and the offerers themselves were to spend the night at Jerusalem.

> *"...So the LORD brought us out of Egypt with a mighty hand and an outstretched arm, with great terror and with miraculous signs and wonders. He brought us to this place and gave us this land, a land flowing with milk and honey; and now I bring the firstfruits of the soil that you, O LORD, have given me." Place the basket before the LORD your God and bow down before him (Deut. 26:8–10).*

THE WORD 'FIRSTFRUITS' IN THE NEW TESTAMENT

Turning from this to what may be called its higher application, under the Christian dispensation, we find that the word rendered 'firstfruits' occurs just seven times in the New Testament. These seven passages are: Rom. 8:23; Rom. 11:16; Rom. 16:5; 1 Cor. 15:20–23; 1 Cor 16:15; James 1:18; Rev. 14:4. If we group these texts appropriately, one sentence of explanation may suffice in each case. First, we have (1 Cor. 15:20, 23), as the commencement of the new harvest, the Lord Jesus Himself, risen from the dead, the 'firstfruits'—the first sheaf waved before the Lord on the second Paschal day, just as Christ actually burst the bonds of death at that very time. Then, in fulfilment of the Pentecostal type of the first loaves, we read of the primal outpouring of the Holy Spirit, dispensed on the day of Pentecost. The presentation of the firstfruits is explained by its application to such instances as Rom. 16:5, and 1 Cor. 16:15 (in the former of which passages the reading should be *Asia*, and not *Achaia*), while the character of these first-

> *But Christ has indeed been raised from the dead, the firstfruits of those who have fallen asleep....But each in his own turn: Christ, the firstfruits; then, when he comes, those who belong to him (1 Cor. 15:20, 23).*

And they sang a new song before the throne and before the four living creatures and the elders. No one could learn the song except the 144,000 who had been redeemed from the earth. These are those who did not defile themselves with women, for they kept themselves pure. They follow the Lamb wherever he goes. They were purchased from among men and offered as firstfruits to God and the Lamb (Rev. 14:3–4).

fruits is shown in James 1:18. The allusion in Rom. 11:16 is undoubtedly to the 'first of the dough,' and so explains an otherwise difficult passage. The apostle argues, that if God chose and set apart the fathers—if He took the first of the dough, then the whole lump (the whole people) is in reality sanctified to Him; and therefore God cannot, and 'hath not cast away His people which he foreknew.' Finally, in Rev. 14:4, the scene is transferred to heaven, where we see the full application of this symbol to the Church of the first-born. But to us all, in our labour, in our faith, and in our hope, there remain these words, pointing beyond time and the present dispensation:

'Ourselves also, which have the firstfruits of the Spirit, even we ourselves groan within ourselves, waiting for the adoption, to wit, the redemption of our body' (Rom. 8:23).

'Glory to God on account of all things.'—St. Chrysostom.

DID THE LORD INSTITUTE HIS "SUPPER" ON THE PASCHAL NIGHT?

⁕

The question, whether or not the Saviour instituted His Supper during the meal of the Paschal night, although not strictly belonging to the subject treated in this volume, is too important, and too nearly connected with it, to be cursorily passed over. The balance of learned opinion, especially in England, has of late inclined *against* this view. The point has been so often and so learnedly discussed, that I do not presume proposing to myself more than the task of explaining my reasons for the belief that the Lord instituted His "Supper" on the very night of the Paschal Feast, and that consequently His crucifixion took place on the first day of Unleavened Bread, the 15th of Nisan.

From the writers on the other side, it may here be convenient to select Dr. Farrar, as alike the latest and one of the ablest expositors of the contrary position. His arguments are stated in a special *Excursus*,[1] appended to his *Life of Christ*.[2] At the outset it is admitted on both sides, "that our Lord was crucified on Friday and rose on Sunday;" and, further, that our Lord *could* not have held a sort of *anticipatory* Paschal Supper in advance of all the other Jews, a Paschal Supper being only possible on the evening of the 14th of Nisan, with which, according to Jewish reckoning, the 15th Nisan began. Hence it follows, that the Last Supper which Christ celebrated with his disciples must have either been the Paschal Feast, or an ordinary supper, at which He afterwards instituted His own special ordinance.[3] Now, the conclusions at which Dr. Farrar arrives are thus summed up by him:[4] "That Jesus ate His last supper with the disciples on the evening of Thursday, Nisan 13, *i.e.*, at the time when, according to Jewish reckoning, the 14th of Nisan began; that this supper was not, and was not intended to be, the actual Paschal meal, which neither was nor could be legally eaten till the following evening; but by a perfectly natural

---

[1] *Excursus 10.*

[2] Vol. 2, pp. 474-483.

[3] Dr. Farrar rightly shrinks from the conclusions of Caspari (*Chron. Geogr. Einl. in d. Leben Jesu*, p. 164, etc.), who regards it as what he calls "a *Mazzoth*-meal" without a Paschal lamb. The suggestion is wholly destitute of foundation.

[4] *Life of Christ*, 2, p. 482.

identification, and one which would have been regarded as unimportant, the Last Supper, *which was a quasi-Passover, a new and Christian Passover,* and one in which, as in its antitype, memories of joy and sorrow were strangely blended, got to be identified, even in the memory of the Synoptists, with the Jewish Passover, and that St. John silently but deliberately corrected this erroneous impression, which, even in his time, had come to be generally prevalent."

Before entering into the discussion, I must confess myself unable to agree with the *à priori* reasoning by which Dr. Farrar accounts for the supposed mistake of the Synoptists. Passing over the expression, that "the Last Supper was a quasi-Passover," which does not convey to me a sufficiently definite meaning, I should rather have expected that, in order to realise the obvious "antitype," the tendency of the Synoptists would have been to place the death of Christ on the evening of the 14th Nisan, when the Paschal lamb was actually *slain,* rather than on the 15th Nisan, twenty-four hours after that sacrifice had taken place. In other words, the typical predilections of the Synoptists would, I imagine, have led them to identify the death of Christ with the slaying of the lamb; and it seems, *à priori,* difficult to believe that, if Christ really died at that time, and His last supper was on the previous evening—that of the 13th Nisan,—they should have fallen into the mistake of identifying that supper, not with His death, but with the Paschal meal. I repeat: *à priori,* if error there was, I should have rather expected it in the opposite direction. Indeed, the main dogmatic strength of the argument on the other side lies in the consideration that the anti-type (Christ) should have

died at the same time as the type (the Paschal lamb). Dr. Farrar himself feels the force of this, and one of his strongest arguments against the view that the Last Supper took place at the Paschal meal is: "The sense of inherent and symbolical fitness in the dispensation which ordained that Christ should be slain on the day and at the hour appointed for the sacrifice of the Paschal lamb." Of all persons, would not the Synoptists have been alive to this consideration? And, if so, is it likely that they would have fallen into the mistake with which they are charged? Would not all their tendencies have lain in the opposite direction?

But to pass to the argument itself. For the sake of clearness it will here be convenient to treat the question under three aspects:—How does the supposition that the Last Supper did not take place on the Paschal night agree with the general bearing of the whole history? What, fairly speaking, is the inference from the Synoptical Gospels? Lastly, does the account of St. John, in this matter, contradict those of the Synoptists, or is it harmonious indeed with theirs, but incomplete?

How does the supposition that the Last Supper did not take place on the Paschal night agree with the general bearing of the whole history?

1. The language of the first three evangelists, taken in its natural sense, seems clearly irreconcilable with this view. Even Dr. Farrar admits: "If we construe the language of the evangelists in its plain, straightforward, simple sense, and without reference to any preconceived theories, or supposed necessities for harmonising the different narratives, we should be led to conclude from the Synoptists that the Last Supper was the ordinary Paschal meal." On this point further remarks will be made in the sequel.

2. The account of the meal as given, not only by the Synoptists but also by St. John, so far as he describes it, seems to me utterly inconsistent with the idea of an ordinary supper. It is not merely one trait or another which here influences us, but the general impression produced by the whole. The preparations for the meal; the allusions to it; in short, so to speak, the whole *mise en scène* is *not* that of a common supper. Only the necessities of a preconceived theory would lead one to such a conclusion. On the other hand, all is just what might have been expected, if the evangelists had meant to describe the Paschal meal.

3. Though I do not regard such considerations as decisive, there are, to my mind, difficulties in the way of adopting the view that Jesus died while the Paschal lamb was being slain, far greater than those which can attach to the other theory. On the supposition of Dr. Farrar, the crucifixion took place on the 14th Nisan, "between the evenings" of which the Paschal lamb was slain. Being a *Friday*, the ordinary evening service would have commenced at 12.30 p.m.,[5] and the evening sacrifice offered, say, at 1.30, after which the services connected with the Paschal lamb would immediately begin. Now it seems to me almost inconceivable, that under such circumstances, and on so busy an afternoon,[6] there should have been, *at the time when they must have been most engaged,* around the cross that multitude of reviling Jews, "likewise also the chief priests, mocking him, with the scribes,"

which all the four evangelists record (Matt. 27:39, 41; Mark 15:29, 31; Luke 23:35; John 19:20). Even more difficult does it seem to me to believe, that after the Paschal lamb had been slain, and while the preparations for the Paschal Supper were going on, *as St. John reports* (John 20:38, 39), an "honourable councillor," like Joseph of Arimathæa, and a Sanhedrist, like Nicodemus, should have gone to beg of Pilate the body of Jesus, or been able to busy themselves with His burial.

I proceed now to the second question: *What, fairly speaking, is the inference from the Synoptical Gospels?*

1. To this, I should say, there can be only one reply:—The Synoptical Gospels, undoubtedly, place the Last Supper in the Paschal night. A bare quotation of their statements will establish this:—"Ye know that after two days *is the Passover*" (Matt. 26:2), "Now *the first day of unleavened bread* the disciples came to Jesus, saying unto Him, Where wilt Thou that we prepare for Thee *to eat the Passover?*" (Matt. 26:17) "*I will keep the Passover* at thy house" (Matt. 26:18); "*They made ready the Passover*" (Matt. 26:19). Similarly, in the Gospel by St. Mark (Mark 14:12-17): "*And the first day of unleavened bread, when they killed the Passover,* the disciples said to Him, *Where wilt Thou that we go and prepare, that Thou mayest eat the Passover?*" " The Master saith, Where is the guest-chamber, *where I shall eat the Passover with my disciples?*" "There make ready for us." "*And they made ready the Passover.* And in the evening He cometh with the twelve. And as they sat and did eat

---

[5]See page 174.
[6]See the chapter on the "Paschal Rites."

…"And in the Gospel by St. Luke (Luke 22:7-15): *"Then came the day of unleavened bread, when the Passover must be killed;"* *"Go and prepare us the Passover, that we may eat;"* "Where is the guest-chamber where I shall *eat the Passover with my disciples?"* "There make ready;" *"And they made ready the Passover."* "And when the hour was come He sat down;" *"With desire have I desired to eat this Passover with you* BEFORE I SUFFER." It is not easy to understand how even a "preconceived theory" could weaken the obvious import of such expressions, especially when taken in connection with the description of the meal that follows.

2. Assuming, then, the testimony of the Synoptical Gospels to be unequivocally in our favour, it appears to me extremely improbable that, in such a matter, they should have been mistaken, or that such an "erroneous impression" could—and this even "in the time of St. John"—have "come to be generally prevalent." On the contrary, I have shown that if mistake there was, it would most likely have been rather in the opposite direction.

3. We have now to consider what Dr. Farrar calls "the *incidental* notices preserved in the Synoptists," which seem to militate against their general statement. Selecting those which are of greatest force, we have:—

(*a*) The fact "that the *disciples* (John 13:22) suppose Judas to have left the room in order to buy what things they had need of against the feast." But the disciples only *suppose* this; and in the confusion and excitement of the scene such a mistake was not unintelligible. Besides, though servile work was forbidden on the first Paschal day, the preparation of all needful provision for the feast

was allowed, and must have been the more necessary, as, on our supposition, it was followed by a Sabbath. Indeed, the Talmudical law distinctly allowed the continuance of such preparation of provisions as had been commenced on the "preparation day" (Arnheim, *Gebetb. d. Isr.*, p. 500, note 69, *a*). In general, we here refer to our remarks at p. 195, only adding, that even now Rabbinical ingenuity can find many a way of evading the rigour of the Sabbath-law.

(*b*) As for the meeting of the Sanhedrim, and the violent arrest of Christ on such a night of peculiar solemnity, the fanatical hatred of the chief priests, and the supposed necessities of the case, would sufficiently account for them. On any supposition we have to admit the operation of these causes, since the Sanhedrim confessedly violated, in the trial of Jesus, every principle and form of their own criminal jurisprudence.

Lastly, we have to inquire: *Does the account of St. John contradict those of the Synoptists, or is it harmonious, indeed, with them, but incomplete?*

1. Probably few would commit themselves to the statement, that the account of St. John necessarily *contradicts* those of the Synoptists. But the following are the principal reasons urged by Dr. Farrar for the inference that, according to St. John, the Last Supper took place the evening before the Paschal night:—

(*a*) Judas goes, as is supposed, to buy the things that they have need of against the feast. This has already been explained.

(*b*) The Pharisees "went not into the judgment-hall, lest they should be defiled, but that they might eat the Passover." And in answer to the common explanation that "the Passover" here means the 15th day, *Chagigah*,[7] he adds, in a foot-note, that "there was nothing specifically Paschal" about this *Chagigah*. Dr. Farrar should have paused before committing himself to such a statement. One of the most learned Jewish writers, Dr. Saalschütz, is not of his opinion. He writes as follows:[8] "The whole feast and *all its festive* meals were designated as the Passover. See Deut. 16:2, compare 2 Chron. 30:24 and 35:8, 9; *Sebach.* 99, *b*, *Rosh ha Sh. 5, a*, where it is expressly said, 'What is the meaning of the term Passover?' (Answer) 'The peace-offerings of the Passover.'" Illustrative Rabbinical passages are also quoted by Lightfoot[9] and by Schöttgen.[10] As a rule the *Chagigah* was always brought on the 15th Nisan, and it required Levitical purity. Lastly, Dr. Farrar himself admits that the statement of St. John (John 18:28) must not be too closely pressed, "for that *some* Jews must have even gone into the judgment-hall without noticing 'the defilement' is clear."

(*c*) According to St. John (John 19:31), the following Sabbath was "a high day," or "a great day;" on which Dr. Farrar comments: "Evidently because it was at once a Sabbath, and the first day of the Paschal Feast." Why not the second day of the feast, when the first

omer was presented in the Temple? To these may be added the following among the other arguments advanced by Dr. Farrar:—

(*d*) The various engagements recorded in the Gospels on the day of Christ's crucifixion are incompatible with a festive day of rest, such as the 15th Nisan. The reference to "Simon the Cyrenian *coming out of the country*" seems to me scarcely to deserve special notice. But then Joseph of Arimathæa *bought* on that day the "fine linen" (Mark 15:46) for Christ's burial, and the women "prepared spices and ointments" (Luke 23:56)[11]. Here, however, it should be remembered, that the rigour of the festive was not like that of the Sabbatic rest, that there were means of really buying such a *cloth* without doing it in express terms (an evasion known to Rabbinical law). Lastly, the Jerusalem Talmud (*Ber. 5, b*) expressly declares it lawful on Sabbaths and feast-days to bring a coffin, graveclothes, and even mourning flutes—in short, to attend to the offices for the dead—just as on ordinary days. This passage though, as far as I know, never before quoted in this controversy, is of the greatest importance.

(*e*) Dr. Farrar attaches importance to the fact that Jewish tradition fixes the death of Christ on the 14th Nisan.[12] But these Jewish traditions, to which an

---

[7] Page 170 etc., and page 199, etc., of this vol.

[8] *Mos. Recht,* p. 414. The argument and quotations from the Talmud are also given in Relandus, *Antiq.,* p. 426. For a full treatment of the question see Lightfoot, *Horæ Hebr.* p. 1121.

[9] *Horæ Hebr.* p. 1121, etc.

[10] *Horæ Hebr.* p. 400.

[11] It should not be overlooked that these supposed inconsistencies appear in the accounts of the Synoptists, who, according to Dr. Farrar, wished to convey that Christ was crucified on the 15th Nisan. If really inconsistencies, they are very gross, and could scarcely have escaped the writers.

[12] I have not been able to verify Dr. Farrar's references to *Mishnah*, Sanh. 6.2 and 10.4. But I agree with Grätz (*Gesch. d. Juden.,* 3, p. 242, note), that much in Sanh. 7 bears, though unexpressed, reference to the proceedings of the Sanhedrim against Christ.

appeal is made, are not only of a late date, but wholly unhistorical and value-less. Indeed, as Dr. Farrar himself shows,[13] they are full of the grossest absurdities. I cannot here do better than simply quote the words of the great Jewish historian, Dr. Jost:[14] "Whatever attempts may be made to plead in favour of these Talmudic stories, and to try and discover some historical basis in them, the Rabbis of the third and fourth centuries are quite at sea about the early Christians, and deal in legends for which there is no foundation of any kind."

(f) Dr. Farrar's objection that "after supper" Jesus and His disciples went out, which seems to him inconsistent with the injunction of Ex. 12:22, and that in the account of the meal there is an absence of that *hurry* which, according to the law, should have characterised the supper, arises from not distinguishing the ordinances of the so-called "Egyptian" from those of "the permanent Passover." On this and kindred points the reader is referred to Chaps. 11, 12.

(g) The only other argument requiring notice is that in their accounts the three Synoptists "give not the remotest hint which could show that a *lamb* formed the most remarkable portion of the feast." Now, this is an objection which answers itself. For, according to Dr. Farrar, these Synoptists had, in writing their accounts, been under the mistaken impression that they *were* describing the Paschal Supper. As for their silence on the subject, it seems to me capable of an interpretation the opposite of that which Dr. Farrar has put upon it. Considering the purpose of all which they had in view—the fulfilment of the type of the Paschal Supper, and the substitution for it of the Lord's Supper—their silence seems not only natural, but what might have been expected. For their object was to describe the Paschal Supper only in so far as it bore upon the institution of the Lord's Supper. Lastly, it is a curious coincidence that throughout the whole Mishnic account of the Pascal Supper there *is only one isolated* reference to the lamb—a circumstance so striking, that, for example, Caspari has argued from it[15] that ordinarily this meal was what he calls "a meal of unleavened bread," and that in the majority of cases there was no Passover-lamb at all! I state the inference drawn by Dr. Caspari, but there can scarcely be any occasion for replying to it.

On the other hand, I have now to add two arguments taken from the masterly disquisition of the whole question by Wieseler,[16] to show that St. John, like the Synoptists, places the date of the crucifixion on the 15th Nisan, and hence that of the Last Supper on the evening of the 14th.

(a) Not only the Synoptists, *but St. John* (John 18:39) refers to the custom of releasing a prisoner at "the feast," or, as St. John expressly calls it, "at the Passover." Hence the release of Barabbas, and with it the crucifixion of Jesus, could *not* have taken place (as Dr. Farrar supposes) on the 14th of Nisan, the morning of which could *not* have been designated as "the feast," and still less as "the Passover."

---

[13] *Excursus*, 2, p. 452.
[14] *Gesch. d. Judenth.*, 1, p. 405.
[15] *Chronol. Geogr. Einl. in d. Leben Jesu Christi*, p. 164.
[16] *Chronolog. Synopse der 4 Evang.* p. 333, etc.

(*b*) When St. John mentions (John 18:28) that the accusers of Jesus went not into Pilate's judgment-hall "lest they should be defiled; but that they might eat the Passover," he *could not* have referred to their eating the Paschal Supper. For the defilement thus incurred would only have lasted to the evening of that day, whereas the Paschal Supper was eaten *after* the evening had commenced, so that *the defilement of Pilate's judgment-hall in the morning would in no way have interfered with their eating the Paschal Lamb.* But it *would* have interfered with their either offering or partaking of the *Chagigah* on the 15th Nisan.[17]

2. Hitherto I have chiefly endeavoured to show that the account of St. John is harmonious with that of the Synoptists in reference to the time of the Last Supper. But, on the other hand, I am free to confess that, if it had stood alone, I should not have been able to draw the same clear inference from it as from the narratives of the first three gospels. My difficulty here arises, not from what St. John says, but from what he does not say. His words, indeed, are quite consistent with those of the Synoptists, but, *taken alone*, they would not have been sufficient to convey, at least to my mind, the same clear impression. And here I have to observe that St. John's account must in this respect seem equally incomplete, whichever theory of the time of the Last Supper be adopted. If the Gospel of St. John stood alone, it would, I think, be equally difficult for Dr. Farrar to prove from it his, as for me to establish my view. He might *reason from* certain expressions, and so might I; but there are no such clear, unmistakeable statements as those in which the

Synoptists describe the Passover night as that of the Last Supper. And yet we should have expected most fulness and distinctness from St. John!

Is not the inference suggested that the account in the Gospel of St. John, in the form in which we at present possess it, may be incomplete? I do not here venture to construct a hypothesis, far less to offer a matured explanation, but rather to make a suggestion of what possibly may have been, and to put it as a question to scholars. But once admit the idea, and there are, if not many, yet weighty reasons, to confirm it. For,

1. It would account for all the difficulties felt by those who have adopted the same view as Dr. Farrar, and explain, not, indeed, the supposed difference— for such I deny—but the incompleteness of St. John's narrative, as compared with those of the Synoptists.

2. It explains what otherwise seems almost unaccountable. I agree with Dr. Farrar that St. John's "accounts of the Last Supper are incomparably more full than those of the other evangelists," and that he "was more immediately and completely identified with every act in those last trying scenes than any one of the apostles." And yet, strange to say, on this important point St. John's information is not only more scanty than that of the Synoptists, but so indefinite that, if alone, no certain inference could be drawn from it. The circumstance is all the more inexplicable if, as on Dr. Farrar's theory, "the error" of the Synoptists was at the time "generally prevalent," and "St. John silently but deliberately" had set himself to correct it.

3. Strangest of all, the Gospel of St. John is the only one which does not

---

[17] This argument is already mentioned by Lightfoot, *u.s.*

contain any account of the institution of the Lord's Supper, and yet, if anywhere, we would have expected to find it here.

4. The account in John 13 begins with a circumstantiality which leads us to expect great fulness of detail. And yet, while maintaining throughout that characteristic, so far as the teaching of Jesus in that night is concerned, it almost suddenly and abruptly breaks off (about ver. 31) in the account of what He and they who sat with Him *did* at the Supper.

5. Of such a possible *hiatus* there seems, on closer examination, some internal confirmation, of which I shall here only adduce this one instance—that chapter 14 concludes by, "Arise, let us go hence;" which, however, is followed by other three chapters of precious teaching and intercessory prayer, when the narrative is abruptly resumed, by a strange repetition, as compared with 14:31, in these words (18:1): "When Jesus had spoken these words, He went forth with His disciples over the brook Cedron."

Further discussion would lead beyond the necessary limits of the present *Excursus*. Those who know how bitterly the *Quartodeciman* controversy raged in the early Church, and what strong things were put forth by the so-called "disciples of John" in defence of their view, that the Last Supper did not take place on the Paschal night, may see grounds to account for such a *hiatus*. In conclusion, I would only say that, to my mind, the suggestion above made would in no way be inconsistent with the doctrine of the plenary inspiration of Holy Scripture.

ANALYSIS OF CONTENTS

✧

is cut up—The *third* and *fourth* lots are cast—Prayer of the priests—
Service of burning the incense—'Silence' in the Temple—Prayers of
priests and people—Burning the sacrifice on the altar—The priest's blessing—The drink-offering accompanied by Temple music—The Evening

CHAPTER 9—SABBATH IN THE TEMPLE

Meaning and object of the Sabbath—Rabbinical ordinances of Sabbath
observance, and their underlying principles—Differences between
the schools of Hillel and Shammai—'The eve of the Sabbath'—
Commencement of the Sabbath, how announced—The renewal of the
shewbread—When and how it had been prepared—The table of shewbread—How the bread was arranged upon it—Service of the priests in
removing the old and putting on the new shewbread—Meaning of the
shewbread—The Sabbath service in the Temple—Sabbatical years—
Rabbinical ordinances on the subject—Scriptural ordinances—Were
debts wholly remitted, or only deferred on Sabbatical years?—The
'*Prosbul*'—Rabbinical evasions of the Divine law—Sabbath observance

CHAPTER 10—FESTIVE CYCLES AND ARRANGEMENT OF THE CALENDAR

The number *seven* as determining the arrangement of the sacred year—
The three festive cycles of the year—Difference between the *Moed* and the
Chag—Three general characteristics of the great feasts—Post-Mosaic
festivals and fasts—Duty of appearing three times a year in the Temple—
The 'stationary men' Israel's representatives in the Temple—Their
duties—The Hebrew year lunar—Necessity of introducing leap-years—
How the appearance of the New Moon was officially ascertained and
announced—'Full' and 'imperfect' months—New Year's Day—Origin of
the Hebrew names of the months—The 'civil' and the 'sacred' year—
Jewish era—Division of the day and of the night—Jewish calendar

CHAPTER 11—THE PASSOVER

Difference between the Passover and the Feast of Unleavened Bread—
Threefold reference of the Passover to nature, history, and grace—Time of
the Passover—Meaning of the term *Pesach*—Difference between the so-
called 'Egyptian' and the 'Permanent Passover'—Mention in Scripture of
seasons of Paschal observance—Number of worshippers in the Temple at
the Passover—Preparations for the feast—The first and the second
Chagigah—The 'eve of the Passover'—Search for, and removal of all
leaven—What constituted leaven—Commencement of the feast on the
forenoon of the 14th Nisan—At what hour it became duty to abstain from
leaven, and how it was intimated—Selection of the Paschal Lamb—At
what hour it was slain—Division of the offerers into three companies—

CHAPTER 15—THE NEW MOONS: THE FEAST OF THE SEVENTH NEW MOON, OR OF TRUMPETS, OR NEW YEAR'S DAY

CHAPTER 16—THE DAY OF ATONEMENT

How 'the commandment' bears testimony to its inherent 'weakness and
unprofitableness'—Specially so in the services of the Day of Atonement—
Peculiar solemnity of that day—Its name—Significance of its occurrence
on the 10th day of the seventh month, and previous to the Feast of
Tabernacles—The high-priest officiating in a peculiar white dress—
Symbolical meaning of this—Threefold sacrifices of that day—Their
order—Number of priests employed—The high-priest prepares for the

Day of Atonement seven days before its occurrence, and takes up his abode in the Temple—The night of the fast—The high-priest himself performs all the day's services—How often he changed his raiment and washed his body, or else his hands and feet—The ordinary morning service —The high-priest puts on his linen garments for the first time—The sin-offering for the high-priest and his family—Confession over it—The ineffable name of *Jehovah* is ten times pronounced on that day—Mode of casting the lot over the two goats—The two are really one sacrifice—A tongue-shaped piece of scarlet cloth is tied to the horn of the goat for *Azazel*—This goat standing before the people, waiting till their sins should be laid upon him—Confession of sin for the priesthood, and sacrifice of the bullock—The high-priest enters the Most Holy Place for the first time to burn the incense—Prayer of the high-priest on coming out—The high-priest enters the Most Holy Place a second time with the blood of the bullock—And a third time with that of the goat for Jehovah—The sprinkling towards the veil, of the altar of incense, and of that of burnt-offering—The high-priest lays the personal sins and the guilt of the people on the so-called 'scape-goat'—Peculiar mode of confession over it—The goat is led away into the wilderness—And pushed over a precipice—Meaning of the scape-goat—Reference to the coming of Christ, as He who would take away sin—Meaning of the expression *la-Azazel*—The high-priest's reading and prayers in the Court of the Women—The high-priest puts on the golden garments to offer the festive, burnt-, and other sacrifices—He again puts on his linen garments to enter the Most Holy Place for the fourth and last time—On the afternoon of the day, dance and song of the maidens of Jerusalem in the vineyards—Views of the Synagogue about the

CHAPTER 17—POST-MOSAIC FESTIVALS

Object of these feasts—The Feast of *Purim*—Its origin and time—Was it ever attended by the Lord?—Services on the Feast of Purim—When and how the *Megillah* was read—Modern ceremonials—The Feast of the Dedication of the Temple—Its origin and duration—The 'Hallel' sung on each day of its duration; the people carried palm branches, and there was a grand illumination of the Temple and of private houses—Suggestion that the date of Christmas was taken from this feast—Practice as to the illumination—The Feast of the Wood-offering on the last of the nine seasons of the year, when such offerings were brought in the Temple—Rabbinical accounts of its origin—Maidens dance in the vineyards on the afternoon of that day—Fasts, public and private—Memorial fasts—The four great fasts mentioned in Zech. 8—Mode of observing public fasts

CHAPTER 18—ON PURIFICATIONS

Symbolical meaning of Levitical defilements and purifications—The purification of the Virgin Mary in the Temple—Defilement by contact

with death—*Six* degrees of defilement—Sacrifice of the red heifer—
Preservation of its ashes, and use of them in purification—Symbolical
meaning of this purification—Analogy between the red heifer, the scape-
goat, and the living bird let loose in cleansing the leper—Why was the
heifer *wholly* burnt?—Meaning of the use of the ashes of the red heifer—
Rabbinical tradition about Solomon's ignorance of the meaning of this
rite—Selection of the red heifer—Ceremonial in its sacrifice and burning—Selection of one so free from suspicion of defilement as to administer this purification—Children kept in special localities for that purpose—
Ceremonial connected with the purification—How many red heifers had
been offered from the time of Moses—Symbolical meaning of leprosy—
Lepers admitted to special places in the synagogue—How the priests were
to examine and pronounce judgment on leprosy—Explanation of Lev. 13.
12, 13—Two-fold rites in restoring the healed leper—First, or social stage
of purification—Second stage after seven days' seclusion—The rites to be
observed in it—Rabbinical account of the service—The meat-offering at
the purification of a wife suspected of adultery—Symbolical meaning of
it—The priest warns the woman of the danger of perjury—The words of
the curse written upon the roll, washed in water from the laver—This
mixture, with dust of the sanctuary, drunk by the woman—In what cases
alone the Rabbis allowed this trial—How the accused appeared dressed in
the Temple—How she had to drink the bitter water—Divine judgments
upon the guilty—Cessation of this rite shortly after the death of our
Lord—Remarks of the *Mishnah* in recording this fact . . . . *Page 275*

INDEX

INDEX TO SCRIPTURE REFERENCES